# Revolution, Reform and Regionalism in Southeast Asia

Geographically, Cambodia, Laos and Vietnam are situated in the fastest growing region in the world, positioned alongside the dynamic economies of neighboring China and Thailand. *Revolution, Reform and Regionalism in Southeast Asia* compares the postwar political economies of these three countries in the context of their individual and collective impact on recent efforts at regional integration. Based on research carried out over three decades, Ronald Bruce St John highlights the different paths to reform taken by these countries and the effect this has had on regional plans for economic development.

Through its comparative analysis of the reforms implemented by Cambodia, Laos and Vietnam over the last 30 years, the book draws attention to parallel themes of continuity and change. St John discusses how these countries have demonstrated related characteristics whilst at the same time making different modifications in order to exploit the strengths of their individual cultures. The book contributes to the contemporary debate over the role of democratic reform in promoting economic development and provides academics with a unique insight into the political economies of three countries at the heart of Southeast Asia.

**Ronald Bruce St John** earned a Ph.D. in International Relations at the University of Denver before serving as a military intelligence officer in Vietnam. He is now an independent scholar and has published more than 300 books, articles and reviews with a focus on Southeast Asia, North Africa and the Middle East and Andean America.

# Routledge contemporary Southeast Asia series

# Revolution, Reform and Regionalism in Southeast Asia

Cambodia, Laos and Vietnam

**Ronald Bruce St John**

Routledge
Taylor & Francis Group

LONDON AND NEW YORK

First published 2006
by Routledge
2 Park Square, Milton Park, Abingdon, Oxon OX14 4RN

Simultaneously published in the USA and Canada
by Routledge
270 Madison Ave, New York, NY 10016

*Routledge is an imprint of the Taylor & Francis Group*

© 2006 Ronald Bruce St John

Typeset in Times by Wearset Ltd, Boldon, Tyne and Wear
Printed and bound in Great Britain by MPG Books Ltd, Bodmin

*British Library Cataloguing in Publication Data*
A catalogue record for this book is available from the British Library

*Library of Congress Cataloging in Publication Data*
A catalog record for this book has been requested

ISBN 0-415-70184-8

**To Carol, Alexander and Nathan**
**who shared the journey**

# Contents

# Preface

My study of the political economies of Cambodia, Laos and Vietnam began in 1970 as a freshly minted captain in the U.S. Army. I served as an intelligence officer in the Strategic Research and Analysis Section of Headquarters, Military Advisory Command, Vietnam. Working under cover as a "topographical engineer," my duties included the supervision of a small, dedicated group of highly educated analysts, detailed to brief the commander-in-chief daily on the impact of political events on the military conduct of the war. In attempting to understand and explain the organization and operation of the so-called Viet Cong Infrastructure, I earned the equivalent of an M.A. in Southeast Asian Studies to accompany advanced degrees in international relations earned earlier at the Graduate School of International Studies, University of Denver. At the same time, I grew increasingly disenchanted with the American role in Southeast Asia. Out of that disillusionment grew a lifelong fascination with the often troubled, ever-changing political economies of Cambodia, Laos and Vietnam.

Following my tour in Vietnam, I resigned my commission and pursued a dual career in academia and international commerce, living much of the next two decades in Europe, Africa and the Middle East. I returned to Southeast Asia in 1987, living first in Hong Kong and later in Bangkok. Employed as a regional manager for Caterpillar Inc., I traveled widely throughout the region, most especially in Cambodia, Laos and Vietnam. My duties varied widely from mine clearing operations on the Poipet-Battambang road to drafting reports on the political economies of Cambodia and Laos to testifying before the Senate Foreign Relations Committee in 1991 in support of lifting the multinational embargo and resuming multilateral aid to Vietnam. Eventually, I returned to the United States and took early retirement to work full time as an author and independent scholar. In recent years, I have continued to travel frequently to Cambodia, Laos and Vietnam.

Based on research begun in the 1970s, this book explores the economic and political reforms implemented by the governments of Cambodia, Laos and Vietnam over the last three decades. A focal point is the different paths to reform taken by three neighbors long considered to be intimately related, if not a single entity. The impact of their divergent reforms on regional plans for economic development through the Association of Southeast Asian Nations in general and the Greater Mekong Subregion in particular is a secondary focus. Grandiose schemes abound and publicists tout success; however, as is often the case, the devil is in the detail.

In writing about a diverse geographical area, I have followed a simple rule regarding the spelling of place names discussed. I have tried to use the most common contemporary spelling even when this means that current usage is at variance with earlier decades. Fortunately, the difference in most cases between present and past usage is not great. The official title of the state and government of Cambodia is an exception as it has varied considerably over the last four decades. Unless reference to a specific regime adds clarity or emphasis, I have generally referred throughout the book to the country and government simply as Cambodia. Widely known Vietnamese toponyms like Hanoi or Danang are recorded as a single word while less well known place names like Ben Tre or My Tho are cited in their common Vietnamese form. The terms "Laos" and the "Lao People's Democratic Republic" or "Lao PDR" are used interchangeably as they are in English-language publications by the Vientiane government. The term "Lao" is used to denote citizens of the Lao PDR as well as ethnic Lao. The different usages should be apparent in their context. The full complement of diacritical marks is not used as a matter of printing convenience. Where references to place names are contained within quotations from earlier periods, I have retained the contemporary usage.

In the course of completing this book, which has been in progress for almost two decades, I have received assistance from a variety of sources which have facilitated access to materials and information in many different ways. The library staffs at Carnegie Mellon University, Knox College and Bradley University have been especially gracious of their time and talent over a prolonged period. I would also like to thank the staff at the Orientalia Section in the Library of Congress and at the U.S. National Archives in College Park, Maryland for their research support. I am grateful for the assistance I received at the Bibliothèque Nationale and the Archives Nationales in Paris and the Centre des Archives, Section Outre-Mer, in Aix-en-Provence. The library staffs at Georgetown University, Northern Illinois University and Yale University also facilitated selected aspects of my research endeavors.

Over time, I have become indebted to a large number of teachers and scholars whose research and writing, often accompanied by counsel and guidance, have shaped my own thinking. While a mere listing of names cannot do justice to their manifold contributions, I would like to take this opportunity to recognize some of them. The late Mikiso (Miki) Hane, Szold Distinguished Professor Emeritus of History and a gifted scholar and talented teacher, first sparked my interest in Asian studies when I was an undergraduate student at Knox College. Peter Van Ness later helped grow my understanding of Asia when I was a graduate student in international relations at the University of Denver. My Vietnamese language training commenced at the Defense Language Institute at Ft. Bliss, Texas under the strict tutelage of some wonderfully warm and caring Vietnamese teachers who succeeded in inculcating in me a love of the culture as well as the language of Vietnam. Major Arnold Catarina, a foreign area officer specialist on Southeast Asia and officer commanding during my Vietnam tour, was an informed teacher and a sensitive individual, highly knowledgeable about the region but serving in an impossible situation.

Among those active in Vietnamese studies, I would like to thank especially Douglas Allen, Melanie Beresford, Mark Philip Bradley, Pierre Brocheux, Nayan Chanda, Patrice Cosaert, Henrich Dahm, Dang T. Tran, William J. Duiker, Adam Fforde, Frances Fitzgerald, Frédéric Fortunel, Nick J. Freeman, Bernard Gay, Ellen J. Hammer, Daniel Hémery, Hue-Tam Ho Tai, Huynh Kim Khanh, Neil L. Jamieson, John Kleinen, Gabriel Kolko, Börje Ljunggren, David G. Marr, Albin Michel, Patrice Morlat, Martin J. Murray, Ngo Van, Ngo Vinh Long, Nguyen Van Canh, Milton E. Osborne, Eero Palmujoki, Douglas Pike, Doug J. Porter, Gareth Porter, Lewis M. Stern, Philip Taylor, Carlyle A. Thayer, Tran Thi Que, Andrew Vickerman, Vo Nhan Tri, Vu Tuan Anh and Alexander Barton Woodside.

In Lao studies, I would like to acknowledge Yves Bourdet, Kennon Breazeale, MacAlister Brown, Jean Deuve, Arthur J. Dommen, Grant Evans, Geoffrey C. Gunn, Mayoury Ngaosrivathana, Pheuiphanh Ngaosrivathana, Jonathan Rigg, Martin Stuart-Fox, Christian Taillard, Joseph L. H. Tan, Mya Than, Leonard Unger, William E. Worner and Joseph J. Zasloff.

I am grateful for inspiration and assistance in Cambodian studies from Elizabeth Becker, Jacques Bekaert, David P. Chandler, Chang Pao-Min, Ros Chantrabot, Justin Cornfield, Jean Delvert, Thomas Engelbert, Craig Etcheson, Alain Forest, Christopher E. Goscha, Evan Gottesman, Caroline Hughes, Karl D. Jackson, Raoul M. Jennar, Ben Kiernan, Judy Ledgerwood, Michael Leifer, Marie Alexandrine Martin, Stephen J. Morris, Sorpong Peou, François Ponchaud, David W. Roberts, William Shawcross, Serge Thion, Thu-huong Nguyen-vo, John Tully and Michael Vickery.

In Laos, a number of friends, sponsors and colleagues have assisted me in a variety of ways over the years, including Bounleuang Insisienmay at the Ministry of Trade and Tourism, Bountheuang Mounlasy, Bountiem Phissamay and Bounnhang Sengchandavong at the Ministry of External Economic Relations, Himmakone Manodham, Oudone Vathanaxay and Phetsamone Viraphanth at the Ministry of Communication, Transport, Post and Construction, Khamphan Simmalavong at the Ministry of Commerce, Khamphou Laysouthisakd at the Chamber of Commerce and Industry, Liang Insisiengmay at the Tax Department, Noktham Ratanavong at the Ministry of Commerce and Tourism, Sitaheng Rasphone at the Ministry of Agriculture and Forestry and Sommano Pholsena at the Ministry of Industry.

Richard M. Millar and Maurice Dewulf with the United Nations Development Programme, William F. Beachner and Geoffrey W. Hyles with the United Nations International Drug Control Programme, Randall C. Merris with the Asian Development Bank, and Arne Hansson and Martin Kerridge with SWECO contributed helpful information and insight on development issues in Laos. From the private sector, I would like to thank Olle Andersson with SweRoad, Lee Bigelow with the Hunt Oil Company, Chanphéng Bounnaphol with Entreprise Oil, Harold Christensen and Panh Phomsombath with Lao Survey and Exploration Services, Ted Gloor at Petrotech, Bjarne Jeppesen at Champion Wood Investment, Thommy Johansson with Skanska International Civil Engineering, Sumphorn Manodham at Burapha Development Consultants and Virachit Philaphandeth at Phatthana Trading Company for their assistance in understanding contemporary socioeconomic issues. I also owe a real debt to Jonathan Rigg at the University of Durham for his support of my work in Laos.

In Vietnam, I owe a special thanks to Ambassador Le Van Bang who was in the gallery when I testified before the U.S. Senate in 1991 and has continued to be a source of both inspiration and guidance. I also want to thank Dao Minh Loc at the Ministry of Water Resources, Le Dang Doanh at the Central Institute for Economic Management, Le Ngoc Hoan at the Ministry of Transport, Nguyen Dinh Lam at the National Coal Export-Import and Material Supply Corporation, Nguyen Minh Thong at the Ministry of Agriculture and Food Industry, Pham Chi Lan and Nguyen Duy Khien at the Chamber of Commerce and Industry and Tran Danh Tao and Tran Ngoc Hien at the Ho Chi Minh National Academy for Political Science. Virginia Foote at the United States–Vietnam Trade Council has provided welcome support and assistance, including the organization of numerous personal interviews in Vietnam, for many years.

In Cambodia, I would like to thank several people for assistance at different times, including David W. Ashley when he worked in the Ministry of Economics and Finance, Sophal Ear and Michael Hayes, editor of the *Phnom Penh Post*.

An earlier version of part of Chapter 4 appeared in *Asian Affairs: Journal of the Royal Society for Asian Affairs* vol. 24, no. 3, October 1993, pp. 304–14 and in *Asian Affairs: An American Review* vol. 21, no. 4, Winter 1995, pp. 227–40. An earlier version of part of Chapter 5 appeared in *Contemporary Southeast Asia* vol. 17, no. 3, December 1995, pp. 265–81 and in *Contemporary Southeast Asia* vol. 19, no. 2, September 1997, pp. 172–89. I would like to thank Triena Noeline Ong, Managing Editor of *Contemporary Southeast Asia*, Michael Sheringham, editor of *Asian Affairs: Journal for the Royal Society for Asian Affairs*, and Jannette Whippy, managing editor of *Asian Affairs: An American Review*, for their assistance both in guiding the above articles through publication as well as for their gracious consent to reproduce the material here in a revised and updated form.

From the beginning to the end, my family has shared with me both the frustrations and the rewards of this project. In the process, we have all enjoyed the opportunity to travel widely in Cambodia, Laos and Vietnam. Therefore, I would like to dedicate this book to my wife, Carol, and our sons, Alexander and Nathan.

Ronald Bruce St John

# Acronyms

| | |
|---|---|
| ADB | Asian Development Bank |
| AEM | ASEAN Economic Ministers |
| AFL-CIO | American Federation of Labor–Congress of Industrial Organizations |
| AFTA | ASEAN Free Trade Area |
| AMBDC | ASEAN Mekong Basin Development Cooperation |
| APEC | Asia Pacific Economic Cooperation |
| ASEAN | Association of Southeast Asian Nations |
| BLDP | Buddhist Liberal Democratic Party [Cambodia] |
| CDC | Council for the Development of Cambodia |
| CGDK | Coalition Government of Democratic Kampuchea |
| CIA | Central Intelligence Agency |
| CIB | Cambodian Investment Board |
| CIDA | Canadian International Development Agency |
| CIF | Cost, Insurance and Freight |
| Comecon | Council for Mutual Economic Assistance |
| COSVN | Central Office for South Vietnam |
| CPK | Communist Party of Kampuchea |
| CPP | Cambodian People's Party |
| CRDB | Cambodian Rehabilitation and Development Board |
| DK | Democratic Kampuchea |
| DRV | Democratic Republic of Vietnam |
| DRVN | Democratic Republic of Viet Nam |
| ECAFE | Economic Commission for Asia and the Far East |
| EGAT | Electricity Generating Authority of Thailand |
| ESCAP | Economic and Social Commission for Asia and the Pacific |
| EU | European Union |
| EWEC | East-West Economic Corridor |
| FBIS | Foreign Broadcast Information Service |
| FCDI | Forum for Comprehensive Development of Indochina |
| FDI | Foreign Direct Investment |
| FFC | Fact Finding Committee |
| FULRO | United Front for the Struggle of the Oppressed Races |

| | |
|---|---|
| FUNCINPEC | Front Uni National Pour un Cambodge Indépendant, Neutre, Pacifique, et Coopératif or National United Front for an Independent, Neutral, Peaceful and Cooperative Cambodia |
| GDP | Gross Domestic Product |
| GFI | Gross Fixed Investment |
| GMS | Greater Mekong Subregion |
| GNP | Gross National Product |
| GVN | Government of [South] Vietnam |
| HCMC | Ho Chi Minh City |
| HIV/AIDS | Human immunodeficiency virus/acquired immunodeficiency syndrome |
| HRD | Human Resource Development |
| ICBV | Industrial and Commercial Bank of Vietnam |
| ICORC | International Committee for the Reconstruction of Cambodia |
| ICP | Indochinese Communist Party |
| IDBV | Investment and Development Bank of Vietnam |
| IDRC | International Development Research Centre of Canada |
| IMC | Interim Mekong Committee |
| IMF | International Monetary Fund |
| ISEAS | Institute of Southeast Asian Studies |
| ITP | Indochinese Trotskyite Party |
| JBIC | Japan Bank for International Cooperation |
| JIM | Jakarta Informal Meeting |
| JPRS | Joint Publications Research Service |
| KKK | Struggle Front of the Khmer of Kampuchea Krom |
| KNP | Khmer Nation Party |
| KNUFNS | Kampuchean National United Front for National Salvation |
| KPNLF | Khmer People's National Liberation Front |
| KPRP | Khmer People's Revolutionary Party |
| KR | Khmer Rouge |
| Lao PDR | Lao People's Democratic Republic |
| LCMD | Lao Citizens Movement for Democracy |
| LPDP | Lao People's Democratic Party |
| LPF | Lao Patriotic Front |
| LPLF | Lao People's Liberation Front |
| LPRP | Lao People's Revolutionary Party |
| MACV | Military Assistance Command Vietnam |
| MBDC | Mekong Basin Development Cooperation |
| MDRN | Mekong Development Research Network |
| MFA | Multifiber Agreement |
| MFN | Most Favored Nation |
| MIA | Missing In Action |

| | |
|---|---|
| MITI | Ministry of Trade and Industry [Japan] |
| MRC | Mekong River Commission |
| NEM | New Economic Mechanism |
| NGO | Nongovernmental Organization |
| NLF | National Liberation Front [South Vietnam] |
| NLHS | Ne Lao Hak Sat (Lao Patriotic Front) |
| NTR | Normal Trade Relations |
| NUFK | National United Front of Kampuchea |
| NVA | North Vietnamese Army |
| NVN | North Vietnam |
| ODA | Official Development Assistance |
| OPIC | Overseas Private Investment Corporation |
| PAVN | People's Army of Vietnam |
| PDK | Party of Democratic Kampuchea |
| PGNU | Provisional Government of National Union |
| PL | Pathet Lao |
| PLA | People's Liberation Army [Vietnam] |
| PNGC | Provisional National Government of Cambodia |
| PRC | People's Republic of China |
| PRG | Provisional Revolutionary Government [South Vietnam] |
| PRK | People's Republic of Kampuchea |
| RGC | Royal Government of Cambodia |
| RGNU | Royal Government of National Union [Cambodia] |
| RKG | Royal Khmer Government |
| RLA | Royal Lao Army |
| RLG | Royal Lao Government |
| RVN | Republic of Vietnam |
| SARS | severe acute respiratory syndrome |
| SCCI | State Committee for Cooperation and Investment |
| SEATO | Southeast Asia Treaty Organization |
| SNC | Supreme National Council [Vietnam] |
| SOC | State of Cambodia |
| SPA | Supreme People's Assembly [Vietnam] |
| SRP | Sam Rainsy Party |
| SRV | Socialist Republic of Vietnam |
| SVN | South Vietnam |
| TVA | Tennessee Valley Authority |
| UBCV | Unified Buddhist Church of Vietnam |
| UN | United Nations |
| UNDP | United Nations Development Program |
| UNF | United National Front [Vietnam] |
| UNHCR | United Nations High Commission for Refugees |
| UNTAC | United Nations Transitional Authority in Cambodia |
| VBA | Vietnam Bank for Agriculture |
| VCP | Vietnam Communist Party |

| | |
|---|---|
| VML | Viet Minh League |
| VNQDD | Viet Nam Quoc Dan Dang [Vietnamese Nationalist Party] |
| VWP | Vietnam Workers' Party |
| WHO | World Health Organization |
| WTO | World Trade Organization |

# 1   Same space, different dreams

"Indochine" is an elaborate fiction, a modern phantasmatic assemblage
invented during the heyday of French colonial hegemony in Southeast
Asia. It is a myth that never existed and yet endures in our collective imagi-
nary.

> Academic Panivong Norindr, *Phantasmatic Indochina*, 1996

I'd bet my future harp against your golden crown that in five hundred years
there may be no New York or London, but they'll be growing paddy in
these fields, they'll be carrying their produce to market on long poles,
wearing their pointed hats.

> British Novelist Graham Greene, *The Quiet American*, 1955

It's the tragedy of a small nation, to have to depend on foreigners.

> Vietnamese Novelist Ma Van Khang, *Against the Flood*, 2000

Southeast Asia by the middle of the nineteenth century had become an
arena of imperial rivalry between Britain and France. There was growing
interest in both countries in exploring the regions that abutted China
because the fabled riches of the Middle Kingdom were believed to be a
potential source of enormous commercial opportunity.[1] A British army
officer in 1837 traveled from Burma into China in search of future trade
routes between newly established British colonies and the Chinese empire.
Two decades later, a French expedition departed Saigon with orders to
explore the Mekong River to the fullest extent possible in an effort to dis-
cover an effective means to join, on a commercial basis, the upper reaches
of the river with Cochinchina.[2]

Epic in concept and execution, early explorations of the Mekong
highlighted the practical difficulties involved in harnessing the river and
promoting commercial development. In consequence, as the historian
Milton Osborne has noted, the colonial administration in Indochina eventually adopted a more realistic view of the French role as well as the real
potential for subregional trade and development in Cambodia, Laos and
Vietnam.

The grudging recognition, at the beginning of the twentieth century, that the Mekong could not become the major commercial artery hoped for by so many Frenchmen coincided with the end of what they and their metropolitan admirers frequently called "The Heroic Age" of colonialism in Indochina. ... Central to the use of the term was the view that with the passing of the heroic age *Notre Indochine* had become a settled group of French possessions. What now existed, the publicists proclaimed, was a territorial ensemble in which the prospects for economic success were real, made greater by the rapid expansion of rubber estates in the 1920s, and the necessary firmness of colonial rule was balanced by the worth of France's civilising mission.[3]

## Disparate states

Imperialists, colonialists, internationalists and nationalists, for almost two centuries, have shared a vision of economic and political union in Indochina. Discounting the reality that Cambodia, Laos and Vietnam are three very different countries, numerous individuals and groups have promoted various levels of subregional cooperation and development since the middle of the nineteenth century. Most recently, the Asian Development Bank and other international bodies have advanced the concept of a Greater Mekong Subregion, integrating Cambodia, Laos, Myanmar, Thailand, Vietnam and the Yunnan Province of China into a joint development zone.[4]

Cambodia, Laos and Vietnam sit squarely in the middle of this nascent development zone; consequently, sustained economic progress in these three states is vital to the success of more ambitious plans for both subregional and regional integration. All three states have moved, to a greater or lesser degree, from centrally planned to market economies in recent years. But political reform has been slower and less uniform than economic reform. The ongoing efforts of Cambodia, Laos and Vietnam to recreate themselves raise important internal and external issues. Is it realistic to think Cambodia, Laos and Vietnam can duplicate the economic success of the booming industrial "Tigers" of Asia in the 1980s and early 1990s? How far can economic development progress in these three states without concomitant political change? Do past and present attempts at Indochina-wide cooperation facilitate or hamper efforts at subregional and regional development? What is the future economic and political role of Cambodia, Laos and Vietnam in the region and the world?

Cambodia, located in the center of Southeast Asia, bordered on the west by Thailand, on the east by Vietnam, on the north by Laos and on the south by the Gulf of Thailand, is a relatively small country, slightly smaller than the state of Oklahoma. Unlike its giant neighbors to the east and west whose populations are much larger, the population of Cambodia is less than 13 million people. Khmers comprise over 90 percent of the population, Vietnamese 5 percent and ethnic Chinese 1 percent. The Cambodian economy is dominated by small-plot agriculture with some 80 percent of the labor force engaged in rice cultivation.[5]

Slightly larger than Cambodia, the Lao People's Democratic Republic (Lao PDR) approximates the size of the state of Utah and is bordered by Burma, Cambodia, China, Thailand and Vietnam. It is the only landlocked country in Southeast Asia. At the time the French annexed Laos in the late nineteenth century, it was divided into several principalities. Numbering no more than six million people today, it is the least populous country in the Indochinese Peninsula with a population less than half that of Cambodia and only 7 percent that of Vietnam. Laos has the lowest population density in the subregion, but one of the highest rates of population growth. The Lao are the dominant ethnic group in Laos but account for a much smaller proportion of the total population than is true of the dominant ethnic groups in Cambodia and Vietnam. Ethnic composition, together with the fact that a large number of its citizens live outside the lowland, Buddhist-centered cultural universe, differentiate Laos from Cambodia and Vietnam. Theravada Buddhism is the main religion in Laos. But unlike neighboring Cambodia and Vietnam where the vast majority of the people are ethnic Khmer or ethnic Vietnamese as well as Buddhist, less than 60 percent of the people in Laos are ethnic Lao and Buddhist with the remainder composed of diverse minorities practicing animism.[6]

Subsistence agriculture accounts for approximately half the GDP of Laos and provides 80 percent of total employment; nonetheless, arable land constitutes only 3 percent of land surface. The infrastructure of the Lao PDR remains primitive with no railroads, a rudimentary albeit expanding road system and limited internal and external telecommunications. Electricity is widely available only in urban areas. Historically, Laos has depended heavily on trade with neighboring Thailand. Sharing the Mekong Basin with six neighbors, Laos occupies 26 percent, Thailand 23 percent, China and Myanmar collectively 22 percent, Cambodia 20 percent and Vietnam 9 percent. Despite a well-endowed natural resource base, including forests, water and minerals, the Lao PDR remains one of the world's least developed states.

Vietnam is bordered on the west by Cambodia and Laos, on the north by China and on the east by the South China Sea which the Vietnamese, sensitive to Chinese maritime claims, term the East Sea. Vietnam is 40 percent larger than Laos and almost twice the size of Cambodia. With a population exceeding 80 million, there are six Vietnamese for every Cambodian and 14 for every Lao. A poor and densely populated country, Vietnam has achieved substantial economic progress in recent years; however, the economic reforms implemented by the government originated from an extremely low base. The Vietnamese economy is more diversified than that of either Cambodia or Laos with 35 percent of GDP from industry, 25 percent from agriculture and 40 percent from services.

## French plan for Indochina

In the latter half of the nineteenth century, France brought together in *l'Union Indochinoise* the five distinct territories of Annam, Cambodia, Cochinchina, Tonkin and eastern Laos, areas that were not tightly integrated at the time and enjoyed no common political life or cultural heritage. Cambodia and Laos were strongly influenced by Indian civilization while Annam, Cochinchina and Tonkin owed much to China. The hill tribes in the subregion were a people apart, attached only loosely to Annam, Cambodia, Laos and Tonkin. French rule did little to promote subregional integration as a contemporary French observer noted at the end of World War II:

> French Indo-China is thus a hotchpotch of very different peoples. A Cambodian, for example, differs far more from an Annamite than an Englishman does from an Italian. There is a much greater difference between a Laotian living on the western slope of the Annamite Cordillera and an Annamite on the eastern than there is between a Savoyard and a Piedmontese living on opposite sides of the Alps. These different peoples dislike one another and do not live at peace voluntarily.[7]

In establishing the Indochinese Union, the French created a new geopolitical entity, reversing demographical and geographical patterns long characteristic of the subregion. The peninsula of Southeast Asia was broken by mountain chains, river valleys and coastal plains that generally ran north and south. There were the Irrawaddy, Menam and Mekong river valleys; the Arakan, Chan, Tenasserim and Annamite mountain ranges; and the coastal plains of Vietnam. Ancient Burmese, Annamite, Lao and Siamese invasions followed the river valleys and coastal plains moving north to south. Where Siam was built on the Menam Valley and Burma on the Irrawaddy and Sittang valleys, French Indochina was built south to north and east to west on the Mekong River and the coastal plains of the South China Sea.[8]

After occupying the region, the French moved initially to "civilize" the disparate peoples of Indochina on the assumption their benign task was to assimilate them into French culture and civilization. "Only gradually did it become apparent that haphazard and piecemeal attempts to gallicize the Indochinese resulted chiefly in their demoralization." The subsequent policy of association through the Indochinese Union proved contradictory as it sought to maintain the cultural integrity of the indigenous population within a framework of total economic, political and social domination by the French. The administrative, fiscal and legal policies implemented by the colonial government undermined native family units and created a dependent peasant proletariat. French education imbued the privileged few with ideals of equality, political freedom and self-government, but the political machinery established by the French prevented adequate political representation of native interests. "This situation, which included the usual European attitudes of superiority, could hardly build up the capacities and self-respect of the Indochinese or lead them wholeheartedly to accept either their own or French civilization."[9]

The growing unrest in Indochina spurred movements for change throughout the subregion. Ranging in approach from mild reform to violent revolution, these movements were driven by a reservoir of unrest as well as growing nationalist sentiments. In the inter-war years, opposition to French rule took the form of legal and illegal political groups and actions including secret societies, nativistic religious cults and isolated acts of terrorism.[10] French officials clung tenaciously to an economic policy that viewed Indochina largely in terms of its usefulness to France. In so doing, French political policy wavered between strict repression and meaningless concessions that served to fuel nationalist discontent. In the process, "the people of Indochina suffered in almost indescribable ways from the barbaric nature of French colonialism." Even the liberal Popular Front government in France in 1936–8 proved unable to reverse traditional colonial policies as it was forced to compromise virtually all the reforms it did propose for Indochina.[11]

Although French rule of Indochina was anything but benign, some of the barriers between the peoples of the subregion did begin to erode under French administration. For example, half a million Vietnamese, encouraged to do so by the French, settled in Cambodia during the colonial era and eventually came to dominate certain sectors of the local economy like fishing on the Tonlé Sap, rubber plantation labor and skilled crafts in the towns. Moreover, hundreds of Vietnamese at any given point were employed in the colonial civil service. Cambodia was also closely linked economically with Cochinchina during the colonial period. Because Cambodia had no deep water port, colonial trade controlled by the French passed through Saigon.[12]

To the north, French administrators realized the economy of landlocked Laos could not develop without a modern transportation system. Consequently, they built a road the entire length of the Mekong Valley, linking Luang Prabang in the north with Pakse in the south. Other roads were constructed through the mountains to the east, linking Laos with Vietnam and the South China Sea. Unfortunately, a proposed project to build a railroad from Savannakhet to the Vietnamese coast never materialized.[13]

The desire of the French "to carry out a colonial civilizing mission produced a certain unity of policy" in Cambodia and Cochinchina as well as elsewhere in the subregion; nonetheless, it must be emphasized that "the comparison is chiefly one of contrasts" both in terms of fundamental social differences and French methods of government.[14] Paul Doumer, governor

general of Indochina from 1897 to 1902, carried out an aggressive administrative reorganization that produced strong centralized leadership from
Hanoi as well as from the *résidents supérieurs* in the provinces; however,
he failed to create an entirely homogenous political or administrative
entity. For example, in the highlands of Annam, Cambodia, Laos and
Tonkin, the French negotiated separate deals with local tribal leaders,
created new political entities and organized the population for purposes of
tax collection and conscript labor. In the main, the French mostly pre-
served existing structures throughout Indochina either because they
lacked the manpower to administer modified structures or because locals
resisted French efforts to change them. As the distinguished historian,
Arthur J. Dommen, later emphasized, the result was a hodgepodge of disparate administrative structures and services.

> So French Indochina consisted of, on the east, a Vietnam divided into
> three parts consisting of a colony and two protectorates under the
> nominal suzerainty of the emperor, and on the west two protected
> kingdoms and a handful of directly administered provinces forming a
> bulwark against Siam. Even this scheme, a hodgepodge not much less
> heterogeneous than the British dominions in North America in the
> previous century, was to be further complicated by large-scale recruit-
> ment of Vietnamese cadres into the Indochinese civil service and by
> encouragement of Vietnamese migration into Laos and Cambodia.
> These developments led, in turn, to a lively debate about whether the
> inhabitants of these diverse territories owed an allegiance to
> "Indochina," or indeed whether there was such an entity at all.[15]

## Indochinese Communist Party

Marxism-Leninism entered French Indochina in the inter-war period via
Vietnam. The Indochinese Communist Party (ICP), founded in Hanoi in
1930, was the product of Soviet initiatives to form a communist party to
combat French colonialism throughout the subregion. Under the leadership of Ho Chi Minh, the communist parties operating in the north, center
and south of Vietnam merged into a single communist party and adopted
the slogan "Complete Indochinese Independence!." With the exception of
a brief period between February and October 1930, this slogan would
define the revolutionary domain of Vietnamese communism until a few
days before the August Revolution in 1945. The ICP was officially recognized by the Comintern, an organization in Moscow for promoting
communism abroad, in April 1931. Encouraged by the Soviet Union, Vietnamese revolutionaries toiled over the next decade with little success to
recruit members in Cambodia and Laos.[16]

   Dictated from abroad, the Vietnamese vision of an Indochina-wide
communist movement was illusory from the outset. The thinking of young

Vietnamese activists focused on Tonkin, Annam and Cochinchina; and if such thinking occasionally expanded westward to Cambodia or Laos, it was almost always limited to the Vietnamese communities found there. As a result, the Vietnamese residents of Cambodia and Laos, as well as Thailand, formed the bulk of early recruits. Opposed to French imperialism, Vietnamese revolutionaries talked much of the need for radical reform but seldom mentioned the roles of their Cambodian and Lao counterparts. For example, Indochinese Communist Party cells were established in Phnom Penh in late 1930 with others established later in Kandal, Kratie and Kompong Cham; however, they all acted sporadically and none was ever linked systematically with the larger Party network operating in Cochinchina or elsewhere. In addition, the Party cells established in Cambodia were generally led by Vietnamese who, according to an internal study of the Cambodian Party:

> had difficulties with the [Cambodian] language, customs, and enemy [French] repression. But the main problem was that the ICP did not reach into Cambodian masses. Party bases had not yet taken hold in Cambodia and they had not yet succeeded in making the cause of the ICP the chief cause of the Cambodian people. This weakness can be attributed to the ICP's failure to understand clearly the ethnic question (*van de dan toc*) ... and thus Party members in Cambodia only made efforts to work among the overseas Vietnamese populations, without paying attention to the matter of reaching into the masses of Cambodian workers, peasants, intellectuals, and working peoples in general.... Every Party cell [in Cambodia] was filled with overseas Vietnamese, with only one party member (an alternate) being Cambodian. Even the question of organizing the masses was effectively limited to working among the overseas Vietnamese. In such a situation, one could not have a truly nationalist movement [in Cambodia].[17]

French efforts to breathe life into their vision of Indochina stimulated and reinforced nascent Vietnamese concepts of an Indochinese nation. Vietnamese nationalists prior to the arrival of the French generally held traditional Vietnamese notions of economic and political space, but those ideas mingled after 1887 with the geopolitical entity the French shaped in the form of *l'Indochine française*. French promotion of colonial policies that emphasized the Vietnamese content of the union also encouraged the Vietnamese to think in terms of Indochina. The employment of Vietnamese in lower level bureaucratic postings throughout the colonial administration had the same effect.

> It would not be an exaggeration to say that by the 1930s, the Lao and Cambodian bureaucracies were remarkably dependent, *at the ground*

*level*, on Vietnamese civil servants. In turn, this increasing number of literate Vietnamese bureaucrats working in western Indochina allowed for publication of numerous Vietnamese-language papers, distributed widely among the expanding Vietnamese communities in Lao and Cambodian urban centres. Meanwhile, French business interests in Laos and Cambodia preferred tapping the dynamic Vietnamese labour force to work on their plantations and mines or for building the *Trans-Indochinois* transport system. In an irony which was not lost on several Vietnamese writers at the time, by targeting the Vietnamese in the Indochinese education system, by staffing the Lao and Cambodian bureaucracies with Vietnamese, and by sending thousands of Vietnamese labourers to Cambodian rubber plantations and Lao mines, the French had facilitated the Vietnamese rethinking of the space around them.[18]

Despite inducements for an Indochina-wide, anti-colonialist movement, Vietnamese political activities in Cambodia and Laos remained at relatively low levels. In Cambodia, the recruitment problems referred to earlier, combined with a brief relaxation of French controls on political expression in 1936–9, resulted in the dissolution of secret, Vietnamese-led Party structures. Vietnamese revolutionary work in Laos was more productive but largely confined to the Vietnamese communities already in existence there. As early as the end of World War I, anti-colonialists from north-central Vietnam had begun using Vietnamese communities in Laos as stepping stones to key resistance bases in Thailand. Significantly, most of these bases were located in the northeastern part of Thailand as opposed to further south on the Thai–Cambodian border. Consequently, when the Indochinese Communist Party came to life in 1930, it inherited an active network of liaison bases in western Lao towns like Vientiane, Savannakhet and Thakhek. Laos became a corridor for Vietnamese revolutionaries working in Thailand in the late 1920s and early 1930s, but Vietnamese efforts to recruit the Lao themselves were not much more successful than their work with the Cambodians.[19]

Northern Vietnamese played a key role in the creation of the Siamese Communist Party in 1930; and a special revolutionary organization known as the Indochinese Assistance Section served briefly as the ICP's Central Committee following heightened French repression in north-central Vietnam in the 1930s. In addition, Vietnamese communists operating in Laos and Thailand established a provisional Lao Regional Committee to oversee revolutionary activities ranging from northern Vietnam to northeastern Thailand and Bangkok. Southern Vietnamese communists attempted unsuccessfully to establish a similar network running from Cambodia to Thailand in the mid-1930s. The French crackdown on southern communists in the wake of the failed 1940 uprising in Cochinchina made the success of additional efforts even more difficult.[20]

At the beginning of World War II, Vietnamese communists attempted to incorporate Cambodia and Laos more closely into their revolutionary activities. With a promise of self-determination, they sought to situate both Lao and Cambodian revolutionaries within two Vietnamese-led political bodies, the National United Anti-Imperialist Front of Indochina, and following the planned revolution, the Federal Government of the Democratic Republic of Indochina. Two years later, having breathed new life into the Vietnamese Independence League or Viet Minh, Vietnamese revolutionaries organized in 1941 a Cambodian Independence League and a Lao Independence League. The three organizations collectively were intended to form part of a larger body which the Vietnamese envisioned to be the Indochinese Independence League. The subsequent failure to establish a viable Indochinese Independence League proved a crucial juncture in Vietnamese communist thought about Indochina. From this point forward until Saigon fell in April 1975, "Vietnamese communist discourse on Indochina would be dominated by this strategic maxim attaching overriding importance to access to rearguards in Laos and Cambodia as a means to securing Vietnam's western flank." Viewed as a prerequisite for communist action in Vietnam, the "Indochinese Battlefield" was put in motion.[21]

The dialog among Vietnamese communists as to the limits of revolutionary action in Indochina continued into the period following the Japanese overthrow of the French in March 1945. When the Viet Minh came to power in August 1945, they could easily have proclaimed a Republic of Indochina; instead, Ho Chi Minh on 2 September 1945 revived his 1930 Vietnamese line, announcing creation of the Democratic Republic of Vietnam. The slogan "Complete Indochinese Independence!" was also quietly changed to "Complete Vietnamese Independence!." The rationale behind the decision to revert to the Vietnamese line remains a matter of conjecture. Given the recognized discrepancies in Indochinese base-building, the Vietnamese were surely concerned with the tactical dangers associated with creation of a Vietnamese-dominated Indochinese Republic, especially in terms of regional relations with China and Thailand. Nevertheless, tension between the Indochinese and Vietnamese lines persisted in the wake of the August Revolution. For example, *National Salvation*, the official publication of the Viet Minh, soon carried the new slogan "Complete Vietnamese Independence!" but the ICP's *Revolutionary Flag* continued to call for "Complete Indochinese Independence!" well into the postwar period.[22] Even after the Indochinese Communist Party became the Vietnamese Workers' Party in 1951, "the Indochinese model remained the guiding geo-political state structure for the top Vietnamese communist ideologues in the Vietnamese Workers' Party."[23]

## French Indochinese Federation

At the end of World War II, the French government hoped to regain its former influence and position in Indochina. On 24 March 1945, French officials announced a plan long in preparation that called for creation of an Indochinese Federation within the French Federal Union. Couched in general terms, the declaration indicated that Indochina would become autonomous, although the French government would still control its foreign interests. The proposal called for the Indochinese people to become citizens of both the new Indochinese Federation and the existing French Federal Union; however, the process for defining citizenship was left for future determination. While provisions were made for a state council and an elected assembly, both had only advisory powers, and the declaration did not suggest a radical change in the representation of indigenous as opposed to French interests. The Indochinese Federation also promised additional economic freedoms, increased education, more effective labor policies and less discrimination. In addition to the rationale found in public pronouncements, at least two other considerations motivated the French proposal. First, Paris felt it must offer Indochina singular inducements to return to the French community, if for no other reason than to counteract the impact of a Japanese offer of independence. Second, the French government was very concerned that its World War II allies would propose an international trusteeship for Indochina if France did not make a serious gesture of liberalism.[24]

Despite a plethora of evidence to the contrary, one of the myths advanced at the time by proponents of a revived French Indochinese Federation was that colonial rule had been benign and that a federation would return peace to the subregion. As the French geographer Pierre Gourou noted in glowing terms:

> Out of various mutually alien and hostile elements France molded a peaceful whole from which domestic wars were excluded. Irrespective of France's right to intervene in Indo-China, the fact is that she brought about a state of affairs which, viewed in terms of the peaceful relations established among the peoples of the Federation, was certainly not undesirable. Accordingly, the Federation deserves to survive.[25]

Considered in Paris to be a statement of good intentions, the French government felt the creation of an Indochinese Federation marked the beginning of a new era. French Foreign Minister Georges Bidault remarked only three days later that "France has no lessons to learn from anyone in such matters."[26] While independent observers generally disagreed with the arrogant attitude of the French foreign minister, most of them recognized the proposed Indochinese Federation marked a new departure in French colonial policy.

In pursuit of subregional federation, French authorities concluded a modus vivendi with Cambodia on 7 January 1946. Acknowledging King Sihanouk's autonomy in internal affairs, the agreement provided for a French high commissioner, French advisers at ministerial and provincial levels, and French control over defense, foreign affairs and minority populations. Power over matters of subregional concern was to be shared by the government of Cambodia and the Indochinese Federation. While the agreement was not particularly generous, the promise of semi-autonomy for Cambodia represented a significant change from the indirect but total control previously exercised by France over the Cambodian protectorate.[27]

Taking the Franco-Cambodian agreement as a model, a subsequent French pact with Laos in effect restored the latter's prewar status. A provisional modus vivendi, concluded on 27 August 1946, formally endorsed the unity of Laos as a constitutional monarchy within the French Union. But the arrangement involved only a limited devolution of authority as the French again remained responsible for defense and foreign affairs as well as for a variety of other functions from customs and postal services to meteorology and mines. The real power in Laos rested not with the prime minister but with the French commissioner, who retained the right to veto even royal decrees.[28]

A more significant pact, signed by Vietnamese and French authorities on 6 March 1946, followed the modi vivendi signed with Cambodia and Laos. Concluded after six months of difficult talks, this agreement recognized the Democratic Republic of Vietnam as a free state forming a part of the Indochinese Federation and the French Union but with its own government, parliament, army and finances. In addition, Paris agreed to ratify decisions made by the Vietnamese people in a popular referendum on the union of the three Vietnamese provinces of Nam Ky (Cochinchina), Trung Ky (Annam) and Bac Ky (Tonkin). In signing this agreement, the Vietnamese erroneously thought the French would consider Cochinchina to be an integral part of the Republic of Vietnam, at least until such time as the promised referendum directed otherwise. Less than three months later, the French announced the establishment of an independent Cochinchinese Republic within the Indochinese Federation and the French Union. This move to maximize French power in Cochinchina met with very strong objections from the Vietnamese government in Hanoi and contributed to the failure of otherwise promising negotiations.[29]

While Indochina remained their guiding structure, the French later transformed the still-born Indochinese Federation into the Associated States of Cambodia, Laos and Vietnam. Nationalists in Cambodia and Laos proved reluctant to join the Indochinese Federation because the structure left the Vietnamese numerically, and thus politically, predominant. "The dominant role the Vietnamese had played in building Indochina was no longer acceptable for consolidating postwar Laotian and Cambodian states." In this regard, it was no accident that both the Lao and the Cambodians had demanded local as opposed to federal control over immigration and security affairs as a precondition for joining the Indochinese Federation. These were viewed as key juridical tools in over-turning what both governments viewed as the "prewar 'Vietnamisation'" of Cambodia and Laos by the French.[30]

## Special relationships

Vietnamese communists actively engaged in revolutionary work in Laos as early as the 1930s; nonetheless, the essence of the "special relationship" that developed between them and their Lao counterparts was forged in the three decades after World War II.[31] During these difficult years of struggle against the French and Americans, the revolutionary elite of the neighboring states developed close ties based on common ideology and shared revolutionary experience. With many senior Lao cadre educated in Vietnam or married to Vietnamese, historic ties were cemented by the personal relationships forged between members of the two communist movements.[32]

After 1975, the Lao People's Democratic Republic and the Socialist Republic of Vietnam formalized the close relationships developed over the previous years in a series of agreements, the most important of which was a 1977 treaty of friendship and cooperation. In conjunction with these agreements, all important areas of decision making in the early years of the Lao PDR government, from foreign policy to economic planning to military security, were strongly influenced by Vietnamese advisers or made with Vietnam very much in mind. Some observers characterized the prevailing Lao–Vietnamese relationship as a form of Vietnamese colonial-ism. On the contrary, it was more a situation in which, after decades of common struggle, Lao officials felt natural in consulting with their Viet-namese counterparts as to what was best for the Lao People's Revolution-ary Party (LPRP), for Laos and for Indochina as a whole. In this regard, the Kaysone Memorial Museum, created after the death of Kaysone Phomvihane in 1992, literally spoke volumes about the close nature of the Lao–Vietnamese relationship. Most of the books on display in the per-sonal library of the former General Secretary of the LPRP were in Viet-namese, as were his personal notes on a table.[33]

Concrete revolutionary action by Vietnamese communists in Cam-bodia, unlike the Lao experience, did not predate the end of World War II. The reasons for this difference are not completely clear, but the Viet-namese certainly placed greater strategic emphasis on northern Laos and northeastern Thailand than they did on eastern Cambodia. In any case, the failure of southern Vietnamese communists to form bases in Cam-bodia before World War II hampered attempts to influence events there after 1945. At the same time, the Vietnamese communists were the only real allies the Cambodians had for much of the period between the

Geneva Conference in 1954 and the overthrow of the Sihanouk government in 1970.[34]

Suffering heavy losses in 1954–9, the Cambodian communist leadership
pushed Hanoi to adopt a new course of action that would include armed
struggle against the Sihanouk regime. North Vietnam adamantly opposed
this policy because Sihanouk's neutrality protected the western flank of
Vietnam and was thus of enormous strategic importance. A June 1965
meeting in Hanoi between the Secretary General of the Cambodian communist movement and various Vietnamese communist officials marked an
important turning point in Cambodian–Vietnamese relations. When the
Vietnamese again refused to take up armed struggle against the Sihanouk
government, the Cambodians resolved to separate from their Vietnamese
patrons and to carve out a revolutionary program that was uniquely Cambodian albeit strongly influenced by the Vietnamese example.[35] This policy
decision, which contributed to an often uneasy Cambodian–Vietnamese
alliance over much of the next decade, eventually led to the establishment
of Democratic Kampuchea in 1975.

In the late 1960s, a number of significant developments also occurred
internationally which affected events in Southeast Asia. The Sino-Soviet
dispute entered a more acute phase reflected in a growing rivalry between
Moscow and Beijing throughout the subregion. In turn, the escalation of
the Second Indochina War forced Vietnam to depend increasingly on the
more sophisticated military assistance available from the Soviet Union. As
one result, the Soviets eventually replaced the Chinese as the main supplier
of military goods to Vietnam. A related source of tension was the rapprochement between China and the United States, a move Hanoi viewed as
a betrayal. As Sino-Vietnamese relations deteriorated, Beijing responded
by shaping Cambodia into a tool to contain the expansion of Vietnamese
influence in Indochina. In supporting an independent and neutral or pro-
Beijing Cambodia, China hoped to block Vietnamese attempts to dominate
the subregion as well as Soviet efforts to expand their influence in
Indochina, long an integral part of China's security environment.[36]

Throughout this period, the communist leadership in Hanoi continued
to favor an Indochinese federation; however, given the international political climate, they avoided any public discussion of their support. The
Soviet ambassador to Vietnam in a February 1973 political report to
Moscow outlined what he considered to be Hanoi's longer term objectives:

> The program of the Vietnamese comrades for Indochina is to replace
> the reactionary regimes in Saigon, Vientiane, and Phnom Penh with
> progressive ones, and later when all Vietnam, and also Laos and Cam-
> bodia, start on the road to socialism, to move toward the establish-
> ment of a Federation of the Indochinese countries. This course of the
> VWP [Vietnam Worker's Party] flows from the program of the former
> Communist Party of Indochina.[37]

Two years later in the wake of the collapse of Saigon, several factors combined to force Hanoi to undertake a tactical retreat. First, the Vietnamese were reluctant to jeopardize an increasingly uneasy relationship with China, a state which had long laid claim to a role in determining Cambodia's future. Beijing was clearly committed to an independent Cambodia as evidenced by its material and ideological support for the Khmer Rouge insurgency and its nominal head, Prince Sihanouk. Second, Hanoi realized that the successful creation of an Indochina Federation would be dependent on Vietnam's ability to control the military and political situation in both Cambodia and Laos. The Khmer Rouge purge of Khmer Viet Minh in the early 1970s preempted internal control of the Cambodian revolution. And the Khmer Rouge seizure of Phnom Penh two weeks before Hanoi took Saigon precluded a fraternal Vietnamese invasion of its neighbor under the guise of assisting the Khmer Rouge to liberate Cambodia. The leadership in Hanoi may have hoped in 1975 for a resurgence of pro-Vietnamese elements within the Khmer Rouge leadership, but this was not to be the case.[38]

With revolutionary movements now in power in Cambodia and Laos, Vietnam was left to bide its time as it continued to emphasize the special relationship existing with its Indochinese neighbors. At the Fourth Party Congress in 1976, for example, Foreign Minister Nguyen Duy Trinh stressed the importance Vietnam placed on solidarity and fraternal friendship with Cambodia and Laos:

> We attach high importance to the solidarity between the three countries: Vietnam, Laos and Cambodia. The close solidarity between the three countries is of vital importance to the three nations, and a strong source of inspiration for the struggle waged by the peoples in Southeast Asia for genuine peace, independence, democracy and neutrality.[39]

When the People's Republic of Kampuchea, under Vietnamese tutelage, later replaced the Khmer Rouge regime in 1979, Cambodia and Vietnam immediately concluded a 25-year treaty of peace, friendship and cooperation modeled closely after the Lao–Vietnamese pact signed two years earlier. The Cambodian–Vietnamese treaty attached great importance to the tradition of friendship between the Cambodian, Lao and Vietnamese peoples and pledged to strengthen this long-standing relationship.[40]

## Mekong TVA

With the conclusion in 1954 of the First Indochina War, American policy makers began to develop plans to thwart the spread of communism in Southeast Asia through regional economic development projects centered on the Mekong River. The central objective of such projects, as detailed in a proposal prepared by the National Security Council in 1956, was to "deny the general area of the Mekong River Basin to Communist influence or domination."[41] The exact manner in which the U.S. government planned to accomplish its stated objective was left unclear in this and other early documents since there was only limited technical information available about the river or its tributaries.

In formulating policy, the Eisenhower administration drew upon a study, *Reconnaissance Report–Lower Mekong River Basin*, issued in March 1956 by the U.S. Bureau of Reclamation. Proposing a variety of potential sites for hydropower development, this 36-page report included five detailed appendices and constituted a thorough examination of the available data.[42] It also reflected a view popular in American policymaking circles that the lower Mekong River, defined as the river from the Burmese border to the South China Sea, could be developed along the lines of the Tennessee Valley Authority (TVA), a system of dams and other engineering works initiated by the Roosevelt administration in the 1930s. A treasure trove of information, the Bureau of Reclamation report, thereafter, became one of the basic Mekong documents.[43]

At the time, the U.S. government was aware of and concerned with the growing involvement in the area of the Economic Commission for Asia and the Far East (ECAFE), a regional United Nations body. ECAFE had published in May 1952 an 18-page document entitled "Preliminary Report on Technical Problems Relating to Flood Control and Water Resources, Development of the Mekong – An International River" that offered exciting possibilities for subregional development along the Mekong. Washington desired to be the prime mover in the greater Mekong subregion, an area of the world American policy makers had come to view as having great strategic importance. In the face of U.S. opposition, ECAFE later sponsored an independent survey of the Mekong in 1956 and produced a report in 1957, entitled "Development of Water Resources in the Lower Mekong Basin," that influenced plans for subregional development for many years.[44]

The 1957 ECAFE study reiterated many of the arguments found in its 1952 report and reprinted in full the recommendations of the 1956 Bureau of Reclamation study. To exploit the Mekong's resources, the 1957 report called for the construction of a series of five dams on the mainstream of the river. The recommendations reflected a broad consensus at the time that the construction of large dams on the Mekong should be a major part of any plan to exploit the river's resources. In so doing, the 1957 ECAFE report suggested the proposed projects would generate exports, principally electric power and rice, worth an estimated $300 million annually. As a related benefit, the report argued that all of the projects, even those located in a single country, would benefit two or more countries in the subregion.[45]

The U.S. government promoted the idea of a Mekong TVA for most of the following decade. From his first trip to Saigon in 1961, for example, Lyndon B. Johnson was intrigued with the idea of developing the river to provide food and power on a scale so large as to dwarf even the TVA.[46] President Johnson saw a future for the lower Mekong basin similar to his vision of the Texas hill country some four decades earlier when dams had first been built to bring electricity, water and hope to poor American farmers. It was a future full of new houses, schools, hospitals and roads.[47]

In a key speech on Vietnam delivered at Johns Hopkins University on 7 April 1965, President Johnson coupled his resolve to continue the fight against communism with an offer of $1 billion to develop the lower Mekong basin.

> These countries of Southeast Asia are homes for millions of impoverished people. Each day these people rise at dawn and struggle through until the night to wrest existence from the soil. They are often wracked by disease, plagued by hunger, and death comes at the early age of 40.
>
> The American people have helped generously in times past ... and now there must be a much more massive effort to improve the life of man in that conflict-torn corner of our world....
>
> The United Nations is already actively engaged in development in this area.... And I would hope tonight that the Secretary-General of the United Nations [would] initiate, as soon as possible, with the countries of that area, a plan for cooperation in increased development.
>
> For our part I will ask the Congress to join in a billion-dollar American investment in this effort as soon as it is underway.[48]

A recognized master of pork-barrel politics, Johnson believed he could buy communist support with a little old-fashion patronage. The president outlined in his speech a UN project to promote regional economic development by constructing dams along the Mekong in Cambodia, Laos, Thailand and Vietnam. Riddled with doubts, as was often the case with Johnson, the president commented after the speech, "old Ho can't turn me down." But he later told staff members: "If I were Ho Chi Minh, I would never negotiate."[49] One year later, Johnson commented in a speech to the American Federation of Labor–Congress of Industrial Organizations (AFL-CIO): "I want to leave the footprints of America in Vietnam." He added: "We're going to turn the Mekong into a Tennessee Valley."[50] The future as envisioned by President Johnson was filled with promise if only Hanoi would stop its crazy war and join in the task of improving Vietnamese society.

President Johnson's pledge in Baltimore to commit $1 billion in economic aid to develop the lower Mekong basin was still-born. The North Vietnamese government never responded officially to Johnson's proposal to turn the Mekong into an Asian TVA.[51] However, Premier Pham Van Dong did emphasize in a speech before the UN General Assembly the following day that his government was prepared to negotiate only on the basis of the four points contained in the 1954 Geneva Agreements on Vietnam. In so doing, he specifically ruled out UN participation in any initiative or plan.[52]

## Mekong Committee

Founded in 1957 under UN auspices, the Committee for the Coordination of Investigations of the Lower Mekong Basin, generally known as the Mekong Committee, was charged with promoting regional projects throughout the lower Mekong basin. A child of the Cold War, committee membership consisted of the four riparian states located on the lower course of the river (Cambodia, Laos, Thailand and Vietnam), all of which were dependent on U.S. aid. A fifth riparian state, Burma, expressed no interest in membership; and in the early years of the Cold War, no thought was given to Chinese participation.[53]

Governed by one representative each from Cambodia, Laos, Thailand and Vietnam, half the staff of the Committee was drawn from the four member states and half were foreign experts. The Mekong Committee had a statute, *Statute of the Committee for Coordination of Investigations of the Lower Mekong Basin*, to which the four member governments subscribed and which they envisioned one day would become a charter for a Lower Mekong Basin Authority. The primary function of the Mekong Committee was to establish priorities for the various projects envisioned for the subregion.[54]

Reflecting the determination of the U.S. government to play a major role in the area, a reconnaissance team led by Lieutenant General Raymond A. Wheeler, a retired officer in the U.S. Army Corps of Engineers, completed a survey in late 1957 of the lower course of the Mekong. The Wheeler Report called for a basin-wide development plan and suggested several sites for mainstream dams. Its recommendations for the location of dams paralleled those of the 1956 ECAFE report. Accepted by the Mekong Committee in February 1958, the Wheeler Report largely shaped the work of the Committee until the Second Indochina War ended any hope of completing major development projects on the Mekong itself.[55]

In its early years, the Mekong Committee performed an important role in a subregion torn by conflict. At a time when the four member states often bickered with one another, committee members met three or four times annually to discuss the challenges and opportunities of the river. Moreover, they were able to raise over $100 million from 26 countries, 15 international organizations, four private foundations and several private business enterprises. Reflecting American interests, the United States was the largest contributor, and an American became administrative head of the Mekong Committee. Contributions were used to study the flow of the river, possible dam sites on the mainstream and tributaries, and the socio-economic patterns of the 25 million people living in the four member states.[56]

Even as the war escalated in Indochina, the Mekong Committee in 1970 commissioned a team of independent consultants to create a comprehensive 30-year development plan. Known as "The 1970 Indicative Basin Plan," the resulting study constituted a detailed plan for integrated development through the year 2000. Identifying 180 possible projects, the plan called for mainstream and tributary endeavors to generate electric power, control flooding, increase irrigation and improve navigation on the Mekong. Implementation of the plan was later thwarted by growing regional instability. The end of the Second Indochina War subsequently brought new forms of government to Cambodia, Laos and Vietnam which severely impeded the work of the Mekong Committee. All three states failed to appoint plenipotentiary members in 1976 and 1977; and although Laos and Vietnam renewed their participation in 1978, the Khmer Rouge regime in Cambodia did not. The governments of Laos, Thailand and Vietnam later formed an Interim Mekong Committee in January 1978; however, subregional political conditions throughout the 1980s were not conducive to substantive progress.[57]

## Conflicting dreams

In the process of creating *l'Indochine française*, the French government ended traditional patterns of subregional relationships that the peoples of Cambodia, Laos and Vietnam had enjoyed with China and Thailand (Siam), replacing them with the outlines of an emerging French colonial space. Between the two world wars, Indochinese revolutionaries adopted this revised geopolitical framework and sought to fashion from it an Indochina-wide revolutionary movement. Neither the French nor their revolutionary opponents were wholly successful in these competing endeavors; nonetheless, French policy remained largely unchanged throughout the First Indochina War.

During the Second Indochina War, the approach of the United States and its Western allies to economic development in the Mekong Basin, in terms of direction and emphasis, largely mirrored the French view, as opposed to more traditional demographical and geographical patterns. Focused on the Mekong Valley and east-west communication and migration, the Americans promoted large-scale, multi-country projects with a strong emphasis on dam construction on the Mekong and its tributaries. The growing intensity of the war eventually doomed significant practical progress in this regard; however, economic development plans developed in the 1950s and 1960s would be revisited before the end of the century.

American interest in Cambodia, Laos and Vietnam waned with the end of the Second Indochina War, leaving its communist rulers free to continue after 1975 their efforts to promote Indochina-wide cooperation and unity. The concept of a unified French Indochina proved apocryphal before 1975 as would the vision of an Indochina-wide communist movement after 1975. However, communist dreams of a monolithic Indochina would affect the economics and the politics of the region for much of the next two decades.

# 2 Rush to socialism

In our society, there are only two respectable types of people: the proletariat – avant-garde of our society, the beacon of the revolution – and the
peasantry, faithful ally of the proletariat in its struggle for the construction
of socialism. The rest is nothing. The merchants, the petty tradespeople,
they're only exploiters.

> Vietnamese Novelist Duong Thu Huong, *Paradise of the Blind*, 1988

Peace? Damn it, peace is a tree that thrives only on the blood and bones of
fallen comrades. The ones left behind in the Screaming Souls battlegrounds
were the most honourable people. Without them there would be no peace.

> Vietnamese Novelist Bao Ninh, *The Sorrow of War*, 1991

The special, pure, consistent, exemplary and rarely-to-be-seen relationship
that has bound Vietnam to Laos constitutes a factor of utmost importance
that has decided the complete and splendid victory of the revolution in
each country.

> Joint Lao–Vietnamese Statement, 1976

In Cambodia, Phnom Penh fell to the Khmer Rouge on 17 April 1975; and
in Vietnam, Saigon fell to the North Vietnamese Army on 30 April 1975.
In contrast, the communist march to complete power in Laos was more
deliberate and less violent. King Savangvatthana was pressured to sign a
decree on 13 April dissolving the National Assembly, but the Pathet Lao
did not declare Vientiane "completely liberated" until August. And it was
only in early December 1975 that the monarchy was abolished and the Lao
People's Democratic Republic formed.

   With the conclusion of the Second Indochina War, the governments of
Cambodia, Laos and Vietnam quickly initiated "socialist" revolutions. The
speed of implementation was particularly surprising in Vietnam where the
communists had long promised a gradual reunification of North and
South. The communist government in Laos took a more relaxed approach
to the social transformation of the countryside; however, it soon followed
the Vietnamese example, implementing its own program of economic

reforms. In Cambodia, Khmer Rouge radicalism led to an orgy of death and destruction as the government of Democratic Kampuchea (1975–8) returned that hapless state to Year Zero. An unintended victim of the accelerated march to socialism in Cambodia, Laos and Vietnam was the notion of a fraternity of communist states in Indochina.[1]

## Policy vacillation in Vietnam

The Democratic Republic of Vietnam (DRV), before the sudden collapse of the Republic of Vietnam (RVN), had long hinted that reunification of the country would take place in stages over a period of a decade or more. Consistent with this thinking, the "Program of the South Vietnam National Liberation Front" in December 1960 called for the progressive, peaceful reunification of Vietnam.

> The urgent demand of our people throughout the country is to reunify the fatherland by peaceful means. The *South Vietnam National Liberation Front* undertakes the gradual reunification of the country by peaceful means, on the principle of negotiations and discussions between the two zones on all forms and measures beneficial to the Vietnamese people and their fatherland.[2]

In mid-1968, the Alliance of National, Democratic and Peace Forces, a pro-NLF coalition of noncommunist intellectuals and political figures, adopted a manifesto affirming that South Vietnam would be "an independent and fully sovereign state with a foreign policy of nonalignment" and that "national reunification cannot be achieved overnight."[3] The "Action Program of the Provisional Revolutionary Government," announced in June 1969, later repeated the call for gradual reunification.

> The unification of the country will be achieved step by step through peaceful methods and on the basis of discussions and agreement between both zones, without coercion by either side.[4]

Soon after the fall of Saigon, the communist leadership in Hanoi reversed course and decided at the 24th Central Committee Plenum, meeting in July–August 1975, to eliminate the South Vietnamese regime and to proceed with immediate reunification. Excluded from this decision, the National Liberation Front and Provisional Revolutionary Government were obliged in November 1975 to vote themselves out of existence. The decision to proceed with the immediate reunification of North and South Vietnam ignored "the political, psychological, moral, and economic differences between the North and the South and among Vietnam's various peoples," setting the stage for five long years of failed experiment in the South.[5]

Hanoi's decision to proceed to immediate reunification, as Robert K. Brigham stressed in his landmark study of guerilla diplomacy, was the product of a long-standing debate.

> The division of Viet Nam in 1954 posed unique problems for the revolution, compelling it to adopt twin goals: to develop socialism in the North and to wage a war of liberation in the South. These two goals often competed for limited resources and at times were mutually exclusive. Whereas some Party members granted primacy to socialist development in the North and so sought to protect northern interests, southerners saw national liberation as the Party's priority and acted accordingly. The result was an often fierce debate within the Party that led to the South's estrangement at the war's end.[6]

Nationwide elections in April 1976 selected a national assembly which approved in June a government for the newly unified Socialist Republic of Vietnam. Later in the year, the Fourth Party Congress, meeting in Hanoi in December 1976, laid out extremely ambitious, totally unrealistic goals for the complete socialist transformation of the South by 1980.[7]

## North versus South

When Vietnam was reunified in 1975, the North Vietnamese economy had already achieved a high degree of socialism. Most peasants were members of cooperative units, and the bulk of staple food production was carried out by these cooperatives. The industrial segment was also well incorporated into the socialist sector. The state owned relatively modern industrial plants at the central and provincial government levels. Cooperatives at the district level, or within agricultural cooperatives, ran handicrafts. On the other hand, the development of a relatively high level of socialization of ownership was not accompanied by the development of truly effective forms of socialized production. A limited understanding of the economic problems created by this paradoxical situation had begun to emerge by the end of the war. However, full recognition was not widespread because the difficulties of managing a wartime economy and the availability of foreign aid had understandably diverted attention from them.[8]

Unfortunately, the program formulated in Hanoi for the economic transformation of South Vietnam took the establishment of similar institutions in the South for granted. Not only did like institutions not exist, the condition of the agricultural sector in the South at the end of the war was very different from that of the North in 1954 or even in 1975. A series of land reform programs had been implemented in the South in 1956–74 which largely enabled farmers to overcome problems of high land rents and skewed land distribution. The land distribution program implemented in South Vietnam in 1970, known as the "land-to-the-tiller program," redistributed 1.3 million hectares of agricultural land to more than 1 million farmers. Completed in 1974, the results of this program compared favorably to those of the land reform program implemented in North Vietnam in the 1950s. Agriculture in the South was also more highly mechanized than in the North; and in many rural areas in the South, the division of labor was more highly specialized with well developed production servicing and marketing systems.[9]

Despite these differences, the transition model followed in the South after 1975 was very similar to that followed earlier in the North, a model Swedish economists Adam Fforde and Stefan de Vylder rightly noted had already led to hardships there.

> Following a similar procedure to that adopted in the north after 1954, the authorities sought to bring about the "Socialist Transformation" of the south, which essentially meant the imposition of the institutional models of the DRV [Democratic Republic of Vietnam]. In large-scale industry, factories were brought under the direct control of central Ministries who sought to manage them according to central-planning methods, allocating quantity targets for output and requiring that production units submit to the administrative allocation of inputs and outputs. Pressure was brought to bear upon the Mekong delta peasantry for them to join cooperatives and "production collectives." In the centre of the country these measures were quickly successful, but in the south, and especially Ho Chi Minh City, they encountered considerable resistance. . . .[10]

In a keynote address to the National Assembly in July 1976, General Secretary Le Duan provided an official, albeit unimaginative and unconvincing, explanation of how the socialist North and the nonsocialist South could march together down the road to socialism.

> We must immediately abolish the comprador bourgeoisie and the remnants of the feudal landlord classes, undertake the socialist transformation of private capitalist industry and commerce, agriculture, handicraft and small trade through appropriate measures and steps. We [must] also combine transformation and building in order actively to steer the economy of the South into the orbit of socialism and integrate the economies of both zones in a single system of large-scale socialist production.[11]

But if the model was no longer appropriate to the North itself, the special conditions existing in the South created even greater problems there. At the time, these difficulties either were not well understood or were ignored by the Hanoi leadership. As a result, it seems clear in retrospect that the main motives for Hanoi's uncompromising line were political as opposed to economic. Tran Thi Que, a senior researcher at the National Center for Social Sciences and Humanities of Vietnam, later described how the economic process of agricultural collectivization was held captive to the political process.

> It could be said that the collectivization process, or in other words, the process of changing the form of production in accordance with political objectives, was very successful in meeting its official targets. But behind those successes were concealed many factors of instability which were constantly challenging the cooperative form of organization and, to a certain extent, these factors were recognized by the authorities. However, due to the absolute confidence placed in the model, no correct appraisal was made of the nature of the problem and no effective measures were taken to deal with these problems, whose growth was to lead to the ultimate weakening of the collectivization model.[12]

The main cause for the rapidly deteriorating economic situation in Vietnam after 1975 was the decision to impose the economic development strategy followed in the North after 1954 on the South in a wholesale, precipitate manner. In support of this conclusion, Vo Nhan Tri, head of the World Economy Department at the Institute of Economics in Hanoi in 1960–75, cited the overemphasis on heavy industry as well as the strong opposition to agricultural collectivization in the South.[13] In addition, enormous socioeconomic problems faced southern Vietnam at the end of the war, including extensive war damage and the breakdown of basic economic systems and institutions. Social dislocations ranged from war refugees, prostitution, drug addiction and unemployment to hostile political elements.[14]

Nonetheless, it soon became clear to Vietnamese inside and outside the Communist Party that a substantial proportion of the economic problems in the South could not be attributed to colonialism, imperialism or war. Instead, they were the product of the Party's counterproductive economic policies. On this question, the Vietnamese leadership in the immediate postwar period was generally split into two broad tendencies. On the one side, conservative elements demanded ideological purity and insisted on the immediate transformation of the economy in the South to socialism. On the other side, moderates or pragmatists favored granting concessions and offering capitalist incentives, most especially to increase agricultural production in the South. Consequently, as the ideological winds shifted, regime policies vacillated from token liberalism in 1975–6 to rigidity in 1976–8 and back again after 1980 to limited private trade and manufacturing along with practical incentives for farmers.[15]

## Transition to socialism

After decades of struggle, members of the Vietnamese Communist Party were understandably in a rush to implement socialism throughout the country. In line with this thinking, as the Hanoi government realized the scope of the problems it faced in the South, so the answers appeared to lie in tighter control of the wayward southerners. This point was later emphasized by Philip Taylor in his superb study of contemporary southern Vietnamese society:

> The attempt to extend North Vietnamese political culture into the unfamiliar social terrain of the southern half of the country was accompanied by a sustained critique of the way of life associated with the former regime. Such criticisms were based on the assumption that the DRV, despite having unfolded under very different circumstances, embodied an authentic model for the newly unified Vietnamese people.[16]

Initially, the new regime pursued a policy of economic restoration in the South; however, the Party Central Committee in August 1975 declared the nation's economy had entered a period of transition to socialism. This new phase of revolution, namely the socialist revolution, aimed at liberating the nation from hunger and the working people from the exploitation and oppression of capitalists and feudalistic landlords. The X-1 Campaign, launched in August 1975, targeted landlords, big businessmen and war profiteers who had collaborated with the United States and the Saigon regime. The first currency reform, enacted one month later, replaced the old piaster with a new southern dong. In theory, all piasters held by private citizens in the South could be exchanged for the new currency. In reality, each family possessing less than one million piasters was allowed to exchange no more than 100,000 piasters with the remainder deposited in the Central Bank. In consequence, this initial currency reform was not really a reform at all but rather the first step in the socialist revolution.[17]

The Fourth National Congress of the Vietnam Communist Party, meeting in December 1976, adopted the Second Five-Year Plan (1976–80), aimed at a socialist transformation of the South. To achieve this result, the entire country was focused on achieving a so-called "leap forward" in agriculture while at the same time vigorously developing light industry. In the plan, heavy industry appeared to take a secondary role in support of the development of agriculture and light industry; nevertheless, its actual role remained ambiguous. In effect, the thrust of the Second Five-Year Plan, officially designed to unite the two halves of the country, was to leave the rich South concentrating on agriculture and the North on industry. In this regard, the plan took little notice of the resistance of the peasantry in the South to collectivization, and it was overly optimistic in thinking the land would generate sufficient surpluses to fund industrialization. It also under-estimated the damage inflicted on the country by decades of war and was wildly optimistic in its expectations for international funding for postwar economic reconstruction. Embarking on an early unification of Vietnam and thereby forcing the South to adopt the economic practices of the North, the leadership in Hanoi reduced the capability of the Vietnamese economy to expand output at the very time that expansion was most needed.[18]

Predictably, the decision in 1976 to pursue a rapid socialist trans-formation in the South along northern lines precipitated an economic crisis throughout the country. A variety of policies and actions contributed to the developing emergency. They included forced collectivization in agri-culture, an inefficient and rigid administrative supply system, price distor-tions and a tax system heavily biased in favor of distribution and cooperativization. In the first full year of the Second Five-Year Plan, industrial output reached a respectable growth rate of 10.8 percent, but Gross Social Product grew only 4.4 percent. This poor result was due largely to the dismal performance of agriculture. The production of food crops declined from 13.5 million tons in 1976 to 12.6 million tons in 1977, contributing to a 5.7 percent decline in agricultural output.[19]

Priority to heavy industry, which had long occupied a central role in the socialist grand scheme for Vietnam, was officially deferred in the postwar period due to the exigencies of the situation in the South. The Second Five-Year Plan relegated development of heavy industry to second place; and in the Third Five-Year Plan (1981–5) and the Fourth Five-Year Plan (1986–90), it slipped to fourth place. The reality of the situation, on the other hand, was far different from the declared intention of the planners. In 1976–82, Gross Fixed Investment (GFI) in heavy industry grew at an annual rate of 10.2 percent while GFI in light industry fell at an annual rate of 9.2 percent. In terms of investment, the priority accorded to heavy industry was clear, irrespective of claims to the contrary in successive five-year plans. Nevertheless, its capital productivity in 1976–9 declined at a rate of 18 percent per annum. In 1980–2, capital productivity continued to decrease an average of 3.2 percent annually while that of light industry increased by 24.8 percent.[20]

Economist Tran Thi Que accurately explained the discrepancy between expressed priority and actual practice in the following terms:

> It is clear that the country's leaders realize the primary importance of agriculture, not only for its own sake, but for the development of other sectors of the economy as well. Nevertheless this seemed to be an awareness only in theory with the expressed intentions to concen-trate resources to achieve a leap forward in agriculture, existing only in official documents. In practice, the first priority was given to indus-try. Agriculture seems to be providing resources rather than receiving investment because of lower economic investment effectiveness.[21]

The Vietnamese leadership agreed in November 1975 to a step-by-step approach to the collectivization of all sectors of the southern economy. In agriculture, this was understood to mean peasants would first be asked to join labor-exchange teams and later to form low-level cooperatives which would eventually be upgraded. In an abrupt policy reversal, the Communist Party decided at its Second Plenum in July 1977 to accelerate the pace of collectivization. The declared aims of the new program were to steer peasants toward large-scale socialist production, eradicate rural exploitation, mechanize agriculture and mobilize resources for irrigation. Private ownership of land was abruptly ended, and the option to join labor-exchange teams disappeared. Implementation of agricultural collectivization was relatively successful in the central coastal provinces and central highlands of Vietnam. Further south, the peasants strongly resisted collectivization. They objected in particular to a social welfare burden requiring them to support a large number of nonproductive members like Party cadre, the unemployed and the poor.[22]

Even though the government continued into the 1980s to push for enhanced collectivization, the failure of the program was obvious to independent observers by the beginning of the decade. Of the relatively small number of cooperatives established in the South by the end of 1979, most had disintegrated or existed only *pro forma* barely one year later. At the same time, agricultural production continued to deteriorate, mostly due to the dampened individual initiatives that resulted. In a country in which the agricultural sector accounted for some 50 percent of GDP, and in which over 80 percent of the population was living in rural areas, the Vietnamese government in 1976–80 was forced to import 5.6 million tons of food.[23]

The postwar economic crisis also impacted negatively on Vietnam's international trade position as the trade deficit increased an average of 14.8 percent in 1976–9. The deterioration in the balance of trade was due in part to the multiple exchange rate system and the exchange controls adopted by the government. The multiple exchange rate system encouraged importation and gave incentives to expatriates to send goods, instead of hard currency, to relatives in Vietnam. The system thus defeated any attempt to improve export capability or to promote import substitution. In addition, the persistent overvaluation of the Vietnamese dong discouraged sales overseas as well as the supply of exports by local producers since the latter were paid domestic prices for their products.[24]

Recognizing the importance of exports, the Vietnamese government was slow to acknowledge the deterioration in its external trade position. Foreign Trade Minister Dang Viet Chau, as late as December 1978, was still painting a positive albeit totally inaccurate picture of export performance.

> In the last three years, our economy has achieved remarkable progress. As a result, our exports have increased rapidly. In 1976 they

surpassed those of the two zones taken together before reunification, and in 1977 they increased by over 40 percent as compared with 1976. I can say with firm confidence that in the current five-year plan (1976–1980), our exports will probably grow at the average annual rate of over 40 percent.... The prospects for our foreign trade are very bright.[25]

## China, Kampuchea and Vietnam

Foreign policy decisions also impacted directly, and for the most part negatively, on the performance of the Vietnamese economy in the immediate postwar era. By 1977, the People's Republic of China had ended all economic aid of any consequence to the Hanoi government. At the same time, expanded Chinese military aid to the Khmer Rouge encouraged the latter to increase attacks against Vietnamese border provinces. Vietnam responded by invading Kampuchea in late December 1978, and Beijing retaliated by invading Vietnam in mid-February 1979. Premier Pham Van Dong in a February 1979 interview outlined the official Vietnamese position on the growing conflict with China.

> The root cause of the tense situation at the border between Vietnam and China is Beijing's hegemonistic ambitions regarding Vietnam and the other Southeast Asian countries. An independent, unified and socialist Vietnam is a big obstacle to this ambition. That is why, since the Vietnamese people's spring 1975 victory, Beijing's policies toward us have become increasingly hostile. On the other hand, the Beijing leadership incited the Hoa [ethnic Chinese] in Vietnam to riot. It conducted sabotage and cut aid to cause difficulties to Vietnam, and at the same time it intensified armed provocations at the Vietnam–China border and launched an anti-Vietnam campaign of propaganda throughout the world.[26]

While Pham Van Dong's official statement addressed the public aspects of the dispute, other elements were more complex and deep-seated. The genesis for the border disputes between Cambodia and Vietnam stretched back to 1869–1942 when the French administration redrew the borders of Indochina, often to the disadvantage of Cambodia. Well before seizing power in 1975, Khmer Rouge forces had attacked Vietnamese border villages. Those attacks increased in number and intensified in scale as the paranoia of the Pol Pot regime grew after 1975. Over the same period, the Hanoi government had begun to tilt toward the Soviet Union in its competition with China.[27] Analyst Stephen J. Morris best captured the cluster of factors, including the clash of regional ambitions, that impacted on Sino-Vietnamese relations in general and the Vietnamese decision to invade Cambodia in particular.

The background cause was the imperial ambition of Vietnam's leadership, which had always wished to dominate the entire region of what was formerly French Indochina. The immediate or triggering cause, without which the invasion was unlikely to have taken place, was the provocative military attacks upon the communist Vietnamese by the communist Cambodians. These attacks occurred intermittently over a five-year period, peaking in 1977–78.

Among the secondary factors relevant to the outbreak of the war was North Vietnam's foreign policy behavior during the previous decade. By aligning itself with the Soviet Union, in a process that began in the late 1960s at the height of China's conflict with the Soviet Union, North Vietnam had needlessly antagonized China. Vietnam's subsequent decision to purge and begin to expel its ethnic Chinese minority population and to join the Council for Mutual Economic Assistance (Comecon), the Soviet-dominated economic bloc, further antagonized China.[28]

The adverse impact on Vietnamese economic development of the overlapping conflicts with China and the Khmer Rouge was considerable and proved to be much greater than anticipated in Hanoi. The six northern provinces of Vietnam were largely destroyed by the Chinese invaders. The conflicts with China and Cambodia also diverted a large percentage of the population from productive development activities to nonproductive military affairs as well as displacing large numbers of Vietnamese citizens. Finally, in response to the invasion of Cambodia and the resulting pressure from the U.S. government, the capitalist countries cut off virtually all economic assistance to Vietnam. The loss of both Chinese and Western aid was disastrous for a country heavily dependent on foreign resources. In the end, the total cost of the Vietnamese invasion and occupation of Cambodia remains difficult to quantify; however, it likely served to retard Vietnamese economic development for at least a decade.[29]

The Chinese invasion of Vietnam had an especially deleterious impact on the Chinese community in Vietnam which enjoyed a significant presence in the Vietnamese economy. Well before the Europeans arrived, ethnic Chinese played an active role in many sectors of the Vietnamese economy, including commerce, mining and handicraft. The French colonial administration practiced a "divide and rule" policy in which they promoted a separate status for the Chinese minority, a practice that sparked both envy and animosity among the Vietnamese majority. The French welcomed this friction between the Chinese and Vietnamese communities as it reduced the antagonism of the two peoples toward the French, enabling the latter to play the role of peacemaker.[30]

With the departure of the French, the Ngo Dinh Diem government, in an attempt to break what it viewed as a Chinese stranglehold on the South Vietnamese economy, extended its control over the Chinese, seeking to integrate them into the Vietnamese community. In 1956, all Chinese born in Vietnam were granted Vietnamese citizenship and expected to take Vietnamese names. At the same time, all non-Vietnamese nationals were forbidden to engage in 11 occupations, all of which were dominated by the Chinese community and most of which related to retail trade. The impact of these measures was contradictory as the government appeared to push the Chinese out on the one hand and to welcome them in on the other. The Chinese community refused to believe it would be treated on an equal footing with the Vietnamese in matters of trade and was furious with having what it considered to be an inferior nationality thrust upon it. Vietnamese businessmen, on the other hand, complained the Chinese stranglehold on trade actually had been strengthened instead of broken. After a period of internal resistance, most Chinese complied with the citizenship requirement, and the Chinese community largely retained its traditional position in the Vietnamese economy.[31]

The collapse of the Republic of Vietnam (RVN) in 1975 heightened the vulnerability of the Chinese community to a government in Hanoi intent on a rapid transformation from capitalism to socialism. The prosperous business community in southern Vietnam suffered in toto, but it was the Chinese contingent that suffered the most. Victimized in the restructuring of the Vietnamese economy, the deteriorating international situation aggravated local conditions for the Chinese because the government in Hanoi viewed them as a potential fifth column. Following a series of measures undertaken against the ethnic Chinese community, General Secretary Le Duan was able to boast, in an October 1977 conversation with the Soviet ambassador to Vietnam, that the Hoa community no longer posed a threat to the Vietnamese leadership. Whereas ethnic Chinese had previously controlled 80 percent of economic activity in the South, Le Duan indicated that basic positions in the industrial sphere were now firmly in the hands of the "people's authority." The fallout from Chinese involvement in the dispute between Vietnam and Cambodia prompted an exodus of refugees from Vietnam in the second half of the 1970s, a large number of whom were ethnic Chinese, further exacerbating Sino-Vietnamese relations.[32]

## In Laos, old habits continue

The government and people of Laos have enjoyed a long, involved history of foreign aid dependence. From 1968 to 1973, over $74 million in foreign aid annually was pumped into the Royal Lao Government (RLG), making the Lao nationals living in the Vientiane-controlled zone among the highest per capita aid recipients in the world. Unfortunately, most of this money was spent, not in developing the economy, but to feed war refugees and to maintain a high standard of living for the small foreign community. Members of the traditional aristocracy reaped special benefits from the aid bonanza with many of them growing wealthy by channeling aid to their own purposes. Unfortunately, few of the aid dollars corralled by the elite were invested in productive ventures with most dissipated on luxury goods.[33]

The abrupt termination of U.S. aid in 1975, combined with an end to multilateral budgetary assistance, resulted in the virtual collapse of the economy in the former Vientiane-controlled zone. From this perspective, as the anthropologist Grant Evans has emphasized, it was the Second Indochina War, and not internal social change, which led to revolution in Laos.

> It was not internal social change that led Laos to revolution, but America's commitment to rolling back communism in neighboring Vietnam, which in turn made it imperative for the North Vietnamese to support the Pathet Lao and thence led to U.S. intervention in Lao political affairs throughout the 1950s and 1960s to ensure that only solidly pro-U.S. governments ruled in Vientiane. Thus, because of the foreign policy priorities of the world's strongest state the Lao lost control of their destiny.[34]

In the Pathet Lao-controlled zone, massive U.S. bombing destroyed once prosperous villages and reduced many peasants to subsistence living.[35] Guerrilla leaders presided over a primitive economy in a limited area that received large amounts of commodity assistance from China, the Soviet Union and North Vietnam.[36] At war's end, the communist leadership of the newly formed Lao People's Democratic Republic (Lao PDR) inherited a virtually bankrupt state. The flight to Thailand of a substantial segment of the country's limited skilled personnel, together with severe droughts in 1976–7, added to the misery of the Lao people. Rampant inflation plagued the new state as postwar expenditures increased, revenues declined, the movement of goods to market slowed and newly created state enterprises operated at a loss.[37]

Ideologically, the Lao PDR viewed suppression of the laissez-faire economy as an essential stage in its consolidation of the socialist revolution. Nevertheless, the Lao People's Revolutionary Party (LPRP), at the outset, wisely eschewed the path of radical socioeconomic transformation and instead promised gradual change. Unlike in Cambodia and to a lesser extent in Vietnam, there was no headlong rush to a social transformation of the countryside. Instead, Lao peasants were encouraged to embrace a collective way of life and to form solidarity and labor-exchange units through which they would learn to appreciate the advantages of forming cooperatives.[38]

Once the LPRP assumed power, it took time for the flow of non-military aid to regain momentum. That said, the total value of commodity aid received by Laos in the 1975–8 period was estimated at more that $100 million with project aid and technical assistance worth an additional $126.5 million. The sources of revenue for the Lao PDR, as early as 1977, mirrored those of the previous regime in that foreign aid accounted for 81 percent of the total. Approximately 60 percent of multilateral aid came from the United Nations with the remaining 40 percent sourced from OPEC financial agencies. Multilateral aid rose significantly in 1978, largely reflecting increased lending by the Asian Development Bank (ADB) and the World Bank through the International Development Association.[39]

Bilateral assistance from socialist states remained an important source of aid for Laos after the new government took power in December 1975. The Soviet Union proved the dominant player in this regard, especially after 1978, when both China and North Korea suspended bilateral assistance. Following a January 1978 Comecon delegation visit to Laos, fresh agreements on economic and technical assistance were concluded with the USSR as well as Czechoslovakia, Bulgaria and Hungary. Later expanded to cover Poland, these agreements became increasingly sector oriented as the aid effort intensified. In terms of bilateral aid from nonaligned states, Sweden was the most prominent donor and the first to make a significant contribution after independence. Australia, France, Japan, the Netherlands and the United Kingdom also contributed aid in the early years of the revolution. The U.S. government, despite the socialist orientation of the Lao PDR, extended modest amounts of food aid annually in 1977–9. The Vietnamese presence in Laos, dominant in the military sense by the end of the decade, later led to charges that food aid, both from the East and the West, was diverted to feed Vietnamese military and civilian advisors.[40]

## Economic reform in Laos

Following a secret two-day meeting of the Congress of People's Representatives in early December 1975, the general public was told the six-century-old monarchy had been abolished and replaced by the Lao PDR. The full rationale behind the abrupt timing of this announcement remained a matter of speculation; however, it was surely influenced by the simultaneous decision in Hanoi to proceed with the immediate reunification of North and South Vietnam. The severe economic impact of the blockade Thailand imposed on Laos from November 1975 to January 1976, following an exchange of fire along the disputed border, also likely impacted the decision. Evidence of limited, active resistance to the regime, especially among selected ethnic minorities, may also have encouraged the accelerated move to the next phase of the revolution. At the time, an estimated 30,000 Vietnamese troops were stationed in Laos to help deal with the insurgents.[41]

The Lao PDR announced in 1976 that it intended to build an independent, national economy that would progress, step by step, toward socialism without first passing through a stage of capitalist development. Its initial program consisted of three core elements. First, the government planned to reduce the service sector in favor of the state sector, implying the nationalization of some private sector assets, together with the implementation of measures to control petty traders. Second, it intended to develop the state sector, including banking, internal trade, transportation and export trade. Third, it planned to emphasize the agricultural sector, including the development of irrigated rice production, multiple cropping and the rationalization of labor use. In industrial policy, the government aimed to maintain existing artisanal and industrial production, construct agro-industries and develop the mining and hydropower sectors. Finally, the Lao PDR announced its intent to reduce the nation's dependence on the flow of goods through Thailand and to increase trade through Vietnam.[42]

The economic reforms introduced in the second half of the 1970s focused on the marketing and distribution systems, property rights and the agricultural taxation system. Not all reforms were implemented at the same time, with changes in the marketing system and tax policies preceding reform of the property rights system. Laos established in 1976 a public trading network and made inter-provincial trade a state monopoly. Salaries and wages of civil servants were kept at low levels as were government-subsidized prices of basic commodities, like rice, fish sauce and kerosene, sold in newly created state stores. Two price systems emerged with the administrative price system, consisting of prices fixed by the government in the public distribution network, paralleling a free market system determined by conditions of supply and demand. As the economy deteriorated, the government also implemented a series of strong fiscal measures. The Vientiane kip in June 1976 was demonetized and replaced by the Liberation kip at a conversion rate of 20 to one. As poor budgetary discipline and state enterprise deficits combined to expand the money supply, the Lao PDR introduced additional measures to improve budgetary discipline, control monetary expansion and reduce state enterprise losses.[43]

Significant changes in the agricultural taxation system, intended to generate revenues to support the state apparatus and to supply the state distribution network with basic foodstuffs, accompanied reforms made to the marketing and distribution systems. In October 1976, the Lao PDR introduced a progressive tax that took up to 30 percent of a farmer's rice production. Non-rice crops, when they provided the principal source of income, were taxed at a flat rate of 8 percent. In its defense, the communist government had little option but to turn to taxation to replace the budget subsidy provided by the United States before 1975. At the same time, the introduction of new agricultural taxes, without a concerted effort to explain their need, soured relations with the very Lao peasantry the government claimed to represent. In contrast, the previous regime had not collected rice taxes; and with landlordism not a serious problem in Laos, few farmers had ever paid rents in kind. The unpopularity of rice taxation, together with an equally unpopular rice purchase policy in which the government purchased rice at below market prices, fostered distrust with the subsequent policy of collectivization. In retrospect, the agricultural tax policy proved the clearest signal to date that the government planned a new role for Lao peasants in the nation's economic development.[44]

Dissatisfaction with the agricultural tax program was so widespread that government officials were forced to defend publicly the new policies, an unusual tact in the Lao PDR. An article in *Sieng Pasasonh*, the Party journal, exemplified the official government line.

> We must make it clear to our people that paying agricultural taxes to the state now is different from paying taxes to the reactionary clique in the past. Then it only served to increase the wealth of a group of persons or their men and did not help the nation or the people; today it contributes to national construction and to the improvement of the people's living conditions.[45]

The Lao PDR in March 1978 launched an interim three-year development plan, intended to bring state planning in line with the five-year planning cycle of Vietnam and the Comecon states. The objective of the plan was to attain by 1980 self-sufficiency in food grains, most notably rice. The government planned to achieve this goal by increasing the cultivated area, expanding irrigation and increasing yields. To accomplish these targets, the government allocated new funds to industry and manufacturing to increase inputs to agriculture as well as to accelerate the processing of timber. Reflecting geopolitical concerns, the government also emphasized a variety of transport and communications projects, including construction of an all-weather road to Vietnam.[46]

## Social and political reform in Laos

As the Lao PDR struggled to remake the economy, it embarked on a concerted effort to reestablish Lao cultural identity and national sovereignty. The immediate need was "to integrate the many scattered villages and districts into a single country with a common identity," a task never before accomplished. Divided into principalities at the time of the French takeover, the creation of the modern Lao state was the product of French concessions to Lao sovereignty in the 1946–54 period when Laos was recognized as an independent state. At that time, dialogue centered on the king and Buddhism.[47]

In contrast, post-1975 discourse evidenced a new, socialist world in which the king had abdicated and Buddhism was no longer recognized as the state religion. The revolutionary government first sought to duplicate throughout Laos the administrative structures in place in the liberated zones before 1975. This process involved increased control by political cadre, a thorough reorganization of village administration, creation of mass organizations at village level and emphasis on political correctness. The increased political and social control that resulted prompted an estimated 300,000 people, approximately 10 percent of the population, to make their way to refugee camps in Thailand. It took the Lao PDR many years to recover from this loss of much of its educated citizenry. Government policies regarding national integration had far-reaching consequences for ethnic minorities in particular. Attempts to rationalize upland farming and to promote paddy rice production led to the relocation of upland villages to lowland areas. While some ethnic minorities had supported the Pathet Lao during the war, others sided with the Royal Lao Government and concerns for the political reliability of the latter motivated some relocations. Implementation of the relocation policy resulted in social disruption, and in some cases high mortality. Associated promises of land clearance and school and clinic construction were not always kept.[48]

Buddhism occupied a central place in the nationalist ideologies of other Southeast Asian states, like Cambodia and Thailand, but not in Laos because it was the religion of the ethnic Lao population only and not that of hill tribe groups. A major wartime achievement of the Pathet Lao was their elaboration of a nationalist ideology that recognized ethnic minorities as part of the Lao nation. Once in power, the new regime moved quickly to bring Buddhism under its influence. The Buddhist *sangha* was reorganized in 1976 with the supreme patriarch displaced by a committee from the newly created Lao United Buddhist Association. Regime militants, arguing monks were part of the unproductive, former ruling class because they were dependent on alms, forced them to till their own gardens. This injunction, together with food shortages in 1976–7, led monks to abandon their *wats* with some becoming forest monks. In turn, many believers, concluding monks who worked were not really monks, stayed away from their *wats*. As a result, a revival of both spirit worship and consultations at the village level took place in the early years of the revolution. It thus proved ironic that a policy aimed at mobilizing Buddhism for state ends led to a revival of "superstitious practices" outside the *wats* as well as the alienation of many lowland Lao.[49]

In promoting change, the Lao PDR recognized the importance of symbolism. In December 1975, a series of resolutions related to the Lao language, national anthem and national flag were adopted in an effort to reconstruct the past. The new national anthem, for example, replaced references to Buddhism and to a singular Lao race with references to all Lao ethnic groups. At the same time, the music of the old anthem was retained in an apparent effort to maintain phonic continuity. Over time, "through gesture after gesture, the new regime distanced itself from the old regime, and then embarked on modifying old rituals and symbols and creating new ones." The Lao PDR implemented dramatic breaks with the past, such as abolishing the monarchy, but also adjusted to existing realities. For example, Vientiane kip notes were destroyed in ceremonial burnings in June 1976 and replaced with the new Liberation kip. But old stamps remained in use, as long as the word "kingdom" was crossed out so that only "Laos" remained. Unlike its comrades in Cambodia and Vietnam, the Lao PDR also decided it was unnecessary to rename the streets of the main cities of Laos.[50]

### Agricultural collectivization campaign

At the outset of 1977, the Lao PDR appeared to be preparing for a relatively slow, steady march to socialism. Not yet in command of the countryside, its administrative reach was limited and its control of the economy fragile. With the overall situation poised to improve, external and internal events combined to spur the regime to take more aggressive measures. A deterioration in relations with Thailand led to another blockade in 1977. Growing tensions between Vietnam, the closest ally of Laos, and both China and Democratic Kampuchea, further increased the insecurity of a landlocked state seemingly surrounded by threatening powers. Serious natural calamities compounded the impact of mounting international tensions to lead the LPRP leadership to initiate an accelerated economic and social transformation of the countryside.[51]

Official pronouncements in the second half of 1977 promoted the collectivization of agriculture; and in early 1978, the Political Bureau of the LPRP announced a formal policy of collectivization based on the creation of village-based cooperatives. The government had made no mention of cooperatives when it came to power in late 1975, but the increased use of both mutual aid groups and solidarity teams paved the way for the launch of the new program. Officials emphasized economic reasons for the change, arguing collectivized agriculture would boost production by increasing the amount of land under cultivation and facilitating the use of irrigation and technology. Ideological and political considerations were also cited in support of the decision to establish cooperatives.[52]

The socialist transformation of agriculture in Laos focused on the creation of village-based cooperatives, as opposed to land reform, leading to the formation of over 1,732 such units by the end of April 1979. By the time the program was suspended three months later, the government claimed 2,800 cooperatives existed, incorporating some 25 percent of peasant families. The program also involved the creation of a few state farms; however, the emphasis of the movement was on rice cultivation which occupied some 85 percent of all agricultural land. The rapid growth of village-based cooperatives resulted in declining agricultural outputs and increasing peasant resistance. Opposition to the policy took a variety of forms, including smuggling to Thailand, destruction of agricultural output, emigration and cultivation in remote areas where administrative control was lacking.[53]

In response, the Lao PDR in mid-1979 abruptly suspended the forced creation of agricultural cooperatives and called for the consolidation of existing ones. At the same time, the government accommodated those peasants who had been forcibly organized and now wished to withdraw. The manifold reasons for the failure of collectivization have been grouped by historian Martin Stuart-Fox under a few central headings.

> These include peasant attachment to traditional lifestyles, lack of understanding of the value of cooperatives, fear of effects of joining, the shortage of trained cadres, their failure to understand and implement the Central Committee directive and their use of coercion, failure of the government to provide material support, and the effectiveness of anti-government propaganda in exploiting peasant distrust of government motives.[54]

The decision to suspend the creation of agricultural cooperatives, when coupled with reforms in the agricultural taxation system, signaled a major policy shift. The basic error as Kaysone Phomvihane, Prime Minister and General Secretary of the LPRP, admitted in late 1979 was that the government had adopted an over-centralized model of socialism in which the state sector was unable to fulfill its prescribed role. Socialism remained the ultimate goal of the Lao PDR, but increased production and an improved standard of living were recognized as immediate needs for the stability of the regime.[55]

In this regard, it should be remembered that the Lao PDR decision to embark on an ambitious program of agricultural collectivization followed in the wake of a similar decision in Vietnam. There was a limited economic rationale for the policy in southern Vietnam; however, there was no possible justification for its introduction in Laos, except ideological conviction in the superiority of the socialist mode of production. Given the extent of small-scale, individual landholdings in Laos, any widespread move towards collectivization necessitated careful preparation and introduction if it was to have any chance of success; however, this was never done. Consequently, widespread peasant opposition to collectivization, especially when it was preceded by unpopular changes to rice taxation and purchase policies, was to be expected. By mid-1979, both the Soviets and the Vietnamese were counseling the Lao PDR to suspend the program indefinitely. Of some 2,800 cooperatives organized after 1978, as few as 65 retained any organizational basis by 1980.[56]

## Heightened economic reform

The decision to terminate plans to collectivize Lao agriculture a little more than a year after their announcement represented a clear victory for pragmatism over ideology. Food production was now accorded the number one priority in an effort to reduce imports and overcome the nation's food deficit. Coming as it did halfway through the interim three-year plan, the abandonment of the policy of collectivization heralded similar rethinking on the broader economic front. The change was recognized officially in December 1979 in the Seventh Resolution of the Supreme People's Assembly. In a truly remarkable document, the regime candidly admitted its shortcomings and announced sweeping economic reforms to address the problems arising from earlier policy decisions.

> In guiding economic activities, we have failed to firmly grasp and implement the details of the economic line, plan and policy of the party and state. We still have some weak points in organizing the implementation of the plan and policy. In addition, there has been a delay in formulating many necessary plans on economic activities. Some plans or systems on economic activities, which we have already adopted, do not conform with the true situation in the country.[57]

The package of reforms embodied in the Seventh Resolution touched virtually every aspect of the Lao economy. In the current stage of economic development, General Secretary Kaysone admitted, recourse would have to be made to both capitalist and socialist economic laws in an effort to promote economic growth. The government officially recognized five separate economic sectors – individual subsistence, joint state-private, private capitalist, collective or cooperative, and state-socialist – all of which would have to be developed for the welfare of the nation. In short, the government agreed to recognize private investment by small traders as well as the investment of private capital in larger enterprises, either privately run or operated in conjunction with the state.[58]

In line with the overall objectives of the Three-Year Plan (1978–80), the Seventh Resolution emphasized agricultural production in particular.

> In the immediate future, all cantons, districts and provinces must review their past experiences in implementing plans for agricultural production, outline new plans and tasks for 1980, organize a thorough implementation of the above-mentioned measures together with periodic inspections, and pay attention to learning from 1979 lessons in mobilizing the people to set up agricultural cooperatives to prepare for the 1980 production season....[59]

Among the steps introduced to stimulate the production and distribution of goods, the most significant initiatives liberalized restrictions on private participation in manufacturing, commerce and internal trading. The government called for private involvement in communications and transportation in order to overcome bottlenecks in state procurement and distribution services. And it made major concessions in the area of internal trade where past policies had been especially restrictive. In an effort to boost agricultural production, curtail inflation and improve the overall economic climate, the Lao PDR reduced the tax on rice. The Seventh Resolution also introduced important new reforms in pricing, finance and economic management. In so doing, the government admitted that it was unable to control prices. In an unexpected currency reform, the Bank kip replaced the Liberation kip, implementing an effective devaluation of 60 percent against the U.S. dollar.[60]

The Seventh Resolution represented a major policy reorientation in the Lao PDR's transition to socialism, and its central themes were reiterated at the Party's Third Congress in 1982 and Fourth Congress in 1986. The revised LPRP economic strategy legitimized small-scale capitalism and petty commodity production; however, the state sector still controlled the "commanding heights" of the Lao economy. A significant policy shift, the Seventh Resolution did not constitute a basic reappraisal of capitalism. For the communist leaders of Laos, "the long-term superiority of socialism over capitalism remained unquestioned."[61]

## Subregional collaboration

Vietnam began to characterize its relations with Laos as a "special relationship" well before the Pathet Lao came to power in late 1975. With the establishment of the Lao PDR, Hanoi reaffirmed this symbiotic relationship, together with its view of Indochina as a strategic unit, retracing the roots of the Indochinese Communist Party back to the 1930s. Vietnamese General Secretary Le Duan put special emphasis on the strategic interdependence of the two states: "Neither of our two countries could live and work in peace, independence and freedom, so long as the security and territory of the fraternal country was threatened and encroached upon by imperialism." His remarks reflected the threat to Laos and Vietnam posed by Thailand, because of its collusion with the United States, as well as Hanoi's growing suspicion of China.[62] General Secretary Kaysone officially endorsed the "special relationship" in a visit to Hanoi in February 1976:

> The special relationship ... is the great, constantly consolidated and enhanced comradeship between two Parties which both issue from the Indochinese Communist Party. ... The special, pure, consistent, exemplary and rarely-to-be-seen relationship that has bound Vietnam to Laos constitutes a factor of utmost importance that has decided the complete and splendid victory of the revolution in each country. This is also the firmest basis for the solidarity and cooperation between the two Parties and the two countries, and for the victory of the revolution in each country in the new stage.[63]

The close economic and political relationship enjoyed by Laos and Vietnam, in which Vietnam remained the dominant external power within Laos, was cemented in a 25-year treaty of friendship and cooperation in July 1977. The second article of the pact accorded Vietnam legal justification to maintain large numbers of Vietnamese advisers in Laos.[64] The two states also concluded a border delimitation treaty, forming a joint border commission which divided the frontier into 19 sectors and completed a pilot demarcation in March 1979. The remainder of the frontier was demarcated between July 1979 and August 1984.[65]

On the first anniversary of the Lao–Vietnamese Friendship Treaty, Kaysone issued a statement publicly committing Laos to the Vietnamese side in the latter's disputes with both Cambodia and China.

> We once again reaffirm that we always stand by the struggle to defend their [the Vietnamese people's] independence, sovereignty and territorial integrity against threats, pressures, trouble-making, provocation, violation, slander and sabotage, committed by the imperialists and the international reactionaries.[66]

In December 1978, a large-scale Vietnamese invasion of Cambodia ended almost four years of Khmer Rouge rule. The Chinese government responded in February 1979 with a three-week punitive attack on the northern border provinces of Vietnam. In response, Laos denounced China by name for the first time in March 1979, and its rhetoric against China was soon indistinguishable from that of Vietnam. In April 1979, Lao PDR President Souphanouvong outlined the accusations against China:

> The Chinese powerholders who are pursuing a counterrevolutionary policy of regional hegemony and big-nation expansionism. . . . are ruthlessly carrying out schemes to swallow up our country as well as Vietnam and Kampuchea so as to proceed with annexing other countries in Southeast Asia. . . . We must maintain high vigilance against the adventurous, warmongering schemes of the Chinese powerholders.[67]

Lao PDR officials complained of alleged Chinese aid to anti-government rebels, especially Hmong remnants of General Vang Pao's army, as well as the resettlement of Lao refugees in Yunnan province near the Lao border. One of the reasons for the December 1979 currency reform was the fear Beijing, which held the printing plates for the Liberation kip, might sabotage the Lao economy by circulating illegally printed currency. Given the vehemence of its propaganda campaign, China took a surprisingly indulgent stance toward the Lao PDR, largely blaming Vietnam and the Soviet Union for the provocative statements of the LPRP.[68]

In its relations with the Association of Southeast Asian Nations

(ASEAN), Laos continued to follow the lead of Vietnam. Following the communist takeover in Laos, the governments of both Laos and Vietnam proclaimed their desire to improve relations with the ASEAN member states but denounced ASEAN itself as an American-sponsored, anti-communist body. And they later decried an ASEAN resolution calling for creation of a zone of peace, freedom and neutrality after it was introduced at a summit of nonaligned nations in August 1976. Attitudes began to change as the decade ended and the growing rift with China led Laos and Vietnam to seek a more active, harmonious involvement in regional affairs, a policy supported by the Soviet Union.[69]

A joint Lao–Thai communiqué in January 1979 promised to transform the Mekong into a river of peace, friendship and mutual benefit. Nevertheless, Thailand in mid-1980 used a shooting incident on the Mekong as a pretext to again close its border with Laos. Thailand probably took this action more as a means to display its opposition to Vietnam's occupation of Cambodia than as a punitive measure against Laos. The border closure also signaled Bangkok's displeasure with a recent Vietnamese strike at Khmer refugee camps inside Thailand. Finally, it encouraged Vientiane to reconsider its close ties with Hanoi and to recognize the importance of friendly relations with Thailand. While the Chinese government firmly supported Thai policy, it continued to stress its friendship for the Lao people, claiming its grievances were with the Lao PDR leadership. Two months later, Thailand reopened two border crossings near Vientiane, citing humanitarian concerns for the Lao people.[70]

The evolving nature of the Lao–Vietnamese relationship led many seasoned Southeast Asian observers to conclude that Laos by 1980 had sacrificed its independence to its larger, stronger neighbor to the east. Academics Brown and Zasloff, referring to Kaysone's statement on the first anniversary of the conclusion of the Lao–Vietnamese Friendship Treaty, together with other official utterances, spoke of Hanoi's "domination" over Laos.

> The national interest of weak little Laos, if she could act independently, would be to remain neutral in a conflict between her two powerful neighbors, Vietnam and China, and to steer a middle course in the Sino-Soviet dispute. Laos's forthright assumption of the Vietnamese and by extension the Soviet side in this conflict seems to have resulted from Vietnamese pressure, presumably with Soviet endorsement.[71]

In turn, historian Arthur J. Dommen argued that "Vietnam has replaced France as the colonial power in Indochina" with Laos essentially "a satellite of Vietnam." At the same time, he rightly viewed Hanoi's policy toward Laos as reflective of a return to the concept of a unified Indochina.

The stationing of Vietnamese troops in Laos today is obviously aimed at defending the independence, sovereignty, territorial integrity and economic and cultural construction not of Laos, but of a Greater Vietnam, envisioned by Ho Chi Minh's successors and supported by the Soviet bloc. This Greater Vietnam will make Laos far more a part of Vietnam than the Indochinese Federation Ho envisioned when his preoccupation was the expulsion of the French.[72]

## Vietnam leads – Laos follows

Throughout history, successful revolutionaries have often proved more adept at war and revolution than at peace and reconstruction. This proved to be the case in Vietnam. By early 1979, it was increasingly clear to outside observers that the economic policies developed in the North and fostered on the South were not addressing the economic and social problems of the newly unified country.

The crisis of 1979–80 above all affected the central state management system. Western and Chinese aid cuts reduced directly the volume of resources controlled by the state trading monopolies. At the same time bad weather and resistance to the collectivization drive in the Mekong delta made it extremely difficult for the authorities to secure rice supplies. There was a sharp fall in domestic supplies of staples to the state in 1978 and 1979. At the same time, imports fell off as Western countries and China responded to the deterioration in international relations and the Vietnamese invasion and occupation of Kampuchea in the winter of 1978–79.[73]

While the Communist Party Central Committee eventually initiated tentative steps in the direction of economic reform, years would pass before there was a broader recognition in Vietnam that the rush to unite the North and the South under a single communist government was a major historical error. As Gareth Porter, a noted Vietnam scholar, later concluded:

A separate Southern regime would have avoided the policies of forced collectivization of agriculture and elimination of the Chinese-dominated trading system by confiscating the assets of merchants and sending the merchants to the countryside. It would have established business links with the overseas Chinese communities in East Asia and maintained a freer press that might have prodded the party leadership to begin the process of economic and political reform much sooner than it did.[74]

In short, a separate regime in the South after 1975 would have put Vietnam in a much stronger position in the late 1970s to implement the economic and social reforms that, because of forced unification, it was eventually able to adopt only in the late 1980s.

The full extent to which internal policies in Laos trailed Vietnamese decisions in the first half-decade of the revolution was remarkable. Comparing the sequence of events in Laos and Vietnam in the period 1975–80, major domestic policy decisions in Laos almost invariably followed similar decisions in Vietnam. This was definitely true in the case of agricultural policy in Laos where a decision to move forward with an accelerated drive toward collectivization in 1977–8 was soon followed by an abrupt decision to suspend the same movement. Other economic policies implemented in Laos after 1976 also mirrored Vietnamese practice as did the decision to relax economic controls and move toward a market economy in 1979. In the colorful words often employed in the official communications of both states, Laos and Vietnam were like "lips and teeth."[75] Given the close correlation between the Lao and Vietnamese approaches, in both domestic and foreign policy, the Seventh Resolution of the Lao People's Revolutionary Party, introduced in December 1979, suggested the beginning of an important new emphasis by the Lao PDR to develop Lao solutions to Lao problems.

Interrelated to a certain degree, it must be recognized in the end that the post-1975 revolutions in Laos and Vietnam were undertaken in vastly different circumstances. As they evolved, each assumed a singular character. Consequently, the economies of Laos and Vietnam remained significantly different in important areas from the agricultural sector to investment policies to the management of state enterprises. A comparative look at selected aspects of economic and political reform in these states directs attention to the unique approach to economic growth each pursued. It also highlights the different rules, regulations and procedures in place or coming into place. Such policy differences threatened to inhibit the ability of their respective economies to participate fully in the growing number of proposals for subregional and regional development later advocated by private and public bodies.

# 3   Tentative reforms

The king of the mice agreed to pay the woodcutter a gold coin daily not to cut down the tree where he lived. The woodcutter's wife told him to fell the tree because the mouse-king hid a pile of gold underneath it. The wood-cutter did as he was told, but there was no gold to be found, and the mouse-king had run off, too. That night, the mouse-king and some of his subjects crept up to the woodcutter's house and took back the gold pieces he had collected earlier, so he was soon as poor as ever.

"The Woodcutter and the Mouse-King," Cambodian Folk Tale

My life seems little different from that of a sampan pushed upstream towards the past. The future lied to us, there long ago in the past. There is no new life, no new era, nor is it hope for a beautiful future that now drives me on, but rather the opposite. The hope is contained in the beautiful pre-war past.

Vietnamese Novelist Bao Ninh, *The Sorrow of War*, 1991

On the economic front, we also indulged in subjectivism, failed to grasp economic laws and to strongly promote the people's mastery as a motive force.

LPRP General Secretary Kaysone Phomvihane, 1982

The governments of Cambodia, Laos and Vietnam cautiously initiated in 1979 a limited process of economic reform. Predictably, the output of many of these reforms was soon compromised by internal, ideological debates over the optimum pace and direction of socialist transformation. Consequently, this first wave of reforms yielded disappointing results, setting the stage for renewed efforts in the second half of the decade.

At the time, all three states faced related development challenges; therefore, it was not surprising that many of the reforms implemented appeared on the surface similar in origin, sequence and substance. Selected reform programs were interrelated to some degree; however, they were mostly undertaken in different circumstances, and each gradu-ally assumed a unique character. The ongoing emphasis by the communist leadership in all three states on their "special relationship" added to the confusion. Official statements implied the three neighbors were proceeding down parallel development paths when the reverse was more often the case.

## Early reforms in Vietnam

It was clear by early 1979 that the economic policies instituted in Vietnam after 1976 were not reducing the serious economic and social problems facing the newly unified country. The industrial sector had ceased to grow; food production was erratic; GNP was barely equal to that of 1976; and population growth had reduced the per capita GNP figure. When General Secretary Le Duan acknowledged the difficult situation Vietnam faced at the outset of the 1980s, he placed the blame squarely on the socialist policies pursued by the Party after 1975.

> The deep root cause of the difficulties in the economy and daily life is the following: Our economy is still primarily one of small production, and moreover suffers the extremely heavy aftermaths of prolonged war and of colonialism....
> On the other hand, the difficulties have also stemmed from shortcomings and mistakes of the party and state agencies, from national down to grass-roots levels, in economic leadership and management and in the running of our society.
> In some definite aspects, these shortcomings and mistakes in leadership and management have mainly caused or aggravated the social and economic difficulties in the past years. The party Central Committee sternly criticizes itself before the congress.[1]

In response to the deteriorating situation, the Sixth Plenum of the Party Central Committee, meeting in August 1979, retreated from its policy of a rapid socialist transformation of the economy and initiated instead a policy of cautious economic reform. Criticizing what was described as a "haste tendency," the Vietnamese leadership took steps to provide incentives to producers, to encourage individual initiative, and to grant greater autonomy to local authorities and production units. Reflecting the power wielded by conservative Party elements, this initial attempt at economic reform was limited in scope.

> To encourage production establishments to fully use all their potential for producing as many goods, especially consumer goods, as possible ... on 2 August [1979] the Council of Ministers promulgated the following policies:
> Boldly encourage state-owned, collective and privately-run production establishments to accelerate the production of commodities which

are not under state control and which are not produced with state-supplied materials.

Local economic units are authorized to establish direct relations and contracts with each other in order to accelerate production and circulation of these goods.

State enterprise, joint state-private firms and collectively, and privately, run economic units will be allowed to purchase agricultural, forestry and fishery by-products as well as other locally available raw materials which are not under state control for the production of commodities, provided that they do not involve themselves in competitive buying of those raw materials for which the state has planned the buying in the localities concerned.[2]

The Party's call for greater economic efficiency, less central control and more attention to individual interests stimulated a number of concrete changes in the Vietnamese economy.[3]

In both agriculture and industry, "spontaneous bottom-up" reforms were the first steps taken to adjust to the new economic conditions. Peasants in Vinh Lac district of Vinh Phu province had initiated the output contract system in 1967–8. It was later adopted in the late 1970s by a cooperative in Do Son district of Haiphong city. Severely criticized by Vietnamese officials at the time, the Party now endorsed the output contract system as an innovative effort to raise production. Under Instruction 100 CT, widely known as Contract 100, the Party Central Committee in January 1981 made the output contract system national policy. Contract 100 proved to be the initial legal document in the economic reform of Vietnamese agriculture.[4] As economist and Vietnam expert Melanie Beresford later observed, "the adoption of this system [the output contract system] represented a virtual revolution in official thinking on collective agriculture."[5]

The government aimed to keep the cooperative agricultural system intact but to enhance the role of individual initiative and productivity in both output and reward systems.[6] The driving force of Contract 100 was its return to peasant households of control over some links in the farm production process.[7] Through a production group or cooperative, the output contract system allocated plots of land to individual farmers; and a delivery quota, based on average yield over the last three years, was then established for each farmer. The cooperative furnished the farmer with adequate inputs to achieve the contracted output level. But household farms retained for sale in the free market all output in excess of the preestablished delivery quota.[8]

At the outset, the Contract 100 system was limited in application to northern and central Vietnam. Due to continuing opposition to agricultural cooperatives, the Party was unwilling to implement immediately this new form of contractual arrangement in the South. Consequently, there was a specific reservation in Instruction 100 CT:

> For cooperatives in the mountainous regions and cooperatives and
> production collectives in the south, the Ministry of Agriculture will,
> along with the provinces, study and give specific guidance on the
> proper application of the various forms. With regard to the contract-
> ing out of production quotas to groups of workers, or individual
> workers, experiments must be made with this form before expanding
> its application.[9]

Ignoring the spirit if not the letter of this directive, a number of districts in
the South proceeded to assign output contracts without the endorsement
of the central government. The result was highly positive as yields
increased as did the willingness of peasants to take part in collective
duties. In response, the Party Secretariat issued a communiqué in November 1981 which authorized implementation of the output contract system
in southern Vietnam.

Contract 100 had a positive impact on rice production which grew annually at a rate of 2.8 percent in 1982–7 compared to 1.9 percent in the
1976–81 period. Most of this increase was due to an increase in output per
hectare as opposed to an expansion in the area cultivated. In the South,
aggregate rice output increased by 2.5 million tons from 1980 to 1987 while
the corresponding increase in the north was around two million tons for
the same period. The Contract 100 system undoubtedly served Vietnam
well in the formative years of economic reform; however, as agronomist
Vo-Tong Xuan later recognized, notable drawbacks led to its eventual
replacement in 1987.

> The success of the contract system could not be sustained over the
> long term due to the following reasons: 1) top-down planning on land
> use and crop choice without consideration of farmer preferences and
> local market conditions; 2) the government's frequent inability to
> procure all the contracted production at harvest time; 3) as a con-
> sequence, seasonal surpluses at the farm gate led to a crash in private
> rice price in several regions, which, while benefiting the urban poor,
> had severe negative effects on farmers; 4) the persistence of central-
> ized input supplies resulted in inadequate and untimely provision of
> inputs to farmers; and 5) lack of security of land tenure resulting in
> inadequate farm-level investments for maintaining long term land pro-
> ductivity.[10]

At the same time, it must be emphasized that the strengthening of land
use rights for Vietnamese farmers at this point in the reform process contributed mightily to the economic resurgence later in the decade. The new
approach reversed a process of nationalization and collectivization that
started in 1954 and accelerated in the 1960s in the North and after reunification in the South. It culminated in a clause in the 1980 constitution that

all land belonged to the state. The decommunalization of agriculture began as early as 1981 with the household officially replacing the farm cooperative as the basic economic agent in agriculture. General Secretary Le Duan ratified this policy shift in a 1982 report to the Fifth Party Congress in which he spoke of the need "to correctly combine the building of the central economy with a vigorous development of local economies in a unified national economic structure."[11] The cooperative retained indirect control over the activities of the farming household; however, households were allocated specific plots of land on short-term contract in return for a portion of the crop and their contribution of labor to production on communal lands.[12]

In the Vietnamese industrial sector, bottom-up reform may have begun as early as 1977 although no specific instances were recorded. Individual factories in this period began to apply the term "fence-breaking" (*pha rao*) to their efforts to break through the constraints of the central planning system. When materials were short, factory managers were known to sell goods on the open market in order to raise cash to buy supplies or to pay bonuses to raise worker productivity. Technically illegal, the use of initiatives became more and more widespread. In January 1981, Vietnam enacted Decision 25/CP, providing guidelines for the development of both initiatives and financial autonomy in state enterprises. Recognizing earlier practices, these initial reforms in the industrial sector allowed factories to acquire and employ resources as necessary to increase their supply outputs as long as they reported all activities outside the official plan.[13]

The bottom-up reforms in agriculture and industry generated both positive and negative results. Gross industrial output, like agricultural output, increased significantly from 1979 to 1982, triggering a fairly rapid economic recovery in the early 1980s. By raising agricultural productivity, the output contract system expanded the range of products available on the free market while greater autonomy for state enterprises meant a higher percentage of sales at market prices. Predictably, the demand for goods grew more rapidly than the supply which fuelled inflation. The higher prices of the free market also meant the government had to raise the salaries of government employees as well as the purchasing prices for which the state bought goods from various agricultural and production units. In June 1981, the Vietnamese government granted substantial salary increases which only served to push up further prices in the free market. The rate of inflation nearly doubled in 1979 and by 1982 approached 90 percent, erasing any gains from public sector wage and salary increases. So-called "negative phenomena," such as smuggling, speculation and corruption, accompanied the run-up in inflation. The Hanoi leadership associated such negative phenomena with Ho Chi Minh City which had captured 37 percent of the country's gross industrial product by 1982. In response, a Council of Ministers resolution in September 1981 limited the free market activities of state industries, a decision impacting most heavily on Ho Chi Minh City.[14]

## Fifth Party Congress

Conservative elements at the Fifth Party Congress in March 1982, gener-ally pleased with the economic results of the limited reforms introduced but concerned with their downstream ideological ramifications, directed a retreat from the so-called "reformist tendency." With the opening phase of economic reform drawing to a close, cautious Party leaders moved to correct what they saw as some of the most acute imbalances and to curb some of the more undesirable side-effects of reform.[15] In opening remarks to the congress, Central Committee member Truong Chinh signaled the need to reevaluate Party policies.

> This fifth congress of our party will review the implementation of the line set forth by the fourth congress, correctly assess achievements and shortcomings, recognize the actual prevailing economic and social conditions and analyze the causes of successes and difficulties. It will also set forth the main economic and social orientations, tasks and targets for 1981–85 and for the 1980s.[16]

Reflecting the shift in policy, Nguyen Van Linh, Party Secretary in Ho Chi Minh City, was removed from the Politburo and the Central Committee Secretariat.[17]

In early 1983, the government issued new directives in an attempt to slow both the rate of inflation and the resurgence in private trading. It also imposed steep taxes on private enterprises operating in sectors considered nonessential to the growth of production. And it introduced a new system of taxation in agriculture intended to encourage cultivation efforts in the collective sector. In the South, the drive to collectivize agriculture con-tinued, accelerating in 1984–5. The government clearly viewed the collec-tivization of the main grain surplus area of Vietnam as an essential part of its overall development strategy. Responding to the renewed emphasis on collectivization, many farmers in the South destroyed their crops and abandoned the farm sector altogether. In a related move, the government in 1983 revoked the freedom of industrial enterprises to buy and sell outside official channels.[18]

. Despite the on-again, off-again approach, this initial period of economic reform had a positive impact on the Vietnamese economy. Real GDP per capita rose in 1980–5 even as the population continued to grow. The agri-cultural sector performed well as agricultural production, employment, labor productivity and capital productivity all increased in the wake of reform. Employment and capital productivity in the industrial sector grew faster than in the pre-reform period, but growth in production and labor productivity actually slowed. The private sector in industry gained the most while the socialist sector and heavy industry were less able to take advantage of the opportunities opened by the reforms. The transportation sector, in particular, was left untouched by the reforms; and similar to what had happened in Cambodia and Laos, it later became a development bottleneck in Vietnam. Finally, inflation worsened as the state sector, at a growing disadvantage in competition with the private sector, groped to adjust to the new economic mechanisms. As various reform measures generated upward pressure on prices, the central bank expanded the money supply, seemingly oblivious to its inflationary impact.[19]

The Eighth Plenum of the Fifth Central Committee, meeting in June 1985, once again combined personnel shifts with major policy change. The Party reinstated Nguyen Van Linh first to the Politburo and later to the Central Committee Secretariat. In turn, new economic policies adopted by the Party moved the economy from central planning toward a market system. The Party abolished state subsidies with future wages and salaries to be paid on a straight cash basis. State enterprises were instructed to implement socialist accounting measures and to fix prices on the basis of costs. The amount of currency in circulation was a cause for concern; unfortunately, subsequent currency reforms were ineffective and inflationary. Following this preliminary series of reforms, the rate of inflation from September 1985 to September 1986 surged to 700 percent, threatening a major defeat for the reformers. Instead, the failure of currency and price reforms prompted the government to enact even more radical reform measures the following year.[20]

## Origin, timing and scope of reform in Vietnam

The origin of the economic reform movement in Vietnam quickly became a controversial subject and remained one for many years. One school of thought argued that Vietnamese economic policies were heavily influenced by China, even in periods of open hostility between the two neighbors. This was a major theme in Vo Nhan Tri's study of Vietnamese economic policy after 1975. He argued the policies of land reform and cooperativization implemented by the Party in 1955–75 were inspired by Maoist thought and practice and executed under the close guidance of Chinese advisers. He also contended the Stalinist-Maoist model of development continued to be implemented, despite piecemeal and makeshift measures adopted after 1979, until late 1986. Tri concluded the leadership of Vietnam, "until 1986 was much more influenced by Mao than by Marx."[21]

Carlyle Thayer, on the other hand, argued the main impetus for reform in Vietnam came from within the Party.

> It is clear from field work conducted in Vietnam that the main impetus for reform and change in Vietnam is coming from within the Vietnam Communist Party itself, both as a reaction to events in Eastern Europe and the Soviet Union, but more particularly as part and parcel of the internal processes of *doi moi* begun in 1986.[22]

Vu Tuan Anh also stressed that Vietnam did not follow external models in charting its reform process; instead, it slowly worked out its own reform scenario.

> The nature of Vietnam's reforms was not merely one of switching from an old model that no longer worked to one borrowed from another country.... As there is no ready reform scenario or general "road map" available that Vietnam could use as a guide, it has to work out its own short-term action plans, treading slowly and tentatively, and ready to shift gear when necessary.[23]

The question of the timing of the reform process in Vietnam, often tied closely to the issue of origin, also generated considerable controversy. The Pacific Basin Research Institute argued that a conservative backlash to the 1979 reforms occurred in 1982. In their words, "draconian" measures were introduced in late 1982 which led to a return to a more orthodox Marxist-Leninist model, lasting until mid-1985. At that time, a resolution of the Eighth Plenum of the Communist Party Central Committee on price, wages and currency reintroduced production incentives and price liberalization measures.[24] Dang T. Tran made a related point in emphasizing that liberalization policies introduced after 1979 promoted competition and market processes but did not go far enough.[25] In turn, Thayer rightly argued the impetus for economic reform in Vietnam dated back to the later half of the 1970s although very little was accomplished prior to 1986.[26]

Neither the issue of timing nor the question of Chinese influence can be resolved conclusively. However, the clear success of Chinese economic reforms by 1986, coupled with the success of Vietnam's East Asian non-socialist neighbors, did not go unnoticed in Hanoi. On the contrary, these events surely influenced post-1979 decisions in favor of economic reform. In turn, Vietnamese efforts to reform economic policies influenced similar plans, first in Laos, and later in Cambodia.

Collectively, the economic reforms introduced in Vietnam in 1979 had a positive impact on the Vietnamese economy. Tentative steps in the direction of economic liberalization promoted market processes and competition, rewarded efficiency in the private sector, and penalized the state sector for rigidity, inefficiency and wastefulness. That said, the administrative supply system remained intact, and structural changes introduced to raise productivity did not go far enough. The government also failed to eliminate multi-tier price and multiple exchange rate systems. Ideological checks also remained in place. The first round of economic reforms were mostly piecemeal, makeshift measures that could best be described as minor surgery when major surgery was required. Throughout the first half of the decade, much of the Party leadership appeared to be residing in a halfway house between growing disillusionment with the development strategy in place and a serious commitment to a new approach.[27] In this milieu, the most promising development in Hanoi was a growing appreciation that the old policies were bankrupt and significant reforms desperately needed.

## First Lao five-year plan

The year 1981 proved to be highly significant in the history of the Lao PDR as it marked the outset of the First Five-Year Plan (1981–5). On 6 January 1981, General Secretary Kaysone presented to the Supreme People's Assembly a five-year plan for economic and social development which was unanimously approved two days later. Although Laos was not a member of the Council for Mutual Economic Assistance, the presentation of the plan was timed to coincide with the long-term plans of the Comecon states, most especially the Soviet Union and Vietnam. On the surface, the plan was balanced, pragmatic and not overly ambitious. However, the failure of the government to achieve the goals of the Three-Year Plan (1978–80), the economic foundation for the 1981–5 plan, led contemporary observers to question whether even the modest goals articulated in January 1981 could be met.[28]

The First Five-Year Plan, better known as the Eighth Resolution of the LPRP Central Committee, together with Ordinance 408 of the Lao PDR Council of Ministers, issued on 28 November 1980, established in broad outline the goals and priorities of the government for the first half of the decade. In presenting the plan, Kaysone highlighted the achievements of the regime over the previous five years, particularly the period of the interim three-year plan, in the face of what he termed the counter revolutionary alliance of American imperialism and Chinese international reactionism. He admitted the country faced severe economic problems, such as poor management experience, a shortage of educated cadre, poor use of labor and the failure to implement economic policies. But Kaysone suggested such problems were largely the product of the particular stage of transition to socialism in which the Lao PDR found itself. Drawing lessons from the past, he underscored the need to understand the Party line, improve management, strengthen internal unity and promote international solidarity with Kampuchea, Vietnam, the USSR and other socialist countries.[29]

General Secretary Kaysone stressed two fundamental objectives in the five-year plan. First, the government aimed to "normalize the material and cultural life of the people of all nationalities." Second, it planned to "concentrate on building those enterprises which are strategically important to our [the Lao] economy and national defense, with the aim of gradually and firmly building material and technical bases for the national economy."[30] To achieve these objectives, Kaysone highlighted seven priorities: promote agricultural production, build strategically important enterprises, consolidate the economic bases of state enterprises, train economic managers and technicians, complete the literacy campaign, consolidate and restructure the organizations managing the economy and state, and acquire and efficiently utilize foreign economic assistance. Thereafter, a government slogan repeated ad nauseam called on the Lao people to "fulfill the two objectives and seven priorities."[31]

The targets for the First Five-Year Plan, published in Council of Government Ordinance 408 on 28 November 1980, were difficult to assess as they were conveyed as percent increases over unstated production figures for 1980. For example, the government expected gross social product to increase by 65–68 percent in 1981–5 while national income from domestic production would grow 38–40 percent. Total agricultural production was targeted to increase 23–24 percent over the period with gross industrial production expected to double. The five-year plan emphasized a number of strategic initiatives, all of which aimed at reducing Lao dependence on Thailand for the purchase and transshipment of goods. These projects included completion of Route 9 as an all-weather road linking Laos and Vietnam, construction of a cement factory north of Vientiane as well as oil pipelines from Vietnam to Laos and the creation of a motorized transport unit for the import-export of goods.[32]

The five-year plan accorded first priority to increasing agricultural and forestry output. A related goal of the interim three-year plan had been self-sufficiency in food production, and Kaysone openly admitted this had not been achieved. On the contrary, Laos remained a net food importer even after some 10 percent of the population fled the country in the wake of the communist takeover. Ordinance 408 set clear goals for increases in agricultural production but not specific targets for increases in forestry production. Nevertheless, the export of timber, together with electricity from the Nam Ngum Dam, constituted major sources of foreign exchange. Brown and Zasloff later estimated the completion of the second phase of the Nam Ngum Dam enabled Laos to increase its annual export earnings from around $2 million in 1978 to more than $8 million the following year. Moreover, even after Thailand closed its border with Laos in 1980, electricity continued to flow.[33]

General Secretary Kaysone also emphasized the rights and duties of state-owned enterprises to contribute to the success of the five-year plan through what he termed a "system of balanced and profitable management." Following approval of capital investment and production goals, state enterprises would be granted considerable autonomy in management. They would be free to establish labor requirements, wage increments, marketing and pricing policies, and levels of reinvestment. This decentralization of authority and decision making was to be extended to all areas of the economy with managers and technicians largely freed of the political controls of the past. "Administrative organizations such as ministries," Kaysone emphasized, "shall not directly interfere in production management work and the business of an enterprise."[34]

In addition, the five-year plan called for stricter management in construction and a more efficient use of investment funds. In the area of foreign trade, the plan foreshadowed a further easing of restrictions. On the one hand, official state policy continued to call for transactions with foreign countries to be conducted on the basis of a gradual state monopoly of foreign trade. On the other, the five-year plan allowed for private trade at border crossings as long as government monopolies were respected, duties paid, and there was no hoarding. Internal trade was also liberalized. The government called on state trading enterprises to increase purchases from individual farmers and cooperatives. On the crucial issue of retail pricing, Kaysone indicated the government would continue its two-price policy. The plan also called for increased private enterprise participation in a number of key economic sectors. Kaysone summarized its goal as "the socialist transformation of capitalist industry, trade and agriculture," arguing it provided "a method aimed at ensuring victory for socialism in the struggle of who is overcoming whom during the bypassing capitalism stage in our country." In short, Lao capitalists would be used, manipulated and transformed as state enterprises and cooperative forms were advanced.[35]

Finally, Kaysone emphasized the success of the First Five-Year Plan was dependent on Laos continuing to receive foreign aid and investment. He described economic cooperation with fraternal countries as strategically significant because it would provide the capital necessary to build the material and technical foundations of socialism. Consequently, solidarity with the Soviet Union, as well as with Cambodia and Vietnam, were ingredients essential to success.

> We affirm that our relations, solidarity and all-round cooperation with the great USSR and other fraternal socialist countries are the cornerstone of our foreign policy and a solid guarantee for our cause of national defense and socialist construction.[36]

At the same time, Kaysone cautioned that Laos could not expect unlimited amounts of foreign aid. On the contrary, diplomatic work would be required to obtain contributions from sources outside the socialist bloc. He also stressed the need for national unity, a reflection of ongoing Chinese and Lao-exile efforts to exploit ethnic differences to undermine the government.[37]

## Disappointing results in Laos

The rural reforms introduced after 1980 concentrated on the three policy arenas, marketing and distribution, property-rights and taxation, most affected by the socialization policies implemented in the latter 1970s. Reforms began gradually over the next decade with modifications to agricultural taxation preceding changes in the marketing and property-rights systems. And reforms to property-rights focused on user rights as opposed to private ownership. Predictably, the reforms enacted had only a limited impact on agricultural performance. The agricultural sector continued to be an extensive albeit low productivity system characterized by low input and output. Irrigation was rare, double cropping scarce and land quality highly variable. The forestry and rice subsectors, in particular, performed poorly while selected non-rice subsectors, together with livestock, experienced stronger growth. Supply and demand factors, like ineffective agricultural services and weakly developed marketing opportunities, combined to result in the low productivity characteristic of Lao agriculture. The situation prevailing in the rural areas strongly contrasted with that in urban areas where economic reforms raised living standards. The poor economic results achieved in Laos also contrasted with the experience of other socialist countries like China and Vietnam.[38]

External factors outside the control of the government, such as droughts and floods, impacted negatively on agricultural performance. However, government policies in areas like pricing and resource allocation were the principal cause of low growth. The resulting poor performance was compounded by insufficient coordination and sequencing of reforms within the agricultural sector as well as between rural reforms and those implemented in macroeconomic and other areas. Inadequate transportation and communication systems, because they discouraged regional specialization and trade, also contributed to the problem. The geographical, social and economic realities of Laos, most especially rural isolation in mountainous districts, constituted serious impediments to the rapid development of a socialist economy.[39]

In the public sector, a gradual process of economic decentralization began after 1979 in which state enterprises, previously little more than government departments, became semi-autonomous. They developed their own internal accounting systems and began dealing with the state and state-owned firms as external rather than internal agents. Political Bureau Resolution 11, introduced in mid-1981, instructed state enterprises to meet a dozen compulsory plan targets, determined by supervising authorities. Beyond these targets, the state enterprises assumed a new degree of operating autonomy and retained 10 percent of their profits for reinvestment. The government in 1983 granted selected enterprises additional autonomy that allowed them to keep 40 percent of their profits and a proportion of overseas earnings as well as to engage in limited direct sales on the open market. The Lao government later expanded these measures with the result that by 1988 a majority of state-owned firms had become, in effect, autonomous state enterprises.[40]

That said, five separate and distinct forms of economic organization coexisted in Laos by the mid-1980s. First, there was a state sector consisting of the largest industrial firms, the banking sector and state farms, together with state construction, transportation and trading enterprises. Second, there was a collective economy mostly consisting of agricultural cooperatives. Next, there was a relatively small individual economy made up of self-employed farmers, handicraft producers and small traders. Fourth, the capitalist economy consisted of industrial, trading and transportation companies owned by private entrepreneurs in larger towns like Vientiane. Finally, there was a state-private economy representing joint ventures between state and private capital. General Secretary Kaysone openly recognized this plethora of economic structures, suggesting they might coexist for some time:

> in our country there are still nearly all the modes of production, from primitive to contemporary modes of production, mankind has gone through. All these sectors exert an inter-effect on one another, depend on one another and remain united in an economy still in the period of transition to socialism.[41]

On the other hand, despite the multitude of economic forms in operation after nearly ten years of experimentation, there was little change in the basic structure of the Lao economy. The relative share of state versus private control of that economy also remained largely unchanged.[42]

At the macroeconomic level, the Lao PDR in the decade after the 1975 revolution pursued import substitution, accommodating fiscal and monetary policies, and a fixed exchange rate system. High and persistent inflation was one result of these policies with 56 percent being the average in the 1980–6 period. High rates of inflation, combined with a fixed exchange rate system, contributed to the overvaluation of the kip. A very restrictive trade regime was another element of macroeconomic policy in this period. High tariffs and quantitative restrictions on most imported products aimed at protecting domestic industries and supporting the state apparatus. By increasing the price of industrial goods, this restrictive trade policy negatively altered terms of trade between the agricultural and industrial sectors. Taken as a whole, the hostile macroeconomic environment prevailing after 1975 restrained growth in agriculture, in particular, diluting the impact of rural reforms.[43]

With the economic results of the First Five-Year Plan at best mixed, the internal debate over the optimum process and pace for socialist transformation intensified. The so-called "two-line struggle" pitted proponents of a gradual pace of transformation against those Party members endorsing a rapid transition to socialist modes of production. The proponents of a gradual pace of reform argued that a mixed economy, consisting of both a state-owned-cum-cooperative sector and a state-private-cum-private sector, was both an inevitable and indispensable step in the transition to socialism. In turn, those conservatives supporting the extension of state control over all facets of economic production and distribution argued the

various attempts to liberalize the economy were nothing more than ideological backsliding that retarded the advent of socialism in Laos. Given the
failure of hard-line policies in 1976–8 and the LPRP's endorsement of a
gradualist approach after 1980, the persistent dialogue over the appropriate reform pace was a clear indication that no consensus had been
reached.[44]

## External dependence

Politically, the close association of the Lao People's Revolutionary Party
with Cambodia, Vietnam and the Soviet Union heightened its isolation
from the nonsocialist world. However, as historian Martin Stuart-Fox has
emphasized, it did not reduce its dependence on other states.

> The problem of dependency is one which Laos has always faced, and
> the transference of that dependence from Western capitalism (particu-
> larly the United States and Thailand) to Soviet socialism (particularly
> the Soviet Union and Vietnam) has done little to reduce it. The
> geopolitical reality is simply that Laos is underpopulated, militarily
> and economically weak, yet strategically vital to the interests of its
> neighbours. Consequently, it is so vulnerable to outside pressures that
> the only realistic choice open to its leaders is which patron they prefer.
> But this is a choice which depends internally not on economic, but
> on political and ideological considerations, and externally on global
> and regional power balances. Laos is now locked into both the
> Vietnamese-dominated Indochina solidarity block (consisting of
> Vietnam, Kampuchea, and Laos), and the Soviet camp, with all this
> entails for Lao relations with China and the West, both of which have
> provided considerable assistance for the Lao five-year plan.[45]

With the outbreak of hostilities between China and Vietnam, the Lao
government in March 1979 asked China to suspend its road construction
assistance and withdraw its road construction cadre. The Lao PDR's close
alignment with Vietnam was the primary determinant in the subsequent
Chinese decision to terminate all economic assistance to Laos. For a time,
there was even concern that China might apply a "second lesson" on
Vietnam through northern Laos. Its close association with Vietnam also
entailed for Laos serious economic as well as political costs from the West.
The policy of the United States, China and the ASEAN member states, as
long as Vietnam occupied Cambodia, was to isolate Vietnam. A similar
albeit less stringent policy was applied to its Lao ally. As a result, Laos
received much less Western technical assistance and economic aid in this
period than would otherwise have been the case.[46]

Nonetheless, the Lao PDR remained heavily dependent on external
assistance throughout the period with foreign aid in 1982 estimated to be

some 80 percent of its annual revenue. The Soviet Union was the principal benefactor in the early years of the decade as it provided, with help from its East European allies, approximately 60 percent of the country's external assistance in 1980. An August 1981 report from Moscow indicated the Soviet Union intended to build some 54 economic projects in Laos in the 1981–5 planning period. In contrast, the Vietnamese economy was in such dire straits that Hanoi provided little if any economic assistance. At the same time, the 6,000 Vietnamese civilian advisers and up to 50,000 Vietnamese troops stationed in Laos in 1984 made a strong political imprint on the economic policies of the country. Sweden remained the most generous Western donor with other Western states, including Australia, Japan and France, also offering assistance. The International Monetary Fund was Laos's most important international agency donor in the first half of the 1980s, providing direct support as well as guidance. U.S. law prohibited all but humanitarian aid to Laos; however, some food donations and medicines were sent in years of hardship and in support of efforts to recover the remains of U.S. servicemen.[47]

Even though the Lao government enjoyed some success in replacing the United States with the Soviet Union and its socialist allies as primary donors, its limited ability to absorb aid and achieve the self-generating growth envisioned in the five-year plan remained a basic problem. The paucity of skilled administrative, managerial and technical manpower was a serious deficiency which the government was unable to overcome. This was largely a self-inflicted wound as policy choices in the early days of the regime drove away many well-trained professionals and administrators from the former Royal Lao Government. At the same time, the Lao PDR often made very poor use of the few experienced managers remaining.[48]

## Internal political developments

A major political event in the brief history of the Lao PDR occurred in April 1982 with the convening of the Third Congress of the Lao People's Revolutionary Party (LPRP). The Second Congress had been held a decade earlier when the Lao communist movement was still locked in a revolutionary struggle with the Royal Lao Government. In a remarkable display of continuity, the Third Congress reconfirmed each of the seven members of the Politburo, the top LPRP leadership since the late 1950s, with only one change in formal rank between the fifth and sixth positions. Unlike many communist regimes, the LPRP leadership eschewed a cult of the personality, like Mao in China or Ho Chi Minh in Vietnam, in favor of a collective profile. In post-1975 visits to government offices, for example, it was common to see group photographs of the total Politburo as opposed to individual photos of Kaysone or other leading members. All 27 incumbent members of the Central Committee of the LPRP were also reappointed with 28 new members elected to join them. In addition to bringing new talent to the senior echelons of the Party, the appointment of 28 new members increased functional representation on the Central Committee, especially in military and security affairs, and improved provincial representation.[49]

The Lao PDR government was also reshuffled in 1982. Like the Party, continuity and stability were the twin themes of governmental leadership after 1975, and this was the first major reorganization in seven years. A harbinger of change was the promulgation by the Supreme People's Assembly of a regulation in July 1982, providing for a change in the size and organization of the Council of Ministers. When the new government was formed in the fall of 1982, continuity was assured as there was no change in the role of veteran leaders; however, the government was revamped and enlarged in January 1983 in line with the new administrative law. In March 1983, the middle echelons of the government underwent a mini-purge following charges of corruption and other irregularities.[50]

There were no comparable changes in Party structure; instead, the LPRP focused on consolidating its organization in areas of strength and expanding its apparatus in areas of weakness. To increase managerial and ideological competence, senior cadre attended courses at the Party's Marxist-Leninist School while the Party newspaper was renamed *Pasason* (The People) and its format modified to make it a more effective means of communication. Considerable effort was also expended to strengthen the Lao Front for National Construction, the umbrella body for mass organizations, and Party affiliated groups like the Lao People's Revolutionary Youth Union. A first step toward writing a constitution was taken in 1984 with the creation of a constitutional commission. The country had been without a constitution since the Congress of People's Representatives met in December 1975 to establish the organs of state power. Since that time, LPRP decisions had the force of law for Lao citizens. The following year, the Lao PDR completed a national census making it the first country in postwar Indochina to generate fairly reliable data on the size and distribution of its population.[51]

At the same time, Laos began to relax its close control of Buddhism with even Party members allowed to enter the monkhood for short periods of time. In part, this "efflorescence of Lao Buddhism" was due to the growing prosperity which resulted from the modest economic reforms begun in 1979. Some of the surplus income generated in ensuing years went toward the construction of new Buddhist monuments or the repair of existing *wats*, both well-established, highly visible forms of merit-making. While the revival of Buddhism was partially due to nascent economic reforms, anthropologist Grant Evans was correct to suggest that it was also motivated by "an accumulating existential crisis within the Lao leadership." With Marxist-Leninism largely quiet on issues like personal tragedy and bereavement, Lao funeral rites were an area which witnessed "the gradual reemergence of non-secular Buddhist rituals at the level of the state." As early as 1980, the communist regime began to relax its control over a number of traditional religious rituals. With the death in 1984 of Prince Souvanna Phouma, a long-time advocate of neutralism and the architect of three coalition governments in 1957–75, the Lao PDR was finally ready for the high-style Buddhist funeral it accorded the Prince.[52]

## Political economy of the People's Republic of Kampuchea

When the Vietnamese Army reached Phnom Penh in early January 1979, the Kampuchean People's Revolutionary Council, a Council of Ministers created to implement the directives of the ruling Kampuchean People's Revolutionary Party (KPRP), announced the formation of the People's Republic of Kampuchea (PRK). Heng Samrin, a former Khmer Rouge division commander who defected to Vietnam in October 1978, was named president with most other leadership positions filled by dissident Khmer Rouge cadre and the few surviving members of the Khmer Issarak movement, formed in the 1940s. The new government was not recognized by ASEAN or the United Nations and was denied economic assistance by the Western powers.[53]

On 18 February 1979, Kampuchea and Vietnam concluded a 25-year Treaty of Peace, Friendship and Cooperation remarkably similar to that signed by Laos and Vietnam less than two years earlier. Recalling historical ties between the two countries, the pact emphasized the need for the signatories to develop and defend their enduring tradition of "militant solidarity and fraternal friendship" against reactionary forces and international imperialists. The agreement also addressed the peaceful resolution of bilateral disputes, in particular the border issue. Finally, the signatories attached "great importance to the long-standing tradition of militant solidarity and fraternal friendship between the Kampuchean, Lao and Vietnamese peoples" and pledged "to do their best to strengthen this traditional relationship." In so doing, the agreement confirmed the de facto situation in Indochina, a close-knit, three-nation military alliance under the leadership of Vietnam. The Kampuchea–Vietnam treaty was soon followed by a similar pact between Kampuchea and Laos, completing the third leg of the Indochina solidarity bloc.[54]

The People's Republic of Kampuchea faced a difficult economic situation when it came to power in January 1979. Democratic Kampuchea (DK) had succeeded in creating a classless society, but it did so at the price of neglecting almost all sectors of the economy except agriculture and a few related industries. Emphasizing poor peasants as the only worthwhile class, the Khmer Rouge had ignored skilled, trained personnel when they did not kill them. Basic infrastructure at all levels from roads to transport to buildings had deteriorated. There were no banks, no currency, no private exchange, no personal income and no taxes. In addition, there had

been no written records, formal judicial proceedings, codified laws or conservation of archives in Democratic Kampuchea.[55]

The PRK government immediately reversed core DK policies. Early
socioeconomic restructuring in Cambodia, unlike in Vietnam and to a
lesser extent in Laos, was almost totally laissez-faire. Suddenly, there was
freedom of movement, freedom of work choice and freedom of trade. The
PRK later moved to create a mixed planned and market economy in which
currency, banking and commercial transactions would be restored. This
meant reviving the urban sector, schools, public facilities, formal administration and personal possessions. Private ownership of land was not reintroduced; but the means of production, mostly draft animals, could be
owned privately. Land remained the property of the state, and it could not
be used for speculation or loan collateral. Equally important, it could not
be lost due to nonpayment of debt.[56] As Michael Vickery later noted, the
Cambodian approach necessitated a class revolution of a very different
sort from that adopted in either Laos or Vietnam.

> The PRK proposed to create from scratch a nonproductive adminis-
> trative and service sector, reactivate and restore a small essential
> industrial sector, and persuade the majority food-producing sector to
> support the administration and industry with minimal return for the
> immediate future. That is, the PRK inherited a truly classless society,
> yet in order to move toward socialism they had to recreate social
> classes.[57]

Religious tolerance was another policy arena in which the PRK distinguished itself from the Khmer Rouge. The DK regime had guaranteed
freedom of religious worship but also declared "reactionary" religion to be
forbidden. In practice, Buddhist monks were among the more prominent
victims of incessant DK purges; and it soon became evident that no ideology beyond the militant ideological purism of the Khmer Rouge was
really allowed. In contrast, the PRK stressed the right to freedom of
religion and pledged to help repair and maintain temples, pagodas and
historical relics destroyed by the Khmer Rouge. Despite official pronouncements, however, only limited religious freedom existed in practice
after 1978 with significant restrictions frustrating full freedom of religious
rights. Among other disincentives, the PRK authorized only one pagoda
per commune, and only unproductive elderly men were allowed to take
the monk's habit. Half of all offerings to the monks went to the
commune's revolutionary committee, and all religious celebrations
required the approval of the authorities.[58]

As it moved to govern the country as opposed simply to presiding over
it, the PRK modified its initial laissez-faire approach. The 1981 constitution consecrated three distinct economic sectors: the state, cooperatives
and the family with the latter referring mostly to small-scale agricultural

and artisan work. Industry, finance and transport remained in the public sector which also retained a major role in the distribution of rice and other necessities. The government established a system of central planning, with physical production targets and administrative controls, and also determined key prices and wages. A private sector was subsequently added, following the Fifth Party Congress in October 1985, in which individuals could hire labor and invest funds in small-scale manufacturing. The PRK introduced a new Cambodian riel in 1980 after a five-year period in which there was no currency. The success of monetary and fiscal policies in winning popular acceptance of the new currency, while avoiding extreme inflation, evidenced a certain amount of intelligent planning, especially when compared to Vietnam. At the same time, the Khmer Rouge abolition of currency continued to impact negatively on economic recovery in that it reinforced Cambodian reluctance to use local currency as a store of value, preferring gold, silver or U.S. dollars as accepted means of exchange.[59]

The Cambodian government reintroduced taxation in 1983; nevertheless, a large percentage of its budget continued to come from aid and long-term loans from the socialist states. As in Laos, this practice was consistent with historical experience in that no Cambodian regime since independence in 1954, with the arguable exception of Democratic Kampuchea, had survived on its own resources. Industrial and consumer goods, supplied with the help of the Soviet Union and its allies, generated the revenues necessary to pay government expenditures.[60]

Early PRK economic policies were strongly influenced by Vietnamese advisors detailed to assist enthusiastic, albeit inexperienced, local leadership in rebuilding the economy. An early history of the Kampuchean People's Revolutionary Party stressed that:

> *As an authentic Marxist-Leninist Party, our Party closely associates authentic patriotism with brilliant proletarian internationalism* [italics in the text]. The line of the Party is to raise high the two banners of patriotism and international solidarity, solidarity with the Soviet Union which is the strong bulwark of peace and socialism in the world, solidarity with every socialist country, solidarity with the revolutionary forces and progressive forces in the world, and, foremost solidarity with Vietnam to develop the alliance of the three countries of Indochina.[61]

The extent of Vietnamese control over the PRK government was most systematic in foreign affairs and defense policy, together with issues concerning the expansion of the Kampuchean People's Revolutionary Party. The influence of the Vietnamese was much less in policy areas such as tax collection and the collectivization of agriculture. Moreover, a close examination of both government and Party documents suggests that KPRP emphasis on a long history of revolutionary struggle and cooperation with its Vietnamese counterpart was often undertaken by the Cambodians with some reluctance. In many cases, the constant allusion to close Kam-puchean-Vietnamese relations "amounted to the simple repetition of vague slogans, whereas, in parallel with this," PRK officials stressed constantly "the importance of preserving national independence and the important role plaid [*sic*] by the Cambodian forces themselves." Cambodians deeply resented any sign of Vietnamese superiority or condescension and took care to present themselves always as on an equal footing with their Vietnamese allies.[62] As Chanthou Boua observed, having spent considerable time in Cambodia in 1980–2, the activities of ethnic Vietnamese were an especially sensitive issue in the 1980–1 period.

> The presence of ethnic Vietnamese civilians in Kampuchea became a subject of debate in 1981 when it was obvious that their movements were getting out of control. Some were establishing themselves as farmers, fishermen, traders and technicians. They included former residents expelled by Pol Pot and Lon Nol, but many Khmer leaders and ordinary people objected to their presence.... Differences consisted of how and when to expell [sic] the migrants. One official told me at the time: "It must be done discreetly and now is obviously not the time for it."[63]

## Agricultural cooperatives in Cambodia

The restoration of agricultural production was the most urgent task facing the new regime in Phnom Penh. The agricultural sector had long been fragile due to a combination of irregular rainfall, limited water control and poor quality soils. Modern implements and techniques were little developed, fertilizers seldom used and high-yielding seed varieties virtually unknown.[64] In response to the need to increase agricultural production, the government organized agricultural producers into cooperative units called production solidarity groups (*krom samakki*), a creative and appropriate response to the demographic nightmare produced by the Khmer Rouge. Official plans for the agricultural sector envisaged a three-tier structure of progressively collectivized groups ranging from traditional family farms to largely collectivized groups. The government continued to advocate a policy of agricultural collectivization until 1989, but implementation of the policy was lackadaisical and poorly received throughout the country.[65]

Designed to function as enlarged families providing economic and moral support to all members, *krom samakki* responded to an equally important problem, the disappearance of cadastral plans and plot demarcations in the wake of Khmer Rouge attempts to remodel the Cambodian countryside. Production solidarity groups also served as instruments of government policy at local levels where the organizations facilitated political control and indoctrination as well as military conscription. In theory, each *krom samakki* consisted of 10–15 families tilling the land and sharing the harvest. In practice, few communes were formed. The bulk of the *krom samakki* functioned more like village mutual help groups with the bulk of the land assigned to individual families. Farmers were permitted to sell most of their produce on the open market after paying the 10 percent production tax and reimbursing the state for seed, farm equipment and fertilizer. In this sense, as Chanthou Boua has emphasized, they differed from the land reforms implemented in Vietnam after 1979:

> It is worth pointing out that the *krom samaki*, a form of what might be called "advanced mutual aid teams" ("advanced" in the sense that the land each team works is owned by it collectively), appear to have no parallel in Vietnamese rural organization, which is now a mixture of private farming, mutual aid teams, cooperatives and state farms. It seems that the destruction of life and property under Pol Pot, the security factor, and broad socialist ideological preconceptions, rather than adherence to a strictly Vietnamese model, were the important factors leading to the creation of the *krom*.[66]

Collectivized farming remained the ideal in Cambodia for much of the next decade; however, statistics released throughout the 1980s revealed an opposite trend in which production was increasingly dominated by individual producers. Theoretically, all land belonged to the state, but administrators distributed parcels of 1,500–2,000 square meters to households to use in addition to the plots they farmed as part of production solidarity groups. In this regard, even the highest level of *krom samakki* corresponded to a low level of socialist organization. When the PRK initiated economic reform in October 1985, it formally legalized private land ownership and recognized the right to inherit land. In the second half of the decade, free markets were widely tolerated, both for agricultural produce and manufactured goods. As one result, as the author observed personally on many occasions in the 1987–92 period, a brisk trade grew up along the Thai–Cambodian border.[67]

## Isolation all around

After almost six years in power, the PRK enjoyed full diplomatic relations with only 27 states, including all of the East Bloc states, except Romania and Yugoslavia, and 11 states in Africa. In Asia, in addition to its Indochinese neighbors and India, only Afghanistan and Mongolia, close allies of the Soviet Union, recognized the PRK, and in Latin America, only Nicaragua and Panama. Cambodia's seat at the United Nations and other international organizations was held initially by Democratic Kampuchea and later by the Coalition Government of Democratic Kampuchea (CGDK) established in June 1982. Norodom Sihanouk served as president of the CGDK with Son Sann, a former prime minister and head of the Khmer People's National Liberation Front (KPNLF), as vice president. Khieu Samphan represented remnants of the Khmer Rouge in the role of prime minister.[68]

Unlike Democratic Kampuchea, the diplomatic isolation visited on the People's Republic of Kampuchea was not self-imposed. On the contrary, it was the product of a complex interplay of regional and global interests. The Cambodian policy of most states reflected their policy toward Vietnam. In turn, their policy toward Vietnam was more often than not a result of their policy toward China. For example, the approaches to the Cambodian conflict of both the United States and the Soviet Union were driven generally by their respective attitudes toward Vietnam which were strongly influenced, if not governed, by their China policies. The same relationship generally applied to the policies of the ASEAN member states, Europe and Japan.[69]

Less than a decade after the end of the Second Indochina War, the ASEAN countries joined the People's Republic of China to aid Cambodian rebels against the Soviet-backed Heng Samrin regime. And the U.S. government actively supported an ASEAN formula that called for Vietnamese withdrawal from Cambodia followed by popular elections. The ASEAN approach was adopted at a UN-sponsored conference in 1981 and gained strength the following year when noncommunist resistance factions joined forces with Khmer Rouge remnants to form the Coalition Government of Democratic Kampuchea. The creation of the CGDK shored up the international coalition that had denied UN admission to the PRK after 1979. International opposition to the PRK in turn isolated Vietnam economically and helped restrain it militarily. The global campaign against the PRK also checked Soviet ambitions in the region. The USSR retained its bases in Vietnam at an estimated cost of $2 billion in aid to Indochina. But its support of Vietnamese policy earned few other dividends and generated considerable ill will throughout the region. Washington in turn played a secondary role, at least in public, supporting the diplomatic initiatives of friendly Asian regimes working for a political settlement.[70]

The ASEAN strategy incorporated a carrot-and-stick approach. On the incentive side, it offered Vietnam a series of forums and formulas to resolve the Cambodian issue, most of which centered on the final resolution adopted in July 1981 by the International Conference on Kampuchea. This resolution called for the complete withdrawal of Vietnamese troops from Cambodia with internationally supervised, free elections to follow. In so doing, ASEAN conceded that an acceptable political solution would have to include provisions for Vietnamese security. The United States later indicated that a Cambodian solution acceptable to ASEAN would open the way to normalized relations between Washington and Hanoi and a resumption of Western aid to Vietnam. ASEAN disincentives included a continuation of the policy of denying the PRK admittance to the United Nations as well as ongoing pressure on UN member states to freeze assistance and financial credits to Vietnam and to withhold diplomatic recognition of the PRK. UN support for the ASEAN approach was so strong that Vietnam after 1983 no longer attempted to seat the Heng Samrin regime at the United Nations. In a related disincentive, the ASEAN states worked with China to forge the three-member CGDK and subsequently provided its noncommunist elements with material assistance and training.[71]

## Checkered economic success in Cambodia

A serious crisis in agricultural procurement was an important consequence of the PRK failure to secure complete political control of the countryside. The state trading service as late as mid-1986 had failed to purchase one-third of its planned target for 1985–6 despite the fact the harvest was better than the previous year and almost as good as 1983–4 which was the best since the late 1960s. For government employees, the situation was critical as they relied on the state trading system for food. The rice shortage fuelled inflation rates and price increases as government employees turned to the private market for food. With no overall shortage in food production in 1985–6, the procurement crisis in 1986 reflected the failure of the government to control both state cadre, among whom corruption was rampant, and the peasantry. The ongoing civil war, difficulties in reforming the state procurement system and a prolonged drought in 1986 compounded problems in the agricultural sector, especially in rice production.[72]

In turn, the industrial sector remained stagnant. In the best of times, Cambodian industry produced only a limited inventory of goods, like beer, cigarettes, cloth, paper, vehicle tires and soap. Output of even these basic industries remained well below capacity in 1986 with more than 40 percent of the country's pre-1975 factories still inoperative. Operation of the plants which had reopened was seriously hampered by shortages of raw materials and spare parts due to scarce amounts of hard currency and the PRK's international isolation. Although industrial performance offered little possibility for significant improvement in the immediate future, developments in the communication and energy sectors offered some promise for limited economic recovery in the longer term. Electric power generation capacity increased as Soviet-funded power plants came into operation. At the same time, road and waterway projects planned or under construction promised improved access to Laos and Vietnam.[73]

Given the economic embargo in place, Comecon trade dominated Cambodia's external links in the mid-1980s. In its First Five-Year Plan

(1986–90), Cambodia linked its future development to the economies of Vietnam, the Soviet Union and the Soviet bloc countries. Trade agreements concluded in March 1986 projected a doubling in the volume of PRK-USSR trade in 1986–90. In addition to Comecon, Cambodia also maintained significant economic links with Laos and Vietnam. The ministers of economic and cultural cooperation for Cambodia, Laos and Vietnam held their sixth annual conference in January 1986 and agreed to cooperate in the areas of primary production, communications and transport and to increase mutual trade. Based on the Laos-Vietnam experience, so-called twin province agreements became an increasingly important part of the total Cambodia-Vietnam relationship with Vietnamese provinces providing aid and assistance to their "twins" in Cambodia. To generate hard currency and promote an image of stability, the PRK regime in late 1986 again began to welcome tourists to Cambodia, especially to Angkor Wat.[74]

In spite of the crisis in the agricultural sector, industrial stagnation and diplomatic and economic isolation, the private sector of the Cambodian economy was booming by the middle of the decade. In October 1985, the Fifth Congress of the Kampuchean People's Revolutionary Party officially recognized that the private sector was essential in the transition to socialism. Previously, only the state, cooperatives and the family had been sanctioned as economic units. The National Assembly in February 1986 legalized the private sector; and shortly thereafter, the government began collecting annual license fees, utility fees and rent, together with substantially increased tax rates, from private businesses. The revitalized private sector also benefited public sector employees as it provided a source for supplementary income.[75]

## Indochina ties

Cambodia, Laos and Vietnam initiated market reforms in 1979 that broadened in scope and impact in the coming decade. The revolution in the Lao PDR, even as it continued to bear similarities to its Vietnamese counterpart, increasingly assumed a Lao character as the decade progressed. In Cambodia, the Vietnamese invaders replaced the Democratic Kampuchea regime with a sympathetic government, consisting of Khmer Rouge defectors and Cambodians who had previously sought refuge in Vietnam. Even as the new Phnom Penh government restored many of the institutions abandoned or destroyed by the Khmer Rouge, its control of political issues and events remained tight. The situation left most Western observers to agree with David Chandler "that Vietnam's occupation of the country fitted into a long-term strategic plan to join the components of Indo-China into a Vietnam-dominated federation."[76] On the other hand, economic reforms in Cambodia increasingly assumed forms outside the Vietnamese model. Vietnamese communism, which had not influenced the revolution in Cambodia to the extent it impacted the Lao revolution in the three decades after World War II, guided but did not dominate Cambodia in the post-1979 period of Vietnamese occupation. Although the full extent of Vietnamese influence in Cambodia in the first half of the 1980s remains a contentious issue, it appears most appropriate to describe Cambodia as a satellite but not a colony of Vietnam.[77] Over time, the three revolutions increasingly acted independently of each other even though a high level of fraternal fellowship continued to characterize the Lao–Vietnamese relationship in particular.

At the same time, the communist party leadership in all three states perpetuated the fiction that their "special relationship" had deep historical roots. In presenting the history of the Kampuchean People's Revolutionary Party, PRK documents insisted on the importance of the links of militant solidarity shared by Cambodia, Laos and Vietnam as they struggled for freedom, independence and socialism. Stressing that militant solidarity had its origins in the colonial era when the three Indochinese countries were subjected to the same colonialist yoke, KPRP historiography emphasized that the KPRP had its origins in the Indochinese Communist Party.[78]

Lao leaders, together with their Cambodian counterparts, professed themselves to be in a common front with Vietnam against the Chinese "expansionist hegemonists" who had by the early 1980s replaced French colonialists and American imperialists as the primary threat to a united Indochina. General Secretary Kaysone echoed the feelings of his neighbors when he said:

> We believe that solidarity and mutual co-operation and assistance among Laos, Vietnam and Cambodia will be as firm as and last as long as the Truong Son Mountain Range and the Mekong River.[79]

To guide the policies of its junior partners, the Socialist Republic of Vietnam created a number of formal and informal mechanisms. Most important were the special structures at the apex of each party organization to facilitate liaison among the fraternal Indochinese parties. Frequent exchanges of high-level party and state officials took place as did similar exchanges between advisory staffs in each country. The mounting overlay of trilateral agreements, commissions and conferences included semi-annual meetings after 1980 of the ministers of foreign affairs of Cambodia, Laos and Vietnam as well as periodical Indochina summit meetings after 1983. The three states also formed Committees for Economic Cooperation in 1983 which met twice yearly thereafter to coordinate economic development policies. Indochina-wide committees were also established to coordinate the policies of their national Mekong Committees within the Interim Mekong Committee. Laos and Vietnam renewed their participation in the Interim Mekong Committee in 1978, but Cambodia did not rejoin until after the 1991 Paris Peace Agreement. One negative consequence of the increasingly complex web of Indochinese relations, seldom recognized at the time, was that it effectively blocked any possibility of wider regional cooperation with noncommunist neighbors like Thailand.[80]

Hanoi maintained a fiction of political equality at these trilateral gatherings, but there was no question as to which state determined the policy line. Long-term Vietnamese aspirations for Indochina-wide institutions were more debatable. The Chinese government repeatedly charged that the creation of each new institution moved Vietnam closer to its dream of a Federation of Indochina; however, Hanoi's explicit rejection of such a formula, which reeked of the French colonial past, made this approach appear impolitic and thus improbable.[81] At the same time, it was clear that Vietnam intended to remain the dominant power in the subregion.

# 4 Reform accelerates

Our Party struggles for communist ideology; it is an organization of people who fight with determination against oppression and exploitation, and who have sacrificed all for our national independence, freedom, and reunification.

Vietnamese Novelist Ma Van Khang, *Against the Flood*, 2000

As for political qualifications, the candidates must maintain a line of thinking that explicitly distinguishes friends from foes and a certain ability level for implementing the line and policies of the Party and state.

Lao People's Revolutionary Party Central Committee Secretariat, 1988

A small boat shouldn't try to be like a large boat.

Cambodian Proverb

The economic reforms initiated by the governments of Cambodia, Laos and Vietnam at the outset of the 1980s enjoyed limited success but failed to achieve many of the objectives set by the ruling communist parties. Faced with disappointing results, officials in all three states elected to accelerate reform efforts after 1985 in an effort to improve economic performance and thus forestall political reform. The substance of this new round of economic reforms varied in content and emphasis from state to state; and while the results were generally encouraging, the decade ended with much remaining to be done. Nascent political reform languished in both Laos and Vietnam; however, in Cambodia, successful peace talks set the stage for nationwide elections and important steps toward increased political pluralism.

## *Doi moi* in Vietnam

Economic reform, both as a theoretical and a practical concept, has enjoyed a long history in Vietnam; nevertheless, the years 1985–6 remain an important benchmark. The half-hearted reform measures pursued throughout the first half of the decade were unsuccessful in containing

inflation and reducing serious fiscal imbalances. In response to the deteriorating situation, Vietnam introduced in 1985 price and currency reforms in
an attempt to stabilize the economy. Largely ineffective, these new measures marked the outset of fundamental changes in government policy.
Ultimately, the full extent of changes were reflected in resolutions adopted
by the Sixth Party Congress meeting in Hanoi in December 1986.

The package of reform measures adopted by Vietnam at the end of
1986 focused on six policy areas in an attempt to quicken the pace of what
the government termed *doi moi* (renovation). First, Hanoi established the
independent status of public enterprises with the intent they would
operate according to socialist accounting principles, a concept calling for
economic and financial independence. Second, price liberalization policies
moved the entire economic system from administratively determined
prices toward market determined prices. Third, ownership diversification
reforms encouraged nonstate ownership and provided for partnerships
between the state, cooperative and private sectors. Fourth, segments of
the economy were opened to commercial relations with foreigners with
attendant encouragement for foreign investment. Fifth, the Party strengthened both agricultural incentives and institutional support for agriculture
in a reversal of the earlier emphasis on the industrial sector. Finally,
Vietnam undertook a fundamental reform of the financial system to separate central banking and commercial banking functions. At the same time,
it implemented adjustments in official exchange rates and liberalized
foreign exchange regulations.[1]

The economic reforms adopted by the Vietnamese in 1986 were widespread and of considerable historical significance. *Doi moi* represented a
sustained attack on the central planning model; thereafter, market-type
relations existed alongside the central planned economy throughout
Vietnam. The Sixth Party Congress thus represented an important retreat
by the Party as the latter was forced to admit that central planning had
been a failure. At the same time, the Congress insisted on retaining Party
rule even as it adopted the goal of economic reform along market lines. In
effect, Party members at the end of 1986 offered the Vietnamese people a
deal: we give you the opportunity to find new economic space and you
leave us in control of politics. No communist-ruled society had been successful to that time with this approach. On the one hand, the Chinese
example appeared to offer the Vietnamese leadership some promise of
success in this endeavor. On the other, the experience of the Soviet Union
and its East European satellites suggested meaningful economic reform,
because it necessitated popular support, could only be successful once the
Party had been dislodged from power.

Initially, implementation of the *doi moi* reform package was sluggish
and incomplete, as economist Dang T. Tran later recognized; consequently, the new reforms were inadequate to halt the progressive deterioration in economic conditions.

The implementation of the second reform was slow at first. Party bureaucrats had been hesitant about *Doi Moi* (Renovation). Only when twenty-one people died of starvation in Thanh Hoa Province and famine threatened the central part of the country in March 1988 did the Vietnam leaders finally realize that they had to push hard for reforms or millions would perish. The Politburo decided to return the land confiscated from the peasants during 1975–1983. It downgraded the role of agricultural cooperatives and allowed farmers to perform individually most tasks in the rice-growing cycle.[2]

After achieving a fairly respectable level of economic growth in the first half of the decade, the period 1986–8 witnessed a dramatic slowdown, principally due to the near disastrous performance of agriculture. A series of natural calamities compounded the negative impact of a long period of neglect and forced collectivization. Consequently, agricultural production stagnated throughout the period with an actual decline in output in 1987. Although official statistics showed continued growth in industrial output, many observers, including the author, believe government data for the period was overstated and that industrial performance also deteriorated. Industrial enterprises experienced increased difficulties in securing intermediate inputs, especially from abroad, due to growing foreign exchange shortages. Domestic demand for industrial goods slowed as the agricultural situation worsened and agricultural incomes stagnated. The economic crisis also assumed a regional dimension in that it provoked a new outpouring of boat people. The number of Vietnamese illegal arrivals in neighboring countries jumped to 45,000 in 1988 and 50,000 in the first half of 1989. Most of them came from northern Vietnam where the food crisis hit the hardest, but departures from the South also increased.[3]

Frustrated with the lack of progress, Vietnam in 1988 launched several comprehensive and well coordinated new reform measures. Reversing earlier monetary policies, Hanoi imposed tight credit ceilings by controlling the growth of reserve money, introducing cash reserve requirements and increasing interest rates. Commercial bank access to state bank credit was restricted, a policy supported by stricter control of the budget deficit and government borrowing from the state bank. Expenditure restraint, revenue mobilization, improved tax administration and new tax measures helped reduce the budget deficit. In the area of exchange policy, the government unified the exchange rate near the level of the parallel market and devalued the ruble rate to the more realistic level of the cross-exchange rate. Traditional foreign trade monopolies, jealously guarded by state companies, were largely dismantled with new public enterprises, as well as private traders, allowed to engage in foreign trade.[4]

The agricultural reforms introduced in Vietnam in 1988–9 recognized both cooperatives and production teams as voluntary, self-governing economic units. Tenure periods of 15–20 years or longer became common, and contracts often included inheritance and transfer rights. Peasants gained the right to sell agricultural produce freely, and at their discretion, to engage in exchanges with the state. As a result, the initiative in northern Vietnam, as well as in the South, clearly passed from collectives to households although the net effect of the process was far from uniform in each area. In the South, where collective agriculture had never really taken root, new reforms forestalled rather than overturned collectivization.[5]

The movement to strengthen property rights accelerated in 1988 with the implementation of the land law approved earlier by the National Assembly. The new land law maintained state ownership of land; however, it also recognized private land use rights awarded by the state. Granted without charge for a fixed term, these rights carried an obligation to observe a variety of regulations and controls and to pay taxes on the land. But land use rights still could not be transferred, and the lack of transferability meant they could not be pledged as loan collateral.[6]

By 1992, six million out of seven million hectares of cropland in Vietnam were farmed under direct household land use rights with the land either leased directly from state farms or allocated by collectives or former state farms. Many state farms had been dissolved and the land distributed to employees and local farmers. Most of the remaining state farms were expected to be dissolved or to lease out their land in the near future. Even large portions of state forest operations had been given over to smallholders. The 1988 land law did not permit the transfer or inheritance of land use rights; however, a number of de facto land sales took place as the economy surged.[7]

## Party reform in Vietnam

The Party elected Nguyen Van Linh, a long-time southern activist and organizer and twice chairman of the Ho Chi Minh Party Committee, General Secretary of the Vietnamese Communist Party at the Sixth National Party Congress in December 1986. Under his leadership, Party reform accelerated as the political consequences of economic transformation encouraged Party leaders to shape a parallel reform movement within the Party. Establishing himself as a forceful and forward-looking leader, Linh committed to a measure of economic change and Party transformation that was far more ambitious than the reformist goals of his predecessors. Among other measures, the new reforms empowered local Party organizations to assume responsibilities parallel to the growing economic autonomy gradually being granted to state enterprises.[8]

Linh also worked to improve the training of Party managers and advocated a more flexible style of management that relied increasingly on modern organization skills and management techniques. He sought to confine the Party to a more limited role as the conscience of the revolution responsible for fashioning social and political direction while allowing accountability for daily governance to pass to a body of elected and appointed officials. Emphasizing the need for the Party to share power with the Vietnamese polity, Linh strongly urged that Party building should properly include non-Party entities. At the same time, he took pains to stress the extent to which the Party would remain central to the political process and continue to exert a strategic influence.[9]

At the outset, General Secretary Linh successfully nurtured the ability to compromise, change political habits and alter institutional rules. He also achieved limited, early success in turning the Party into a more flexible, responsive body able to undertake organizational change. Nonetheless, the Party after three years was still incapable of coping with a noncommunist movement or anti-Party activism. Rules stating that the Party was the preeminent political voice in Vietnam were still on the books, slightly bent but hardly supplanted.[10]

Nguyen Van Linh eventually proved unsuccessful in pushing beyond the conservative majority, as well as his own faith and political beliefs, to achieve extensive, permanent change in the Vietnamese political system. On the contrary, the Party responded to the change in Eastern Europe and the improved domestic economic climate at the end of the decade with a retreat from the modest gains recognized by Linh. As Vietnam entered the decade of the 1990s, the Vietnam Communist Party had yet to redefine its concept of socialism or alter its modus operandi to an extent that foreshadowed a multi-party system or significant pluralism. The contradictions inherent in this dual commitment to economic reform and political dogma constituted a major imponderable in any assessment of the future direction of economic reform in Vietnam.[11]

## Structural reform and foreign investment

In support of the package of economic reforms introduced in 1988–9, Vietnam expanded and strengthened its structural policies. Hanoi extended price reforms through the liberalization of virtually all commodity prices. As a result, only a handful of prices remained subject to administrative controls. The government also modified agricultural contracts to link output and input prices more closely to market developments. The remunerative package of public sector employees was restructured with most subsidies in kind removed. Enterprise autonomy, with a few notable exceptions like petroleum and electricity, was strengthened by reducing the number of compulsory plan targets. Finally, the government introduced an improved system to monitor the performance of public enterprises.[12] The revised reform package in place by the end of the decade represented the most radical, comprehensive set of reforms adopted by any socialist country to that time.

The Vietnamese National Assembly first approved a foreign investment law in late 1987. Although it resembled a 1979 Chinese law, the 1987

Vietnamese version was, in some areas, more comprehensive and liberal. For example, the Vietnamese statute stipulated maximum terms for joint ventures, specified tax rates and set criteria for priority tax treatment. Elsewhere, the Vietnamese law was identical to its Chinese counterpart in that it allowed joint ventures, business cooperation contracts and 100 percent wholly owned foreign enterprises. Even though it still entailed bureaucratic problems and delays, the investment approval process in Vietnam was designed to avoid many of the problems encountered earlier in China. Vietnam established one control body responsible for all foreign investment projects, the State Committee for Cooperation and Investment (SCCI). This body reviewed and approved all foreign investment applications, playing the same role as the Ministry of Foreign Trade and Economic Cooperation in China. In theory, the SCCI was designed as a one-stop shop, and all relevant ministries were represented on it. SCCI approval specified tax rates, tax holidays, import duties and other matters related to financing. In practice, there was also a second approval level, the local people's committee at the site of the proposed investment. In a few cases, project approval also involved a third level as the Politburo could become involved in major projects.[13]

The 1987 foreign investment law aimed to create attractive conditions for overseas investors, especially those from Western and noncommunist countries. In the process, Vietnam hoped to lay the basis for expanded foreign economic relations and increased integration within the world economy. Desperate to develop alternate sources of foreign exchange, Hanoi was prevented from doing so, not by the progressive introduction of market-oriented reforms, but by the constraints of the U.S.-led embargo. When introduced, the terms of the 1987 law on foreign investment were considered to be among the most liberal in Asia. Overseas response to the law was very positive; and by the end of 1989, Vietnam had granted investment licenses for projects totaling $832 million with half of them in operation.[14]

A December 1992 revision to the 1987 foreign investment law set the maximum limit of foreign investment at 50 years with a possible extension to 70 years. The government then issued a decree in April 1993 which detailed new regulations for contractual business cooperation, joint ventures and enterprises with 100 percent foreign capital. In addition, it included sections on export processing contracts and zones, technology transfer, labor relations, financial matters and foreign exchange controls. Finally, the 1993 decree established a base tax rate of 25 percent with lower rates available for special projects or projects located in designated areas of Vietnam.[15]

The initial impact of the economic reforms implemented in Vietnam in 1989 was positive, especially in the area of disinflation. The rate of inflation dropped sharply from the spring of 1988 to the summer of 1989. There were other notable successes as well. Hard currency exports doubled as a result of the trade liberalization policy and the exchange rate devaluation. These earnings enabled Vietnam to replace lost Soviet assistance with purchases of necessary imports from the convertible area. National savings also increased dramatically, more than offsetting the loss in foreign savings. As one result, both the growth rate and the investment rate in 1989 increased over the previous year. On the other hand, money creation continued at an unacceptably high level preventing the government from consolidating the gains of the disinflation program. Inflation soon reemerged at a disturbingly high level and real interest rates were once again negative. In addition, reduced Soviet assistance, combined with the failure of new sources of finance to materialize, contributed to a sharp decline in public investment as well as a return to excessive financing of the national budget through credit creation. National calamities throughout the first half of 1991 added to the growing list of economic problems. However, the relatively high, excessively volatile rate of inflation continued to be the major obstacle to successful growth in Vietnam.[16]

Vietnam joined Comecon in 1978; and during the 1980s, the Soviet Union was Vietnam's largest single trading partner as well as its largest creditor and aid donor. But as the Soviet Union began to crumble, its economic relationship with Vietnam deteriorated; and its economic support faded. Vietnam was increasingly preoccupied with extracting itself from Cambodia, ending its international isolation and participating in the economic prosperity of its neighbors. For Vietnam, the changes that took place in the Soviet Union and Eastern Europe meant the loss of political allies, economic aid and its largest market. In addition, the already large ranks of the unemployed swelled further with the return of thousands of contract workers from the Soviet bloc. Visits to Moscow in May 1991 convinced senior Vietnamese leaders they could no longer count on political or economic support from the Soviet Union. The leadership in Hanoi thus concluded that the rigorous pursuit of economic reform was the best survival course for the Communist Party of Vietnam.[17]

## Economic reforms continue in Vietnam

It was against this background that the Party held its much delayed Seventh Party Congress in June 1991. At the congress, the reformer Vo Van Kiet, previously Deputy Prime Minister for Economic Affairs, was elevated to the post of Prime Minister replacing the more conservative Do Muoi who became General Secretary of the Communist Party. Phan Van Khai, another leading reformer, replaced Kiet as Deputy Prime Minister in addition to serving as Chairman of the State Planning Commission. The elevation of recognized reformers to key government positions increased their respective influence over the central organs of the state. Otherwise, the Congress did not witness significant change in regional or local interests and influence as reflected in provincial and lower bodies. More to the point, it refused to extend market economy reforms by any measure that might diminish Party control. In his closing speech, Do Muoi argued, on the one hand, that economic reform was the keystone of Party policy, and on the other, that the Party remained unshakable in its determination to follow the path of socialism.[18]

Where the Seventh Party Congress had leaned toward order, constitutional amendments drafted at the ninth session of the National Assembly, which opened at the end of July 1991, dropped most references to socialism and emphasized the building of a multi-sector commodity economy according to a state-guided and regulated market mechanism. In turn, the Party Central Committee, meeting at the end of the year, called for a strengthening of the economic reforms undertaken in the last five years and proposed new measures to resolve the current economic crisis. It also reaffirmed Vietnamese adherence to socialism, together with the leading role of the Party in both government and society.[19]

Recognizing the need for additional change, Hanoi continued its measured pace toward economic reform. Government spokesmen repeatedly emphasized the need to boost economic growth with special emphasis on controlling inflation, expanding foreign trade and promoting foreign investment. The National Assembly adopted a new constitution in April 1992 which institutionalized the market-oriented policies adopted by Vietnam over the preceding five years. In Article 15, the 1992 charter described the economic system as "a multi-component commodity economy functioning in accordance with market mechanisms under the management of the State and following a socialist orientation." Among other things, the new constitution encouraged foreign investment, specifically mentioning investment by Vietnamese living abroad.[20]

In providing for private ownership and enhancing the protection offered by the state for such ownership, the 1992 constitution formally established three types of ownership: people (state ownership), collective and private, all three of which received legal protection from the state. Nationalization of the private property rights of individuals and organizations was expressly prohibited while any necessary seizure of property had to be compensated. The rights of inheritance and transfer were also protected. The revised charter stipulated that land remained the property of the state but could be allotted for long-term use and transferred by the user. And it guaranteed that neither foreign-owned nor Vietnamese-owned property could be nationalized. The new code also recognized the right of citizens to own means of production, to start their own businesses and to enter into joint ventures with foreign companies. Other reforms included changes to the foreign exchange and banking codes. A modified foreign investment law permitted private businesses to enter foreign joint ventures and gave tax and operating concessions to overseas investors. The government also took tentative steps toward the privatization of state-owned companies.[21]

In 1990, some 12,000 registered state companies operated in Vietnam, ranging from large industrial concerns to small retail stores. With total assets estimated at $12 billion and total employment around 2.3 million, state enterprises were relatively small compared to the former Soviet Union and its East European satellites; however, they played a significant role in the national economy. The existence of a large number of state-owned firms at provincial, district and local levels distinguished Vietnam from Cambodia and Laos as well as other socialist countries like China. Size was another notable feature of state enterprises in Vietnam; an over-whelming majority of them were very small in terms of assets. The majority of small and medium enterprises belonged to provincial and local authorities and the Party apparatus. The smaller enterprises were the least efficient with an estimated 40 percent losing money and another 30 percent barely breaking even.[22]

The Vietnamese government after 1991 made a real effort to reform state enterprises by granting more autonomy to management and requiring more financial discipline. Such efforts produced minimal results, largely because the attempted reforms faced strong resistance from Party cadre managing the enterprises. Vietnam, according to a report based on 1992–3 data, estimated that at least one-third of its 12,000 state enterprises were bankrupt. To address this situation, the World Bank called on Vietnam to take three related steps. First, it encouraged Hanoi to adopt a clear policy as to the sectors of the economy in which the government would continue to invest. Second, it suggested the government strengthen the procedures in place for closing bankrupt enterprises and for auctioning assets, especially land use rights. Finally, the Bank called on Hanoi to implement a pilot program to privatize profitable enterprises in non-strategic sectors. In effect, these policy recommendations constituted a de facto privatization policy in that thousands of state firms would cease operation with many of their assets and employees shifting to the private sector. The World Bank report concluded that additional reforms, in particular procedures for transferring the land use rights of failed enterprises, were needed to make the government's implicit strategy for state enterprises more formal.[23]

A major revision to the 1988 land law was drafted in 1992–3 and approved by the National Assembly in July 1993. The new law created a role for the state in land management similar to that of governments in market economies. The continued ownership by the state of all land was viewed as essentially a legal basis for regulating and taxing land use in ways not dissimilar to that in many capitalist countries. For example, the State was to determine prices applicable to each category of land for purposes of tax calculation, revenue collection, valuation of property and compensation for damages when land was recovered.[24]

The 1993 land law provided that land use certificates would be issued for agricultural land and urban residential land. The certificates could be exchanged, transferred, rented, inherited and mortgaged during the period for which the land was allocated. These changes further strengthened the incentives in place for agricultural production; however, they left the length of tenure for commercial and urban industrial land use rights to implementing regulations. The length of tenure for agricultural land, set at 20 years for annual crops and 50 years for perennial crops, was renewable. Residential land was allocated on a permanent basis, recoverable only upon fairly narrow, specified conditions. In the 1993 land law, the people's committees at all levels were given authority, on behalf of the state, to administer land within their respective local areas and within the scope of their respective authority.[25]

A fundamental reform of the Vietnamese banking system began in July 1987 when basic banking functions were carefully delineated between the State Bank and the commercial banks. Under the new system, the State Bank undertook to regulate the supply of money and credit and hence safeguard the value of the national currency. Commercial banking functions were assumed by two newly established commercial banks, the Vietnam Bank for Agriculture (VBA) and the Industrial and Commercial Bank of Vietnam (ICBV). Regrettably, these early reforms were not implemented to the fullest extent. Consequently, the government in 1990 introduced additional reforms that separated the State Bank from a commercial role, giving it instead responsibility for conducting monetary policy and regulating a more complex financial system.[26]

In the post-1990 banking structure, the state-owned and operated Investment and Development Bank of Vietnam (IDBV) assumed responsibility for the transfer of budgetary appropriations earmarked annually for basic infrastructure and various government investment projects. Funded by the government for both equity and working capital, the IDBV functioned as the development bank for the central government. Three state-owned and operated institutions, the Bank for Foreign Trade, the Industrial and Commercial Bank of Vietnam and the Vietnam Bank for Agriculture, handled banking operations on a commercial basis. Joint-stock banks were the third category of credit institution established. In addition, an extensive network of credit cooperatives had operated in northern Vietnam since the early years of national independence. Modest in scope, these cooperatives catered to the limited banking needs of local communities. Credit cooperatives also emerged in southern Vietnam after independence.[27]

## Positive impact of Vietnamese reforms

By mid-1993, the package of economic reforms initiated in 1986 and expanded after 1989 was having an increasingly positive impact on the Vietnamese economy. The level of economic growth in 1992, generally estimated at around 8 percent, was a marked improvement from less than

5 percent in 1991. At the same time, the rate of inflation dropped from almost 700 percent in 1986 to around 18 percent in 1992. As the currency stabilized and reserves grew, the trade deficit virtually disappeared. Public sector subsidies were reduced or eliminated although the privatization of Vietnamese state enterprises proceeded at a much slower pace than expected. The private sector was now responsible for almost 75 percent of the value of national goods and services. All in all, it was a credible performance for an economy that had recently suffered the sudden disappearance of $1 billion in annual Soviet non-military aid together with a continuation of both the prohibition on multilateral funding and the U.S. embargo.[28]

In July 1993, the U.S. government finally ended its prolonged opposition to loans to Vietnam from international lending institutions. This cleared the way for implementation of a French proposal to refinance Vietnam's $140 million debt to the International Monetary Fund (IMF), a move which enabled Hanoi to clear its arrears, restructure its debt and attract new international funding. Clearance of IMF arrears set the stage for the World Bank and ADB to inject substantial amounts of project aid to rebuild Vietnam. Meeting in Paris in November 1993, the world financial community responded enthusiastically to the above developments. Praising Vietnamese progress in moving toward a market economy, participants pledged $1.8 billion in aid. Japan emerged as the single largest donor to Vietnam with a pledge of $560 million for 1994 alone.

## Lao PDR adopts Second Five-Year Plan

Nouhak Phoumsavanh, a member of the Central Committee of the Lao People's Revolutionary Party, presented the Second Five-Year Plan (1986–90) to the Fourth Party Congress in 1986. In most respects, the new plan did not depart from the previous one, largely following guidelines outlined in 1981. The goal in the agricultural sector was to meet the basic food requirements of the population as well as to expand production for export and for the development of agricultural processing industries. To meet these objectives, planned expenditure for agriculture was set at 20 percent of the total investment budget with much of this expenditure targeted for the development of small irrigation projects to support double cropping. To stimulate growth in forestry, the plan allocated an additional 10 percent of expenditure to forestry-related projects. Collectively, the agricultural and forestry sectors were allocated almost one-third of total budgeted investment, an indication of the high priority the government placed on them.[29]

In the period of the First Five-Year Plan, the performance of the industrial sector, despite heavy government investment, was the worst of any sector of the economy. Where targeted growth was 17 percent annually, actual output was negative, dropping more than 10 percent in 1980–4. The

poor performance in industry was due in large part to a decline in manufacturing as most Lao factories operated below capacity. The new plan
revised growth targets downward and shifted emphasis from capital inten-
sive industries to light industry to better meet consumer demand for goods
and handicrafts. With the sale of electricity and minerals a major source of
foreign exchange earnings, the Second Five-Year Plan provided for continued expansion in these areas.[30]

The lack of physical infrastructure in Laos has long been identified as a
major impediment to economic and social development. With this in mind,
it was not surprising that the new plan allocated some 20 percent of total
government investment to the improvement of transportation and communications. It targeted the construction or rehabilitation of 1,500 kilometers
of road network with priority placed on routes 8, 9 and 10 as well as sections of route 14. Improvements in air and river transport, together with
the postal and telecommunications systems, were also priorities in the
plan.[31]

In the trade sector, the Second Five-Year Plan focused on the development of internal trade to increase the volume of goods in circulation. It
also called for increased external trade with the Soviet Union and other
socialist countries, especially Cambodia and Vietnam. In the social development sector, education and health remained priority areas as they had
been in the First Five-Year Plan. While Laos had made impressive gains in
expanding to the village level both education and primary health care, the
quality of services remained poor.[32]

Observers in and out of the Lao PDR generally agreed the development priorities articulated in the Second Five-Year Plan were realistic and
appropriate for a poor country like Laos. At the same time, many worried
the targets set were too ambitious given the nation's mediocre performance in the First Five-Year Plan and its ongoing shortage of material and
manpower resources. A land-locked position, immature economic structures and a poor communications system were correctly cited as serious
obstacles to rapid economic development.

## New economic mechanism in Laos

Openly acknowledging its poor performance, the LPRP leadership
launched a new round of economic reforms in conjunction with the
presentation of the Second Five-Year Plan. Decrying an excess of centralization in a thinly populated country with virtually no infrastructure,
LPRP officials admitted there was little scope for building socialism in a
subsistence economy. Therefore, the Party decided that administration
must be decentralized, with economic management developed from the
grass roots up, while the economy underwent a capitalist phase before it
moved beyond subsistence activities. Focused on improvements in economic management, the new reforms were entitled the New Economic

Management Mechanism or simply the New Economic Mechanism (NEM). According to General Secretary Kaysone, the new management system was designed to correct the serious shortcomings of the old approach.

> At present, our mechanism of economic management is fraught with bureaucratic centralism and based on state subsidies. The essence of this mechanism is that the State must provide the capital, equipment and all materials needed for running business and the enterprise must hand in its products to the State. The enterprise's economic accounting is merely perfunctory, as a result the enterprise's profit is inaccurately determined. As a matter of fact, the enterprise is not fully responsible for its operation.[33]

To end "economic operations which are based on wishful thinking and administrative orders from top levels," the LPRP replaced the former management system with what Kaysone termed "socialist economic accounting." In the new system, state enterprises would be responsible for their operations based on factors such as capital availability, production capacity, labor productivity and profitability.[34]

The New Economic Mechanism implied a substantial decentralization of administrative controls on pricing, production targets and wages. Under the new system, policy decisions in these areas were delegated either to local economic units or the management of state enterprises. To the uninitiated, the new approach appeared to be a bold departure from past practice. In reality, it was a classic example of Lao pragmatism. Elements of the new system had been quietly implemented on a trial basis by larger state enterprises after 1983. When the experiment achieved positive results, the Party elected in 1986 to extend the system to all enterprises and to grant additional autonomy. Support for the new strategy came from a wide variety of sources, including Hanoi and Moscow who were also experimenting with new methods. Western aid donors, like the World Bank and the International Monetary Fund, also welcomed the change.[35]

The most far-reaching policy adopted in the New Economic Mechanism was the one market, one price principle, eliminating the dual price system. Unification of multiple exchange rates began in 1986 when the government devalued the commercial exchange rate of the kip. Introduction of a market exchange rate, together with the unification of official exchange rates, supported development of an export-oriented cash economy. Moves to stimulate domestic and foreign competition through private sector promotion and import substitution complemented price and exchange liberalization measures.[36]

The introduction of a market exchange rate, together with the unification of official exchange rates, were major policy adjustments in support of the development of an export-oriented cash economy. The Lao PDR by mid-1987 had moved to a pricing system reflective of the new economic structures coming into place. It abolished virtually all administered prices as well as the multi-tiered foreign exchange rate, lifted barriers to internal trade and granted state enterprises direct access to international markets. The reform process was further consolidated in March 1988 when the fifth session of the Council of Ministers passed several important decrees related to the economy. These new measures included revised policies on taxation, finance and banking, state pricing, goods circulation and the private sector.[37]

To implement the one-price concept, the Lao PDR took three major policy decisions in March 1988. First, it set official retail prices, with very few exceptions, at a level equal to the parallel market price. Prices at the wholesale level, on the other hand, were to be freely determined by buyers and sellers. Second, the government permitted state enterprises to fix their own output prices. Finally, it increased the price of the 22 basic goods available in state shops with coupons to the same level as the parallel market price. This last decision, in line with the policy to eliminate consumption subsidies to state workers, was scheduled for implementation over a period of two to three years due to the size of the adjustments involved.[38]

Other important policy changes introduced in late 1987 included the removal of restrictions on the internal trade of agricultural products as well as an end to the state setting producer procurement prices for a wide range of crops. In the future, prices were to be set by mutual agreement. For example, the procurement price of rice in 1988, which had been around 30 percent of the parallel market price in 1987, was increased to market level. In addition, the procurement price of rice paddy was now determined on a contract basis between farmers and cooperatives. Through these policy adjustments, the government hoped to boost the incomes of farmers trading with the state and thus encourage increased food production. At the same time, consumption subsidies to state employees fell 25–35 percent in 1988. Unfortunately, the inadequate road system in Laos continued to be a major barrier to the internal movement of goods and services, limiting the trade in rice between provinces. Large price differentials between regions compounded the problem.[39]

A distinctive feature of the early Lao approach to reform was the speed and intensity with which the new economic measures were implemented. The ability of the government to execute quickly a profound reorientation of its economy was due in no small part to its underdeveloped nature. Given the resistance to socialist reforms in the first decade of the revolution, the challenge to the government was not so much dismantling an entrenched socialist system as it was reorienting a largely subsistence system to market demands.

### State enterprise reform in Laos

The Lao government in 1986 switched four state enterprises to the new business accounting system and granted them business autonomy. The four enterprises were the Lao Electricity Company, Beer and Soft Drink Company, Lao Tobacco Company and Lao Plywood Company. In this initial stage of state enterprise reform, these four companies registered increased profits, adding considerable revenue to the state budget.[40]

Mandatory production targets were abolished in 1988 with each state enterprise free to decide which commodities to produce and how to produce them as long as it met its targeted tax payments. A March 1988 decree implemented the principle of "self-financing" in which all indirect and direct costs of production were to be financed by state enterprises without state subsidies. Under this policy, only newly created enterprises (or new activities within an existing firm) were entitled to receive investment funds from the government. Once enterprises were operating normally, both investment and working capital were to be financed from after-tax profits or credit extended by the banking system. Any new bank loans extended would be based on normal commercial criteria.[41]

The policy of empowering additional state enterprises to decide upon prices, investments and wages was not successful. Autonomy did not improve their performance, and financial results continued to fall short of official expectations. In some cases, autonomy resulted both in greater managerial discretion and increases in current savings at the expense of investment and thus in a decapitalization of the enterprise.[42]

When efforts to reform state enterprises fell short of expectations, Laos launched in 1989 a program of privatization covering some 260 state firms. Initially, the privatization process proceeded rapidly with some 30 enterprises transferred to the private sector through mid-1990. The process then slowed due to the absence of a competent authority to handle privatization. Dissatisfaction also arose over the valuation of enterprises and the tendering procedures adopted by the government. The absence of key elements of a privatization infrastructure, like a legal contract system, accountants, a functioning capital market and merchant bankers, also slowed the process. Finally, resistance to privatization increased among civil servants hoping to retain the more profitable state enterprises in the public sector.[43]

In 1990, the Lao PDR expected the 141 enterprises under central government control to contribute 19.3 billion kip to the state budget. However, during the first five months of the year, state firms paid only 643 million kip or 3 percent of the annual target. Most of the factories were old and lacked spare parts, and many were confused as to how to implement the liberalization measures. The government responded to their production problems by trying to sell them to private interests. In April 1990, for example, Laos offered 70 of its state enterprises for joint venture agreement, lease or sale. This total included 20 factories and six hotels. When the number of such enterprises had decreased only slightly by year end, the government issued a decree in March 1991 that accelerated its disengagement from state firms. Some 37 state enterprises were privatized in 1991–2 alone with more than half considered medium to large in terms of number of employees. Privatization in agriculture was also relatively rapid with 22 state enterprises under the Ministry of Agriculture and Forestry privatized in the same period.[44]

## Reform tempo increases in Laos

The year 1988 marked a watershed in the tempo of reform in the Lao PDR. Faced with ominous signs that the economy was in serious financial difficulty, the government mid-way through the Second Five-Year Plan introduced bold new policy initiatives, expanding reforms initiated in 1986. This new stage of reform promised to change fundamentally the structure of the Lao economy both in terms of an enhanced private sector and wider commercial relations with capitalist countries. In the process, the communist leadership, casting off whatever remained of Stalinist economic doctrines, broke dramatically with the past. Stressing the importance of international trade and private foreign investment to the transformation of domestic economic structures, the government revised the exchange rate structure linked earlier to the one market, one price principle. It also adopted a relatively liberal foreign investment law which allowed for wholly owned enterprises, equity joint ventures and contractual business arrangements.[45]

The Lao PDR also continued to encourage private holdings in agriculture with a mid-1988 announcement that no preferential treatment, credit or subsidies would be provided to cooperatives. In addition, the Party added a new economic sector, termed "the economy of small goods," to the existing five sectors of the Lao economy (individual subsistence, private capitalist, collective, joint state-private and state socialist). Instead of moving directly from subsistence to collective farming, the government now encouraged peasant families to enter the small goods economy by trading surplus production for commodities. To promote the newly recognized small goods economy, Resolution 6, adopted in June 1988, gave farmers long-term tenure rights and allowed them to pass land to their children or to sell it, charging for improvements made. These changes followed other reforms in late 1987, including the removal of restrictions on the internal trade of agricultural products. The state also stopped setting low producer procurement prices for a wide range of crops.[46]

In March 1988, the Lao PDR initiated a radical reform of the state-controlled banking system as part of its promotion of the new management system. The responsibilities of the state bank, heretofore the sole financial intermediary in Laos, were now confined to the monetary functions generally expected of a central bank. Management of foreign exchange, as well as commercial and development banking functions, were reassigned to other autonomous banking institutions.[47]

Commercial banks in Laos no longer received government subsidies and were fully responsible for their operations, including remittance of 60 percent of profits to the government. At the same time, foreign banks were offered facilities in the country. The government later streamlined the functions of the State Bank in a mid-1990 law which established the State Bank of the Lao PDR. Finally, in January 1992, the Lao PDR enacted new regulations governing commercial banks as well as other financial institutions.[48]

In consequence, private ownership in Laos had become, by the early 1990s, the dominant form of property rights in the rapidly expanding service sector as well as in the agricultural sector. However, it remained a minor property rights form in the industrial sector. On the other hand, the scope of private activities in the industrial sector expanded throughout the second half of the decade as the result of the privatization of state enterprises and the emergence of new private firms, most especially in construction. Taken as a whole, this meant that private property rights, although occasionally defined imperfectly, could be said to predominate in Laos.[49]

Unfortunately, the rules and regulations necessary to support market institutions and private property rights trailed the implementation of market-oriented reforms. Contract, inheritance and property laws, for example, were not passed until mid-1990. On the other hand, the 1991 constitution did guarantee the security of private property and foreign investment. And new insurance and accounting systems, adopted in 1990, were followed in 1991 by laws covering the settlement of commercial disputes, bankruptcy and liquidation. The government also expanded the banking reforms initiated in early 1988, announcing plans to privatize state-owned commercial banks.[50]

Until 1988, all investment in Laos was funded by the state which relied in turn largely on foreign assistance to fund public sector investment. At that point, the private domestic savings rate was negative and foreign investment was negligible. With the release of a new foreign investment code in July 1988, the government initiated a drive to attract external investment. The code was comparatively liberal and excited much interest, especially in Thailand, a target of the new policy. The objectives of the code were to expand economic and technological cooperation with foreign investors and to boost ailing state enterprises. It allowed for 100 percent wholly owned enterprises, equity joint ventures with a 30 percent minimum foreign share, and cooperative or contractual business ventures. The new code also provided guarantees against seizure and nationalization, allowed the remittance of profits and salaries, and extended tax concessions or exemptions in specific circumstances. Tax rates on profits varied with a minimum of 20 percent set for areas where the government was eager to attract capital and a rate of 35 percent or more for trading or hotel businesses. Unfortunately, long-standing impediments to investment, including an underdeveloped legal framework, poor infrastructure and remoteness from world markets, combined to limit the positive effects of the new investment regulations.[51]

## Lao external relations

Lao relations with neighboring Thailand were not good at any time after 1975 and were especially tense in 1984–6 following a border confrontation involving three small villages in the province of Sayaboury. The conflict erupted over differing interpretations of a 1907 treaty between France and Thailand delimiting the border between Laos and Thailand. Tensions eased in 1986 when the foreign ministers of Cambodia, Laos and Thailand, meeting in Hanoi, publicly endorsed a statement by Kaysone Phomvihane, indicating the Lao government was ready to do its utmost to normalize relations with Thailand. The foreign ministers of Laos and Thailand met later in the year to discuss improving diplomatic and commercial ties. After another short, but intense, border war in the winter of 1987–8, Thailand announced its intent to turn Indochina from a battlefield into a marketplace. Trade between Laos and Thailand burgeoned in 1988 with Thailand reducing from 273 to 30 the list of strategic goods that Thai companies were forbidden to trade in Laos. Relations continued to improve over the next two years. In March 1989, Laos and Thailand established the Lao–Thai Commission for Economic, Cultural, Scientific, and Technical Cooperation, an event which led to frequent exchanges on both sides of the Mekong. In November 1989, Thailand lifted its ban on the export of strategic goods to Laos, a list that once included 363 items. Finally, Thai Princess Maha Chakkri Sirinthon made an eight-day visit to Laos in March 1990.[52]

The withdrawal of Vietnamese troops from Laos in 1987 gave the Lao PDR additional latitude to develop both diplomatic and commercial ties with its neighbors. Relations with Vietnam remained close throughout the period, extending from political work at the party, administrative and military levels to the twinning of provinces, districts and communes. Although the dramatic improvement in Lao–Thai relations was a significant development, it did not presage a shift in the "special relationship" between Laos and Vietnam. As William Worner noted in a perceptive article on the Lao PDR, "the art of foreign policy-making in Laos has been to recognize the practical limits imposed by the 'special relationship.'"[53]

While it went largely unpublicized at the time, there was a much freer movement of goods and people across the Lao–Chinese border after 1985. Toward the end of 1987, the governments of China and Laos elevated their diplomatic relations to the ambassadorial level, opened borders closed since 1979, and in 1988, reestablished commercial relations. The exchange of ambassadors between China and Laos took place against the background of Vietnamese troop withdrawals from the Lao–China border and assurances from Beijing that it was terminating support for anti-government guerrillas in Laos.[54]

The Lao PDR also continued its close relationship with the Soviet Union. Soviet aid accounted for approximately half the total economic assistance received by Laos in 1988. At the same time, Moscow continued to criticize the Lao government for what it felt was an often inefficient and wasteful use of Soviet assistance. In part, Moscow's attitude reflected its position as the dominant donor to a country under severe constraints in its ability to absorb aid. For this reason, the Soviet Union welcomed an increase in Western influence in Laos as a means to reduce Soviet financial investment at minimal political cost.[55]

Diplomatic relations with the United States in the second half of the 1980s focused on the issues of American MIAs (servicemen missing-in-action since the Vietnam war), drug trafficking and political prisoners. Responding to Lao cooperation in the search for MIA remains, the U.S. Congress in December 1985 removed the ten-year-old ban on direct aid to Laos. This action led to exploratory talks on possible areas of cooperation but not to an immediate resumption of significant quantities of financial aid. The State Department in May 1988 issued a report that implicated Laos in the international narcotics trade. These charges were vehemently denied by the Lao government, but direct proof of Lao involvement later surfaced when several people were convicted of running an illegal heroin factory in Oudomxay province in northern Laos. After temporarily decertifying Laos in 1989 for failure to curb the production and distribution of illicit opium, Washington in 1990 provided assistance to initiate crop substitution programs intended to replace opium production. The question of political prisoners was largely defused before the end of the decade when the government closed political reeducation camps as part of an effort to attract expatriates to return to Laos.[56]

Laos also enjoyed a wide range of bilateral relations with other foreign countries and support from international financial institutions, like the World Bank, United Nations Development Program (UNDP) and Asian Development Bank (ADB). Foreign Minister Phoune Sipaseuth in March 1988 made the first official visit of a Lao foreign minister to Japan since the founding of the Lao PDR. The visit highlighted Lao interest in obtaining development assistance from Japan as well as Tokyo's reluctance to increase the level of aid before a Cambodian settlement was reached. Eighteen months later, Kaysone visited Japan and France, his first visits to countries outside the socialist bloc. These excursions to the West were meant to signal to the capitalist world that Laos was committed to strengthening its economic and political ties with the nonsocialist world. Laos also continued to maintain close ties with Australia and Sweden, countries that had long provided generous amounts of aid.[57]

## Political developments in Laos

The Lao approach to reform could best be characterized as *perestroika* without *glasnost* or economic change without political reform. Even as the LPRP cast off Stalinist economic doctrines and broke dramatically with the socialist past, it refused to share political power. In this context, the April 1988 decision of the Supreme People's Assembly (SPA) to hold elections, the first to be held in Laos since the regime took power in 1975, was a major political development which complemented efforts to liberalize the economy. Nationwide elections were scheduled in three stages with the first, local council elections in June, followed by provincial assembly and SPA ballots at the end of the year.[58]

The mechanics of the election law were clearly designed to broaden participation in the selection of representative institutions without challenging the Party's authority. A 15-member national election committee, under the direction of the Supreme People's Council Standing Committee, was established to oversee the election process, and all candidates standing for election were nominated by the LPRP as opposed to representing competing party platforms. Candidates were required to "be faithful to the country and socialism" as well as to "be obliged to implement the party's line and policies." Determined to retain its preeminent position in Laos, there was clearly no intent on the part of the LPRP to permit political plurality in the form of competing political parties.[59]

At the same time, despite the control exercised by the state and Party, the 1988 elections were more than simply a matter of confirming government candidates. With 4,462 candidates vying in the first round for 2,410 seats in 17 provinces, most voters had a choice. Only 360 single candidates were elected unopposed. Delayed for a month, the provincial assembly elections were held on November 20 and resulted in the formation of 16 provincial assemblies as well as a municipal assembly for Vientiane city.[60]

Turnout for the SPA election, which was delayed until March 1989, reached a level of more than 98 percent, according to official sources, and the Party acknowledged "weak points and shortcomings" in the administration of the balloting. A total of 121 candidates campaigned for 79 seats in the SPA so Lao voters again were granted a limited choice. The newly elected representatives included 65 LPRP members, 66 lowland *Lao Loum*, and five women, a number consistent with the low level of females in Party and government positions.[61]

The first major undertaking of the Supreme People's Assembly, which convened in May 1989, was the preparation of a draft constitution. The absence of a constitution was not a major issue in the early years of the revolution; however, it had surfaced frequently in the 1980s in conjunction with the trend toward liberalization. Without the protection of a legal umbrella, prospective business entrepreneurs and individuals felt exposed to the whims of powerful Party and government officials with broad interpretive powers. On 14 August 1991, the SPA unanimously endorsed the first constitution promulgated since the formation of the Lao PDR in 1975. Logically constructed and legally correct, it detailed the structures and duties of branches of government and defined certain basic citizen rights. On the other hand, the new constitution was rather quiet as to the limits of government authority.[62]

The 1991 Lao constitution stood in marked contrast to those of the Socialist Republic of Vietnam and the People's Republic of Kampuchea, both published ten years earlier, in that it was much less ideological in tone and content. In the cultural, economic and social spheres, both Cambodia and Vietnam were obviously more committed to socialism at that point than Laos was a decade later. There were also similarities in the three documents, notably in their structure and in the political institutions endorsed. The Lao constitution owed much to its Indochina neighbors and the Soviet Union, but it was "a unique document reflecting specifically Lao needs and conditions which apply, in the words of the Preamble, 'at this new period' in the history of the state."[63]

A major reshuffle of government ministries, evidence of the government's determination to consolidate the position of its supporters, occurred without public announcement in 1988. The State Planning Committee and the Ministry of Finance merged into a new State Committee for Economic Planning and Finance. Politburo member Sali Vongkahmsao was named chairman of this powerful new committee with Khamsai Souphanouvong, son of the ailing Lao PDR president, as first deputy chairman. In addition, a new State Committee for Foreign Economic Relations and Trade under Phao Bounnaphon, former Minister of Transport, Communications, and Posts, assumed responsibility for the foreign component of economic development strategy. Finally, the appointment of Thongsavat Khaikamphithoun, former ambassador to the Soviet Union, to the post of first deputy foreign minister, reflected the shift in Lao foreign policy vis-à-vis the socialist bloc. Knowledgeable observers agreed that these changes in key government structures and personnel signaled the determination of the Lao government to press ahead with its new development strategy.[64]

The Lao government also registered a shift in its attitude toward Buddhism in a March 1989 national meeting of the *Sangha* in Vientiane. The structural rules for the *Sangha* adopted at this meeting made it clear that the government intended to "take the religion forward along the road of socialism under the leadership of the party." Young men were accorded the right to enter *wats* as long as they received permission from local authorities; and "before leaving the *Sangha* they must have a good reason and carry it out according to the customs of Buddhism." While not restricting the beliefs of the Lao people, the Lao United Buddhist Association reserved "the right to decide on all problems relating to the world of the *Sangha*." The document also reiterated the government's opposition to superstitious beliefs in spirits and *thevadas*, together with any form of intoxication or gambling. Subsequently, Lao monks were permitted to travel to Thailand for study and to organize, on a temple-to-temple basis, Thai assistance with Buddhist teaching texts. This latter concession marked a radical departure from the recent past when the Lao government had actively discouraged any contact with Thai Buddhists.[65] The 1991 constitution later upgraded the status of Buddhism from one religion among many to the one specific religion named in the document.[66]

## Cambodia's First Five-Year Plan

At the end of 1985, the People's Republic of Kampuchea had survived for seven years, longer than either the Khmer Republic or Democratic Kampuchea. Supported by massive economic and military aid from the Soviet Union and Vietnam, the PRK made notable progress in rebuilding its economy and reestablishing at least some of the attributes of a functional nation state. At the same time, numerous obstacles remained to the sustained, peaceful reconstruction of the economy, in particular the absence of an international settlement to the diplomatic and military conundrum plaguing Cambodia after 1978. It would take another six years of shifting power relations and diplomatic maneuvering before an agreement was reached which brought independence and peace to Cambodia.

President Heng Samrin, in his political report to the Fifth Party Congress, introduced the PRK's First Five-Year Plan (1986–90) in October 1985. Described as a program of socioeconomic restoration and development, the plan emphasized agriculture, establishing aggressive production targets for four economic spearheads – food supplies, rubber, aquatic production and timber. Targets for the industrial sector, given its underdeveloped nature, were more modest. The plan called for the selective restoration of existing industrial production capacity and the gradual construction of small and medium industrial bases appropriate to Cambodian requirements.[67] The First Five-Year Plan also called for an expansion of the socialist trade network under the motto:

> For the peasantry, selling rice and agricultural products to the state is patriotism; for the state, selling goods and delivering them directly to the people is being responsible towards the people.[68]

Decisions taken at the Fifth Party Congress also resulted in important changes in the political leadership of Cambodia. The balance of power in the PRK continued in 1986 to shift from Khmer Viet Minh, former members of the Communist Party of Indochina who had remained in exile in Vietnam for long periods, toward former members of the Khmer Rouge. Khang Sarin, Minister of Interior, and Chan Pin, Minister of Finance and Trade, both Khmer Viet Minh, were replaced by deputy ministers who were not Hanoi exiles. Other ministerial changes and appointments to Party posts also reflected a consolidation of power by former Khmer Rouge cadre. The evolving complexion of the PRK leadership had significant albeit uncertain implications for the future direction of Cambodian reform efforts. At the very least, the changes clearly suggested a move toward a more Cambodian-oriented, less Vietnamese-inclined leadership.[69]

It should also be recognized that these important leadership changes had little or no impact on the legitimacy of the regime in the eyes of most Cambodians, the majority of whom were unsophisticated, rural peasants. Throughout the decade, revolutionary changes in institutions, policy and process, with the exception of the question of land ownership, were implemented with little public notice, interest or debate. For example, elections to the National Assembly, scheduled for mid-1986, were postponed in February 1986 until 1991 under a constitutional proviso which allowed the National Assembly to prolong its term of office "in the case of war or under other exceptional circumstances."[70]

The tenuous security situation throughout much of Cambodia continued to undermine efforts to rebuild the political economy. Three separate resistance groups, the National Army of Democratic Kampuchea (former Khmer Rouge), the Khmer People's National Liberation Front (former Prime Minister Son Sann), and the Nationalist Sihanoukist Army (Prince Sihanouk group), operated on the Thai–Cambodian border. With the Soviet Union and Vietnam supporting the PRK government, Chinese support of the Khmer Rouge, coupled with American and ASEAN support of their respective clients, sucked the major world powers into the Cambodian vortex, vastly complicating any potential settlement.[71]

As journalist Steven Erlanger noted at the time, power politics in Cambodia in the 1980s were largely a reflection of regional rivalries before and during the Second Indochina War:

> For China, rivalry with the Soviet Union and long enmity with Vietnam made the humiliation of its ally, the Khmer Rouge unacceptable – whatever its crimes. While the Soviets supported Vietnam, the Chinese revived the Khmer Rouge as the best way to harass Hanoi and Moscow. Thailand, always fearful of Vietnam's expansionist ambitions, facilitated Chinese aid to the Khmer Rouge, happy to take a cut and to have a buffer of Khmer Rouge soldiers and Cambodian civilians between itself and Vietnam. The United States, traumatized by its military defeat in Indochina and preferring improved relations with China over those with Vietnam, sided with the Chinese and thus, ironically, with the Khmer Rouge.[72]

To complicate matters, the three Cambodian resistance groups, loosely tied after 1982 as the Coalition Government of Democratic Kampuchea (CGDK), were often at odds with each other.

Despite difficult economic and political obstacles, Cambodia's economy improved over the next three years. Self-sufficiency remained elusive, but annual rice production increased after 1984, with the exception of a setback in 1988. Industry on the other hand was slow to recover in part due to a lack of raw materials and power. And the composition of manufacturing output continued to be heavily state-controlled. The trade balance continued in deficit with any increase in exports offset by an increase in imports. Most foreign trade continued to be conducted in the Comecon zone, but cross-border trade with Thailand also grew. In 1988, Cambodia concluded a trade protocol with Vietnam in which the signatories agreed to expand by 20 percent the volume of goods exchanged. The PRK also negotiated agreements with the Soviet Union to provide construction, vocational training and geological mapping to facilitate mineral exploration.[73]

## Economic liberalization in Cambodia

Beginning in the spring of 1988, Cambodia initiated a series of economic liberalization measures to strengthen the role of the private sector. In the area of private property, the growing dominance of family farming continued a trend visible for much of the decade with the government eventually abandoning its policy of agricultural collectivization.[74] With the possession of land, albeit not ownership, already guaranteed in Article 15 of the 1981 Constitution, a February 1989 constitutional amendment granted limited land ownership, although it did not alter Article 14 which stipulated that all land was state property. Article 15, as amended in early 1989, gave citizens the right to manage and use land as well as the right to bequeath and inherit land granted by the state for the purpose of living on or exploiting it.[75] The new rules, as Viviane Frings noted, accorded Cambodian peasants secure tenure rights:

> Contrary to what was said by most analysts at the time, the constitutional amendment did not provide for a privatisation of land ownership, but rather for some kinds of usufruct rights for the people who cultivate the land, with all the land theoretically remaining the property of the State.
> Nevertheless, what was important was that the peasants were thenceforth given secure tenure rights on the land they cultivated and that land could not be redistributed.[76]

Traveling in Cambodia in mid-1989, journalist H. D. S. Greenway cited anecdotal evidence to exemplify the importance of secure tenure rights to Cambodian peasants.

> François Grunewald, a French agronomist who does a lot of travelling in the Cambodian countryside, told me that for the first time in ten

years peasants are planting sugar-palm trees. Because it takes from ten to twelve years for a sugar palm to mature, Grunewald sees the planting as a sign that the peasants have enough confidence in the government and in their own tenure on the land to plan for the future.[77]

While rice production increased steadily in the second half of the 1980s, the primary aim of the government's land reform program was to increase domestic political support as opposed to boosting agricultural output. Land reform was a significant political gesture in a period of intense peace negotiations with the CGDK resistance groups. The reforms helped rally popular support for the PRK as it prepared to face the challenge of an emboldened resistance following Vietnamese troop withdrawals. Economic liberalization measures also helped compensate for unpopular policies like increased conscription. In reality, the PRK land reforms simply legalized the existing situation since the land in most cases had been distributed several years earlier.[78]

Cambodia in mid-1989 promulgated a liberal, if somewhat deficient, foreign investment code. It also established a national committee to review foreign investment decisions. Early attempts to open the cross-border trade with Thailand were encouraging, if problematical, as they threatened a loss of state control over valuable resources. The rubber sector appeared firmly in state hands; however, the prospects for the timber and precious stones industries were far less certain. Over the next three years, Cambodia received more than 200 project applications from some 100 foreign firms. In addition, the lifting in January 1992 of the U.S. economic embargo later eased the flow of foreign direct investment into the country.[79]

Cambodia in late 1989 launched a program of financial autonomy for state enterprises that envisaged them operating within a system of indicative planning but without state interference. State enterprises over time were expected to become financially self-sufficient and to behave as if they were commercial ventures in a market economy. Unfortunately, meaningful autonomy for state enterprises proved difficult to achieve. Faced with worsening budgetary problems, mounting inflation and elections in 1993, the government delayed addressing the short-term social, financial and political problems entailed in a full transition to financial autonomy. Privatization of state enterprises, in the form of partial sales, divestitures and leases, also commenced in 1989. In Cambodia, privatization was seen as an attractive alternative to the protracted restructuring of state enterprises. As early as mid-1992, almost 40 percent of the state enterprises owned by major national authorities, like the Ministry of Agriculture, had been privatized and others were awaiting official approval.[80]

The economic crisis in Cambodia intensified at the end of the 1980s against a backdrop of Vietnamese troop withdrawals and growing turmoil in the Soviet Union and Eastern Europe. Despite some improvement in overall economic conditions, per capita GDP declined by 50 percent from 1968 to 1988. The fate of Cambodia was intimately tied to that of its principal benefactor, the Socialist Republic of Vietnam. After Vietnamese armed forces withdrew from Cambodia in 1989, the PRK doubled its military expenditure to some 30 percent of the national budget. Due to inflation and jittery confidence, the value of the riel plummeted from 150 to 800 to the dollar. The implosion of the Soviet Bloc threatened the sudden disappearance of a development aid flow estimated at around $100 million annually for most of the 1980s at a time when external assistance remained a crucial component of the Cambodian economy.[81]

The year 1990 marked the end of the First Five-Year Plan. The plan had recognized the role of the emerging private sector in creating employment and goods for domestic consumption and export. Economic activities were progressively liberalized after 1988; however, the positive effects of reform were largely offset by ongoing fighting, international isolation and a reduction in economic assistance from the Soviet Union and its allies. Corruption, smuggling and speculation in goods and property contributed to runaway inflation rates. While the First Five-Year Plan set aggressive agricultural production targets, rice yields in 1990 were among the lowest in the world; and timber production was only a little better than half the plan target. Moreover, timber cutting far outstripped replanting which heralded future environmental problems for Cambodia. Rubber production in 1990 approached plan targets, but a lack of capital, trained manpower and research facilities threatened future production increases. Output in freshwater and maritime fish production also approached 1990 targets; and in this sector, the government was successful in negotiating contracts for the export of seafood. Revenues from state-run enterprises, excise, property and other taxes, had also improved. But foreign investment levels remained low, reflecting the prevailing climate of instability as well as the absence of the rules and regulations necessary to support foreign investments.[82]

## Successful peace talks in Cambodia

The Vietnamese government announced in August 1985 that it would withdraw unilaterally from Cambodia no later than 1990. From 1985 to 1989, a series of peace talks occurred in an effort to resolve the decade-long Cambodian civil war. The Jakarta Informal Meetings (JIM I and JIM II) in July 1988 and February 1989 eventually set the stage for a final settlement. The Jakarta talks provided the four warring Cambodian factions, two interested Indochinese states (Laos, Vietnam), and the six ASEAN member states (Brunei, Indonesia, Malaysia, Philippines, Singapore, Thailand) a benign atmosphere to share ideas and build consensus.[83] Neither JIM I nor JIM II produced a formal agreement; however, a consensus had developed by JIM II on the central issues to be addressed in a final settlement:

> 1) achievement through peaceful measures of an independent, non-aligned, politically and territorially sovereign Cambodia; 2) withdrawal of Vietnamese forces from Cambodia by September 1989 and the cessation of all foreign interference in Cambodian affairs; 3) an internationally supervised ceasefire; 4) the establishment of a quadripartite coalition for the convening of a general election; and 5) an international conference to guarantee the resolutions.[84]

JIM I and JIM II also highlighted a reluctance on the part of the Cambodian factions to preempt the major powers and take independent decisions without their sanction. The parties again came together at the Paris International Conference on Cambodia in July–August 1989 but once more failed to reach an agreement. Where only regional players participated in the two Jakarta Informal Meetings, the First Paris Conference included all major international players, including the five permanent members of the UN Security Council, Australia, Japan, India, Canada and Zimbabwe (in its role as chairman of the Non-aligned Movement). Hanoi had announced in January 1989 that it would withdraw all its troops from Cambodia by September 1989. When it claimed to have met that objective on September 26, Hanoi and Phnom Penh asked for UN verification, but their requests were denied.[85]

Diplomacy in early 1990 flowed down multiple tracks. First, the permanent members of the UN Security Council, having formed in 1985 a body known as the "Perm Five" to pursue a settlement in Afghanistan, placed Cambodia on their agenda in December 1989. A second track involved efforts by the Indonesian government to revive the Jakarta Informal Meetings in a different format to preserve a regional initiative. A third track consisted of informal talks between the four Cambodian factions. In September 1990, the four factions agreed to pursue the "Framework for a Comprehensive Political Settlement of the Cambodian Conflict" which the Perm Five had adopted in August 1990. The proposal called for the election of a bipartite Supreme National Council, composed of six CGDK delegates and six from what was now known as the State of Cambodia, to represent Cambodia at the United Nations and to grant the UN a mandate to administer the country. Representatives on the Supreme National Council later proved unable to agree among themselves; consequently, Cambodia's UN seat remained vacant for an additional year. In the interim, prolonged and difficult negotiations, in which the major powers pressed their Cambodian clients to reach a settlement, finally led to the conclusion of a series of agreements in Paris in October 1991.[86]

In the course of the negotiations, the PRK government headed by Prime Minister Hun Sen sought to replace ideological rigidity with a more pragmatic approach. The People's Republic of Kampuchea was renamed the State of Cambodia in April 1989, abandoning the communist-associated moniker of a "people's republic" with its connotation of one-party rule. In mid-October 1991, just before the Paris agreements, a special congress of the Khmer People's Revolutionary Party transformed itself into the Cambodian People's Party (CPP). Several constitutional amendments were also enacted both to move closer to the policies advocated by Prince Sihanouk and to promote Khmer nationalism. Other constitutional amendments abolished the death penalty and made a first step toward installing a separation of powers. Finally, Buddhism regained its pre-1975 status as the state religion, and many of the restrictions long in place, such as an age limit for ordination, were lifted.[87]

The Paris peace accords, concluded in late October 1991, consisted of four separate but related agreements. The "Final Act of the Paris Conference on Cambodia" referenced the Perm Five "Framework" and outlined the terms of the settlement. The "Agreement on a Comprehensive Political Settlement of the Cambodia Conflict" called for the creation of the United Nations Transitional Authority in Cambodia as an interim force to run key government ministries, verify the disarmament of competing factions, and organize and conduct elections for a constituent assembly. The "Agreement Concerning the Sovereignty, Independence, Territorial Integrity and Inviolability, Neutrality and National Unity of Cambodia" detailed the conditions necessary for Cambodia to achieve the status contained in the agreement's title. Finally, the Paris agreement included a "Declaration on the Rehabilitation and Reconstruction of Cambodia" which called for coordinated international assistance for Cambodia's economic reconstruction.[88]

Donor nations meeting in Tokyo in June 1992 pledged $880 million toward the rehabilitation of Cambodia. Japan led with a target contribution of $150–$200 million. The conference also agreed to form an International Committee for the Reconstruction of Cambodia (ICORC) to provide assistance in planning and managing reconstruction programs. Intended from the outset to become operational only after the new Cambodian government was formed, the first ICORC meeting did not take place until September 1993.[89]

## From UNTAC to royal government

By early 1993, the forces of the United Nations Transitional Authority in Cambodia (UNTAC), in accordance with the terms of the 1991 peace accords, were in place and operating throughout the country. UNTAC forces achieved notable success in several areas of their multifaceted mandate, in particular the resettlement of refugees and the organization of nationwide elections. They were less successful in maintaining a cease-fire and demobilizing and disarming competing military forces, primarily because the Khmer Rouge refused to cooperate. They also experienced problems in containing violence and promoting human rights. The run-up to the election witnessed considerable ethnic tension and attacks against Vietnamese living in Cambodia as well as threats to UNTAC personnel.[90]

Even though electoral preparations took place in an atmosphere of threat and intimidation, the actual conduct of elections was a huge success, surprisingly free of violence. An estimated 46 percent of registered voters cast ballots on the first day with voters flocking to polling stations long before they opened, despite driving monsoon rains. Over the planned six-day polling period (23–28 May 1993), more than 89 percent of registered voters, an estimated 97 percent of Cambodians eligible to vote, cast a ballot. When the results were announced, the National United Front for an Independent, Neutral, Peaceful and Cooperative Cambodia (FUNCIN-PEC) had obtained 45.47 percent and 58 of 120 Constituent Assembly seats, the Cambodian People's Party (CPP) 38.23 percent and 51 seats, the Buddhist Liberal Democratic Party (BLDP) 3.81 percent and 10 seats and the small Moulinaka Party 1.37 percent and one seat. The remaining 16 political parties garnered only a handful of votes and no Assembly seats. Exactly what most Cambodians voted for remains a subject of debate. However, William Shawcross probably best captured the prevailing atmosphere at the time. "Over most of the country, people had voted for peace, for reconciliation, for Sihanouk, and, perhaps above all, for change. It was a lot to hope for."[91]

FUNCINPEC emerged from the elections as the largest and most successful political party but one short of a majority in the Constituent Assembly. CPP came second but retained the largest armed force and the most effective administrative structures in Cambodia. With neither party in a position to command the two-thirds majority necessary to secure passage of a new constitution, cooperation between FUNCINPEC and CPP was essential. Following a period of difficult negotiations, the two parties in late June 1993 reached agreement on a power-sharing arrangement in which CPP and FUNCINPEC joined to form the Provisional National Government of Cambodia (PNGC). Creation of the PNGC helped stabilize the immediate post-election period and led to the adoption by the Constituent Assembly in September 1993 of a new constitution, restoring the monarchy with Prince Sihanouk as King. The constitution transformed the Constituent Assembly into the National Assembly and cleared the way for the formation of a new Royal Government of Cambodia (RGC), inaugurated on 29 October 1993.[92]

The new government faced a multitude of pressing problems. A familiar pattern of violence continued to plague the country. Corruption was omnipresent with illicit revenue extraction common at all levels of society. Millions of landmines covered large areas of the countryside. The government struggled to maintain cohesion within its own ranks even as it faced the threat of a weakened but intact Khmer Rouge organization. King

Sihanouk's state of health remained uncertain, often forcing him to be abroad for medical treatment. Economically, Cambodia faced widespread poverty, resource and capital shortages, environmental degradation and economic management shortages. Dependent on external assistance for reconstruction and rehabilitation, only some $10 million or a little more than one percent of the $880 million in financial aid pledged at the 1992 Tokyo Conference had been distributed by January 1993.[93]

When the U.S. government in July 1993 ended its prolonged opposition to loans to Vietnam from international lending institutions, it cleared the way, as noted earlier, for the implementation of a French proposal to refinance Vietnam's $140 million IMF debt. France and Japan subsequently cleared Vietnam's arrears, together with Cambodian arrears of $51 million, at the September 1993 IMF/World Bank meeting. In the Cambodian case, the full amount was raised through cash grants from donor countries with Japan paying more than half the total. The world financial community responded enthusiastically to developments in Cambodia; and at a second ICORC meeting in Tokyo in March 1994, Cambodia received emergency aid pledges totaling $773 million, a figure inflated by the repledging of funds previously committed but not disbursed. Representatives from the 30 nations and 12 multinational bodies attending the second ICORC meeting lauded Cambodia for its progress in curbing inflation, boosting tax revenues and stabilizing the currency.[94]

The conclusion of the UNTAC mandate, followed by the creation of the Royal Government of Cambodia, provided fresh challenges and new opportunities for Cambodian diplomacy. Having regained its status as a full member of the international community, Cambodia immediately pursued contacts with a wide range of states, inside and outside Asia, often with the objective of maximizing foreign assistance. China affirmed its support for the process of reconciliation and moved to improve its relations with the RGC. Cambodian contacts with the ASEAN states also expanded as did its involvement in a variety of regional and international organizations. While it had few problems with neighboring Laos, relations with Thailand and Vietnam were more problematic. Relations with Vietnam were clouded by the volatile issue of ethnic Vietnamese living in Cambodia together with outstanding border questions. The legacy of long years of conflict, and Thai support for Cambodian resistance forces, troubled relations with Bangkok.[95]

## Concluding observations

The theme of a conference held at the Australian National University in 1992 was "the law in Vietnam," but the title of the proceedings, drawn from one of the contributions, became *Vietnam and the Rule of Law*. As David Koh pointed out in an extensive review of the book, this subtle change from the title of the conference to the title of the proceedings masked a fundamental difference in power, scope and emphasis.[96] Any legislative body can enact laws; however, the simple existence of a law does not guarantee adherence. This is particularly true in countries like Cambodia, Laos and Vietnam which have no real tradition of central authority, separation of powers or rule of law. When the ruling powers in these states refer to state rule by law, they generally mean scrutinizing laws, edicts and decrees, codifying them and passing the results through the national assembly. This process incorporates the Confucian principle that the good of society outweighs the individual good. The Confucian system granted a benign ruler final powers of arbitration, but the reality of the situation was more accurately reflected in the Vietnamese adage, "the emperor's writ stops at the bamboo hedge of the Vietnamese village."

In contrast, the concept of rule of law involves not only the passage of law but also enforcement and compliance. It necessitates a clear separation of power between the executive, legislative and judicial branches, together with a consistent body of law and transparent rules and regulations. This separation proved impossible to achieve in the communist-controlled states of Indochina because it was the Party, not the legislature, that made the law; and the Party was above the law. Consequently, the governments of Cambodia, Laos and Vietnam, in the two decades after 1975, faced tremendous obstacles in affecting the rule of law because its implementation involved a basic contradiction between respect for authority and tradition and the legal framework thought by many economists and other scholars to be necessary for a successful market economy.

Responding to serious economic problems, Cambodia, Laos and Vietnam implemented significant reform measures in the second half of the 1980s. Vietnam led the way with Cambodia and Laos, in the early days, often aping the general Vietnamese approach, if not specific measures. Individual approaches to the collectivization of agriculture highlighted the different conditions existing in each state as well as the different paths to agricultural reform pursued. As the years passed, each country increasingly followed its own path to modernization. This was a natural and expected result as the economic problems faced by the three were often very different, necessitating independent solutions.

The end of the Cambodian conflict, as ratified in the 1991 Paris agreements, marked the end of the final phase of the decolonization of Indochina, a process initiated at the end of World War II. The Communist Party of Vietnam in 1945 challenged the resumption of French colonial rule, and the ensuing struggle transformed the entire subregion into a battleground of the Cold War. As the struggle progressed, the Vietnamese leadership viewed Indochina as a single theater which demanded Vietnamese hegemony in the interest of national security. China disliked this strategic perspective but accepted it as long as it viewed the United States as a serious threat.

As the strategic environment changed with the increased threat of the

Soviet Union and a rapprochement with the United States, Chinese opposition to Vietnamese hegemony hardened, leading to a direct military confrontation over Cambodia. This conflict began with the Vietnamese invasion of Cambodia in 1978 and lasted for more than a decade. Throughout this period, the Lao PDR maintained its special relationship with Vietnam, in part by preference and in part in recognition of the practical limits imposed by its dependent affiliation. The competing factions in Cambodia naturally had their own agendas, but all of them were also clients of foreign powers. In the early 1990s, geopolitical shifts divorced Cambodia from the global picture; and the subsequent Sino-Vietnamese rapprochement reduced its regional importance. Collectively, these political developments both set the stage for Cambodia, Laos and Vietnam to act independently of each other in the ensuing decade and enhanced their ability to participate in nascent regional organizations.

# 5    End of the beginning

I think we will have to accelerate our development. Slow development means hunger, don't you think? But at the same time I want to see efficiency and stability. If reform is too fast we will make mistakes. If you run too fast and there is something in the road you may fall down.

> General Secretary Do Muoi, Vietnamese Communist Party, June 1996

It is noteworthy that the imperialists have concentrated on carrying out a strategy of effecting change through peaceful means with the hope of doing away with our party's leadership and moving our country into their orbit. They carry out sabotage and subversive schemes through armed activities while creating problems regarding the implementation of the democratic and multiparty system as well as human rights in our country.

> LPRP Politburo Resolution, October 1992

Le Cambodge s'aide lui-même (Cambodia will help itself).

> Royal Government of Cambodia, 1993

In the final decade of the twentieth century, socioeconomic and political reform in Cambodia, Laos and Vietnam continued to move in divergent directions. On the one hand, reform policy in all three countries contained the core ingredients found in most states in transition. Competing, often conflicting, forces for continuity and change also challenged all three states, albeit in separate ways. On the other hand, the Asian financial crisis in 1997–8 impacted each country differently, highlighting the structural diversity of their respective economies. Finally, the inability of riparian states to reach consensus on the use of the Mekong suggested practical limits to regionalism.

## Vietnam rejoins the world economy

The Vietnamese government achieved notable results in the decade following the introduction of the package of economic reforms known collectively as *doi moi*. The performance of the economy was especially impressive given the collapse of Soviet aid and the loss of Comecon trading partners. As the reform process increased in scope and intensity, Hanoi emphasized external aid and foreign investment but postponed difficult institutional changes, like the privatization of state firms. In addition, it often timed and sequenced economic reforms to fulfill political objectives related to the maintenance of the Party's monopoly of power. Hanoi enjoyed considerable initial success in the execution of economic reforms, but there was growing doubt as to the viability of the current model for the next stage of economic and political reform.

The November 1992 decision of the Japanese government to resume broad economic ties, including the offer of a major loan package, heightened prospects for accelerated change. Unlike the United States, Japan did not break diplomatic relations with Hanoi in the postwar period; but in 1979, after the Vietnamese invasion of Cambodia, it did halt virtually all economic assistance to Hanoi. Japan's decision to resume economic ties increased the pressure on Washington to sanction multilateral economic assistance and to lift the trade embargo on Vietnam.[1]

The Clinton administration responded in mid-1993, ending its opposition to loans to Vietnam from international lending agencies. Further progress toward a normalization of bilateral relations was thwarted by U.S. insistence on first resolving so-called "discrepancy cases," instances where Americans listed as MIAs were known to be alive when they entered Vietnamese captivity. The next major step in U.S.-Vietnamese relations, lifting the trade embargo, occurred in February 1994. The White House delayed taking the final step, normalization of diplomatic relations, fearing the domestic political costs. The end to the U.S. trade embargo was welcomed in Hanoi; however, it also put new pressure on the Vietnamese economy, challenging reforms in place or coming into place.[2]

Vietnamese success in dealing with the new economic climate was due in large part to lessons learned over the last two decades. Real GDP growth in Vietnam in 1991–5 averaged over 8 percent annually compared to an average rate of some 5 percent in the previous five-year period. Flushed with success and full of optimism, the Communist Party, at its Eighth Party Congress in 1996, set an aggressive GDP growth target of 9–10 percent compounded annually over the next five years.[3] In marked contrast to other transitional economies, Vietnam also succeeded in bringing inflation under control. The annual rate of inflation, which approached 700 percent in 1986, decelerated to 17 percent in 1995 with the International Monetary Fund reporting a rate of only 3.2 percent for 1997, the lowest rate since the initiation of economic reforms.[4]

At the outset, economic recovery in Vietnam stemmed from a strong performance in the agricultural sector; however, industrial output, following a period of difficult adjustment, also strengthened, especially petroleum and light manufacturing.[5] The Vietnamese economy thus emerged from its transition period without pervasive subsidies or controls on prices and output but with a reasonably balanced fiscal situation and moderate inflation. For the most part, the economy's response to government structural and stabilization measures was impressive.[6]

At the same time, a variety of concerns highlighted the need for ongoing economic reform. With external debt growing at an alarming rate, the government clearly needed to introduce a system to manage foreign borrowings if it was to avoid the debt problems faced by other transitional economies. In turn, distorted investment incentives underlay widening trade and current account balances that were simply not sustainable. The General Statistical Office put the 1996 trade deficit at $4.15 billion, an increase of 70 percent over the previous year. The trade deficit dropped to $2.35 billion in 1997, but it still remained around 17 percent of GDP. Over the same period, the volume of rice exports increased 20 percent; but the export value of rice actually dropped. Moreover, Vietnam faced tough choices if it hoped to strike an effective balance between economic growth and macroeconomic stability. Without more effective stabilization policies, financial reform could not be successful and might even aggravate macroeconomic imbalances.[7]

## New Vietnamese leadership policies

Politics in 1995 were dominated by the approach of the Eighth Party Congress, scheduled for the summer of 1996, and the Tenth National Assembly, scheduled for 1997. Officially billed as a turning point in Vietnam's shift to heightened industrialization and modernization, the low-key preparations for the Eighth Congress did not presage major changes. Political scientist Brantly Womack accurately termed the period before the congress as "the calm before the quiet" although he recognized that simmering political issues could erupt at any moment.[8]

While some observers predicted a delay, the Eighth Party Congress met on schedule in June 1996. The social composition of both delegates to the Congress and its new Central Committee exemplified new trends in party building. First, the importance of Party cadre from Party organizations, the state sector and the Army increased. Second, there was a renewed emphasis on the centralization of power. Finally, younger delegates and Central Committee members signaled a desire to rejuvenate the Party.[9] Of the three trends, it was the renewed emphasis on control – control of the Party, control of the state apparatus and control over society – at the expense of continued economic reform that was most evident.[10]

The results of the Tenth National Assembly elections, held in mid-1997, did not challenge the go-slow approach of the Party. Of 450 elected candidates, 27 percent were incumbents and only 15 percent were non-Party candidates. Of 11 independent candidates, only three were elected. Tran Duc Luong, a little-known technocrat, was elected President, replacing General Le Duc Anh. Nguyen Thi Binh continued as Vice President and Nong Duc Manh remained Chairman of the Standing Committee of the National Assembly.[11]

At the end of 1997, the Party faced an important policy crossroads when it was forced once again to choose between a fast and a slow track to reform. In selecting a new Communist Party General Secretary to replace the aging Do Muoi, the Party elected Le Kha Phieu, an obscure but hard-line ideologue who had served as the army's political commissar. A representative of the traditional wing of the Party, Phieu was quoted in early 1996 as saying that capitalism would definitely be replaced as it was backward in satisfying the needs of the people. In selecting Phieu, the Party resolved a protracted leadership crisis; but it also dashed hopes for decisive steps to stall economic decline. At the time, little was known of Phieu outside Party circles, but his rise to prominence marked a victory for Party stalwarts eager to cement closer ties between the Party and the People's Army as a means to ensure the Party's survival. Following the election of Phieu, Hanoi reshuffled the top tier of the ruling Politburo, finalizing the new leadership.[12]

At the time, Party regulars were unnerved by peasant revolts in Thai Binh province, sparked by declining rice prices, mounting corruption and the widening gap between urban rich and rural poor. Consequently, they opted for increased control instead of the accelerated economic reforms necessary to promote continued growth and long-term legitimacy. Para-doxically, the unrest in Thai Binh and elsewhere, intended to provoke change, instead revived the political fortunes of the military which capital-ized on the perceived threat to internal stability. In a show of firmness, the government in early January 1998 executed two local businessmen and a government official convicted in the largest corporate corruption scandal in Vietnamese history.[13]

## Crunch time in Vietnam

The election of Le Kha Phieu came at a time when Hanoi faced its most serious economic downturn since it first embraced tentative economic reforms in 1979. The Sixth Five-Year Plan (1996–2000) called for $13 billion in foreign investment, $14 billion from local sources and $7.5 billion from overseas aid. However, Hanoi was far from meeting any of these targets, and the situation appeared unlikely to improve until substantial new economic reforms were announced. Foreign investment pledges in 1997 were down 50 percent from the previous year, the first such decline since the launch of *doi moi*. At the same time, exports were poised to take a battering due to regional currency devaluations; and the banking sector remained in tatters.[14]

In a show of bravado, the Vietnamese government, at the outset of 1998, reaffirmed an estimated annual growth rate of 9 percent. Challeng-ing Hanoi's forecast, informed observers cited the slowdown in GDP expansion over the previous three years and the competitive regional climate for scarce offshore investment following the economic meltdown in Asia.[15] Even as it defended its ambitious target, the Party admitted a rift over the direction of reform, a rare confession casting further doubt on Hanoi's ability to weather the crisis. The official *Vietnam News*, quoting Prime Minister Phan Van Khai, acknowledged people were divided into two camps with some calling for increased reforms and others arguing a domestic slowdown was healthy after years of rapid growth. In a country where any public sign of disagreement within the Party was extremely rare, the Asian financial crisis appeared to widen fissures that had long existed in private, exposing weakness in the communist model.[16]

The limited recognition in official circles of the need for continuing economic reform was evident in policy statements. Prime Minister Khai was quoted in March 1998 as saying capitalism was not an option for Vietnam and additional economic reforms would be implemented at a gradual pace.[17] His comments were taken as an official response to repeated calls by the World Bank and others for lower trade barriers, finance sector reform, currency devaluation and state enterprise privatization. At the same time, the limited impact of current economic policies on principal economic targets, including high growth, low inflation, low unemployment and a positive balance of payments, aptly demonstrated the need to accelerate reforms.[18]

Over the previous three years, GDP expansion in Vietnam had slowed from 9.5 percent in 1995 to 9.3 percent in 1996 to 8.2 percent in 1997. A rapid growth in consumption, together with contracting accumulation and savings rates, combined to stunt the overall growth rate. Revenue collection also fell short of budget targets, and the absence of effective policies to encourage investment choked capital mobilization. In addition, Vietnam continued to face a highly competitive regional climate for limited investment funds. Nevertheless, Hanoi clung doggedly to its 9 percent target throughout the spring of 1998. It was only in July, after the IMF slashed its forecast to 5 percent, that Vietnam reduced the official growth target to 6–7 percent. By that time, many observers felt that even a 5 percent target might be unachievable. Vietnam ended the year at 3.5 percent.[19]

In the area of agricultural reform, the 1993 land law represented a compromise. It recognized partial land ownership in the form of legal rights to use or usufruct land as well as to transfer, lease and inherit such rights. However, the government retained much of the socialist regime of real property rights, in particular the indivisibility of state ownership. A veteran Vietnam observer, Douglas Pike, termed the law "politically correct socialism in title, but market economy in use." To sanction the beginnings of a land market, the 1993 land law circumvented legal and ideological constraints to allow land use rights for extended periods of time. It also diminished the authority of the commune and cooperative

due to their poor performance as administrative units. Additional regulations issued in early 1995 later called into question the powers granted to
property users through land use permits, including the right of transfer.[20]

Outdated, inefficient and uncompetitive state enterprises remained a
core problem in Vietnam.[21] Earlier reforms to the public sector were positive, but additional reforms at a faster pace were required. In 1992–8 only
21 companies, capitalized at less than $20 million, were equitized as the
privatization process was termed in Vietnam. Yet, according to the
Finance Ministry, more than half the country's state-owned firms were
unprofitable. In a study of state enterprise reform, Phan Van Tiem and
Nguyen Van Thanh highlighted the major problems Vietnam faced in the
second half of the decade.

> The legal framework governing the direction of SOE [state-owned
> enterprise] restructuring, issues of state ownership and transferring
> ownership of SOEs, and turning SOEs into joint-stock companies or
> other forms of mixed ownership, is not adequate at present, and stems
> only from the pilot equitizations attempted to date. Also, Vietnam's
> capital market remains underdeveloped, and there has been no active
> preparation for the experimental operation of a stock exchange.
>
> In addition, a master plan for the development of the state sector in
> the coming five, ten, and fifteen years – spanning all branches and
> sectors of the economy and all locations – has not been promulgated.
> Also, the limited ability to mobilize financial resources for the national
> budget means that it is currently difficult to meet the demand for
> expenditure.... Finally, the psychology and training of both managers
> and employees in the state sector are not conducive to their voluntary
> participation in the restructuring of SOEs, and so they do not always
> respond positively to the measures implemented under SOE reform.[22]

Under increasing pressure from international financial bodies, Hanoi
announced in early 1998 plans to speed its privatization program. With up
to half the country's 6,000 state industries as potential candidates, Vietnam
soon fell behind its revised objectives with shares in only 11 state-run firms
offered in the first half of the year. This dismal performance contrasted
with plans announced at the end of 1997 to privatize 150 public enterprises
in 1998 alone.[23]

The rate of inflation also remained a major concern with inflation
targets put to a severe test in 1998. After falling to 3.2 percent in 1997, the
lowest level since the outset of *doi moi*, inflation increased every month in
the following year. Analysts warned the consumer price index, the primary
inflation meter, could jump to double figures unless stringent measures
were implemented to curb price increases. Economists argued that stabilizing the price of rice was one of the most effective ways to control the
consumer price index. Unfortunately, record rice exports in the first half of

1998, coupled with a failure to read global markets accurately, spotlighted inefficiencies in the state-run rice export system. The breakdown in the system raised doubts as to the government's ability to manage the delicate balance between increased rice exports, benefiting farmers and the balance of trade, and the lower rice prices needed to meet inflation goals and avoid social unrest.[24]

The related challenges of job creation and retraining continued to be major obstacles to the speedy reform of the public sector. Unemployment in Hanoi alone was estimated in mid-1998 to be almost 9 percent. And this figure did not include the underemployed or the thousands of rural villagers drifting into the city in search of work. According to official reports, the rate of unemployment in state enterprises approached 10 percent while an estimated 8 percent of the labor force employed in the private sector had experienced redundancies.[25]

## Trade and investment in Vietnam

Prospects for trade diversification improved in 1995 when Vietnam joined ASEAN. Vietnam's accession to full-member status, together with the establishment of diplomatic relations with the United States, were significant moves in the direction of economic and political integration. That said, its entry into ASEAN was not smooth as Vietnam was at a different stage of development compared to older members.

> Whilst gaining full membership of ASEAN is deemed by most to be a positive step for Vietnam, with the prospect of greater trade flows and foreign capital inflows from the region arising from this development, the fruits of acceptance are likely to be evident only in the long term. . . . Prior to that, however, lie a series of challenges that Vietnam must surmount if it is to realize and harness its new-found status in ASEAN. . . .[26]

In the second half of the decade, the level of foreign exchange reserves dropped to worrying levels. Compounding the problem, international donors, to encourage economic reform, began in November 1997 withholding over $500 million in balance of payments support. With a variety of factors impacting negatively on balance of payments in general and exports in particular, the situation was exacerbated by what could best be termed "export gridlock." At a time when its trade patterns had shifted to Asia, neighboring countries were attempting to export their way to growth and recovery and thus had little interest in importing more Vietnamese goods. Vietnam's exports increased in 1998 but no where near the annual average of 27.5 percent in 1992–7. Textile and garment exports to the European Union were a bright spot as they increased rapidly, a trend expected to continue under a three-year agreement, running until 2001.[27]

Hanoi in mid-February 1998 devalued the dong by a little over 5 percent after bankers had complained for months that it was overvalued by as much as 40 percent. In so doing, Vietnam embarked on what its political leadership perceived to be a precarious balancing act between easing market pressure on the overvalued dong and maintaining social stability. With the government reluctant to weaken the currency further due to fears it would lead to rising inflation and difficulties in repaying dollar loans, outside experts soon considered the dong again overvalued. Vietnam later devalued the dong by an additional 7 percent in August 1998 for a combined total devaluation of 16.2 percent between October 1997 and August 1998. In a related event, Decree 63/ND-CP in September 1998 established the dong as the sole legal tender in Vietnam, reducing the country's dependence on the U.S. dollar.[28]

Foreign investment declined in 1997 for the first time in a decade, reflecting the slump in East Asian economies, sluggish domestic demand and inadequate reforms which hampered investment disbursements. And the mid-term outlook was even worse. Hanoi later revised its investment regulations in an effort to address long-term complaints of foreign investors in areas like bureaucracy and corruption. But it was a case of too little, too late. Domestic and regional markets proved smaller than expected while many investors remained skeptical about Hanoi's ability to implement new investment policies.[29]

While the Asian financial crisis impacted negatively on investment, the downward trend actually preceded regional turmoil by several months. Internal reforms had not kept pace with the initial phase of foreign investment; therefore, projects licensed years earlier were still fighting tough trade barriers, an opaque bureaucracy and ever-shifting tax and foreign exchange regulations. Faced with a grim business climate, a growing number of investors pulled out of Vietnam. Foreign representative office openings in Ho Chi Minh City in the first half of 1998, for example, were roughly half the figures for 1995–6 and down 20 percent from the previous year.[30]

In early February 1998, news emerged that three respected Communist Party members had recently warned the Party that it must adopt radical political reforms or face collapse. In a 13-page letter to Party leaders, Tran Do, a former army general and ideology chief, made a sweeping appeal for press freedom, freer elections and reduced Party influence over Vietnamese society. He warned that economic reforms, if not accompanied by vigorous political reforms, would soon reach a dead end. General Do followed his December 1997 letter with a second letter in April 1998 in which he complained of a concerted press campaign attacking his ideas as well as surveillance and intimidation of family members. After Do wrote two more letters calling for greater democracy in Vietnam, the Central Committee of the Communist Party in July 1998 voted to condemn him for writing letters calling on the Party to loosen its grip on power.[31]

Sentiments similar to those expressed by General Do were contained in letters published separately by mathematician Phan Dinh Dieu and former Party Central Committee member Hoang Huu Nhan. In a more dramatic move, Nguyen Van Kinh in mid-April 1998 set himself on fire in broad daylight in Ba Dinh Square, the heart of the Vietnamese state. The incident was reminiscent of the 1960s when Buddhist monks sacrificed themselves to protest the Diem regime in South Vietnam. Kinh's motives were unclear, but the method and site of his self-immolation suggested it was politically motivated. Even if it was not, many in Vietnam viewed the event as a metaphor for political and social decay.[32]

## External relations

In May 1996, President Clinton named Peter Peterson, a former Congressman and ex-POW, as the U.S. ambassador to Vietnam; however, the U.S. Senate did not approve the nomination until the following year. Vietnam remained a relatively unimportant trading partner with the United States. And U.S. investment in Vietnam lagged in 1997–8, due to the absence of clear, enforceable legal standards for commercial transactions as well as the Asian financial crisis. In the summer of 1998, Congress waived the Jackson-Vanik amendment. This meant the Overseas Private Investment Corporation (OPIC) and the U.S. Export-Import Bank could finally provide financial and insurance services to U.S. companies operating in Vietnam.[33]

Congressional discussion of trade issues provided an opportunity for concerned U.S. constituencies to focus debate on other questions, like human rights, religious freedom and labor rights. In turn, Vietnamese officials continued to raise two sensitive questions, Vietnam's own wartime missing and postwar health problems related to the wartime use of defoliants like Agent Orange. An intense, internal policy debate also continued in Vietnam as to U.S. interests in Vietnam and the most appropriate policy for the United States.[34]

Following the collapse of communism in the Soviet Union and Beijing's decision to drop support for the Khmer Rouge, ties between Vietnam and China quickly expanded.

> The similar situations confronting China and Vietnam [after 1990] and their common interests have brought several outcomes for Sino-Vietnamese relations. First, they have enforced contacts between the two countries.... These regular contacts resulted in several joint communiqués, which repeated the will of the two countries to pursue economic cooperation, and not to use force to settle border problems.[35]

China remained the key actor in Vietnamese foreign policy with the most persistent issues being a trio of territorial disputes: the land border in northern Vietnam, territorial waters in the Gulf of Tonkin and ownership of the Paracel and Spratly archipelagos in the East Sea. China began minesweeping operations on the Sino-Vietnamese border in 1993 even as a joint working group struggled to resolve outstanding land boundary questions. In July 1997, the two parties agreed on the year 2000 as the official target for a comprehensive settlement of all open issues related to their disputed land boundary. China and Vietnam also worked to increase cross-border trade which flourished in the second half of the decade. Prime Minister Khai visited Beijing in October 1998. The visit resulted in progress on border dispute questions as well as bilateral trade and investment issues. Sensitive to China's regional interests, Hanoi was careful to keep Beijing well informed throughout the decade as to Hanoi's security discussions with Washington.[36]

A most welcome regional development was the progressive improvement in Vietnamese relations with Thailand. The Thai defense minister visited Vietnam in January 1996, followed three months later by the Thai foreign minister. Vietnam opened a consulate general in Khon Kaen province the same month. Over the next two years, visitations and consultations increased in frequency and broadened in scope. Tran Duc Luong's visit to Thailand in October 1998, the first visit by a Vietnamese head of state, marked an important benchmark. Vietnam and Thailand also concluded the second phase of a program for development cooperation in which Thailand agreed to provide technical support to Vietnam in 1998–2000. And Thailand agreed to send anti-narcotics experts to Vietnam in a joint effort to combat the narcotics trade, one of Vietnam's most serious social problems. Finally, a Thai–Vietnamese memorandum of understanding led to joint naval patrols in overlapping maritime areas.[37]

Border questions and the future of ethnic Vietnamese in Cambodia remained sources of friction between Hanoi and Phnom Penh. Cambodia charged in January 1996 that Vietnamese farmers, supported by Vietnamese army units, had encroached on Cambodian territory in the border provinces of Kompong Cham, Prey Veng and Svay Rieng. In response, Vietnam agreed to convene a border expert working group to determine the January 1995 status quo and to return the boundary to its original position. Violence against ethnic Vietnamese living in Cambodia again occurred during the July 1998 Cambodian elections, and the Vietnamese friendship monument in Phnom Penh was vandalized during a political demonstration. In both instances, Hanoi demonstrated restraint, limiting its reaction to formal protests. Smuggling and border crimes were additional concerns, coloring an already troubled relationship. Political stability in Cambodia remained a policy priority for Vietnam, but Hanoi wisely eschewed unilateral initiatives. Instead, it steered a multilateral course, lobbying on Cambodia's behalf for early ASEAN admission. Hanoi believed regional membership would temper Cambodian foreign policy as well as Chinese influence in Cambodia.[38]

Vietnam continued to pursue its "special relationship" with Laos both on Party and state levels. At the Party level, regular exchanges focused on ideological and cultural issues. At the state level, the two neighbors concluded or expanded a number of cooperation agreements. For example, they signed an agreement on cross-border goods transport in February 1996 and a plan for cooperation in the areas of culture and information later in the year. They also held joint talks on the construction of a port in central Vietnam, important for landlocked Laos, as well as cooperation in improving road links between themselves and other states in the region. Border negotiations also continued although their intensity remained notably lower than Vietnam's corresponding talks with Cambodia and China.[39]

In conjunction with its ASEAN membership, Vietnam established an ASEAN Department in the Ministry of Foreign Affairs together with a National Committee for the Coordination of ASEAN affairs. It also initiated an import tax reduction program as part of its responsibilities as an ASEAN Free Trade Area (AFTA) member and concluded a protocol for dispute settlement in economic relations. In late December 1998, Hanoi hosted the Sixth ASEAN Summit, the first time a meeting of ASEAN leaders had been held in Vietnam.[40]

## Lao economic policy and planning

In March 1991, the Fifth Congress of the Lao People's Revolutionary Party approved a medium-term economic strategy for the period 1991–5. In contrast to the Fourth Party Congress, which endorsed the New Economic Mechanism, the Fifth Congress did not initiate radical changes in economic policy. Instead, it reinforced the direction of reforms in progress. The medium-term economic strategy included familiar goals like self-sufficiency, infrastructure development, sustainable forestry, development of small and medium industry, increased production of consumer goods and basic commodities, and improved education and health.[41]

At the same time, Laos completed a working draft of a Third Five-Year Plan (1991–5). Unlike earlier years, the government later elected not to publish a formal five-year plan, relying instead on an annual planning exercise tied to a rolling five-year public investment program. The continuing uncertainty associated with economic reforms and the poor performance of earlier five-year plans, prompted the Lao PDR to adopt this more flexible approach to planning. The rolling five-year plan, incorporated within the policy framework of the indicative Third Five-Year Plan, was approved in November 1991.[42]

A longer term Socioeconomic Plan (1993–2000), approved by the Sixth Plenum of the Fifth LPRP Central Committee in February 1993, was consistent with both the indicative Third Five-Year Plan and the rolling five-year public investment program. Providing government budget figures for the first time, the long-term plan exemplified Lao PDR efforts to increase transparency and provide greater access to public information. In terms of total state investment, the Socioeconomic Plan (1993–2000) gave priority to communications, transportation, postal services and construction (47 percent); industry and handicrafts (19 percent); agriculture and forestry (15 percent); rural development (9 percent); education (7 percent); public health (2 percent); and information and culture (1 percent). Long-term priorities were later set out in two documents, *Outline Public Investment Program, 1994–2000* and *Socio-Economic Development Strategies*, presented in June 1994 to a round table meeting of aid donors in Geneva.[43]

In support of these policies, the Lao PDR introduced a new land tax in March 1993, replacing an agricultural tax which had proved a serious disincentive to production. A registration tax on housing and property was also introduced.[44] In May 1994, the government repealed the 1988 foreign investment law, replacing it with a new code. Promulgated one month after the official opening of the new Mitaphap (Friendship) Bridge across the Mekong River, the 1994 foreign investment law joined the new bridge in symbolizing the economic opening of landlocked Laos. The law removed key restrictions on joint ventures, reduced corporate tax rates, opened new areas to foreign investment and offered a one-stop service through the Foreign Investment Management Committee. The new regulations also provided for a two-track licensing procedure in which investments below a certain threshold enjoyed a "fast track" approval process.[45]

In conjunction with the new investment regulations, the Lao PDR continued efforts to privatize state enterprises. To accelerate this process, it turned to a decentralized approach in which the central government focused on the privatization of larger enterprises while provincial and municipal authorities took responsibility for the divestiture of medium to smaller ones. The program gained momentum, after limited progress in the early years; and by mid-1995, most medium to small-sized firms, together with a large percentage of larger ones, had been privatized. With some 65 state enterprises remaining in the central government portfolio and approximately 40 remaining at or below the provincial level, the government indicated in 1995 its intention to retain 32 companies in the public sector with the remainder targeted for privatization by 1997.[46]

## New Economic Mechanism, ten years on

In the decade after implementation of the New Economic Mechanism, the Lao PDR made remarkable progress in moving from a centrally planned to a market-oriented economy, especially when compared to other reforming socialist economies. A number of factors contributed to its success, including an agricultural sector that was never more than superficially socialized, a very short period of central planning, and the proximity of

Laos to Thailand which ensured a degree of openness to market influences, regardless of official policy.[47]

Despite large differences between economic sectors, annual GDP growth rates in 1990–6 averaged better than 6 percent, an impressive performance, albeit lower than fast-growing neighbors like Thailand and Vietnam. The industrial sector experienced the most rapid growth followed by services and agriculture. Within industry, manufacturing and construction achieved the best results. The performance of the service sector was mixed with growth varying between the various subsectors.[48]

A subject of concern for some time, agriculture exhibited a highly volatile, relatively weak performance. Several factors combined to explain the poor results obtained, beginning with deteriorating terms of trade for agricultural products after 1990. Another was the subsistence nature of agriculture which was generally isolated from the rest of the economy and characterized by stagnant productivity. High transaction costs, a lack of modern inputs, poor rural infrastructure and weak support services also contributed.[49]

The weak performance of agriculture reinforced the dual nature of the Lao economy and society. Income and wealth distributions became increasingly uneven with standards of living improving in urban regions but stagnating in rural areas. High rates of population growth combined with low rates of agricultural growth to result in a decline in per capita income in some rural provinces.[50]

A strict, non-accommodating monetary policy was a central component of the macroeconomic reforms incorporated in the New Economic Mechanism. As public expenditure declined due to a reduction in the number of civil servants, the Lao PDR tightened fiscal and monetary policy to consolidate reforms. Tax reforms were implemented to increase revenues, and institutional reforms were introduced to improve public finance management and to provide the tools necessary for macroeconomic stabilization. In response, the budgetary situation improved steadily in the early 1990s after which public revenues leveled off and expenditures began to increase. By 1995, multinational bodies, especially the IMF, were pressuring the Lao PDR to revise its five-year public investment program to make it more compatible with anticipated revenues and foreign assistance.[51]

The stabilization policy pursued by the Lao PDR in the early 1990s helped reduce the rate of inflation. But the government later relaxed monetary discipline, resulting in an upsurge in inflation in 1995 which reached double-digit rates for the first time since 1992. At the same time, the exchange rate jumped from around 700 kip to almost 1,000 kip to the U.S. dollar. Monetary policy was tightened in 1995–6, stabilizing the rate of exchange and bringing inflation under control. Integration of the Lao economy into the regional economy also proceeded. Imports plus exports increased from 34 percent of GDP in 1990 to 62 percent in 1995 with the ratio of exports to imports improving from 40 percent to 60 percent.[52]

The Lao PDR's long-anticipated membership in ASEAN was expected to have a positive, if unclear, impact on its economic development. Under the terms of entry, it had until 2008 to meet AFTA requirements to reduce tariffs on most goods to below 5 percent. To meet this goal, Laos would have to encourage trade and investment and introduce fiscal reforms to compensate for the 20 percent of total revenues currently received from tariffs. Regional trade liberalization would be trade-creating and favor export of the products for which Laos had a comparative advantage; however, its overall impact would be limited because the Lao economy was largely complementary to the economies of the ASEAN states. Typically, economic integration among complementary economies has relatively small trade-creating effects. With its ASEAN neighbors viewing overland trade routes as essential to increased trade between Thailand and Vietnam, as well as between Thailand and southern China, road and bridge construction were already priorities. Hydropower dam construction was also expected to continue. In addition to the controversial Nam Theun II dam in central Laos, designed to provide electricity for eastern Thailand, smaller dams were also under construction in northern and southern Laos.[53]

The Lao PDR implemented structural reforms and practiced generally sound economic management under the New Economic Mechanism. These policies fostered a relatively steady movement toward macroeconomic stability, production growth, a small private sector and increased trade and foreign investment. Annual GDP growth in 1992–7 averaged 7 percent, providing some hope Laos would achieve its goal of graduating from the ranks of the Least Developed Nations by the year 2020. Unfortunately, the financial crisis that hit Thailand in mid-1997 triggered a related crisis in Laos in 1997–8. Thailand was the main trading partner and principal source of investment in Laos, and the macroeconomic instability it experienced triggered a sharp depreciation of the kip, together with a widespread loss of confidence in the Lao economy. A weakening domestic reform effort and lax macroeconomic management compounded the impact of the financial crisis. Foreign investment and some key exports, both tied to the sagging Thai economy, took a severe hit. The negative effects of the financial crisis were aggravated by a lengthy consensus-building process. Divergent thinking toward economic reform, which first surfaced in the 1970s, made it impossible for the Lao elite to react quickly and effectively to rapidly changing economic realities. As a result, the reform process slowed and the macroeconomic environment worsened.[54]

The Asian financial crisis thus exposed a major weakness of the Lao political system. The political stability inherent in a one-party state facilitated reform policy at the beginning of the transition process, but as economist Yves Bourdet astutely observed, it turned out to be a hindrance when more balanced economic development was required.

One main lesson from transition in Laos is thus that the existence of the one-party state has facilitated the formulation, adoption and implementation of a comprehensive and relatively rapid transition programme. This has resulted in significantly improved macroeconomic performance in the short and medium-term. But the absence of democracy and transparency in interaction with the specific economic and historical conditions of Laos has contributed to the emergence of a bargaining economy in Laos with a stop-and-go macroeconomic stance and long-term macroeconomic instability.[55]

The Lao PDR initiated a few half-hearted measures to mitigate the crisis, mopping up excess liquidity and raising interest rates, but these tentative steps were not enough to overcome a rapidly deteriorating situation. The most immediate challenge was to institute strong stabilization measures and renew reform efforts to contain both exchange rate volatility and inflation in order to restore the economy's competitiveness. But ideological in-fighting paralyzed the country's leadership at a time when swift, decisive action was required. As late as July 1998, for example, the governor of the Lao central bank, in a front page article in the English-language *Vientiane Times*, blamed the collapse of the kip on "speculative attempts by opportunists," totally ignoring the fact that the kip was among the least-traded currencies in the world. In an adjacent article in the same newspaper, the director of the National Economic Research Institute, a government think-tank, more accurately described the kip's fall as "homegrown" and the product of the Lao PDR's "persistent balance-of-payments deficit."[56]

By the end of 1998, annual GDP growth, shielded in part by the country's large subsistence agricultural base, was still positive but down to 4 percent. The exchange rate had also dropped to an alarming level with the kip less than 30 percent of its July 1997 level, and inflation accelerated to more than 150 percent on an annualized basis, reducing real incomes and purchasing power. Economic targets set by the state for the year 2000 included an annual growth rate of 8–8.5 percent and a per capita income of $500, completely unrealistic goals in the aftermath of the Asian financial crisis.[57]

## Lao domestic politics

The death of President and LPRP Chairman Kaysone Phomvihane on 21 November 1992 was the most significant political event of the early 1990s. Born in the southern province of Savanakhet, he was the son of a Lao peasant mother and a Vietnamese father who was an official in the French colonial administration. Both a brilliant political theoretician and a crafty military chief, he was a leading figure in the Lao revolutionary movement beginning in the 1940s and the most powerful political figure in Laos after the mid-1950s when he became General Secretary of the Lao People's Revolutionary Party. Promoted to the new post of LPRP Chairman in 1991, Kaysone was named President under the new constitution. He was the principal architect of the country's economic reform program. When asked to explain the radical shift in ideology, he acknowledged Laos was simply too underdeveloped to begin socialism.[58]

Throughout Kaysone's career as a Party and state leader, the LPRP leadership assiduously projected a collective profile; but with his death, the state developed a cult of personality around Kaysone in an effort to promote the legitimacy of the regime. A seven-day period of national "deep mourning" was followed by a "state-sponsored sequence of nationalist and religious rites." Throughout the 1990s, the cult of Kaysone was a central part of the Lao PDR's ongoing efforts to invent or reinvent national legitimizing myths. The cult was promoted through the establishment of memorial museums, the erection of statues and busts, and through journalism and speeches.[59]

The Supreme People's Assembly, renamed the National Assembly under the 1991 constitution, elected Nouhak Phoumsavanh President in an extraordinary session on 25 November 1992. Khamtay Siphandone, Prime Minister since August 1991, was elected General Secretary of the LPRP Central Committee. Khamtay was defense minister from 1975 to 1991, and his elevation to the senior Party job exemplified the growing influence of the Lao military in government and Party affairs. Both Nouhak and Khamtay had been close to the center of power for decades, and both were committed to the process of economic reform. Nevertheless, the uncertainty over leadership succession caused by Kaysone's illness caused delays in government actions and decisions in the months surrounding his death. As one observer noted, "inertia and avoidance of difficult personnel decisions are powerful forces in Lao political life."[60]

A reorganization of public administration, expected since the adoption of the new constitution in 1991, was finally approved by the National Assembly in February 1993. One significant change was the division of the Ministry of Economy, Planning and Finance into a separate Ministry of Finance and a Committee for Planning and Cooperation. The reorganization also involved new appointments and a reshuffling of portfolios, strengthening the government's capacity for both economic planning and the implementation of economic reforms.[61]

The National Assembly, elected in December 1992 in only the second nationwide elections since the communists took power in 1975, held its first session in February 1993. As was the case with the Supreme People's Assembly, the candidates for the National Assembly were all screened by the LPRP; and in most instances, the 158 candidates for 85 seats were nominated by Party or government bodies. While the LPRP continued to exercise total control over both the election process and the functioning of the Assembly, the new members, with an average age of around 50, were younger in age and outlook than the senior Party leadership. This offered the potential for fresh, if circumscribed, thinking in the Party and government.[62]

Even as the Party dealt with questions of succession and attempted to restructure, it continued to wrestle with a level of corruption that reached every sector of the economy. In March 1993, Prime Minister Khamtay established an Anti-Corruption Committee to address the issue country-wide. The work of the committee was made more difficult by the omnipresence of corruption due to low salaries paid to civil servants, low levels of respect for the police and legal system, and the growing opportunities for graft as the economy opened to foreign investment. Most observers agreed corruption was especially rampant in the forestry indus-try and in the provision of services. Party officials subsequently stressed in speeches and articles the interrelationship of law and corruption, Party legitimacy and security. If the Party failed to uphold the rule of law, in a time when legal statutes were being published for all to read, it feared popular resentment might undermine Party legitimacy and threaten its hold on power.[63]

During commemoration ceremonies in November 1995, marking the twentieth anniversary of LPRP rule, Party leaders reaffirmed their intent to continue external policies of gradual engagement while promoting stability on the domestic front. Much like the Communist Party of Vietnam, the LPRP offered the Lao people increased economic openness and prosperity in exchange for continued communist domination of the political system. As Yves Bourdet, a long-time observer of Laos, noted:

> There is a clear dichotomy in Laos between the comprehensiveness of the economic reforms and the inertia of the political system. The New Economic Mechanism has not been accompanied by political reforms, and the regime perpetuates itself despite the demise of most of the founding members of the Lao People's Revolutionary Party (LPRP), the Pathet Lao.[64]

## Sixth Party Congress

The Sixth Party Congress was held in Vientiane on 18–20 March 1996, five years after the Fifth Party Congress. The 381 delegates in attendance represented 78,000 Party members (less than 2 percent of the total popu-lation). In terms of reform policy, the Sixth Party Congress was highly significant in that it reinforced the power of Party members advocating a slower reform path with more control over the various effects of reform policy. In effect, it was a victory of "reformers by necessity" over "reformers by conviction." The role of the military in the new top leadership illustrated the change in the balance of power. At the Fifth Party Congress in 1991, the army gained three positions out of nine on the Politburo; but at the Sixth

Party Congress, the number jumped to seven out of nine, six generals and a colonel. Prime Minister Khamtay Siphandone remained number one in the Party hierarchy with General Saman Vignaket, a well-known opponent of comprehensive reforms, occupying the number two position. The appointment of General Sisavath Keobounphanh to the newly created post of Vice President eroded the position of aging President Nouhak Phoumsavanh, fortifying the militarization of the political elite of Laos.[65]

The Sixth Party Congress also reaffirmed the leading role of the LPRP. Party leaders argued economic reform should not be accompanied by political liberalization because a departure from one-party rule could lead to the political instability characteristic of other countries under transition. Another notable result of the congress was the increased political representation of ethnic minorities. Three of the four new members of the Politburo belonged to ethnic minorities. This was particularly significant in Laos both because of the multi-ethnic character of the country and because the NEM had altered income distribution in favor of urban areas. While the increased representation of ethnic minorities could help to correct the insufficient attention given to rural areas in recent years, it was also noted that two of the three new ethnic members were also generals. Consequently, they could prove more inclined to represent the interests of the provincial military-political elite as opposed to the aspirations of rural peasants. Finally, while the changes in the balance of power at the Sixth Party Congress clearly favored advocates of slower economic change, the Party did reaffirm its commitment to reform policy.[66]

As the decade progressed, the Party and general public became increasingly concerned with the problems resulting from an open-door policy, especially its impact on the material and social fabric of Laos. Where less than 15,000 tourists had visited Laos in 1990, the number had swelled to over 400,000 by 1996. Some 50,000 tourists – approximately one per inhabitant – visited Luang Prabang alone in 1996. The pressure on basic infrastructures was tremendous, and the Lao rightly worried that social ills, like prostitution and HIV/AIDS, would follow. The number of American and European visitors increased, but the bulk of tourists remained Thai. With mounting Thai influence a threat to national identity, the government responded with a heightened emphasis on Lao culture and history. It restored historical monuments, erected new monuments to past kings, and conducted seminars on minority culture and the protection of the national heritage. The re-Buddhification of Lao society also continued with Party officials often interweaving Buddhist ideas about seeking truth with the communist idea that there is a single truth which only the Party knows. The Party also emphasized the revolutionary roots of contemporary Lao society. A six-meter-high bronze statue of Kaysone Phomvihone was erected in Vientiane, and the first of an anticipated three statues commemorating Vietnamese killed in Laos during the Second Indochina War was erected on the Plain of Jars.[67]

In January 1998, the National Assembly announced its new member-ship, following elections held in December 1997. Some 160 candidates, almost all of them LPRP members, had contested 99 seats, an increase of 14 seats from the previous session. Out of the 99 members of the new assembly, 68 were from local authorities and 31 from the central govern-ment. One delegate was independent and 21 were women. The retirement of President Nouhak Phoumsavanh precipitated a leadership reshuffle in the spring of 1998. Prime Minister and General Secretary Khamtay Siphandone was elected president; and Sisavath Keobounphanh, a close associate of Khamtay with expertise in foreign affairs, became prime minister. Khamtay's elevation to the presidency made him the most powerful person in Laos since 1992 when Kaysone Phomvihane also held both the top state and Party posts. The leadership changes reaffirmed the Lao PDR's commitment to economic reform; otherwise, they reflected a determination to opt for stability and continuity over change.[68]

## International relations

In July 1992, Laos signed the Bali Treaty of Amity and Cooperation in Southeast Asia, thus becoming an ASEAN observer; and in July 1993, it established diplomatic relations with Brunei, completing the network of associations necessary for inclusion in ASEAN. The Lao PDR applied for ASEAN membership in March 1996 and joined Myanmar in becoming a formal member in July 1997. While most Lao who were aware of ASEAN welcomed their country's membership, there was also concern over whether Laos could meet its diplomatic and financial demands. Based on the experience of bringing Vietnam into ASEAN without proper prepara-tion, a number of seminars and meetings were held throughout the year to better prepare Lao officials, journalists and others. ASEAN membership had an immediate impact on Lao foreign relations. Throughout 1997, a string of ASEAN presidents, prime ministers and foreign ministers visited Vientiane. A wide range of agreements on agriculture, health, narcotics control and cultural exchange were concluded. Both Brunei and Singapore opened embassies in Vientiane. At the annual ministerial meeting in Manila in 1998, Laos opposed efforts by Thailand, supported by the Philippines, to drop ASEAN's long-standing policy of noninterference in the internal affairs of member states and replace it with a policy of con-structive intervention.[69]

The policies of the New Economic Mechanism increased Thai economic and cultural influence in Laos. Thailand became the leading source of private investment as well as its principal trading partner. Thai banks dominated the rapidly expanding banking sector, and Thai television exerted a strong cultural influence on the western parts of the country. As a result, Lao relations with Thailand, marked by strong commercial ties on the one hand and a degree of cultural reserve and suspicion on the other, continued the equivocal pattern of past decades. With relations with all its neighbors in a state of flux, the Lao PDR remained determined not to become an economic or cultural appendage of any state, most especially Thailand. Substantive issues also clouded bilateral relations. These included unresolved border questions and Thailand's eagerness to close down the refugee camp at Ban Na Pho, home to some 12,000 Hmong, most of whom resisted repatriation to Laos. In addition to the economic concerns raised by the Asian financial crisis, Lao–Thai relations focused on the issues of border demarcation and the repatriation of Lao refugees. When Thailand announced in February 1998 that it was suspending work on the border, Laos successfully lobbied to reverse the decision with both sides eventually agreeing to complete its demarcation by 2003.[70]

The Lao PDR's contribution to peacemaking in Cambodia was recognized in July 1993 by the visit to Laos of Cambodian leaders Hun Sen and Prince Norodom Ranariddh. President Khamtay returned the favor later in the year when he traveled to Phnom Penh in what was more than a simple goodwill visit. Reflecting a mutual concern for the unbridled development of the Mekong, the two neighbors issued a joint communiqué during his visit, expressing their determination to cooperate more closely on environmental protection within the framework of the Mekong River Commission. Cambodian Prime Minister Hun Sen returned to Vientiane in April 1997 to conclude economic and cultural agreements with the Lao PDR.[71]

Lao–Vietnamese relations, which remained "special" in the sense the two communist parties continued to feel some degree of solidarity, declined in overall importance. The security concerns that once bound the two neighbors were no longer compelling, and their common search for trade, investment and economic assistance caused both to look elsewhere. Nevertheless, appearances were kept up with a regular exchange of official state visits and delegations at all levels. In contrast to visits with Cambodian or Thai officials, which were carefully defined (border issues, environmental concerns, refugees), the purpose of the manifold meetings with Vietnamese delegations was often vague and concerned with "ideological" questions. The agenda often appeared to be dominated by difficult issues of common concern, such as how to maintain one-party rule within a market-oriented system governed by the rule of law. Agreements on cultural and social development, as well as economic development, tied the two states, but illegal Vietnamese immigration and logging in the border areas constituted minor annoyances. Vietnam's newly elected Party General Secretary, Le Kha Phieu, made his first visit to Laos in March 1998, immediately after the reshuffle of senior Lao Party and state leadership, signing three agreements covering economic cooperation, trade and cultural, and scientific-technical exchange. Prime Minister Sisavath returned the favor in July, concluding agreements on energy, transportation, legal assistance and narcotics control.[72]

Diplomatic and commercial relations with the People's Republic of China expanded throughout the 1990s. China provided aid, arms and trade; however, its most important role was to validate the path followed by the LPRP. If the Chinese Communist Party could adopt market reforms and private ownership while preserving one-party rule, could its Lao comrades be wrong in doing the same? For China, Laos was attractive both for its natural resources, rich hardwood forests and mineral deposits, and for its strategic location as a land bridge and gateway to Southeast Asia. In October 1997, China agreed to provide Laos with a long-term loan of $12 million to build a cement plant, also agreeing to build additional roads in Laos.[73]

Vientiane and Washington finally exchanged ambassadors in 1992 after a hiatus of 17 years. Thereafter, diplomatic intercourse centered on the American fixation with servicemen still listed as missing-in-action (MIA) from the Second Indochina War as well as on drugs and refugees. In May 1995, the United States removed Laos from the list of countries ineligible for foreign assistance; however, lifting the ban proved more symbolic than a precursor to vastly increased aid because of U.S. budget constraints. Washington and Vientiane concluded a draft trade and investment pact in August 1997; and in November 1997, Deputy Secretary of State Strobe Talbott visited Laos, marking the highest-ranking U.S. official visit since 1975. Only days after signing the bilateral agreement, Radio Free Asia, a government-funded corporation mandated by the U.S. Congress, launched a Lao-language service. The move was strongly criticized by the Lao PDR which argued the new broadcasts would create misunderstanding.[74]

Finally, Laos maintained close diplomatic and economic relations with a large number of far-distant foreign donors. The number of bilateral donors increased in the 1990s with the principal ones being Australia, France, Germany, Japan and Sweden. Japan was the main bilateral donor with annual economic assistance approximating $50 million, followed by the European states and Australia with contributions from each generally in the range of $12–14 million. The Japanese presence in Laos was low-key but widely considered to be influential.[75]

## Cambodia's revised strategy for development

In Cambodia, the pace of economic reform accelerated with the successful conclusion of general elections in May 1993 and the subsequent creation of the Royal Government of Cambodia (RGC). Operating under the slogan "*Le Cambodge s'aide lui-même*" (Cambodia will help itself), one of the first undertakings of the RGC was the development of a complex, ambitious program aimed at the economic rehabilitation of the Kingdom. The success of the plan, composed of separate but interrelated initiatives, depended on the RGC's ability to orchestrate a total program in which individual components complemented and reinforced each other.

Envisioned from the outset as a prolonged effort stretching well into the next century, the government rightly deemed progress during the first 18 months to be critical.[76]

A commitment to implement a market economy, together with the fundamental change in the role of the government which that commitment implied, was at the core of Cambodia's new strategy. The 1993 constitution formally adopted the market economy system and accorded citizens the right to sell their products freely. The state was expressly prohibited from imposing on citizens the sale of private products to the state or the use of private products by the state unless authorized by law. In turn, the state assumed responsibility for promoting economic development as well as managing and protecting the environment.[77]

The RGC attached a high priority to integrating the Cambodian economy into both regional and global economies. To achieve this result, it aimed to develop external trade, pursue regional initiatives and attract foreign investment. In so doing, it recognized the interrelationship and mutually reinforcing character of its various goals. On the one hand, export promotion, import substitution and foreign investment had an important role to play in reconstruction. On the other, achievement of desired levels of integration and investment were dependent on revival of productive sectors, rebuilding of physical infrastructure, creation of a modern financial system and maintenance of political and economic stability.

In the external sector, the RGC removed a significant obstacle to free trade with the elimination of import licenses in late 1993. It also commenced negotiations with the U.S. government for the enjoyment of Most Favored Nation (MFN) status, talks complicated by the absence in Washington of a clear legal authority for restoring MFN. Executive Office action had denied Cambodia MFN status in 1975, and the U.S. Congress subsequently confirmed its trading posture in the 1988 Trade Act. The Clinton administration could not simply reverse the 1975 executive order because Cambodia's non-MFN status was subsequently made law by the 1988 Trade Act. Observers estimated MFN status would lower import duties imposed on most Cambodian products by up to 40 percent. Membership in ASEAN also promised to boost economic growth by increasing Cambodian participation in regional economic affairs.

The RGC presented its development plan to the International Committee for the Reconstruction of Cambodia (ICORC) in late 1993. The objectives of the *National Programme* included social justice, national reconciliation and economic growth. In support of these goals, the plan outlined five reinforcing strategies. First, the RGC aimed to promote economic stabilization and growth by creating policies and processes for long-term economic management. At the same time, it hoped to nurture foreign investment and private entrepreneurship. Second, the government planned to reform administrative and judicial institutions through a clarification of the roles and responsibilities of administrators, together with the establishment of effective and fair legal institutions.[78] Third, the Royal Government sought to ensure structural adjustment and sectoral reform through the creation of commercial and investment codes. Fourth, it aimed to provide direct support for sustained development by addressing infrastructure needs, expanding access to social services and upgrading human skills. Finally, it hoped to optimize the sustainable use of natural resources through conservation management and effective protection of the environment. The RGC recognized the plan was ambitious and stated that success depended on the mobilization of the country's resources. It also stressed that considerable international financial support and technical assistance would be essential to success.

In the course of the ICORC meeting, Minister of Economics and Finance Sam Rainsy discussed the national program with members of the international donor community. Declaring the move from a centrally planned to a market economy to be irreversible and irrevocable, Rainsy highlighted the key reforms necessary to achieve this result. Among them, he cited creation of a comprehensive legal framework, transformation of the state apparatus to mirror development of the private sector, disengagement of the state from most commercial activities and continuation of the privatization program. To encourage investment, he promised a new investment law. He also pledged to move Cambodia from a regulated and controlled economy to one based on tariffs and incentives.[79]

## Economic stabilization and growth in Cambodia

In support of RGC policies, the National Assembly in December 1993 unanimously adopted a national budget and new finance laws which collectively set the stage for a sound economic policy. The new regulations called for a single budget, prepared and executed annually, and the closure of all bank accounts held by ministries or other government bodies. All revenues were to be remitted to the National Treasury and all expenditures disbursed by the same body. In effect, the new finance laws stripped ministries, provincial authorities and powerful individuals of long-exercised rights to collect taxes independent of the government. They also separated responsibility for the authorization of public expenditures from the subsequent disbursement of cash and provided greater transparency for the management of state assets.[80]

At the same time, the Royal Government moved to rationalize the tax collection system to increase revenue collected and to make the system more equitable. The Customs Department began to collect both import duties and the consumption tax where the Tax Department had earlier collected the latter. The Ministry of Economics and Finance later unveiled a new tax package intended to improve the balance between direct and indirect taxation and to reduce an unhealthy dependence on customs revenues. Tax revenues at the time approximated only 6 percent of GDP compared to 25–30 percent in a more normal situation, and customs duties provided some 54 percent of total revenues in Cambodia while 15–20 percent would have been more representative. The new taxation measures included a streamlined profits tax, extension of the real estate rentals tax and a new turnover (sales) tax.[81]

The tax reform movement continued throughout 1994 in an effort to increase tax revenues and broaden a revenue base heavily dependent on customs duties. The introduction of new taxes, including increases in the airport departure tax and duties on petroleum products, dramatically increased revenues. Customs duties also increased due to a higher volume of imports and the move to a Cost, Insurance and Freight (CIF) basis to value imported goods. The tax base was again widened in early 1995 when new laws clarified the profits tax and imposed a personal income tax.[82]

The *National Programme*, recognizing the important role confidence in the banking system played in an effective monetary policy, also expanded efforts to transform the banking system into a modern financial sector. The People's National Bank of Cambodia acted as both a central bank and a commercial bank until 1992 when the government reorganized the bank and implemented a commercial banking law. Aimed at transforming the National Bank into a genuine central bank, the new law provided for the establishment and regulation of commercial banks, in particular branches of foreign banks operating in Cambodia.[83]

In March 1994, Rainsy remarked that the monetary policy of Cambodia was devoted to fighting inflation, stabilizing the riel and improving the National Bank's regulatory capacities. He added that regained confidence in financial institutions would facilitate the dedollarization of the economy. He emphasized that the RGC had already implemented a liberal foreign exchange regime and a unified foreign exchange market, introduced a 5 percent reserve requirement on bank deposits and required banks to show minimum paid-in capital. He concluded that the near term goals of the government included enactment of a new Central Bank law guaranteeing National Bank independence, a revised financial institutions act and a more liberal foreign exchange law.[84]

In a June 1994 interview, Radsady Om, Chairman of the Foreign Affairs Committee of the National Assembly, emphasized the need to streamline the existing investment law to make the process more attractive. A new law adopted by the National Assembly in August 1994 combined investment and incentive provisions. It also designated the Council for the Development of Cambodia (CDC) a one-stop service organization responsible for the rehabilitation, development and oversight of investment activity. The new law required CDC to provide a response to investor applications within 45 days.[85]

The terms of Cambodia's new investment law were more liberal than similar statutes in place in Laos and Vietnam, and the response from investors was positive. In January 1995, the Cambodian Investment Board (CIB) circulated a list of 57 private investment projects, totaling $2.2 billion, approved after passage of the new law. However, an estimated $1.3 billion of the total involved a single deal with Ariston, a Malaysian company, to develop a resort complex in Sihanoukville. Critics of the project understandably questioned the utility of a casino to nine million Cambodians, some 80 percent of whom were poor farmers. The issue of political stability also continued to plague Cambodia, and charges of corruption tainted the contract-approval process. An ADB delegation visiting Cambodia in late 1995 rightly emphasized that more needed to be done to make the rules of the game clear and predictable.[86]

The 1994 Foreign Investment Law became the principal legal basis for privatization in Cambodia. Regrettably, the government, especially in the early years of privatization, focused more on speedy execution than on the transparency and equity of deals. In contrast to Vietnam, leasing in Cambodia quickly became the preferred form of privatization, accounting for more than half the deals concluded. The lease option was created to enable local Cambodians with little capital to take over domestic enterprises; however, most investors were foreign. With restrictions in place governing ownership of land, overseas investors regarded leases as less risky in the uncertain economic and political milieu characterizing Cambodia.[87]

## Sustainable development in Cambodia

The Royal Government attached considerable significance in the *National Programme* to managing the reconstruction of Cambodia in a sustainable way, making environmental improvement a principal measure of the success of the overall program. Short-term objectives included strengthening the technical capacities of the Secretariat of State for the Environment, completing provincial land use studies, drafting a comprehensive environmental law and strengthening enforcement capabilities at all levels. Sectoral targets centered on the development of strategies for drainage, irrigation and sanitation; sustainable forestry and fisheries exploitation; and landmine clearance.[88]

The timber sector became a test case for the entire reform process as it focused global attention on the widespread political resistance generated by government attempts to restructure financial regulations and institutions. Economic reforms in Cambodia won loud praise from international lending institutions and donor states, but the traditional power brokers of Cambodia were not pleased to see their incomes and influence eroded. The RGC eased temporarily the timber export ban put in place earlier by the Supreme National Council. At the same time, it implemented new procedures designed to increase national revenues and reduce damage to the environment. These revised procedures required any company intending to export timber to obtain an export permit from the Ministry of Foreign Affairs or an export license from the Ministry of Agriculture.

In large part due to the new control measures, timber exports in the first three months of 1994 generated government revenues close to $23 million compared to total revenues of only $8 million for all of 1993. At the same time, security problems prevented Cambodian customs officials from inspecting a number of frontier crossing points on the Thai–Cambodian border. The amount of timber stockpiled in or exported through these border areas, as well as through Laos, was unknown but was thought to be substantial. Thai customs statistics for 1993 indicated that the amount of timber imported from Cambodia to Thailand alone was more than the total amount of wood licensed for export by Cambodian authorities.[89]

In late June 1994, the Cambodian government, in a decree issued by co-premiers Ranariddh and Hun Sen, transferred oversight responsibility for lucrative logging contracts from the Ministry of Economics and Finance to the Ministry of National Defense. This decision generated intense domestic and international criticism as it was in direct contravention of the new Budget Law which stated that all state revenues must be remitted directly to the National Treasury. The decree also contravened government agreements with international lending bodies, like the IMF, which called for the centralization of government spending. The June 1994 decree was reversed two months later, but the Ministry of National Defense continued into October 1994 to issue licenses for the export of timber.[90]

In late February 1995, Cambodia announced a ban on raw timber exports effective the end of April. In theory, only processed timber could be exported from that date. The RGC hoped this move would encourage investment in the country's timber processing industry, raising export taxes and increasing local employment. It also reserved several million hectares of timber land for concessions to domestic or foreign companies, provided they met regulations for sustainable forestry management. The Malaysian logging company, Samling, signed a memorandum of understanding covering 800,000 hectares; and the Indonesian Panin Group later concluded a deal covering 1.5 million hectares. With both agreements attacked by environmentalists, the timber sector highlighted the complex problems faced by the RGC as it implemented development policies.[91]

As unlikely as it might seem, the precious stones industry proved even more difficult than the timber sector to regulate. The richest gemstone deposits were located in Battambang province around the town of Pailin, an area long dominated by the Khmer Rouge. Government forces briefly occupied Pailin in March 1994 but were unable to hold the town. Reports in early 1995 suggested the number of Thai companies working with the Khmer Rouge to mine gemstones had more than doubled since the latter reoccupied the area. In addition to the loss of customs revenues, mining practices in the area threatened ecological damage to the region and the rivers flowing through it.[92]

Aquaculture proved yet another serious threat to the environment as seaside mangrove forests, among the richest and most diverse ecosystems in the world, were increasingly destroyed for shrimp farms and charcoal. With the mangrove forests in Koh Kong province among the finest remaining in Southeast Asia, environmentalists called for prompt action to curtail shrimp and charcoal production. In a related move, the RGC formed a National Wetland Committee and agreed to sign the Ramsar Convention, an international agreement addressing the preservation of wetland areas.[93]

## Cambodian political culture

The final strategy in the *National Programme*, reform of administrative and judicial institutions, focused on strengthening government bodies through a clarification of roles and responsibilities, reform in corporate functions and improved coordination between central and provincial administrations. The government's strategy here aimed to overhaul the civil service and to promote an effective workforce that accepted the merit system and respected human rights. It also hoped to establish a fair and efficient judicial system.[94] Ironically, it was in this area of administrative reform that domestic and international expectations for improvement were highest while sustained progress proved most difficult.

The UNTAC-sponsored elections were a unique achievement, but they proved insufficient to establish a solid foundation for democratic institutions and practices in a still immature body politic. Instead of spawning change in the political culture of Cambodia, the elections led to a reassertion of the political practices of old. Power brokers continued to practice politics as usual often evidencing the familism, cupidity, narrow horizons and reluctance to tolerate opposing points of view prevalent in the Sihanouk and Lon Nol periods. For Cambodia to prosper, most observers agreed its political culture would have to change. Consequently, the prevailing trend was a discouraging one, hampering progress, not only in judicial and administrative reform, but in the overall development program.[95]

The case of Sam Rainsy, the architect of the nation's economic reform program, illustrated the difficulties involved in changing Cambodia's political culture. As Minister of Economics and Finance, his efforts to root out official corruption and to centralize revenue collection were widely heralded abroad. In contrast, the same reforms prompted a storm of protest at home from politicians, entrenched business interests and the armed forces, sparking efforts at the highest levels of government to remove him from office. Eventually, his critics won out, and Rainsy was sacked in a cabinet reshuffle in October 1994. He was later ousted from the FUNCINPEC party in May 1995 and from the National Assembly in June 1995.

Both prime ministers supported the removal of Rainsy because both viewed him as a serious political rival. At the center of the storm, Rainsy was by no means the only critic targeted by the government. After Prince Norodom Sirivuddh, half-brother of King Sihanouk, secretary-general of the FUNCINPEC party and a deputy prime minister in the government, resigned in solidarity with Rainsy, he was first imprisoned and then exiled to France. At the same time, the RGC argued increasingly that curbs were necessary to keep the press from acting irresponsibly and undermining the people's faith in their leaders.[96]

The ousting of Sam Rainsy and the mounting pressure on the press were the product of heavy-handed government efforts to neutralize any opposition. The National Assembly became little more than a rubber stamp. Voices of even mild dissent often received death threats. The court system, according to human rights lawyers and diplomats, was largely controlled and directed by politicians. The widespread abuse of human rights, accompanied as it was by extensive evidence of corruption, made a mockery of the $2 billion UN peace plan that had led to elections and the subsequent formation of a new government.[97]

Widespread violence also continued to plague Cambodian society. For centuries, Cambodian history has been a chronicle of violence as evidenced by the *bas-reliefs* at Angkor, the cruelties of nineteenth-century uprisings, the sordid political killings of Sihanouk, the Vietnamese massacres of Lon Nol and the murderous purges of Pol Pot. Never a country at peace with itself, it was not surprising that studies of the Khmer Rouge era found that Cambodians were not as shocked as outsiders with its violence because it differed only in scale and intensity from past experience. This predilection to violence was much in evidence in the 1993 election campaign and continued largely unabated after the installation of the new government.[98]

At the March 1994 ICORC meeting in Tokyo, a session which highlighted Cambodia's continuing struggle against banditry, landmines and poverty, the 12 international bodies and 31 donor nations in attendance pledged $777 million in aid to Cambodia, including funds pledged earlier but not yet disbursed. Over the next year, political violence and human rights abuses dampened the donor enthusiasm with many donors complaining of "compassion fatigue." At the March 1995 ICORC meeting in Paris, a chorus of voices, including Amnesty International and Sam Rainsy, condemned the government's human rights record and the limited progress made toward democratization, accusing it of corruption and malfeasance. After the IMF and World Bank emphasized in early 1996 that corrupt practices would no longer be tolerated, major donors at the July 1996 ICORC meeting in Tokyo seized on the new approach, insisting for the first time that Cambodia implement a more transparent forestry policy.[99]

The year 1996 appeared to bring improved prospects for peace, stability and democracy in Cambodia. The ruling coalition experienced periodical crises but managed to stay intact. The two leading parties in the coalition, FUNCINPEC and the CPP, remained at loggerheads with each other, but events suggested that neither could eliminate the other by force, and each appeared willing to contest the other in the national elections scheduled for 1998. In November 1995, ex-minister Rainsy had formed an opposition party known as the Khmer Nation Party (KNP) which claimed membership in 1997 of more than 250,000 people. Most encouragingly, ongoing defections and a loss of foreign support reduced Khmer Rouge capabilities to the point they were largely a spent military and political force by 1997.[100]

As the political and security front improved, Cambodia again suffered what professor Khatharya Um termed its "seemingly limitless capacity for implosive self-destructiveness."[101] In July 1997, the CPP led by Hun Sen launched a preemptive *coup d'état* against the FUNCINPEC party of Prince Ranariddh. The coup itself was not surprising as many had foreseen its making. With an eye on the May 1998 elections, both Ranariddh and Hun Sen had been aggressively competing for the support of Khmer Rouge defectors, and FUNCINPEC was also negotiating a compact with the Khmer Nation Party. Hun Sen's troops and Ranariddh's bodyguards clashed in the weeks prior to the coup, but most analysts agreed it was the political alliance being constructed by Ranariddh that triggered the coup.[102]

While the coup was not unexpected, the brutal manner of its execution shocked most observers, especially the many human rights and pro-democracy groups working in Cambodia. Hun Sen's troops moved swiftly against FUNCINPEC headquarters, military strongholds and the residences of Ranariddh and other FUNCINPEC leaders. Summary executions and custodial deaths were followed by a wave of mass arrests, detentions and the intimidation of any individual or organized opposition.

> Cambodia witnessed a return to state-sponsored violence and *de facto* single-party autocracy in absolute defiance of the spirit of the U.N.-brokered Paris Accords to which all parties were signatories.[103]

The offices of the FUNCINPEC and KNP parties were ransacked. The military and political leaders of FUNCINPEC were pursued, and FUNCINPEC newspapers were shut down. In France, Prince Ranariddh was unable to return to Cambodia. Civil rights activists later verified that extra-judicial killings continued for weeks after the coup. Hun Sen sought to justify the coup by charging Ranariddh with secret Khmer Rouge negotiations, the infiltration of Khmer Rouge units into Phnom Penh, illegal arms shipments and the initiation of a campaign of intimidation and violence. However, most observers saw it as a preemptive strike as the CPP and its adversaries prepared for the 1998 elections. Attempting to legitimize his actions, Hun Sen described the events of July 5 and after as a legal act, not a coup, and promised that free and fair elections would be held in May 1998.[104]

## RGC economic performance

As the Royal Government pursued its economic goals in an environment of considerable political uncertainty, both in terms of the Khmer Rouge insurgency and the political infighting among the coalition leaders, its overall economic performance in 1994 proved credible, if below forecast. The government achieved some degree of macroeconomic stability, containing expenditures and increasing revenues. GDP grew just short of 5 percent, a modest improvement over 1993 but well below the 8 percent target outlined at the March 1994 ICORC meeting. The rate of inflation was a little more than 26 percent which was down from 1993 but well short of the 10 percent target. The exchange rate remained relatively stable throughout the year, contributing to a stronger balance of payments position. But the budget deficit was 6.2 percent of GDP in 1994 which was up from 5.7 percent the preceding year. External economic assistance contributed significantly to Cambodia's fiscal achievements. And the new foreign investment law stimulated business and investment through tax concessions and other incentives to investors.[105]

With the ingredients for a strong and stable economy coming into place, the Council for the Development of Cambodia launched a regional tour in 1995 to publicize the improved investment climate. Advertisements in the United States began with the question, "Why would anyone want to invest in Cambodia?" In addition to a relatively stable exchange rate, respectable GDP growth and a low rate of inflation, CDC officials promoted the positive impact of ASEAN observer status, pending U.S. approval of MFN status and growing confidence among foreign donors. They also touted the potential for American investment in Vietnam to generate economic spillover into Cambodia. The CDC sales pitch was well prepared albeit not wholly convincing.[106]

The Cambodian economy, propped up by massive infusions of foreign aid, continued to struggle over the next two years. GNP growth was 7.6 percent in 1995 and 6.4 percent in 1996, reasonable growth rates when compared to minus 4 percent in 1991 albeit from a low base. Inflation was effectively constrained, and the budget deficit narrowed. The exchange rate remained relatively stable despite uncertainty in the fiscal and monetary sectors. Export growth accelerated thanks to the achievement of MFN status and some European states granting the Generalized System of Preferences. Nevertheless, with total expenditures in 1996 estimated at approximately $580 million, Cambodia still required foreign aid totaling $262 million or more than 40 percent of its entire budget.[107]

Continuing to face serious obstacles to sustained economic growth, the negative fallout from the Asian financial crisis and the July 1997 coup threatened to be devastating, undermining the international support Cambodia so desperately needed. As political tensions increased in the first half of 1997, Cambodia's structural reforms lost steam, decelerating in the second half of the year. Direct foreign investment commitments to Cambodia fell by 35 percent in 1997 and actual flows declined by 45 percent. The Cambodian riel lost value, but it fell less precipitously than other Asian currencies, notably the Lao kip, due to the extensive dollarization of the Cambodian economy. The negative effects of the regional financial crisis and concurrent domestic political unrest were also tempered by the strong increase in 1997 in Cambodian garment exports to Europe and the United States.[108]

## Evolving regional and international relations

At the outset of the 1990s, Thai–Cambodian relations were strained by outstanding bilateral issues like border disputes and Thai support for the Khmer Rouge; however, they gradually improved as the decade progressed. The first meeting of the newly established Thai–Cambodian General Border Committee, held in Bangkok in November 1995, resulted in three border checkpoints being reopened. Shortly thereafter, the two Cambodian prime ministers, in separate deals struck in January and February 1996, granted large timber concessions to 17 Thai logging companies. These deals were followed by a visit to Phnom Penh by Thai Prime Minister Banharn Silapa-Archa in late June 1996, the first such visit since Chuan Leekpai went to Phnom Penh in January 1994 and only the second visit by a Thai prime minister in 42 years. Issues discussed during Banharn's visit included border questions, Thai logging activities and bilateral economic cooperation. The two parties also signed a memorandum of understanding regarding the construction of a hydropower station in Koh Kong province, concluded a trade, economic and technical cooperation agreement and established a joint subcommittee on finance.[109]

Ancient enmities also strained Cambodian–Vietnamese relations. Following the 1993 elections, the Khmer Rouge continued to attack ethnic Vietnamese residents, prolonging the anti-Vietnamese violence of the UNTAC period. In 1993–4, tens of thousand of ethnic Vietnamese fled Cambodia; and more than 5,000 refugees were stranded on the border. High-level Vietnamese delegations visited Cambodia in 1994–5, and King Sihanouk visited Vietnam in December 1995. Tensions between Cambodia and Vietnam increased in 1996 with Cambodia charging Vietnam was moving boundary markers westward into the three border provinces of Kompong Cham, Prey Veng and Svay Rieng. Domestic politics complicated the issue as the co-premiers often advanced conflicting approaches, with Prince Ranariddh usually taking the more aggressive position. In January 1996, he termed alleged Vietnamese encroachments on

Cambodian territory an "invasion," calling them a "complete violation" of existing agreements to preserve the border status quo. The rising tensions between Cambodia and Vietnam were eventually defused; nevertheless, the two neighbors were no closer to a permanent border settlement. Heavy fighting during the 1997 coup again raised concerns among ethnic Vietnamese living in Cambodia, but no evidence surfaced to suggest they were the victims of targeted violence.[110]

Elsewhere, Cambodian policy toward China, Taiwan and Korea moved in new directions. The Chinese government, which terminated its formal ties with the Khmer Rouge in the early 1990s, took steps to strengthen its ties with the RGC, pledging $1 million in non-lethal aid in April 1996. Beijing also moved closer to the Cambodian People's Party, a significant step as it had considered Hun Sen an enemy during the Vietnamese occupation of Cambodia. In the wake of Hun Sen's July 1996 visit to Beijing, Michael Hayes, editor of the *Phnom Penh Post*, highlighted the shift in Chinese foreign policy:

> The Chinese have made a cool calculation. They like the King, but they have to think of their own interests. They waited to see what the coalition would do for three years and now they have decided to back Hun Sen.[111]

In November 1996, a Chinese trade delegation visited Cambodia, signed a cooperation agreement and pledged $10 million in aid. China's major objective in Cambodia was "political stability, not respect for human rights and adherence to democratic principles." It desired, above all, "a stable Cambodia which is not used by anyone to contain China." Taiwan opened a representative trade office in Phnom Penh in 1995, and Cambodia opened a similar office in Taiwan in 1996. But these Taiwanese initiatives were associated with FUNCINPEC, not the CPP, which facilitated Beijing's decision. The Chinese felt betrayed by FUNCINPEC, a party they had supported for a decade when it operated with resistance factions on the Thai border. To curry Chinese favor in the wake of the July coup, Hun Sen closed Taiwan's representative office. By the end of 1997, China had become very active, buttressing claims to regional leadership with high-level political backing, military assistance and investment in Cambodia. The RGC also established mission-level relations with South Korea in 1996, upgrading them to full diplomatic relations in October 1997.[112]

Throughout this period, Japan remained Cambodia's largest aid donor with budgetary support taking up a significant amount of Japanese aid. Like China, Japan did not, at least publicly, seek to tie its financial support to either respect for human rights or adherence to democratic principles, an approach much appreciated by the RGC. In the wake of the 1997 coup, Japan refused to be drawn into the discussion over the legitimacy of the

Hun Sen government, arguing it was more productive to ensure the May 1998 national elections proceeded on schedule. Following a brief interruption in economic aid, Japan quickly resumed its flow to Cambodia and supported ASEAN efforts to find an acceptable solution.[113]

Cambodian relations with the United States also improved, overcoming a number of stumbling blocks. In August 1995, Washington and Phnom Penh concluded an agreement under which OPIC would provide loans, loan guarantees and risk insurance to U.S. companies operating in Cambodia. Angered by U.S. Senate attempts to tie approval of MFN trading status to human rights and democracy improvements, Hun Sen four months later launched a blunt criticism of the United States, protesting its alleged interference in Cambodian affairs. When the U.S. Deputy Secretary of State for East Asia and the Pacific, Winston Lord, visited Cambodia in January 1996, he declined to discuss the issue but suggested "opposition expression and parties" were "important elements" in the domestic affairs of any state. Cambodia finally achieved MFN status in October 1996, a Phnom Penh objective since the beginning of the decade. The U.S. government was the most persistent critic of the July 1997 coup. Condemning the killing, Washington suspended aid, with the exception of humanitarian assistance, until democracy was restored. The White House later looked to the May 1998 elections to legitimize political authority in Cambodia, arguing they must be conducted under international supervision.[114]

As the political situation in Cambodia deteriorated, the European Union joined the United States in taking a tougher line. The European Parliament in May 1996 urged the EU to add conditionality, including support for democracy and human rights, to future aid agreements with Phnom Penh. Elsewhere, a number of Western states, including Australia, Canada, Denmark, France, Germany, Sweden and the United Kingdom, continued to provide generous amounts of financial assistance to Cambodia. Much of this aid went through NGOs; however, France was an exception as it stayed directly involved in the process of state-building. French aid targeted improvement in areas like public health, the judiciary and public administration. Like Japan, France avoided confrontation, using quiet diplomacy to express its concern for human rights and democracy issues.[115]

Cambodia declared an interest in ASEAN membership as early as 1992; and following creation of the RGC, it took the necessary steps to achieve this objective. However, following the July 1997 coup, the ASEAN member states postponed Cambodia's admission which had been scheduled for later in the month. A number of factors contributed to this decision, including the short time between the coup and Cambodia's scheduled membership, U.S.-led international criticism of the coup and Hun Sen's rejection of ASEAN mediation of the issues between his post-coup government and Ranariddh's government in exile. When ASEAN attempted to mediate the dispute, Hun Sen successfully "embarked on a

series of tactical maneuvers that deftly exploited ASEAN's internal con-
tractions," and rendered their efforts ineffective. An early ASEAN initiative was frustrated when ASEAN found itself increasingly isolated in its
defense of Ranariddh as the legitimate head of government. Overruling
both Malaysia and Vietnam, ASEAN later decided to delay Cambodian
membership indefinitely and to consider human rights when reviewing its
decision even though Burma and Laos had stated publicly their support
for Cambodia's immediate accession. In the end, it was Japan, not
ASEAN, that successfully brokered an agreement between Hun Sen and
Ranariddh, enabling the latter to return to Cambodia and participate in
the 1998 elections. In the interim, both the Lao PDR and Myanmar joined
ASEAN on 23 July 1997, a blow to the legitimacy of the Cambodian
government. Largely due to American veto power, the UN Credentials
Committee also left vacant Cambodia's UN seat, dealing another blow to
the prestige of the CPP-dominated government in Phnom Penh.[116]

## Greater Mekong subregion

With the conclusion of the 1991 Paris Peace Agreement, Cambodia joined
Laos, Thailand and Vietnam on the Interim Mekong Committee (IMC).
China and Myanmar refused to join but did agree to participate in the
Mekong Development Research Network, a Canadian initiative. As the
decade progressed, a thaw in Cold War tensions, growing economic liberalization and domestic political events combined to make broader subregional cooperation possible. The emphasis on large dam construction and
hydropower development also continued, despite a growing number of
studies documenting the negative aspects of large dam performance. ADB
alone identified as high potential for economic development over 50
hydropower projects in the six riparian states. Laos remained at center
stage with its large dam at Nam Theun Hinboun among the more controversial projects.[117]

   The Interim Mekong Committee became the Mekong River Commission (MRC) in April 1995 when Cambodia, Laos, Thailand and Vietnam
concluded the *Agreement on the Cooperation for the Sustainable Development of the Mekong River Basin*. The agreement established a new framework for subregional cooperation, calling for the creation of a Mekong
Basin Development Plan. It also established guidelines for the use of
Mekong waters, together with a process to create rules governing water
utilization and inter-basin diversions. Thereafter, the MRC focused on an
inventory of environmental resources, small-scale irrigation and environmental monitoring. As a result, the Nam Ngum Dam in Laos remained the
only significant MRC hydropower project to be completed. China and
Myanmar later became dialog partners in the MRC with the initial dialog
session held in July 1996.[118]

   Upstream, China was busy damming the Mekong to generate

hydropower in Yunnan province. The first dam was completed at Manwan in 1993, and energy production began in mid-1994. Construction of a second major dam, Dachaoshan, in a planned system of seven such dams, began in 1996 with a third, Jinghong, and a fourth, Xiaowan, in the planning stages. The potential downstream impact of these Chinese dams was a source of widespread concern as Milton Osborne later stressed:

> Occasional placatory statements to the contrary, there seems little reason to believe Chinese planners have much concern for the consequences of this dam-building program on the downstream countries through which the Mekong flows. Suggestions that the dams will provide improved water flow during the dry season are a subject of controversy. And talk by Chinese officials of the desirability of blasting an all-season channel along the Mekong, where it runs through the gorges of northern Laos, do nothing to ameliorate worries about the dams' impact.[119]

As the IMC evolved into the MRC, the Asian Development Bank in 1992 initiated a technical assistance program intended to promote economic cooperation among the six riparian states. Emphasizing the importance of coordinated, collective action, ADB President, Kimimasa Tarumizu, stressed the benefits of promoting subregional development and trade within the context of individual national priorities.

> Cambodia, Lao PDR, Myanmar, Thailand, Viet Nam and Yunnan Province of the People's Republic of China share borders and many important natural resources, and as such form a logical grouping for economic cooperation. Recent positive political and economic developments in this subregion provide an excellent opportunity for the Bank to encourage coordinated activities which will enhance the efficiency and competitiveness of the six economies. The most important areas for coordination include trade, investment, transportation, communications, energy, water resources and tourism.[120]

ADB representatives also highlighted the private sector benefits to be derived from the harmonization of investment codes, commercial laws, financial reporting systems, land use and property rights, banking regulations and product standards.[121]

The report of the initial ministerial conference on subregional economic cooperation, which met in Manila in October 1992, emphasized that future projects could involve any number of countries in the subregion but not necessarily all six. In pursuit of the outlined agenda, ADB saw its primary role as being a catalyst for change by "encouraging dialogue, providing forums for that dialogue, and assisting, if requested, in subregional cooperation through project identification and development." ADB officials were also candid from the outset in recognizing existing barriers to subregional cooperation in the transportation, energy and telecommunications sectors as well as in financial services, legal systems and pricing policies.[122]

The riparian states, especially Cambodia, Laos and Vietnam, approached the challenges and opportunities of enhanced subregional cooperation from widely different perspectives. Laos was an enthusiastic, early supporter, seeing subregional cooperation as an avenue to overcome its dual handicap of being small and landlocked. Emphasizing the role of transportation projects as facilitators of trade, together with hydropower projects as trade opportunities, Lao PDR officials voiced concern about debt levels and economic viability. In turn, Vietnam was acutely aware of the need to expand trade horizons following the collapse of its Comecon markets. Hanoi in 1992 was in a difficult position as it attempted to implement structural reforms and develop new markets without assistance from the non-convertible-currency states. Consequently, it viewed subregional cooperation as part of a broader geopolitical strategy aimed at revitalizing the Vietnamese economy through Western aid and foreign investment.[123]

At the outset, Cambodia was the least enthusiastic supporter of the ADB initiative. It agreed that greater cooperation and trade would result in more effective and efficient resource use. However, its ability to pursue cooperative activities was limited by the current state of the Cambodian economy. Phnom Penh rightly argued that any economic gains from subregional cooperation would be marginal compared to what could be achieved from simply stabilizing its domestic macroeconomic climate. On a more positive note, Cambodia recognized the ADB initiative would provide it with a forum to strengthen its domestic and international standing. Moreover, the initiative also provided a weakened state with the opportunity to sit down with its neighbors on an equal footing to discuss a variety of issues important in regularizing trade and reestablishing sovereign control. In the end, Cambodia approached "subregional initiatives with caution, and with high regard for maintaining national sovereignty."[124]

The second ministerial conference on subregional economic cooperation was held in August 1993. In opening statements, delegates expressed their commitment to subregional cooperation. Touting recent political developments, the Cambodian delegate emphasized the successful election, under UN auspices, of a constituent assembly followed by the formation of a national government. He also acknowledged the Cambodian economy remained one of the poorest on earth. "Rehabilitation and reconstruction has been undertaken but due to a lack of resources, the economic activities of the country have not reached the levels achieved in the late 1960s." Again stressing macroeconomic stabilization as its first priority, Cambodia urged ADB to focus its regional plans on the development of transportation, power, tourism and environmental protection.[125]

Highlighting the divergent thinking found at the second ministerial conference, China and Myanmar put road and railway development as their first priorities while Thailand favored the energy sector together with transportation. In turn, Laos considered the telecommunications and energy sectors to be key elements in harmonizing economic cooperation in the subregion. At the same time, it emphasized the need for cooperation in the fields of tourism, trade and services.[126]

In the longest presentation, the Vice Prime Minister of Vietnam tabled five priorities. In transportation, he supported projects to rehabilitate east-west roads from Vietnam to Laos, Cambodia and Thailand. Desiring to upgrade existing transportation systems before considering new ones, he also expressed interest in air, rail and water transport. On the environment, his comments centered on the Mekong, emphasizing the need to develop and utilize "this water resource in line with the latest technology and international laws." In part, his comments here reflected the mounting controversy over the impact of upstream dams on lower Mekong water flows. Vietnamese priorities in the energy sector centered on hydropower projects on the Se San, Ca and Black rivers. Finally, Vietnamese emphasis on both human resource and tourism development echoed similar concerns elsewhere, especially in Cambodia and Laos.[127]

The first two ministerial conferences were followed by a series of subsequent meetings on roughly an annual basis. Over time, delegate presentations tended to become longer, and in some cases, increasingly self-congratulatory. However, core positions and country priorities remained largely unchanged. As time passed, conference proceedings also provided increasingly detailed information on sector development plans. In addition, the scope of the environment as a priority sector expanded to include both the environment and natural resource development. Telecommunications was later added as a seventh priority sector. By the end of 1995, the six governments had endorsed 77 projects, including 34 in transportation, 12 in energy, 11 in environment, eight in trade and investment, seven in human resource development and five in tourism. Early discussions focused on providing the necessary infrastructure for trade and development. Steps aimed at liberalizing trade, such as reducing tariffs and dropping trade barriers, were purposely left out of the deliberations.[128]

## Other subregional initiatives

In addition to the Greater Mekong Subregion (GMS) initiative, an impressive number of other efforts to promote subregional development were underway in the early 1990s. These included the Forum for Comprehensive Development of Indochina (FCDI), established by Japan in 1993 to address opportunities for cooperation in infrastructure and tourism development. FCDI participants included Cambodia, Laos, Myanmar, Thailand and Vietnam. After 1994, Japan, working with ASEAN Economic Ministers and its Ministry of Trade and Industry (AEM-MITI), also promoted

Asian growth in conjunction with strengthening linkages between ASEAN and Indochina. The emphasis here was on market economy transition, infrastructure, investment, trade and industrial policies.[129] Thailand launched the Golden Quadrangle initiative in 1992 to strengthen economic cooperation in line with its concept of "turning battlefields into market-places." This program linked Laos, Myanmar, Thailand and Yunnan province in an effort "to formalize and develop existing cross-border trade, tourism and transport links." The Mekong Development Bank, UNDP, UN/ESCAP, the Canadian IDRC and the private sector were also active in the subregion.[130]

The ASEAN-Mekong Basin Development Cooperation (ASEAN-MBDC) was established in 1995 to promote the well-being of the Mekong subregion through ASEAN assistance to riparian states. This initiative focused on transportation and communication links between ASEAN and the GMS. Concerned that subregional plans reflect regional requirements, officials of the original six ASEAN states spoke increasingly of the need to create "one Southeast Asia" to integrate all ten Southeast Asian countries into a "family of one." In so doing, they developed ambitious – and expensive – plans for regional integration. For example, the development of a trans-Asian rail link from Singapore to Kunming in Yunnan province, a priority project intended to kickstart the area's development, was tentatively estimated to cost at least $1.5 billion. Such grandiose plans, often emphasizing private sector support, raised serious questions as to the source and availability of funds, together with the additional reforms needed in Cambodia, Laos and Vietnam to attract funding. Varying rules, regulations and procedures on matters pertaining to land ownership and transfer, profit repatriation and visas, together with shortcomings in legal frameworks and immigration laws, were barriers to would-be investors.[131]

This potpourri of well-meaning agencies, promoting joint and individual initiatives, sometimes resulted in self-destructive competition between participant states, sponsoring groups and funding organizations over the priority, timing and location of projects. It also provoked occasional criticism as individual governments, organizations and agencies searched desperately for at least a modicum of coordination and cooperation. Some analysts warned of "initiative overload," and an independent observer noted that Mekong region schemes "have proliferated to the extent that there may soon be the need for a scheme to manage the managers of the river."[132]

Sometimes described as an economic growth triangle, the GMS differed from the Greater South China Growth Triangle or the Singapore-Johor–Riau Growth Triangle in important respects. First, the government role was of prime importance in the case of the GMS where market forces were the primary drivers in dynamic Asian growth triangles. Second, unlike the growth triangles developing elsewhere in Asia, which typically involved only selected regions of participating states, the GMS encompassed the entire country in five out of the six states involved and more often than not affected countrywide interests. In the transitional economies found in the GMS, the riparian states were also directly involved in the planning and execution of projects. Fourth, with the possible exception of Thailand and maybe Yunnan province, the financial resources of the participating states were quite limited and thus hindered their ability to invest in subregional infrastructure projects. Finally, differences in factor endowment and economic complementarity characterized the national economies comprising the Greater Mekong Subregion.[133]

From this perspective, the Greater Mekong Subregion could best be described as "a lower level form of subregional economic co-operation" than either "the growth triangles or the ASEAN Free Trade Area (AFTA)" because its programs did not aim at the "economic integration of the participating countries."[134] Pragmatic and results oriented, the "key characteristic of economic co-operation in the GMS" was that it was "activity-driven, involving initiatives in limited transborder linkages."[135] The issue of whether the GMS was or could become an economic growth triangle was more likely one of scope creep as opposed to goal incompatibility. The GMS initiative appeared to be evolving, at least in selected areas, from one whose primary purpose was the development of infrastructure and natural resources to a more ambitious project promising subregional trade and development. That said, the debate over what constituted a growth triangle and the place of the GMS in that debate looked set to continue.[136]

Despite the plethora of ambitious plans, GMS initiatives faced numerous obstacles. With a variety of governmental and nongovernmental bodies involved, inadequate coordination between the various national agendas and international agencies was commonplace. Funding constraints also posed problems as the subregion was estimated to require around $40 billion over the next 25 years. The Asian financial crisis in 1997–8 dampened enthusiasm for such ambitious, expensive development plans. Tensions also surfaced among competing economic and social groups as to optimum water use, and nongovernmental bodies proposed varied, sometimes contradictory agendas. Finally, serious concerns surfaced as to the level of cooperation possible among the major players on the Mekong. When China refused to sign the regional agreement in 1995, for example, it stated that "whatever action it takes to exploit the Mekong's potential is purely an internal matter." For these reasons, the Mekong was accurately labeled "the *realpolitik* dimension of water conflict."[137]

## Conclusions

It was obvious as early as mid-1997 that the leadership of Laos and Vietnam had reached the end of the beginning in terms of economic reform. It was also clear that both states needed to consolidate and build upon the reforms in place to ensure long-term social stability and sustainable growth. Over the next year, the elite in both states appeared to misread the economic tea leaves, moving backwards toward the future. Adrift in a policy vacuum compromised by factional divisions, they seemed to lose their way. Fixated on the appropriate mix of political and economic reforms, they tended to overcompensate for the former, compromising the later. Struggling to get back on course, they were in danger of dismantling and destroying the achievements of more than a decade. Mistaken policy choices, compounded and aggravated by the Asian financial crisis, put the entire reform process at risk in both Laos and Vietnam.

Next door, the development objectives of the Royal Government of Cambodia were ambitious from the outset, especially for a state wracked in recent decades by extreme social, economic and political dislocation. They were doubly difficult because the country was still in the process of building, as opposed to rebuilding, crucial sectors of its economy. In this challenging milieu, Cambodia made considerable progress in promoting economic stabilization and growth as it developed the fundamentals of a market economy. Unfortunately, economic reforms were repeatedly undermined by the domestic political process as a disheartening and disturbing pattern of corruption, incompetence and malfeasance emerged that mirrored past practice and augured ill for future performance. Democratic procedures, respect for human rights and concern for social justice were concepts bandied about but seldom implemented. Instead, the ruling parties returned to the system of clans and clients prevalent in the Sihanouk and Lon Nol eras. Access to power and wealth was sought and achieved through place and position with connections most often determining the level of justice obtained.

The Asian financial crisis in 1997–8 did not bring about a fundamental change in economic policy in Cambodia, Laos or Vietnam. However, it did delay anything more than tentative steps in the direction of regional integration, most especially in the case of Cambodia and Laos. Moreover, the ongoing commitment of the Association of Southeast Asian States to the "ASEAN way" of consultation and consensus building made the development of effective, binding regional initiatives that much more difficult. Whether or not the expanded ASEAN-10 (ASEAN-6 plus Cambodia, Laos, Myanmar and Vietnam) could function with the same degree of trust and cohesion as the original ASEAN-6 also remained unclear. Like many regional organizations, ASEAN-10 promised much, but it had produced little as the decade closed.

One of the world's most untouched rivers only two decades earlier, the Mekong by the late 1990s looked to become one of the most dammed. Upwards of 100 major dams, diversions and irrigation projects were planned, and thousands of smaller schemes already impacted on local residents as well as people downstream. Established to guide the sustainable development, utilization, conservation and management of the river,

# 6 Challenges and prospects

Arriving at Pochentong airport on a Sunday morning, my first sight was a bumper to bumper traffic jam, heading *out* of town, the new middle class of Phnom Penh on their way to the beach at Sihanoukville. The novelty of this was sufficient, it seemed, to mitigate the journey which would take most of the day there and back. Traffic, of course, transforms a city, particularly in the case of Phnom Penh which has seen so little of it, and while its wide boulevards can still handle the modern flow easily, there's the sense that the city's new car owners simply enjoy cruising around.
> Author Michael Freeman, *Cambodia*, 2004

At heart the Lao belong to the past, and it is only by the accident of being located in the middle of Indochina that they have been forced to live amidst the violence of the contemporary world. They have paid a very high price for it.
> Italian Journalist Tiziano Terzani, *A Fortune-Teller Told Me*, 1997

We are not going to undertake political reform in the same way that other countries have because it could easily lead to the collapse of the political and economic system in Vietnam, creating greater instability and disorder.
> Prime Minister Phan Van Khai, Hanoi, 1999

In one sense, revolutions are much like people. While they seldom improve with age, they often become more like themselves. Three decades on, the revolutions in Cambodia, Laos and Vietnam remained a tug of war between economic and political forces, a struggle whose outcome was unclear. In the process, events served to underline the unique character and specific challenges confronting reform efforts in each state. The paradoxes inherent in each revolution, in turn, often masked more practical limits to regional integration and development.

## Vietnam faces economic challenges

Vietnam experienced a drop in foreign trade and a decline in foreign investment as early as 1996. Over the next two years, a series of shocks rocked the Vietnamese economy – declining growth rates, peasant unrest, a crippling typhoon and the aftermath of the Asian financial crisis. Fundamental causes for the deteriorating economic climate included government protection of some 6,000 inefficient, debt-ridden state enterprises and a weak, corrupt financial system. In addition, a combination of internal forces, including excessive red tape, Byzantine rules and regulations and pervasive corruption, impacted negatively on the prevailing investment climate.[1]

A sharp decline in economic growth sparked calls for accelerated reform from international financial institutions and donor countries. The World Bank in 1998 joined the International Monetary Fund in telling the Vietnamese government that certain types of financial assistance would now be contingent on its adoption of appropriate reforms. The global donor community, meeting in Paris in December 1998, endorsed the concept of aid conditionality, tying $500 million in potential Vietnamese assistance to the adoption of an accelerated *doi moi* program.[2] Vietnam responded with a three-point plan of structural and sectoral reform centered on state enterprises, the banking system and trade reform. Hanoi readily agreed to the reform program in late 1998, but it made no effort in the following year to carry out its commitments. As a result, the 1999 donor meeting was largely a rehash of the previous session. Donors again offered a package of conditional aid, totaling $700 million, tied to restructuring state enterprise debt, refinancing the banking system and retraining the unemployed.[3]

The Vietnamese leadership rejected out of hand financial inducements to underwrite reform efforts, fearful the requisite policy initiatives would threaten political stability. This concern and other factors led to what two Vietnam experts, Brantly Womack and Carlyle Thayer, termed reform immobilism, "a middle course of muddling through" with "policies that are conflicting in their effects." Womack concluded, "the structural weakness of immobilism is that it is permanently behind the curve of societal developments."[4]

Economic reforms enjoyed widespread support in Vietnam and continued to be supported publicly by the government; nevertheless, official support for reform continued to be tempered by the Party's concern for retention of political control. In this milieu, ideological conservatives argued that aid conditionality comprised national sovereignty. Some reforms were implemented, but the process as a whole was restrained by "excessive caution and gradualism." Like neighboring Laos, Vietnam failed to develop a comprehensive, coherent strategy for overcoming the economic downturn, electing instead to "tough out" the crisis.[5]

Given dire predictions from all sides, the Vietnamese economy surprised most observers when it revived in the coming year. Real GDP growth in 2000 was 6.8 percent, up from 4.8 percent in 1999, albeit still below the pre-1997 average of 8.2 percent. Strong performances in both exports and industry were the main sources of growth. Exports grew by 21.3 percent, driven by fast-growing manufactured exports and a surge in the value of oil shipments. The resurgence in industrial growth to 9.7 percent was spurred by rising internal and external demand with the domestic nonstate sector outperforming the foreign and state sectors. Agriculture also performed well despite floods in the central region and drought in the north. Imports grew by 29 percent, compared with only 3.8 percent in 1999, reducing the current account surplus to 2 percent of GDP. The slowdown in foreign direct investment also continued. Vietnam followed accommodative fiscal and monetary policies in the year 2000, and inflation continued to fall. Described by some as an under-performing economy, Vietnam's performance in 2000 was highly credible given the shocks experienced in recent years.[6]

A number of high-profile events in 2000 helped restore a buoyant mood to Vietnam. These included implementation of an Enterprise Law effective in January, conclusion of the U.S.–Vietnam Bilateral Trade Agreement and the opening of the Ho Chi Minh City stock exchange in July and the visit of President Bill Clinton in November.[7] Given the recent decline in foreign investment, the new Enterprise Law encouraged the private sector by reducing bureaucratic obstacles thwarting domestic investment. By year-end, 12,000 enterprises had registered under the new law, an exponential increase over the 600 registered in 1995–8.[8]

The Bilateral Trade Agreement opened the way for Normal Trading Relations with the United States which would give Vietnamese goods access to the U.S. market under the same low tariffs accorded other nations enjoying the same trading status. In so doing, it increased Vietnam's attractiveness to foreign as well as domestic investors.[9] In creating a marketplace for investment capital, the stock exchange marked an important step in the development of a market economy.[10] The Bilateral Trade Agreement and the creation of a bourse, together with President Clinton's visit, were of enormous political importance given the ideological discord prevalent within the Party, disagreement which had delayed all three events for many years.

## Long-term economic outlook

Longer term, the ten-year socioeconomic strategy adopted by the Ninth Party Congress in April 2001 set ambitious targets for the 2001–10 period. The goal of the long-term strategy was to lead Vietnam out of underdevelopment, laying the foundations for a modern, industrialized country by 2020. To accomplish this goal, GDP in 2010 was targeted to double that of 2000 while the share of agricultural employment was to drop from 66 percent to around 50 percent. Investment was set to increase to 30 percent of GDP, and exports were targeted to grow at more than twice the rate of GDP growth. As a first step, the goal for annual GDP growth over the coming five years (2001–5) was set at 7.5 percent, a target which proved optimistic. The ten-year plan recognized that Vietnam would have to restructure its economy to make it more competitive, focusing on modernization and industrialization, together with the development of a multi-sector economy. Related targets included improvements in education, the maintenance of social and political stability and a strong national defense.[11]

Despite the global recession which began in late 2000, Vietnam experienced relatively strong GDP growth in 2001–3, averaging 6.4 percent. Vigorous growth of 7.1 percent in 2003, making Vietnam the fastest growing economy in Asia after China, was supported by strong investment and private consumption. Domestic demand grew by 9.4 percent and total investment by 15.8 percent. Strong domestic demand pushed up imports, widening the trade deficit from $1.3 billion in 2002 to $3.38 billion in 2003. The strong growth in imports was the product of higher demand from industry for capital and intermediate goods and of preparations for the Southeast Asian Games held in Vietnam in December 2003. A liberalization of import restrictions also spurred imports. The current account deficit in 2003 was double the previous year but manageable due to inflows from foreign direct investment, international aid and remittances from overseas Vietnamese. The industrial sector grew a robust 9.6 percent with the nonstate subsector growing 18.7 percent. The continuing strong development of the private sector was largely the result of an improved business environment. Initial outbreaks of severe acute respiratory syndrome (SARS) and avian influenza (bird flu) were generally well managed by the government although a fresh outbreak of avian influenza in early 2005 prompted Hanoi to appeal for international assistance in containing its spread. Buoyed by improvements in the business sector and the recovery of external demand, the overall outlook for the Vietnamese economy remained positive.[12]

That said, Vietnam had clearly entered a new phase of economic development. Successful implementation of the Bilateral Trade Agreement, accession to the World Trade Organization (WTO), commitments to the ASEAN Free Trade Area to 2005 and to China's free trade arrangements with ASEAN to 2010, collectively generated new challenges for the Vietnamese economy. Hanoi's pledges to this potpourri of regional groups, donor agencies and international organizations, in effect, constituted a road map for the ongoing liberalization of the country. To remain competitive, Vietnam would have to maintain – or accelerate – reform momentum in a variety of familiar areas, including state enterprise reform, land use rights, access to capital markets, private sector development, banking reform and business and trade liberalization. In so doing, the Vietnamese leadership would have to adapt to an evolving policy-making environment in which economic policy decisions, in particular, were driven increasingly by external as well as internal dynamics.[13]

## Political reform fails to keep pace

As it approached the new millennium, the Vietnamese Communist Party faced daunting challenges in reconciling competing political interests with deepening economic reforms. A wholesale housecleaning appeared in order in the wake of rural unrest caused by local cadre abuse, several banking and smuggling scandals involving state and Party officials and a front-page commentary by former Prime Minister Pham Van Dong, suggesting the people had lost faith in the Party. At the end of the second session of the sixth plenum in February 1999, Party General Secretary Le Kha Phieu launched a three-year "criticism and self-criticism" campaign to restore unity and rid the Party of "bad elements.". Calling on the 2.3 million members of the Communist Party to declare private assets, the campaign also included injunctions against the use of official positions for private gain, deviation from the Party line, and in some cases, participation in private business. In addition to rooting out corruption, the campaign aimed to return unity and discipline to a Party torn by dissension and internecine struggle. As part of the campaign, the Party in November 1999 announced a number of leadership changes, including removal of several senior Party officials for mismanagement or corruption.[14]

As the Ninth Party Congress, scheduled for early 2001, approached, the stewardship of General Secretary Phieu was severely tested by ongoing rural unrest, the aftershocks of the Asian financial crisis and the continuing influence of old guard political leaders. In October 2000, Do Muoi, Le Duc Anh and Vo Van Kiet sent a joint letter to the Central Committee, criticizing Phieu for weak leadership, failure to revive the stagnant economy and inability to root out corruption in the Party. He was also charged with anti-democratic behavior on the grounds he aspired to be both Party leader and state president and with nepotism due to his appointment of cronies from his native Thanh Hoa province. Finally, Phieu was accused of pursuing an overly pro-China foreign policy to the extent of ordering concessions in talks to delineate the maritime boundary in the Gulf of Tonkin.[15]

In February 2001, large-scale demonstrations involving thousands of ethnic minorities broke out in the Central Highlands. The demonstrators protested local government corruption, the appropriation of ancestral lands by ethnic Vietnamese settlers, lack of religious freedoms and denial of basic rights, including education in native languages. A few protestors also called for independence for the Central Highlands region. The demonstrations were expected to fuel growing discontent with Phieu's leadership; however, he skillfully used them to rally his supporters, arguing now was not the time for a potentially destabilizing leadership change. In response, the Politburo in early April 2001 voted 12 to six to recommend his reappointment, but the Central Committee soon overturned their recommendation. By this time, Phieu was also facing charges he had misused the military intelligence services to conduct wiretaps on fellow Politburo members. The Central Committee later reprimanded both the minister of defense and the chief of the general staff for their roles in the affair.[16]

The leadership issue was finally resolved during the Ninth Party Congress which met in late April 2001. Nong Duc Manh, chairman of the National Assembly and a member of the Tay ethnic minority, replaced Phieu as Party head. The congress also reduced the size of the Central Committee from 170 to 150 members with the Politburo reduced from 19 to 15 members. The new Central Committee was largely composed of incumbent officials holding posts in the central government or provincial administrations. Military representation on the Central Committee increased slightly but dropped on the Politburo from three members to one. While some observers viewed the changes as suggesting a decrease in the influence of the military, the relative size of the military-security camp, when military and police members were counted together, actually increased given the reduction in size of the Central Committee and Politburo. The Ninth Party Congress also abolished the Politburo Standing Board, replacing it with a Secretariat. With the former body appointed by the Politburo and the latter elected by the Central Committee, this change represented a concession to supporters of internal Party democracy. Congress also dropped the position of advisor to the Central Committee, effectively eliminating the behind-the-scenes influence of retired senior officials.[17]

Immediately after the Ninth Congress, newly appointed General Secretary Manh instituted several leadership changes, including new appointments to the Central Committee's departments of ideology and culture, organization and internal security. He also initiated a series of new policies, emphasizing that policy implementation would be strengthened through a more proactive Politburo and the use of Party committees within the state apparatus. Thereafter, Manh emphasized six areas: leadership, economic development, state enterprise reform, party-building, redress of ethnic grievances and constitutional reform. Continuing the fight against corruption and the campaign for party-building, he pressed for implementation of Politburo Directive 03-CT/TW, requiring all state and Party officials to disclose their assets. Manh also pushed to give a legal basis to the changes to economic development and political renovation adopted by the Ninth Congress. The Central Committee responded in early November 2001, approving alterations to the 1992 electoral law and 32 amendments to the 1992 constitution. Most of the constitutional amendments subsequently adopted by the National Assembly simply reflected the realities of what the Political Report of the Ninth Party Congress had termed Vietnam's "socialist oriented market economy."[18]

Vietnamese authorities responded to the February 2001 demonstrations in the Central Highlands by dispatching police and military units to restore order. Several alleged ringleaders were arrested and tried later in the year. Initial reports blamed "hostile external forces" for the violence, but it was soon clear to Party leaders that the real cause was encroachment on ancestral forest homelands by lowland settlers in collusion with corrupt local officials. Restrictions on freedom of worship were also a volatile local issue. General Secretary Manh personally addressed ethnic minority grievances, visiting the three affected provinces in September 2001. He ordered increased educational opportunities for ethnic minorities, together with their increased recruitment into government service. While Manh's personal approach appeared to mark a welcome change in official policy, Vietnam's minorities continued to suffer from a mixture of land, religious and ethnic grievances. Government confiscation of land continued after 2001 as did persecution of highland Christians and suspected supporters of the U.S.-based Montagnard Foundation, Inc., an indigenous rights organization. In April 2004, coordinated demonstrations again took place in the Central Highlands to protest long-standing issues of land and religious freedoms together with three years of restrictions on freedom of movement, communication and religious practice.[19]

National Assembly elections were held in May 2002, the third round of national elections since the 1992 election reforms. The revised candidate selection process placed a premium on formal qualifications and ethical probity, and prospective candidates for the first time were required to declare their assets. While a record 762 candidates were certified as eligible to run, this total translated into a low 1.5:1 candidate to seat ratio in the 500 seat National Assembly. After three candidates were disqualified on the eve of the election, the Standing Committee of the National Assembly took the unprecedented step of reducing the number of deputies to be elected from 500 to 498 in order to comply with a 1992 law requiring all seats to be contested. Despite early enthusiasm for candidates from ethnic minorities and the private sector, as well as non-Party affiliated individuals, the results of the election were disappointing in their sameness. The number of non-Party deputies declined from 14.7 percent to 10.2 percent, and only 14 seats were represented by the private sector. Female delegates increased by a mere one percent taking the total to 27.3 percent. Of 161 self-nominated candidates, only two won seats. The incoming delegates faced the daunting task of clearing a substantial backlog from the outgoing legislature as well as bringing Vietnam's laws into compliance with the bilateral trade agreement concluded with the United States.[20]

## Reorganization, repression and reform in Vietnam

Following the National Assembly elections, the Vietnamese government reorganized into 26 ministries and 13 agencies. The revised structure included four new ministries and 15 new ministers, including five deputy ministers who were promoted. In an unusual step, the National Assembly challenged the creation of the four new ministries, arguing they over-lapped existing bodies at a time when the government should be reducing and not expanding the size of the bureaucracy. While the restructure even-tually proceeded, Prime Minister Khai was tasked with reporting back to the assembly as to how the government would prevent overlap between existing and new ministries.[21]

The now infamous Nam Cam scandal began with the arrest in mid-December 2001 of crime boss Truong Van Cam, known as Nam Cam, on ten charges, including drug-trafficking, extortion, fraud, gambling, prosti-tution and murder. The ensuing police investigation revealed an organized crime network stretching from Hanoi to Ho Chi Minh City and involving more than 150 people, including senior Party and state officials. Nam Cam's political ties in Ho Chi Minh City alone were sufficiently strong that outside police forces were brought in to arrest him. The octopus-like extent of his criminal activities combined with his high-level political con-nections to arouse intense public interest in the case. Widespread media coverage soon drew a sharp rebuke from the Communist Party which complained the popular press was not executing the principle of "follow-ing the Party's leadership." The Party expelled 22 members from the Ho Chi Minh City organization in August 2002, and a total of 155 persons were subsequently indicted in November. Politburo and Central Commit-tee members suffered collateral damage due to their alleged involvement in widespread corruption; however, the Party leadership took steps to ensure no member of the political elite was adversely affected. Nam Cam and five accomplices were later sentenced to death in June 2003 with five other defendants sentenced to life in prison and dozens of others receiving shorter sentences.[22]

As the Party wrestled with the corruption issue, it continued to harass its critics, most especially a new breed of political activist – the cyber dissi-dent. At least six cyber dissidents were arrested in 2002 for posting information on the Internet considered illegal by the regime. For example, Nguyen Khac Toan was arrested in January for posting pro-democracy material on the Internet and later sentenced to 12 years in jail followed by three years house arrest. Tran Khue was detained in March 2002 and placed under house arrest for posting on the Internet an open letter to Chinese President Jiang Zemin in which Khue criticized the 1999 Sino–Vietnamese land border settlement. Police then raided the home of Nguyen Vu Binh in July 2002, downloading his computer files and reading personal documents after he took part in a BBC interview series on promi-nent dissidents and provided written testimony to a U.S. Congressional Human Rights caucus.[23]

Reflecting official concern with cyber dissidents, Prime Minister Khai ordered a nationwide inspection of Internet access in mid-2002. The Min-istry of Culture and Information later announced plans to tighten Internet controls, including reinforcement of firewalls to block material threatening national security. In June 2004, Vietnam directed Internet-cafe operators to monitor and record the websites visited by users. Vietnamese attempts to control the Internet mirrored Chinese restrictions on the medium, which were among the most invasive in the world, and contradicted the goal of the sixth plenum to use information technology to spur economic development. International bodies like Human Rights Watch also reported a deterioration in the treatment of other Vietnamese dissidents in 2003–4, including Buddhists, political dissidents and ethnic minority Christians.[24]

Assuming office after a period of drift and discontent, General Secretary Manh championed the fight against "negative phenomena" like red tape, corruption and wastage at state agencies. At the seventh plenum of the Party Central Committee, for example, Manh emphasized:

> Exemplary acts shown by Party officials and members, government employees and their families are of important significance toward the fight against corruption and negative phenomena. It is also necessary to show a strong resolve to effectively combat corruption and negative phenomena, considering this a top criterion to examine the qualifications of each Party official and member as well as government employee, especially the head of each office and organization.[25]

Nevertheless, the campaign against corruption was notably less successful than the campaign against political dissent. Corruption was endemic and touched the highest levels of the state. In June 2004, for example, the Minister of Agriculture and Rural Development was sacked over suspected links to a massive embezzlement case; and in October 2004, the chairman of the management board of the National Shipping Lines was dismissed for illegal authorization of petroleum contracts. Although government efforts to curb graft evidenced some success in 2005, most observers agreed eliminating corruption among Vietnamese officials would require far-reaching changes in the transparency of government decision making and the accountability of public officials.

General Secretary Manh successfully advanced the socioeconomic strategy outlined by the Fifth Party Congress, approaching most of the goals in the Five-Year Plan (2001–5). He also improved the capacity of the Party and state to establish and implement public policy under the rubric of "party-building" and the creation of a "law governed state." As part of this effort, he worked to make Party officials more accountable. For example, the Party in early 2003 introduced new regulations for its key organizations in an effort to institutionalize what was morally acceptable behavior for top Party members. The Central Committee and not the Politburo made the rules, signaling a recognition that authority must come from the larger Central Committee as opposed to the smaller Politburo.

Another reform in governance involved the rotation of senior officials within the bureaucracy to broaden their experience.[26]

At the same time, it must be recognized that Manh's efforts to create a "law governed state" were not necessarily steps in the direction of political liberalization. Intent on maintaining the Party in power, not bringing about its demise, Manh repeatedly stressed the close relationship between political stability and economic development.

> We should know clearly the relationship between stability and development; socio-political stability serves as the precedent for socio-economic development while socio-economic development is the condition for stabilizing socio-political life. Up to now, our country has maintained political stability, but in some places, the situation sometimes became complicated with hidden factors possibly causing instability, that cannot be ignored. At the same time, hostile forces have time and again sought ways to distort, slander, incite and sow the seeds of division among religious sects, the nation and the all-people unity.[27]

The Vietnamese Communist Party in the new millennium executed a carefully paced program of political reform in which the Vietnamese people increasingly enjoyed a limited array of personal freedoms; however, questioning Party rule or assembling to challenge authority were still prohibited. The Party continued to rule the country through the traditional structure of Party cells and Party committees with little real change in the political system inherited from the past.[28]

## Foreign relations

Sino-Vietnamese relations outstripped all others in this period in terms of bilateral exchanges between Party, state and military officials. Vietnam and China reached a comprehensive agreement on their land boundary in late December 1999, delineating their 1,300 km land frontier. The Bac Bo Gulf treaty, completed one year later, delineated their maritime boundary in the Gulf of Tonkin. However, rival claims over the Spratly and Paracel islands remained unresolved. The Ninth Party Congress in April 2002 endorsed plans to build logistical bases and resettle people on the islands as part of Vietnam's economic and defense strategy. In a March 2002 visit to Vietnam, Chinese President and Party General Secretary Jiang Zemin stressed the "Chinese and Vietnamese people have the same ideology" and called for increased bilateral economic ties. Consistent with this thinking, at least ten high-level exchanges at the Politburo and Central Committee levels took place in 2003 tying the two states in a web of relations, ranging from border demarcation to trade and investment to ideological cooperation. At the same time, Vietnam boosted its economic ties with

Taiwan, the number one investor in Vietnam in 2003, whereas China ranked seventeenth. In April 2004, a boatload of 100 Vietnamese tourists sailed on an inaugural voyage to the disputed Spratly Islands despite strong Chinese protests. To promote responsible management of water resources in the Greater Mekong Basin, Vietnam later proposed a so-called "friendly" amendment at the November 2004 World Conservation Congress which suggested construction of hydropower dams on the Mekong mainstream require the prior agreement of all countries in the region. The wording of the amendment upset China which denied its upstream dams had depleted water levels in the river.[29]

Following years of confidence-building, Vietnamese relations with Thailand began to improve with officials from both states regularly exchanging visits. Thai authorities were especially interested in Viet-namese progress towards construction of the East–West Corridor project, a network of roads linking central Vietnam with Laos and Thailand. Thai Prime Minister Thaksin Shinawatra visited Vietnam in April 2001 and returned in February 2004 to participate in the first joint-cabinet meeting between the two governments. A variety of issues were discussed, includ-ing cooperation on narcotics, exchanges among military academies and extradition matters. Thai investors expressed interest in Vietnamese mining, and the Thai government invited Vietnamese enterprises to invest in its energy sector. During the meeting, representatives of Thailand and Vietnam signed two agreements, a Joint Statement on Thailand–Vietnam Cooperation in the First Decade of the 21st Century and a Framework Agreement on Economic Cooperation. The first document outlined the general direction of future relations and established a joint consultation mechanism, co-chaired by their respective foreign ministers, to review implementation of cooperative programs. The second pact identified six areas of economic cooperation comprising trade, investment, finance, infrastructure development, energy and human resource development. Thailand in mid-2004 ranked ninth among foreign investors in Vietnam, and it was the second-leading ASEAN investor after Singapore.[30]

Following ethnic demonstrations in the Central Highlands of Vietnam, relations with Cambodia were turbulent in 2001. The arrest of 24 asylum seekers in Mondolkiri province drew attention to the anti-Hanoi FULRO (United Front for the Struggle of the Oppressed Races) movement whose members were active in the dense forests along the Cambodia–Vietnam border. Cambodia initially agreed to treat the asylum seekers as refugees and to repatriate them to Vietnam. Under pressure from human rights groups and the United States, it later reversed this decision, to the chagrin of Hanoi, and permitted them to leave for the United States where they were granted refugee status by the United Nations High Commission for Refugees (UNHCR). Notwithstanding this prolonged controversy, overall relations with Cambodia remained generally good.[31]

Vietnam maintained traditionally strong ties with fellow travelers in

Laos. Aspects of its close relationship with the Lao PDR resembled China's relationship with Vietnam in that Hanoi provided much needed ideological succor and legitimization to the communists in Vientiane. For example, Vietnam sent specialists to Laos in 2002 to exchange experiences on finance and banking issues, like inflation control and exchange rate balancing; and in 2003, senior Vietnamese officials called for creation of a trade development zone on the Lao border.[32]

Despite close ties with China, Vietnam looked to Russia as its principal source of military hardware and training. In July 1999, the two allies concluded a military agreement providing for comprehensive military-technical cooperation, Vietnamese training in Russian military schools, arms supplies and a service and repair facility in Vietnam for Russian-sourced equipment. Prime Minister Khai later visited Russia, concluding an agreement in September 2000 which resolved the vexing debt issue between the two states. Vietnam agreed to pay Russia $1.7 billion over 23 years with 10 percent in cash and the remainder in business concessions and the provision of goods and services. During Russian President Vladimir Putin's visit to Vietnam, the two sides in March 2001 concluded a strategic partnership which involved long-term economic cooperation and arms sales. The agreement was later devalued when Russia announced in October that it planned to withdraw the last of its military forces from Cam Ranh Bay in early 2002. General Secretary Manh visited Russia in October 2002, and Vietnam continued to purchase Russian weaponry, ordering two air defense batteries in September 2003 at a cost of $300 million.[33]

Japan remained a major donor to Vietnam as well as its largest overall investor. The cumulative disbursed value of Japanese investment in Vietnam in 1988–2003 approximated $4 billion. In November 2003, the two countries concluded a landmark pact which guaranteed Most Favored Nation treatment to investors in both states. The agreement was highly significant because Japanese investment in Vietnam, which was very strong in 1992–7, dropped off sharply in the wake of the Asian financial crisis when regional competition to attract Japanese investment intensified. Representatives of Japan and Vietnam also signed a Joint Initiative in December 2003, an agreement designed to facilitate investment in Vietnam. In the initiative, Hanoi pledged to take a number of steps to improve its investment climate, such as developing a strategic plan, improving local infrastructure and easing investment rules and regulations.[34]

Bilateral relations with the United States reached a new level in March 2000 when William Cohen became the first U.S. secretary of defense to visit Vietnam since the end of the Second Indochina War. The conclusion of the Bilateral Trade Agreement in July set the stage for a November 2000 visit by President Bill Clinton, the first visit to Vietnam by a U.S. president since 1969. Unfortunately, Clinton's meeting with General Secretary Phieu proved a stilted affair in which Phieu lectured his guest, condemning imperialism. Clinton responded with an extended rebuttal of Phieu's description of U.S. aims during the Second Indochina War. Phieu's comments played well with Party conservatives, but reformers viewed his remarks as backward and ill-advised. Responding to the 9/11 terrorist attacks on the World Trade Center and Pentagon, Vietnam offered sympathy and condemned terrorism but warned against a counterproductive U.S. reaction. Vietnam and the United States in October 2003 agreed to resume direct air service; and a U.S. warship visited Ho Chi Minh City in November 2003. Following a trip to Washington by Vietnamese Defense Minister Pham Van Tra, a visit which marked a new stage in U.S.–Vietnamese security relations, Admiral Thomas Fargo, head of the U.S. Pacific Command, visited Danang in February 2004. In mid-November 2004, the first commercial U.S. airliner to fly to Vietnam since the end of the Second Indochina War landed in Ho Chi Minh City.[35]

Ratification of the Bilateral Trade Agreement set the stage for Vietnam to be accorded Normal Trade Relations (NTR) status with U.S. tariffs dropping from around 40 percent to 5 percent. In 2002, the first full year of implementation, Vietnamese exports to the United States more than doubled to $2.4 billion, almost doubling again in 2003. Nonetheless, bilateral trade relations were not without their problems. Vietnamese fish farmers were furious when the U.S. Department of Commerce in June 2003 ruled catfish imports from Vietnam would be subject to anti-dumping duties of 45–64 percent. In the wake of the catfish ruling, the Southern Shrimp Alliance, a coalition of U.S. shrimp producers, lodged a similar anti-dumping petition against six shrimp producing countries, including Vietnam. Washington responded in early July 2004, announcing it would impose preliminary tariffs in the range of 12–20 percent on Vietnamese shrimp imports, applying much lower, company-specific tariffs in November. A garment and textile pact between the United States and Vietnam in April 2003 also set quotas on Vietnamese imports, and Vietnamese manufacturers faced additional quotas following charges Chinese-made garments were being trans-shipped through Vietnam to the United States. The end of the Multifiber Agreement among World Trade Organization members in 2005 left Vietnam, not yet a WTO member, shackled by export quotas under its bilateral trade agreement with the United States. On a more positive note, the U.S. government in June 2004 designated Vietnam a "focus nation" in the global fight against HIV/AIDS, making it eligible for special funding to combat the scourge. Ongoing talks on trade and investment issues, together with preparations for a U.S.–Vietnam summit, also provided ample opportunities for U.S. constituencies to engage Vietnam on other issues of concern like human rights, religious freedom and labor rights.[36]

Vietnam assumed in July 2000 the rotating chairmanship of the ASEAN Standing Committee which contributed to Hanoi's image as an active ASEAN member even though the organization's flexible agenda made few demands on Vietnamese diplomacy. In the role of chairman, Vietnam hosted the ASEAN Senior Officials Meeting, Thirty-Fourth ASEAN Foreign Ministers Meeting, Eighth ASEAN Regional Forum, Fourth ASEAN Plus Three Meeting and the ASEAN Post-Ministerial Conference. Hosting these meetings enhanced Vietnam's position in the international arena and increased ASEAN's confidence in Vietnam's future. Vietnam also took advantage of its temporary chairmanship to shunt aside the constructive engagement approach advocated by Thailand, and it stood firm on the principle of noninterference, steadfastly defending the policy against international pressure. Vietnam hosted a regional conference on immigration in September 2003, calling on ASEAN to establish the framework necessary to achieve visa-free travel within the ASEAN states by 2005. In a four-nation mini-summit on the eve of the November 2004 ASEAN meeting in Vientiane, Burma, Cambodia, Laos and Vietnam later agreed to explore the idea of issuing single-entry visas valid for travel within their four states.[37]

## Severe crisis in Laos

The aftershocks of the Asian financial crisis hit Laos like a tsunami. With the Lao economy heavily oriented toward Thailand, the sharp drop in the value of the Thai baht produced an even sharper drop in the value of the Lao kip, causing hyperinflation and skyrocketing prices for imported goods. Inflation exceeded 90 percent in 1998 and approached 130 percent in 1999. The quasi-insolvent condition of state-owned domestic banks, where nonperforming loans from state enterprises and others constituted around 60 percent of total loans, contributed to the sharp deterioration in the kip. Lao exports also fell off sharply and foreign investment evaporated, contributing to mounting balance of payment and debt repayment problems.[38]

Faced with a severe crisis, the gerontocratic leadership of the Lao People's Revolutionary Party proved incapable of a decisive response. With seven of the nine members of the Politburo sharing military backgrounds and little formal education, their policy priorities remained preservation of both the Party's political power monopoly and the influence of the army. When Western governments and international lending agencies called on Laos to accelerate economic reforms and improve macroeconomic management, Lao authorities turned to Vietnam and China for counsel and guidance. At least four high-level Party exchanges with Vietnam and two with China took place in 1999. It was only toward the end of the year that the Lao PDR began to introduce remedial measures to strengthen the economy.[39]

Macroeconomic conditions improved in 2000 when Laos regained some control over fiscal policy and instituted a tighter monetary policy. Real GDP rose by 5.5 percent as both imports and exports expanded. Increased tax revenues and reduced public expenditures were central components of improved fiscal policy, but expenditure reductions came largely from the social sectors which threatened longer term growth. The central bank improved its control of the money supply, restricting the credit policy of state-owned commercial banks and increasing the sale of treasury bills to absorb excess liquidity. The improved macroeconomic stance contributed to a significant decrease in the budget deficit which reduced both monetary financing of the deficit and the inflation rate. Inflation declined steadily after late 1999, dropping to around 23 percent in 2000. Nevertheless, the rate of inflation rate remained much higher than that of the Lao PDR's major trading partners which meant the kip would again have to be depreciated.[40]

## Measured recovery, worrying trends

The Lao economy continued its recovery in 2001–4. In a September 2003 address to the National Assembly, Prime Minister Bounnyang Vorachit described the overall macroeconomic situation as stable and on track for development. On the negative side, President Saman Vignaket highlighted weaknesses in government administration, low production rates, corruption, illegal trade, drug trafficking and an inefficient use of overseas loans, grants and investment. GDP growth in 2003 was 5.9 percent, similar to growth rates in the previous two years. The overall budget deficit, financed mostly by grants and external concessional loans, was 7.8 percent of GDP in fiscal year 2003, an improvement over the previous year but still over target. Revenue mobilization remained a major and worsening problem, but expenditure control improved. The rate of inflation, averaging 15.5 percent in 2003, was one of the highest in the region. The merchandise trade deficit narrowed to approximately $135 million, continuing a trend evident for several years. While foreign direct investment increased only slightly, approvals increased sharply, raising hopes FDI might return to the higher levels last seen five years ago.[41]

On the other hand, the future of Laos's most ambitious development project, the controversial 1,070 megawatt (MW) Nam Theun 2 hydroelectric power station, continued in doubt. After the Electricity Generating Authority of Thailand (EGAT) agreed to buy its electricity, a dispute arose over the terms of the purchase agreement, delaying finance for the project. Nam Theun 2 was challenged on several grounds, including Thailand's future power needs and the threatened environmental consequences of the project. It was only in November 2003 that EGAT finally agreed to buy 995 MW over 25 years beginning in 2009, and Electricité du Laos agreed to take the remaining 75 MW. Even with the purchase agreement concluded, the project remained contingent on a partial risk guarantee from the World Bank which would open the door to financing from the Asian Development Bank and other international sources.[42]

At the same time, many aspects of the Lao economy, together with the government's management of the economy, evidenced worrying trends. A report published in January 2002 by Focus on the Global South, a Bangkok-based policy research group, highlighted the negative impact centralized decision making had on public policy communication and implementation.

> The current political culture in the Lao PDR is not conducive to formal public debate about macro level policies. Members of the general public and even government officials at mid and lower levels are often unfamiliar with macro development concepts and therefore unconfident in their abilities to engage meaningfully in national planning processes. When policies are put in the public realm, there is little space for dissent, and even fewer channels by which the views and concerns of local civil society can be fed back into the policy development process. So much for World Bank speak about the poor becoming "active participants."[43]

Moreover, the Lao PDR had yet to carry out comprehensive structural reforms. The state banking system clearly required additional reforms to put it on a commercially sound basis. And the government continued to subsidize state enterprises when they needed to be restructured to reduce nonperforming loans, a move which would complement banking reforms. Interventionist policies prevented free market forces from reaching their full potential, and some government policies were counterproductive. When international lending agencies encouraged Laos to increase revenue collection, for example, it raised tariffs on imported goods which contributed to inflationary pressures and increased smuggling. Laos also suffered from mismanagement of foreign aid and often failed to achieve macroeconomic targets. The total external debt stood at approximately $3 billion or around 150 percent of GDP and continued to grow. While this was a significant debt burden, more than half the total was owed to Russia which agreed in June 2003 to write-off 70 percent and to service the remainder over 33 years.[44]

The dual nature of the Lao economy also continued, and in some ways, worsened. As economist Yves Bourdet observed, "the spatial dimension of growth is a critical factor in the development of regional economic disparities that can exacerbate social, ethnic, and political tensions." National income in Laos had long been distributed unevenly among provinces and different types of households. And the economic reforms introduced in the 1990s exacerbated widening provincial income disparities as well as those between urban and rural areas.[45]

Finally and most disappointing, Laos continued to be heavily dependent on foreign aid. In the previous decade, official development assistance had increased to the point it represented around 20 percent of GDP. At the same time, the composition of international aid shifted with grants accounting for an increasingly smaller share and loans a larger one. Among other things, this change in aid composition had important ramifications for the future growth of external debt, threatening creation of yet another debt-strapped Third World state. The concentration of aid dependency in a few sectors, like communications, public health, transportation and social welfare, also had important, albeit unclear, implications. The Asian Development Bank remained the principal source of external assistance. Other donors included Australia, Belgium, the European Union, France, Germany, the International Monetary Fund, Japan, South Korea, Sweden, the United Nations Development Program, the United States and Vietnam.[46]

Professor Hans Luther, an informal adviser to the Lao government for many years, emphasized the downside of foreign aid dependence in a June 2003 interview as he prepared to return to Germany after a decade at the National School of Administration in Vientiane.

> Foreign aid is like a drug. You want more and more of it because it makes development much easier for you. Instead of putting up your own money for building roads and repairing them, you get rich foreigners to do it for you. There are also kickbacks and all kinds of benefits. It is the easy way out in economic development. Now what should a poor country like Laos do? They should be modest and have some clear priorities. But most opt for foreign aid as it seems to promise everything at the same time.
>
> But people forget that with foreign aid, one does not necessarily have ownership. There are grants but also loans which have to be paid back. During the time I have been here the amount of foreign aid contributed to the national budget has doubled.
>
> Therefore, it can in fact be shown that this country is increasing its dependence on foreign aid. Aid is not creating sustainable economic growth, only aid-induced growth.[47]

## Discontent and infighting in Laos

The aftershocks of the Asian financial crisis precipitated both leadership changes and an unprecedented anti-government demonstration in Vientiane. Lao President Khamtay Siphandone in August 1999 dismissed the finance minister and the central bank governor after the latter admitted efforts to combat inflation were "not entirely successful." Amid persistent reports the finance ministry and central bank disagreed over how to deal with the ailing economy, informed observers agreed the dismissals were the result of mismanagement of banking and fiscal policies. Seven weeks later, police arrested several Lao students and teachers in front of the presidential office where they were protesting the failure of the government to address the country's economic problems. A brochure distributed by the students made nine demands, including resignation of the government, dissolution of the National Assembly and conduct of free and fair elections. The students also demanded the release of all political prisoners, amnesty for Lao exiles and dialog with opposition groups. While not the first challenge to the Lao People's Revolutionary Party, this was the first broad-based civil movement involving students, teachers and other professionals dissatisfied with government policy. In the week following the unprecedented public protest, police jailed an additional 25 students implicated in the affair.[48]

The October 1999 protests marked the beginning of an extended campaign of opposition to LPRP rule which included a wave of mysterious bombings. In mid-February 2000, Prince Soulivang Savang, Crown Prince of Laos and heir to the throne, held a press conference in which he raised his resistance profile, calling for assistance in dismantling the communist regime. The prince's grandfather, grandmother and father died in "reeducation camps" after being imprisoned by the communists. Throughout the spring, ethnic Hmong rebels staged hit-and-run attacks in central Laos, prompting foreign embassies to issue warnings against travel in remote areas. In early April, more than a dozen people, including several Western tourists, were injured when a bomb exploded in a popular Vientiane restaurant. The deteriorating security situation prompted Prince Soulivang Savang to issue a press release in late April calling on the United Nations to appoint a special commission to investigate the status of human rights in Laos and the location and condition of all political prisoners. It also prompted the Vietnamese government to dispatch troops and military equipment to Laos to assist the government in putting down the unrest.[49]

The bombing campaign continued throughout 2000, including attacks in Vientiane on the central post office in August and the international airport in November. Another large explosion rocked Vientiane in mid-December, only hours before an ASEAN-EU ministerial conference was set to convene. Termed "an event of great significance" by Prime Minister Sisavath Keobounphanh, the conference was the largest international gathering hosted to that time by the Lao government. Sporadic guerrilla raids also continued throughout the year, including the brief occupation of a border post in early July where rebels raised the royal flag on Lao soil for the first time in almost 25 years. In between periods of denial, the government alternatively blamed the attacks on exiled royalists or foreign-based Hmong led by the former resistance leader, General Vang Pao.[50]

The government responded by cracking down on domestic opposition, imposing an informal curfew in Vientiane in September 2000. It also banned Internet use for anti-government activity, promising to prosecute or expel violators. Aimed at Lao citizens accessing websites created by Lao exiles, the new rules prohibited use of the Internet in the "wrong way" by "lying, deceiving or persuading people inside or outside the country to protest against the Lao People's Revolutionary Party and the government." In mid-November 2000, a little more than one year after the abortive student protest in Vientiane, 15 people were arrested in Champassack province after more than 200 students and civil servants staged a pro-democracy rally. Regime credibility suffered yet another blow in late 2000 when it was confirmed that Khamsai Souphanouvong, son of the Lao PDR's first president, had been granted political asylum in New Zealand.[51]

The year-long opposition campaign did not pose a serious threat to Party rule, but it raised questions about the legitimacy of the leadership elected at the Sixth Party Congress. The 1996 congress represented a clear setback for reform advocates as it strengthened the power of the Party faction opposed to far-reaching reform. The inability of the government to deal effectively with the regional financial crisis and the outbreak of opposition combined to raise new questions about Old Guard leadership. In a stubborn display of normalcy, the Party celebrated the twenty-fifth anniversary of its rise to power in December 2000, four months after the fact and amid very heavy security. A highlight of the celebrations was the inauguration of a multi-million dollar museum memorial to veteran communist leader Kaysone Phomvihane, yet another milestone in the personality cult still being constructed eight years after his death. With Kaysone a trusted Hanoi protégé and ally, Vietnam paid half the memorial construction costs and contributed many of the photographs and documents on display.[52]

According to a widely read article in the *Far Eastern Economic Review* written by Bertil Lintner and Shawn Crispin, two well-respected journalists, dissension within the Party reflected three overlapping conflicts between older and younger members, pro-Vietnamese and pro-Chinese factions and northern and southern provinces. The article also suggested the bombing campaign was the product of internecine struggle within the Party and not the result of opposition groups. Others disputed both the genesis of the intra-Party struggle and the instigators of the bombing campaign. Lao expert Grant Evans, for example, suggested the bombing campaign was conducted by anarchists opposed to the existing system. The principal representatives of the Old Guard, which constituted a majority in the Party, included President Khamtay Siphandone, Prime Minister Sisavath Keobounphanh and Defense Minister Choummaly Sayasone. Foreign Minister Somsavat Lengsawat, an ethnic Chinese from Luang Prabang province in northern Laos, was the main proponent of the relatively more progressive group opposing them.[53]

## Confessions but no concessions

Following months of careful preparation, the Seventh Party Congress opened in Vientiane in March 2001. The 452 delegates to the congress represented approximately 100,000 Party members or roughly 2 percent of the total population. Representatives from the remaining communist states – China, Cuba, North Korea and Vietnam – as well as neighboring countries were also on hand. Preceded by months of intense, secret talks among the Party's senior leadership, the congress itself lasted only three days. It was held amid very tight security measures, given the bombing campaign that had rocked the capital for more than a year.[54]

Veteran Lao watcher Bourdet captured the spirit of the Seventh Party Congress when he styled it "confessions without concessions." In an effort to conciliate the younger generation, the congress ratified cosmetic changes to the composition of both the Politburo and Central Committee. To placate an international donor community financing some 80 percent of Lao development expenditures, it also adopted vague statements promising market-friendly economic reforms and improved governance. Nonetheless, the Old Guard retained its grip on power with State President Khamtay Siphandone continuing as General Secretary of the Party. Seven of the remaining eight members of the Politburo also retained their posts with only the ninth member, deceased Vice President Oudom Khattigna, being replaced. Two seats were added to the Politburo, bringing the total to eleven; however, this change reflected a desire to give the top leadership a younger look as opposed to signaling ideological renewal. Two of the three new Politburo members were educated in Vietnam and the Soviet Union while the third was the military chief of staff. Central Committee membership was also expanded from 49 to 53 seats to add younger Party cadre, but its average age remained relatively high at 56 years.[55]

Elements of surrealism bordering on schizophrenia characterized the Seventh Party Congress. The confirmation of Old Guard control of the Party, together with a proliferation of hammer and sickle flags around Vientiane, contrasted sharply with an implicit repudiation of communist economics. General Secretary Khamtay referred to socialism and stated the Party still adhered to Marxist-Leninist principles but also recognized that corruption and a lack of trained personnel contributed to the policy failures of the 1990s. The Party set an annual growth target of 7 percent for 2001–5 but remained vague as to the market-oriented reforms necessary to achieve this optimistic goal. The long-term objectives approved by the congress, tripling per capita income and eliminating poverty by 2020, were equally unrealistic. With population growth per annum running at 2.8 percent, the population would double by 2025. At the same time, the sectoral distribution of growth remained concentrated in industry and services while poverty was largely a rural phenomenon and could only be addressed by raising rural growth.[56]

The Lao government was reshuffled in March 2001 to reflect changes in the Party hierarchy. Bounnyang Vorachit, a former finance minister and number six in the Party hierarchy, replaced the aging Sisavath Keobounphanh, blamed for the policy failures of the late 1990s, as prime minister.

The elevation of Bounnyang was a compromise between the military faction of President Khamtay and the more ideological wing of former President Nouhak Phoumsavanh, the only living member of the initial resistance government of 1950. Other changes included the appointment of Soukanh Mahalath, a former central bank governor, as finance minister and the designation of Foreign Minister Somsavat Lengsawat as a deputy prime minister. At the same time, Somsavat was not elected to the Politburo; and his command of foreign policy issues appeared weakened by the elevation of Thongloun Sisoulith, chairman of the National Assembly's Foreign Affairs Commission, to the Politburo. Thongloun was also named deputy prime minister in charge of the State Planning Committee.[57]

## Consolidating power in the one-party state

In the National Assembly elections held in February 2002, nearly a year earlier than expected, the Party consolidated its hold on power. The elections were pulled forward to bring them in line with the Five-Year Plan and the Eighth Party Congress in 2006 in addition to accommodating reforms promised to donor countries. All but one of the 166 candidates approved by the Party to contest 109 available seats were Party members with 53 high-ranking Party incumbents, mostly members of the Politburo and Central Committee, running for reelection. No foreign poll observers were invited or allowed, and the foreign media was restricted to monitoring only the political campaign in Vientiane. As a result, the official election results, indicating 99.23 percent of the 2.5 million eligible voters went to the polls, were impossible to verify but questionable in a country where voters in remote areas might have to walk two days to reach a polling station.[58]

President Khamtay carried out an unexpected cabinet reshuffle in January 2003, changing his economic team in a bid to improve the fragile economy. Among the changes announced, Chansy Phosikham, a former governor of the state bank, was named finance minister; and Phoumi Thipphavone was moved from the commerce ministry to governor of the state bank. The cabinet reshuffle consisted of a rotation of old power-holders, as opposed to an injection of new blood into the system, and produced no dramatic changes in economic policy or management.[59]

In February 2003, officials unveiled a statue of the legendary fourteenth century ruler, King Fa Ngum. He ruled over the Kingdom of Lan Xang (million elephants), an expansive empire which stretched from southern China over much of what is now mainland Southeast Asia. The celebration of Fa Ngum lasted four days; and according to Catherine Raymond, Director of the Center for Burma Studies at Northern Illinois University, it "was organized in close accord with classical descriptions of rituals for consecrating Buddha images considered important enough to be patronized by the Lao kings." This appeal to tradition was in stark contrast to the

harsh treatment meted out earlier to the direct descendants of the monarchy. Even more striking, the ruling Party sought to depict itself as the
direct descendant of a Lao monarch that had both unified the Lao people
and introduced them to Theravada Buddhism. A variety of motives were
behind this radical shift in policy. In addition to providing a new basis for
regime legitimization in a "fractiously and ethnically heterogeneous population," a revival of respect for the monarchy served to build bridges to the
Lao exile community. It also countered Thai cultural influence centered
on an increase in the popularity of the Thai royal family among ordinary
Lao.[60]

In a related effort to shore up the one-party-state's legitimacy, the
National Assembly in May 2003 amended the constitution and brought
forward legislation, pending since September 2001, to hold municipal elections for the first time since 1975. The legislation called for pilot elections
in the four provinces of Champassak, Luang Prabang, Khammuan and
Savannakhat to be followed by municipal elections nationwide. The legislation also provided for an increased measure of financial autonomy for
municipal authorities.[61]

As the communist regime moved to buttress its legitimacy, sporadic
ambushes, bombings and dissident acts combined to create an atmosphere
of persistent insecurity. Rebel forces mounted repeated attacks on road
transportation, especially on Route 13 between Vientiane and Luang
Prabang. In June 2003, a bus was bombed near Thakhek in the south; and
in August, another bus was attacked in northern Laos and a bomb
exploded in the capital. Additional incidents were reported in October in
Vientiane and in the southern province of Savannakhet. The perpetrators
of the attacks remained unclear with the government attributing them to
bandits while foreign diplomats ascribed them to a mixture of ethnic
minority rebels, anti-communist exiles and disaffected members of the Lao
armed forces. The Lao Citizens Movement for Democracy (LCMD)
announced in mid-July 2003 the initiation of a revolution to overthrow the
government. Allegedly representing 20 opposition groups, the LCMD
claimed to have begun military operations in 11 Lao provinces.[62]

Thereafter, the U.S.-based Fact Finding Committee (FFC), consisting
of anti-communist Lao exiles and their American supporters, issued a
stream of press releases, making unverifiable claims of military success
against the Lao army. Government officials admitted only that limited
fighting had broken out in a few areas while the Thai military reported
minor incidents along the border. In February 2004, the German-based
Committee for Independence and Democracy in Laos claimed responsibility for small explosions in Vientiane and central Savannakhet province
to call attention and demand regime change towards democracy in Laos.
The upsurge in attacks drew media attention to the sorry plight of the few
remaining Hmong resistance forces. Numbering around 3,000 people,
including women and children, they were surrounded by the Lao army and

allegedly subjected to a deliberate policy of starvation. As the Lao army continued to battle small groups of Hmong rebels, roughly 1,000 of them surrendered their arms and returned to civilian life in early 2004 under a government resettlement program. Ironically, as the rebel threat lessened, Laos faced a new challenge in the form of HIV/AIDS transmission. UN health officials and NGO representatives joined in warning the Lao people were increasingly at risk of contacting HIV/AIDS as a growing number of road projects turned Laos into a regional transportation hub.[63]

Despite a long history of security concerns, there was scant evidence the LPRP was likely to move away from one-party rule in the foreseeable future. Events after 1999 appeared to represent the most serious challenge to Party rule since it came to power in 1975; however, there was little to suggest the attacks, raids and bombings constituted a serious threat to the regime. The Party responded promptly and aggressively with a familiar mix of repressive measures, symbolic gestures and cosmetic reforms. Whatever the claims of groups like the LCMD and FFC, there was no evidence of a sustained, credible threat to the regime. Signs of increased transparency or improved governance were equally scarce.

## Lao foreign affairs

At the ASEAN Ministerial Meeting in July 1999, Lao Foreign Minister Somsavat Lengsawat criticized member states for responding individually, not collectively, to the regional crisis. He also reminded his colleagues of the goals in the 1998 Hanoi Plan of Action, a six-year plan covering the period 1999–2004, to reduce disparities in economic development among member states. With a divided ASEAN offering limited assistance, Laos turned to old friends and allies, China and Vietnam, for counsel and support.[64]

In the aftermath of the Asian financial crisis, Vientiane expanded its ties with Beijing as China moved to increase its influence in Laos as part of a broader strategy of economic expansion into Southeast Asia. Chinese President Jiang Zemin paid the first ever visit of a Chinese head of state to Laos in mid-November 2000, reaching agreement on closer economic and technical cooperation as well as more Chinese aid for Laos. Beijing later praised the appointment of Prime Minister Bounnyang Vorachit in March 2001, a move widely reported in the international press as signaling a more China-friendly Laos. With considerable Chinese aid focused on infrastructure projects, Laos announced in May 2002 the official opening of three new roads, linking Vientiane with cities in China's Yunnan province. Other areas of bilateral cooperation included drug control, trade and transportation and student exchanges. President Khamtay made an official visit to Beijing in June 2003, praising China's economic achievements. With bilateral trade and investment expanding, Chinese Vice Premier Wu Yi visited Vientiane in March 2004, concluding 11 separate agreements in agriculture, chemical production and hydropower exploration.[65] China's economic presence in Laos was poised to expand in the coming years, especially in northern Laos, as Beijing moved to become a regional power-house in Southeast Asia.

Disappointed with the limited regional support available during the Asian financial crisis, Laos turned to Vietnam for guidance and aid, rein-vigorating political ties and expanding commercial relations. At the request of the Lao government, Vietnamese troops intervened in Xiang Khouang province in mid-2000 when the Hmong rebellion escalated and Lao army casualties mounted. The Ho Chi Minh National Politics Institute in Hanoi also offered a series of "refresher" courses for Lao officials. According to the official *Vietnam News Agency*, Lao trainees at the political academy "studied Marxism–Leninism, Ho Chi Minh's ideology, social-ist renovation in Party and administrative building work, and conducted practical studies."[66] Evidence of expanded economic ties could be seen in deeper cooperation between border provinces as well as stepped up cross-border and barter trade. Vietnamese investment increased in strategic sectors of the Lao economy, like agro-processing, construction, forestry and transportation; and Hanoi provided financial and auditing assistance to Vientiane. The Vietnamese provision of foreign aid to Laos was note-worthy because Vietnam at the time was the world's second largest recipi-ent of overseas development assistance. The Lao case illustrated what economist Bourdet termed "international fungibility," a situation in which Western aid to one country (Vietnam) freed domestic resources to be used by that country to expand its influence in another country (Laos).[67]

In May 2002, during an official visit to Vietnam by President Khamtay Siphandone, the two countries reaffirmed their commitment to the Cambodia–Laos–Vietnam Development Triangle first announced in 1999 as well as subregional infrastructure development, such as the East–West Development Corridor linking Laos, Myanmar, Thailand and Vietnam. Laos and Vietnam later concluded Vientiane Agreement 2002, a frame-work for future economic cooperation. Milestones reached in 2002 included the twenty-fifth anniversary of the signing of the Agreement on Friendship and Cooperation and the fortieth anniversary of the establish-ment of diplomatic relations. In June 2003, the chairman of the Lao National Assembly addressed the National Assembly of Vietnam in words suggestive of how little had changed in the official Lao–Vietnamese rela-tionship since the creation of the Indochinese Communist Party in 1930.

> Over the past 70 years, the two nations have stood shoulder to shoul-der in the struggle full of hardships and sacrifices. Following Ho Chi Minh's immortal words "Helping someone means assisting yourself," the Vietnamese people sent their beloved to Laos to help the revolu-tionary cause.
> On behalf of the Lao People's Revolutionary Party, the National

Assembly, the Government, the Fatherland Front, and the Lao people of all nationalities, allow me to express the deep gratitude to the Communist Party, the National Assembly, the Fatherland Front, and the people of Viet Nam for their valuable support to the Lao revolutionary cause.

We are determined to follow the words of President Kaysone Phomvihane: "We should preserve and protect the great friendship, the special solidarity and the all-round Laos–Viet Nam cooperation like protecting the pupils of our eyes and will educate our next generations to be forever faithful to this solidarity, not allowing enemies or opposition forces to destroy it."[68]

Thereafter, the official exchange of visits continued as did expansion of border cooperation and other agreements. For example, Laos and Vietnam in November 2004 concluded an agreement to promote wildlife protection along their border, especially in areas where endangered species were in peril.[69] Vietnam clearly remained the dominant political influence in Laos, but it lacked the resources to compete long-term in the economic sphere with rival China.

Border issues and the resettlement of Hmong refugees resident in Thai camps dominated Lao–Thai relations. Other topics of mutual interest included the creation of special economic zones to promote trade and investment, drug trafficking and the Thai purchase of Lao electricity. Laos's love-hate relationship with Thailand was ever present as exemplified by a rancorous exchange in mid-2001 in which Lao officials strongly objected to a planned film about the Thai patriot and heroine, Thao Suranaree. Thai history books claim she saved her country from Lao aggression in 1826, but Lao historians say the story was fabricated for political purposes. Thailand has long been the dominant cultural influence in Laos due to the similarity of their languages, and "Thai lifestyles and values purveyed by television programmes and other cultural products find a receptive market in Laos." The Thai monarchy is also widely respected. Thai Princess Maha Chakri Sirindhorn visited Laos in May 2001 and again in November 2002.[70]

In June 2001, Laos and Thailand announced plans to create a bilateral tourism network, linking four Thai provinces with two Lao provinces; and in August, the two neighbors established an arbitration panel to resolve commercial and investment disputes. Thailand in June 2002 agreed to extradite 17 Lao nationals who had sought refuge in Thailand after an abortive attack on a Lao border post in July 2000, finally deporting them in mid-2004 after a Thai court rejected their extradition. Amid Lao complaints that anti-Vientiane elements continued to operate in Thailand, Laos and Thailand in October 2003 concluded an 18-point border security cooperation agreement. By the end of the year, 670 kilometers of the land border had been fixed, leaving only 32 kilometers or less than 5 percent of the total to be marked. Laos and Thailand in March 2004 scrapped visa requirements for their citizens in an effort to boost tourism. They also laid the foundation stone for a two kilometer bridge, funded by Japanese loans, linking Mukdahan in Thailand with Savannakhet town and providing a more direct route to the Vietnamese port of Danang.[71] Thailand will remain the dominant cultural influence in Laos, but China's economic presence one day could overtake that of now preeminent Thailand.

Focused on related issues like border security, narcotics control and trade, Lao relations with Cambodia were much less extensive than those with its three big neighbors, China, Thailand and Vietnam, reflecting a lower level of commercial opportunity and ideological concern. In mid-2000, Cambodia and Laos initiated an official survey of their common border, the first such demarcation since Cambodia gained independence from France in 1953. In January 2001, Laos and Cambodia agreed to open their border although officials from both states agreed it would be years before it could be opened completely due to the absence of roads linking Cambodia's interior provinces to Laos. Prime Minister Bounnyang Vorachit made an official visit to Phnom Penh in August 2001 where he highlighted the progress of the joint border commission and encouraged Cambodian Prime Minister Hun Sen to build roads in the border provinces. In turn, Hun Sen encouraged construction of a railroad linking the two states and tied into a proposed ASEAN rail network. As demarcation of the border continued, Laos and Cambodia explored new opportunities to boost bilateral cooperation in other areas related to national development.[72]

Bilateral relations with the United States were dominated by long familiar issues, including human rights concerns, trade talks and the search for MIAs. A new issue involved the fate of two naturalized American citizens, ethnic Hmong and members of an anti-Vientiane organization, the Lao People's Liberation Front (LPLF), who disappeared on the Lao–Thai border in April 1999. Laos claimed to have no knowledge of their whereabouts and participated in at least two joint fact-finding missions to determine their fate; nevertheless, Washington maintained Vientiane was not cooperating fully to resolve the issue. Lao opposition groups, including the Lao Human Rights Council, Laos Institute for Democracy, United Lao Action Center and Hmong International Human Rights Watch, used the issue, together with related human rights abuses, to slow progress in improving Lao–American commercial relations.[73]

Citing increased cooperation in areas like counter terrorism, accounting for MIAs and counter narcotics, the Bush administration in early 2003 supported passage of legislation to normalize trading relations with Laos. Even as the White House continued to support new legislation, opponents in the Lao–American community and their congressional supporters successfully delayed action for almost two years, citing concerns about the two Americans missing since 1999, a U.S. citizen detained in June 2003, imprisonment of pro-democracy activists and the renewed persecution of Christian ethnic minorities. Consequently, the U.S. Congress did not approve normal trading relations with Laos until late November 2004, capping a seven-year effort by successive administrations to end the country's isolation. And the measure passed the U.S. Senate only after opposing senators succeeded in passing a resolution condemning human rights violations in Laos. At the time, U.S. communities were welcoming some 15,000 Hmong refugees from Laos, resettled from holding camps in Thailand. Their transfer largely ended the lingering legacy of the Second Indochina War. Refugee support groups say tens of thousands more Hmong scattered throughout Thailand could claim asylum, but no more were added to the official departure list, and the United States was unlikely to take many more. Meanwhile, the search for American MIAs in Laos continued.[74]

Japan remained the principal donor to Laos. With the Lao PDR in the throes of a severe economic crisis in September 2000, Japan extended a substantial debt relief package; and in December 2001, it approved loans totaling $62 million to fund a second bridge across the Mekong. Japan later wrote off debts owed by Laos for construction of the Nam Ngum Dam; and in December 2003, Laos welcomed a Japanese commitment of $1.5 billion in aid for Mekong River regional development. On the multi-lateral level, the International Monetary Fund approved in principle a three-year, $40 million loan in April 2001, eight years after its last loan in 1993. However, renewed concerns about macroeconomic policies later delayed distribution of the second tranche of the loan. The Asian Development Bank continued its financial assistance to Laos, launching an ambitious poverty alleviation program, with an emphasis on primary education, revenue collection and private sector development. In June 2004, ADB approved a $17.7 million loan to Laos to improve rural roads.[75]

Other aspects of Lao foreign policy were noteworthy. A North Korean delegation, led by Kim Yong-Nam, president of the Presidium of the Supreme People's Assembly and titular head of state, visited Cambodia, Laos and Vietnam in mid-2001 in an effort to shore up international support in the communist world. A 12-point communiqué issued at the end of his visit to Laos reported agreements on public health, double taxation and cultural exchange. During an official visit to Moscow in August 2001, Foreign Minister Somsavat supported Russia's opposition both to an enlargement of NATO and to U.S. plans to scrap the 1972 ABM Treaty. He also hailed Moscow's cooperation with ASEAN and its support for the creation of a nuclear free Southeast Asia. In turn, Foreign Minister Igor Ivanov emphasized Russia's interest in giving "practical content" to its relations with Laos. Russian Foreign Minister Sergei Lavrov reciprocated with an official visit to Laos in November 2004 to discuss economic and trade issues. Less than two years later, as mentioned earlier, Russia agreed to write-off the bulk of its Lao debt. Finally, the Indo–Lao Joint

Commission continued to meet, concluding new agreements on trade cooperation and the protection of investments. India also expanded its defense ties with Laos, including the training of Lao air force pilots, and extended a $10 million loan in support of a power transmission project. In return, the Lao PDR continued to support India's candidacy for a permanent seat on the UN Security Council.[76]

## Foreign aid dependent Cambodia

The Cambodian economy in 1998 suffered its worst performance since the country moved to a market orientation at the turn of the decade. Economic, political and climactic factors combined to reduce economic growth to less than 2 percent with the varying GDP figures reported by different international bodies once again highlighting data collection problems in Cambodia. The suspension of external aid, due largely to Prime Minister Hun Sen's ousting in 1997 of coalition partner, Prince Norodom Ranariddh, contributed to the poor performance as did a decline in fiscal revenues due to tax shortfalls, notably royalties on logging. In addition, the agricultural sector continued to deteriorate in the wake of a series of droughts and floods beginning in 1996. Foreign direct investment in Cambodia, as in Laos and Vietnam, declined sharply since the majority of investors were from the ASEAN states badly affected by the 1997–8 financial crisis. An economic bright spot was the garments sector where exports boomed in the late 1990s after Cambodia concluded normalized trading relationship agreements with the United States and the European Union. Garments became the largest single export item in 1998, accounting for just under 40 percent of all exports.[77]

Economic performance improved after 1998, but the Cambodian economy remained fragile. As the political climate stabilized, bilateral and multilateral donors once again extended financial aid. The Consultative Group for Cambodia met in Paris in May 2000, pledging $548 million in assistance over a 12-month period. The agricultural sector, the mainstay of the Cambodian economy, showed signs of recovery until massive flooding struck in September 2000 just before paddy rice harvesting time. With some 200,000 hectares of paddy destroyed, the adverse effects of one of the worst floods in the last 100 years offset a robust expansion of industry and services. On a more positive note, foreign direct investment increased as the regional financial crisis bottomed out; and exports continued to expand, due largely to the buoyant garment industry. GDP growth averaged 7 percent in 1999–2000, dropping to around 6 percent in 2001.[78]

Despite the improved performance of the Cambodian economy, additional economic reforms were urgently needed. Citing progress in fiscal reform, control of illegal logging and military demobilization, the central theme of the May 2000 meeting of the Consultative Group for Cambodia was the issue of governance, widely recognized as the single biggest obstacle to economic and social development in the country. International donors, along with representatives of the private sector and civil society, urged Cambodia to fight corruption, build credibility in the legal and judicial systems, protect property and individual rights and press ahead with public administration reform. In so doing, participants emphasized that good governance was essential both to the development of a private sector and to attract the foreign direct investment necessary to stimulate long-term economic growth and reduce aid dependency.[79]

Cambodia like Laos remained dangerously dependent on foreign aid. At the dawn of the new millennium, approximately one-third of the government budget came from foreign assistance. International donors increasingly linked aid packages to economic and political reforms, but Cambodia's progress toward those reforms was both slow and spasmodic. In a working paper published in 2000 by the Cambodia Development Resource Institute (CDRI), a private think-tank based in Phnom Penh, several Cambodian specialists examined the impact of large-scale aid on the Cambodian economy.

> The scale of aid is such that it distorts the economy. In an aid-related version of "Dutch disease," a high proportion of Cambodia's scarcest resource, educated people, is pulled toward employment in donor agencies and international non-governmental organizations or attached to projects as salary-supplemented counterparts. At the same time, donors and NGOs virtually take over the funding of education, health care, social welfare, rural development etc., while government spends most of its funds on defense and security.[80]

While elements of the CDRI critique were controversial, the Cambodian case of aid dependency was surely extreme, on a par with that of Laos; and its long-term consequences were deeply concerning, if not always well understood.

## Prospects for the Cambodian economy

The Cambodian economy slowed in 2003 with the Asian Development Bank estimating GDP growth at 5 percent, down from 5.5 percent in 2002, the fourth consecutive year of slowdown. Robust growth in the export-oriented garments sector, combined with a recovery in agriculture, underpinned limited expansion. The garment industry by 2003 was employing 230,000 workers and generating more than 10 percent of GDP and 80 percent of total exports. Activity in the services sector was weakened by lower tourist arrivals due to the SARS scare and domestic political uncertainties. Anti-Thai riots at the beginning of the year, combined with a prolonged delay in forming a new government following July elections, hurt investment and consumption and also delayed official transfers. The fiscal deficit in 2003 narrowed to 6.1 percent of GDP, down from 6.6 percent in 2002, and continued to be financed mainly by grants or concessionary loans. Spending on economic and social transfers was higher than budgeted but defense-related outlays were lower. The inflation rate remained low, at 1.2 percent in 2003, reflecting a strong fiscal stance, relative exchange rate stability and generally stable food prices. Debt repayment remained a topic of discussion, but according to ADB estimates, Cambodia remained the least indebted country in the region with a little over $2 billion in foreign debt compared to almost $2.5 billion for Laos and close to $12 billion for Vietnam.[81]

The short-term outlook for the Cambodian economy remained favorable with ADB forecasting annual GDP growth rates around 4.5 percent over the next two years. Despite donor criticism of the slow pace of reform, the positive outlook for Cambodia reflected the fact that its economic reforms, unlike those in Laos but similar to those in Vietnam, were generally on track. Further growth was contingent on expansion in export-oriented manufacturing, primarily garments, and an upturn in tourism and construction. Both the garment industry and tourism stood to benefit from a stronger world economy. Garment exports to the United States would also benefit from the elimination of a major competitor after August 2003 when the United States imposed an import ban on Myanmar. A forecast increase in global rice prices would boost growth in the agricultural sector, increasing both rural incomes and domestic consumption. Government efforts to redirect expenditures, with the demobilization of the armed forces a prime example, would reduce military spending, leaving additional funds available for economic and social development. Better public financial management and renewed emphasis on structural reforms, together with WTO membership, would help the investment climate. Cambodia was admitted to the WTO in September 2003, albeit under very stringent conditions; but the Cambodian senate did not approve accession until September 2004. Based on China's experience after joining in 2001, Cambodia's accession would likely provide a short-term stimulus to importers and exporters. Ongoing efforts to integrate more closely with neighboring states in the Greater Mekong Subregion, together with infrastructure improvements coming into place as part of GMS initiatives, stood to promote trade and tourism.[82]

At the same time, economic growth in Cambodia, largely centered on the garments industry and tourism, was not broad-based. As a result, long-term prospects for sustainable growth were clouded by diverse challenges in agriculture, industry and services, the three sectors expected to lead the economy. Structural problems hampered expansion in agriculture. Farmers enjoyed limited access to productive land, irrigation, improved seeds and finances, hindering efforts to increase productivity, diversification and commercialization. With the nation's highways and roads in poor condition, it would take a sustained infrastructure development program to improve market access for rural households. Infrastructure improvements were also needed to increase the attractiveness of Cambodia to tourists, a central component of the services sector. The absence of developed infrastructure, combined with more stable political environments in China and Vietnam, also deterred industrial investment in Cambodia (and in Laos). Consequently, China and Vietnam would remain tough economic competitors in both agricultural and garment exports. Cambodian-made garments also faced increasing competitive pressure after 1 January 2005 when WTO rules phased out the garment quota system and Cambodia's bilateral trade agreement with the United States expired.[83]

Direct foreign investment in Cambodia dropped off in recent years due to reduced investment in the garments industry and the closure of foreign banks. Increased competition in the industrial sector made it difficult to reverse the trend. The full benefits of WTO membership remained contingent on improvements in both infrastructure and telecommunications along with passage of the controversial legislation necessary to improve market access. The financial sector remained weak and unable to serve effectively as a bridge between savers and potential lenders; therefore, access to credit continued to limit private sector growth. Public health issues, from tuberculosis to HIV/AIDS to drug use, were other constraints on economic development. Finally, there remained the high transaction costs associated with conducting business in an environment characterized by weak and corrupt governance, including the lack of judicial, legal and regulatory frameworks conducive to private sector development. Unless and until these constraints were rigorously addressed, sustained development and the associated goal of poverty reduction would remain for Cambodia more objectives than realities.[84]

## Hun Sen consolidates power

Cambodians went to the polls in July 1998 in an electoral exercise highly reminiscent of May 1993. Election rhetoric was couched in the lofty terms of democratization, but the electoral process was again clouded by the familiar dynamics of rivalry and intimidation among contending factions. As Cambodian observer Pierre Lizée rightly noted, the elections were in many ways a step backwards as much as a step forwards.

> To that extent, the 1998 elections and the series of political developments surrounding them represented not so much a first step in an overdue process of democratization of the political environment in Cambodia, but rather a movement full circle to precisely the situation of autocracy which these elections were supposed to remedy.

In this context, as Lizée continued, "the elections were not about who would form the next government" as much as "about what the very rules of political power would be" in Cambodia.[85]

In the July 1998 elections, Hun Sen's CPP (Cambodian People's Party) garnered some 42 percent of the vote, Prince Ranariddh's FUNCINPEC (National United Front for an Independent, Neutral, Peaceful and Coop-erative Cambodia) about 32 percent and former Finance Minister Sam Rainsy's SRP (Sam Rainsy Party) approximately 14 percent. With the elections grounded in a proportional representation system, the National Election Committee, dominated by CPP supporters, determined the following seat distribution in the 122-seat National Assembly: 64 seats for CPP, 43 for FUNCINPEC and 15 for SRP. While CPP was awarded a majority of seats, it still lacked the two-thirds majority necessary to form a government. Both FUNCINPEC and SRP protested the formula used to distribute Assembly seats was not in line with election results; however, the decision of the National Election Council remained unchanged. Following an extended period of mutual recriminations marked by out-bursts of violence, Hun Sen and Prince Ranariddh announced in late November 1998 the formation of a coalition government with the former as prime minister and the latter as president of the National Assembly.[86]

After years of turmoil, 1999–2001 marked three years of notable polit-ical stability. Even though the CPP had gained only a slim, contested majority in the 1998 National Assembly elections, Prime Minister Hun Sen was successful in aligning the *de jure* distribution of government power with the *de facto* distribution of bureaucratic and military power. He established dominance over the Cambodian political scene with Prince Ranariddh ceasing to play a meaningful role and his FUNCINPEC col-leagues either cooperating with the CPP or dropping out of politics. In the words of Milton Osborne, a veteran Cambodian observer, Hun Sen remained in that "long tradition of Cambodian rulers for whom politics is a zero-sum game." Sam Rainsy remained the most vocal government critic, but his political effectiveness was diminished by the limited number of SRP seats in the National Assembly and his own tendency to spend large amounts of time outside Cambodia. Continuing in fragile health, King Norodom Sihanouk played an increasingly marginal role.[87]

At the same time, attempts to improve governance in Cambodia faced a political culture with a long history of factionalism and violence, com-pounded by the absence of the rule of law. Even as Cambodians tried to create a democratic culture, corruption remained endemic with the pre-vailing climate most accurately described as a culture of impunity. In March 2000, for example, authorities discovered the existence of over 6,000 "ghost" civil servants who were on the payroll but did not show up for work. In late November 2000, an estimated 70 members of the Cambo-dian Freedom Fighters, a group of anti-communist, anti-Vietnamese Cam-bodian expatriates, attacked multiple targets in Phnom Penh, killing eight people. Two weeks later, a bomb exploded in downtown Phnom Penh. The attacks posed no immediate threat to the stability of the Cambodian government, but they did result in the postponement of a scheduled visit by Vietnamese President Tran Duc Luong. The downstream impact of the violence on tourism, foreign investment and the planned demobilization of the army was uncertain.[88]

The relative calm following the 1998 National Assembly elections enabled the Cambodian government to address a number of long-delayed but important issues, namely a Khmer Rouge tribunal, military demobilization and commune elections. The question of a trial for former Khmer Rouge leaders attracted worldwide interest following the movement's demise in the latter half of the 1990s. The issue sparked ongoing controversy between the coalition government and the international community with Hun Sen's mood swinging back and forth between condemnation and support for a trial. Rejecting a UN-proposed international tribunal, he argued it would violate Cambodian sovereignty and could spark a renewed civil war if former Khmer Rouge guerrillas rose up in support of their old leaders. Apparently willing to let bygones be bygones, Hun Sen remained under heavy pressure from donor states, notably the European Union, Japan and the United States, to establish a tribunal. In January 2001, the legislature finally passed a tribunal bill; however, the Cambodian Constitutional Council later took exception to it on the grounds references in the bill to a 1956 Penal Code could be construed to recognize the outlawed death penalty. It was not until August 2001 that a new version of the bill, without the death penalty, was signed into law by King Sihanouk.[89]

Compared to earlier UN recommendations, the tribunal proposed in August 2001 was a hybrid in that it contained a mixture of Cambodian and international prosecutors and judges. Certain other procedures in the bill were also less than the international community desired in that they failed to address key issues raised by UN legal experts. These included the immunity granted former Khmer Rouge Foreign Minister Ieng Sary in 1996 and the inclusion of international standards aimed an guaranteeing fairness. In the ensuing debate, the global community continued to insist on a trial in the belief the failure to conduct one would have serious ramifications for Cambodia's culture of impunity.[90]

In June 2003, six years of contentious negotiations with the United Nations finally led to a compromise agreement in which the Hun Sen government accepted a mixed tribunal comprising local and international judges operating under Cambodian law. Because the agreement required ratification by the National Assembly, subsequent preparations for the tribunal were delayed almost a year by difficulties surrounding formation of a coalition government after the July 2003 elections. As preparations for the trial continued, some UN member states remained reluctant to quantify in advance financial support for the proceedings.[91]

In part to free up funds for the social sector, the Cambodian government, at the prompting of the international donor community, planned to demobilize by 2004 some 31,500 soldiers out of a total defense force of more than 133,000 personnel. Some 11,500 were to be cut by 2000 with additional reductions of 10,000 each in 2001–2 and 2003–4. In prompting a broader demilitarization of Cambodian society, demobilization was also expected to have a positive impact on the single most serious source of violence in Cambodia, the widespread presence of ill-trained, poorly paid soldiers. Some progress in demobilization occurred in 2000; however, a pilot project aimed at 1,500 soldiers in four provinces was widely criticized on the grounds the reintegration of former soldiers into civilian life was poorly managed, threatening to make them a pool for military entrepreneurship and violence. Related concerns were raised four years later when the Intercontinental Hotel in Phnom Penh replaced striking workers with demobilized soldiers, prompting charges of strike-breaking. A report by the authoritative International Crisis Group described the demobilization program as a "magnet for corruption" concluding an army of 100,000 was still too large for Cambodia's needs. As the troubled demobilization program proceeded, it remained dogged by controversy, causing the World Bank in mid-2003 to reduce its support for the project.[92]

The Council of Ministers approved a draft commune election law in August 2000 whose provisions disappointed international observers because the draft law exhibited an almost total disregard for public opinion as mobilized by election networks. The National Assembly passed the law in January 2001, paving the way for commune elections, planned originally for 1995, to be held in February 2002. With elections scheduled in all 1,621 communes, the elections represented an important step in the process of decentralization as well as a significant opportunity to link local and national power configurations throughout Cambodia.[93]

## Hun Sen in control

The commune elections in February 2002 were the first elections at the local government level held in post-colonial Cambodia. When compared to the two previous general elections, the 2002 commune elections went off rather well with competing political parties and international observers judging their conduct acceptable if not entirely free from violence and intimidation. Enjoying a prolonged monopoly over local government, a well-organized political network and abundant human and financial resources, the CPP won a resounding victory, garnering 62 percent of the votes, 68 percent of the total seats and 97 percent of the top offices. While it won a majority of posts in most councils, the election results marked the first time the CPP would have to share local power with the SRP and FUNCINPEC. In this sense, the elections opened a new vista of competition for the opposition, especially the SRP.[94]

The 2002 commune elections were a wake-up call for FUNCINPEC. The CPP achieved a net vote gain of 20 percent over the 1998 general elections while FUNCINPEC dropped 8 percent. The poor performance of FUNCINPEC was attributed to the poor leadership of Prince Ranariddh, and related to his leadership failure, the party's alliance with Hun Sen's CPP. As Kheang Un and Judy Ledgerwood later pointed out, "FUNCIN-PEC adopted a policy stance based on the principle of 4Cs – coalition, cooperation, and competition without confrontation" vis-à-vis the CPP. The principle of 4Cs brought political stability, but it did not translate into an equal partnership. As a result, many Cambodians no longer saw FUNCINPEC as a viable alternative to CPP. In a state where political patronage remained at the heart of the system, FUNCINPEC had little to offer its members. The widespread perception that royalist party FUNC-INPEC's link to King Sihanouk was no longer a significant factor in national elections left the king deeply disturbed and led to his threat later in the year to abdicate.[95]

As the decade progressed, the question of royal succession became an increasingly important issue. Article 13 of the 1993 Constitution provided for the Throne Council to select a successor within seven days of the death of the king, indicating the organization and operation of the Council should be determined by law. However, no law regulating the Throne Council had been passed by the National Assembly. Even though King Sihanouk was in his early 80s and in poor health, Hun Sen refused to discuss the issue, arguing it would be disrespectful to the monarch to discuss a successor while he was still alive. A suggestion by maverick Prince Norodom Chakrapong that a successor should be chosen by popular vote was rejected by both Hun Sen and Prince Ranariddh. In con-trast to the Lao situation where the regime in recent years had reached out to the memory of the monarchy to buttress its legitimacy, Hun Sen viewed the monarchy in Cambodia as a political threat to be curbed. He made it clear he would not tolerate in the future an activist king able to challenge the prime minister's constitutional powers. In any case, Hun Sen remained in a position to determine a successor to King Sihanouk as the CPP con-trolled a majority of votes in both the Throne Council and the National Assembly. Worried and angry over the issue of succession, King Sihanouk periodically repeated threats to resign in a half-hearted attempt to force Hun Sen to act.[96]

Regime treatment of religion was another arena in which Cambodia differentiated itself both from Laos and Vietnam. An overwhelming majority of Cambodians, well over 90 percent, are nominally Buddhist, with approximately 6 percent Muslim and less than 1 percent Christian. On the surface, Buddhism in recent years made a remarkable recovery from the Khmer Rouge period when it was outlawed and many senior monks were murdered. In traveling around the country today, one sees many new *wats* built or under construction and a growing number of young men entering the monkhood. Recent estimates put the total number of *wats* at 3,980 with almost 60,000 Buddhist monks in the country. On the other hand, anecdotal evidence suggests that many contemporary monks are not well trained in their religion. Moreover, some violate the severe disciplinary code and strict tenets of their faith, participating in worldly pleasures like smoking, drinking alcohol, taking drugs and consorting with females.[97]

The politicization of the Buddhist clergy was also an increasing source of controversy. Activist Buddhist monk Sam Bunthoeun, who spoke out against corruption and in favor of the rule of law, was gunned down at Wat Lanka during the 2003 national election campaign in what some observers viewed as a politically motivated murder. Twelve monks were later threatened with expulsion from their Phnom Penh pagoda after supporting the opposition Sam Rainsy Party in the elections. The participation of monks in the general elections and their broader involvement in Cambodian politics remained an extremely sensitive issue for the *Sangha* and the country at large. The People's Republic of Kampuchea had encouraged a renaissance of Buddhism in the 1980s in an effort to enlist a traditional form of legitimation in support of the regime. Monks were accorded the right to vote, officially recognizing their participation in political activity, but the People's Revolutionary Party of Kampuchea, the forerunner to the CPP, demanded the monks link the Buddhist religion to the revolutionary development of the country. The restrictions placed on the *Sangha* led to the emergence of opposition within the Buddhist hierarchy itself as well as a proliferation of illegal monks, operating outside the sanction of the *Sangha*. While the Hun Sen government was unlikely to be satisfied with anything less than the full support of the *Sangha*, past experience suggested the *Sangha* would only be trusted by the people as long as it was seen as independent of politicians.[98]

Like their Buddhist counterparts, the minority Cham Muslim community faced harsh treatment during the Pol Pot regime. International observers believe the atrocities suffered by both groups could prove key in proving the Khmer Rouge leadership guilty of genocide in any future trials. According to Bjorn Blengsli, a Norwegian anthropologist who has studied religious change among the Chams, the number of religious centers has more than doubled since 1970 from 122 mosques to an estimated 268. In the current war on terrorism, the Muslim community has been a source of public interest and concern for other reasons. In May 2003, the government arrested three foreigners suspected of ties to Jemaah Islamiyah, a clandestine Southeast Asian organization associated with al-Qaeda. The government also closed two Islamic schools and expelled a community of foreign religious teachers. The historically quiescent Cham minority traditionally practiced a syncretic form of Islam, incorporating elements from Buddhism and pre-Islamic belief systems. However, in recent years, religious activists representing the conservative Dawa Tabligh movement and the orthodox Wahabi strain have arrived, preaching a more austere version of Islam. Funded from sources in Malaysia, Saudi Arabia and elsewhere, these organizations want to purify Cham Islamic practice by ridding it of Buddhist influence. Their efforts have been successful with an estimated 40 percent of Chams converting to the Dawa Tabligh and Wahabi branches of Islam. The traditional Cham leadership has long enjoyed close ties with the Cambodian People's Party; however, recent developments were a source of concern to the government. Events in Thailand in April 2004, where Thai security forces killed 107 militants in the mostly Muslim south of the country, sparked new fears and arrests in Cambodia because members of the Muslim minority have long studied in southern Thailand. In November 2004, a UN official suggested Cambodia was in danger of becoming a breeding ground for terrorists, a warning dismissed by the Cambodian government.[99]

National elections held in July 2003 produced significant new gains for the Cambodian People's Party. Its share of the popular vote, with more than 80 percent of eligible voters participating in the election, increased from around 42 percent in 1998 to more than 47 percent in 2003. In turn, the royalist party FUNCINPEC continued its decline, garnering less than 21 percent of the vote compared to almost 32 percent in 1998. The Sam Rainsy Party increased its vote share from a little more than 14 percent in 1998 to almost 22 percent in 2003, surpassing FUNCINPEC for the first time. In the process, a significant rural–urban split in voting patterns surfaced. CPP remained strong in the countryside, but SRP did very well in Phnom Penh and other urban areas, buttressing its claim to have become the principal opposition voice in Cambodia. FUNCINPEC was clearly a diminished factor in national politics, largely due to Prince Ranariddh's inept leadership, factionalism within the party, ineffectual alliances with the CPP and King Sihanouk's marginalized role. UN observers judged the 2003 elections relatively free of corruption and violence, especially compared to previous balloting; however, Human Rights Watch documented a troubling list of rights violations in the run-up to balloting.[100]

Under the proportional representation system, CPP increased its parliamentary majority from 64 to 73 of the 123 seats, FUNCINPEC dropped from 43 to 26 and SRP increased from 15 to 24. While the CPP commanded an overwhelming majority of National Assembly seats, it lacked the two-thirds majority necessary to form a government. Constitutional provisions designed to reconcile warring factions in 1993 had the opposite effect a decade later. Article 82 of the 1993 constitution called for the president, vice presidents and members of each commission of the National Assembly to be elected by a two-thirds majority vote. While the Royal Government of Cambodia was constituted as a separate body, article 100 of the constitution called for the president of the National Assembly, with the agreement of the two vice presidents, to recommend a member of the winning party to the king for the purpose of forming a government. In effect, this meant the CPP needed to form a two-thirds majority coalition in the National Assembly in order to elect a president who could then recommend to the king a CPP member to form a government. The two-thirds requirement, unique in the annals of parliamentary government, posed a major obstacle to a stable transition to a new government.[101]

The 1993 constitution called for the National Assembly to convene within 60 days of the election, but no time limit was set for the formation of a new government. After the 1998 elections, CPP was successful in persuading FUNCINPEC to join a coalition government; however, FUNCINPEC united with SRP in 2003, refusing to form a government with Hun Sen as prime minister. After CPP rejected an SRP proposal from emboldened leader Sam Rainsy to form a tripartite government, the stalemate continued with efforts to reach a power-sharing agreement stretching into 2004. In the interim, sporadic violence, mostly targeted at FUNCINPEC and SRP officials and associates, kept Cambodia in a state of considerable political tension. It was only in June 2004 that Hun Sen and Prince Ranariddh finally reached a power-sharing deal in which Hun Sen retained his position as prime minister and Prince Ranariddh continued as president of the National Assembly. Under the terms of the agreement, which involved an increase in cabinet seats from 80 to 207, CPP took 65 percent of the cabinet seats, including key portfolios like foreign affairs, telecommunications and commerce and FUNCINPEC got the remaining 35 percent. The creation of so many new ministerial positions, done to appease members of both parties by offering them lucrative positions in return for their support, added a heavy burden to the Cambodian economy. The related issue of corruption once again came to the forefront at the end of 2004 with the release of a U.S. Agency for International Development commissioned report depicting a corruption-ridden Cambodian state apparatus.[102]

The formation of a new government meant Cambodia could now deal with crucial legislative business, like ratification of its accession to the World Trade Organization and establishment of a tribunal to try former Khmer Rouge leaders. It also marked the consolidation of Hun Sen's control over the Cambodian political system. FUNCINPEC appeared to be finished as an independent political party, leaving the SRP as the only meaningful opposition. At the swearing-in ceremony for the new government, which the opposition boycotted, Hun Sen spoke of the coalition lasting at least 20–30 years. In complete control of all forms of security in Cambodia, no one in the foreseeable future looked to be in a position to challenge him. Concerned with the future of democracy in Cambodia, King Sihanouk again offered to abdicate, a threat he withdrew a week later after Supreme Monk Tep Vong begged him to remain on the throne. King Sihanouk later announced his retirement and was succeeded in October 2004 by his son, King Norodom Sihamoni.[103] The creation of the coalition government, after a year-long battle in which opponents failed to oust Hen Sen, displayed for all to see his growing inability to tolerate any form of dissent. A win for the culture of impunity, it marked not a benchmark on the road to greater democracy in Cambodia, a signpost which might have served as a beacon for Laos and Vietnam, but instead a serious threat to return Indochina to a region composed of three one-party states.

## Cambodian external affairs

In December 1998, Cambodia regained its seat at the United Nations, suspended in the aftermath of the July 1997 political crisis. Prime Minister Hun Sen later addressed the UN General Assembly in October 1999. Cambodia's entry into ASEAN in April 1999 opened yet another arena for Cambodian foreign policy. ASEAN membership gave Cambodia the opportunity, absent for three decades, to gain leverage in regional affairs. As with Laos, it also enhanced Cambodian security, offering the potential for increased regional trade and investment as well as a venue for conflict resolution. In November 2002, Cambodia hosted summit meetings of heads of state of both the GMS and ASEAN in Phnom Penh, highlighting Cambodia's integration into both regional and global economies. It also hosted the thirty-sixth ASEAN Ministerial Meeting in June 2003 and the ASEAN Economic Ministers Meeting in September. By early 2004, Cambodia was actively seeking a seat on the UN Security Council.[104]

Cambodia maintained traditionally close ties with Vietnam, including frequent official visits at all levels. For example, Communist Party chief Le Kha Phieu, chief commissar of Vietnam's occupation force inside Cambodia in the 1980s, visited Phnom Penh in June 1999. Vietnam also remained a consistent supporter of Cambodia within ASEAN, working to overcome reservations regarding Cambodian accession to membership. It was thus symbolic that Cambodia acceded formally to ASEAN in a small ceremony in Hanoi in April 1999. At the same time, the CPP leadership balanced its close personal relationship with the leadership of Vietnam, dating back to their time as ideological allies, with ancient, grass-roots anti-Vietnamese sentiment in Cambodia. Both FUNCINPEC and SRP resorted to anti-Vietnamese rhetoric during the 2003 national elections, and some Cambodians of Vietnamese heritage were turned away at the polls. Recurrent problems included Vietnamese Hmong highlanders crossing into Cambodia to escape religious or other persecution in Vietnam and Cambodian villagers near the border complaining of alleged Vietnamese encroachments on Cambodian territory. A new note of discord surfaced at the end of 2003 when Cambodia asked Vietnam for compensation for loss of life and property due to flooding attributed to an unannounced release of water from a Vietnamese dam on the Se San River which flows into Cambodia. When Vietnam stonewalled discussions, Cambodia pushed the issue which had wider implications as the Yali Falls Dam on the Se San River was only the first of six dams being constructed there by Vietnam.[105]

In part to balance its relationship with Vietnam, Phnom Penh responded positively to Beijing's overtures to grow China's presence in Cambodia. Accepting the status quo, China appeared content with a situation in which no foreign state, including Vietnam, had a dominant position of influence in Cambodia. In turn, the Hun Sen government welcomed China's benign attitude at a time when Chinese investment was increasingly important to the Cambodian economy. Chinese President Jiang Zemin visited Cambodia in November 2000, a landmark visit which reflected China's growing interest in the region. Following his visit, the dedication of the new National Assembly building, funded by China, illustrated China's growing role. Beijing also opposed a Khmer Rouge tribunal, concerned with global scrutiny of its past support for the Pol Pot regime, and quietly pressured Cambodia not to conduct any trials. In November 2002, Chinese Premier Zhu Rongji announced Beijing was forgiving all foreign debt owed by Cambodia, some of which dated back to the 1960s. Cambodia and China later concluded a military agreement in November 2003 in which Beijing funded equipment and training, and Hun Sen led an official CPP delegation to China in April 2004. In March 2004, Cambodia reached agreement with a state-run Chinese company to conduct a feasibility study for a $39 million hydropower plant, including an option to build and operate the project.[106]

Cambodia's relationship with Thailand remained sound if marred occasionally by outstanding bilateral issues and a resurgence of mistrust. Thai Prime Minister Chuan Leekpai visited Phnom Penh in mid-June 2000, signing a border agreement based on Franco-Siamese pacts concluded in 1904 and 1907. The ceremony was soon followed by a new border controversy in which Cambodian developers, building a cross-border casino, allegedly encroached on Thai territory opposite Poipet. With Thai citizens flocking to the 12 casinos in operation on the Thai–Cambodian border by April 2001, additional casino construction remained a sensitive issue with Thailand. Other bilateral questions included suppression of narcotics and other illegal activity in the borderlands, increased trade and investment and joint fishery ventures. Bilateral relations took a turn for the worse in January 2003 when violent anti-Thai protests in Phnom Penh underscored historical animosities between the two kingdoms. The immediate cause of the violence was a remark falsely attributed to Thai actress Suwanan Kongying, implying Thai sovereignty over Angkor Wat, symbol of Cambodian identity. After Thai diplomats were forced to flee Phnom Penh, Thailand responded by downgrading diplomatic relations, closing the border and suspending trade and technical assistance. Full diplomatic relations were restored only after Cambodia met Thai demands for financial compensation, justice for the perpetrators of the violence and a full accounting of the entire incident.[107]

Despite persistent criticism of the Hun Sen government by domestic and international NGOs, together with selected members of the U.S. Congress, Washington largely refrained from criticizing the Phnom Penh government. At the same time, the United States supported UN efforts to bring former Khmer Rouge leaders to trial as well as the July 2003 electoral process, funding election observers in many Cambodian provinces. Following the elections, the United States resumed direct aid to Cambodia, suspended after the violence in July 1997, notably funding training courses for the Muslim community in an effort to block inroads by religious fundamentalists. The Cambodian government praised the U.S. initiative as part of its support for the war on terrorism. Many Americans also remained very concerned with human rights issues in Cambodia. Members of the U.S. House of Representatives in February 2004 wrote Prime Minister Hun Sen urging him to investigate the murder in January of Chea Vichea, a prominent labor union leader. The Director of the State Department's Office to Monitor and Combat Trafficking in Persons, in a March 2004 press conference, described Cambodia as one of the world's most serious challenges. In July 2004, U.S. congressional leaders, including Senate Majority Leader Bill Frist and Arizona Senator John McCain expressed concern in separate statements that Hun Sen had stepped up threats against Cambodia's democratic opposition.[108]

## Limits of regionalism

In the transition to ASEAN-10, Cambodia, Laos and Vietnam focused largely on subregional development within the Greater Mekong Subregion. The modest progress achieved toward GMS initiatives in the latter half of the 1990s reflected both the enormity of the projects envisioned and the limited resources of the Indochinese states. As Southeast Asian specialists Mya Than and George Abonyi observed: "A central issue facing economic co-operation in the GMS at this stage [was] the mobilization of the extensive resources required for project implementation, especially for infrastructure-related projects." Infrastructure improvement was a key GMS goal because inadequate infrastructure restricted trade and contributed to related socioeconomic and political problems. Lacking both the capital and management resources required to implement desired projects, the GMS states found capital mobilization to be an especially daunting challenge given the obvious gap between future promise and present reality. Project implementation was further complicated by the transborder character of most GMS projects. All of them involved two or more economies, often with very different legal and political jurisdictions. The Asian financial crisis in 1997–8 only compounded existing difficulties in financing GMS initiatives.[109]

   With Southeast Asia in the throes of a severe financial crisis, ASEAN economic and political assistance to the GMS in general and to Cambodia, Laos and Vietnam in particular remained modest. With the exception of the ASEAN-MBDC and AEM-MITI initiatives discussed earlier, there was limited ASEAN policy coordination, financial assistance or other cooperation. The ASEAN Foreign Ministers at their annual meeting in August 2000, in the face of widespread criticism for failing to deal with the economic and social fallout of the regional economic meltdown, refused to modernize structures to deal with the new situation. Instead, they relied on the long-standing ASEAN practices of consultation and consensus building, including noninterference in the internal affairs of member states. After the meeting, Vietnam, in its role as ASEAN chair, affirmed its intent to support the noninterference policy. Asked if ASEAN had rejected a UN proposal to appoint an ASEAN troika to mediate in Myanmar, Foreign Ministry spokesperson Phan Thuy Thanh responded, "ASEAN always operates on the principle of consensus, respect for independence and sovereignty and non-interference into each others' internal affairs."[110] In January 2001, Hans Eichel, the German finance minister, succinctly captured the prevailing situation when he said Asia had "no chance" of creating a common market or a common currency in the near future because the region was too economically and politically divided.[111]

In response, the Indochinese states mostly turned inward for solutions to their economic problems. The prime ministers of Cambodia, Laos and Vietnam met in October 1999 in the first of a series of mini-summits, announcing the creation of an Indochina development triangle, including a shared power grid, expanded aviation and telecommunication ties and upgraded road links. The new subregional initiative raised concern among other ASEAN states who feared the three less developed members were forming a block within the association. Under the GMS umbrella, Laos, Thailand and Vietnam concluded a cross-border trade agreement in November 1999; and Cambodia, Laos, Myanmar and Vietnam signed an air transport agreement in March 2000. Vietnam Airways linked the three Indochinese capitals, Hanoi, Phnom Penh and Vientiane, for the first time with a single flight later in the year.[112]

At a second mini-summit in January 2002, four months after the 9/11 terrorist attacks threatened to rekindle the Asian financial crisis, Cambodia, Laos and Vietnam announced plans to coordinate infrastructure development in the border provinces of Ratanakiri and Stung Treng in Cambodia, Attapeu and Sekong in Laos, and Kontum, Gia Lai and Daklak in Vietnam. This initiative was in line with the 1998 Hanoi Plan of Action which called for a reduction in poverty and the elimination of the development gap among ASEAN members. Cambodia, Laos and Vietnam joined other ASEAN states in condemning the 9/11 attacks, issuing a declaration of joint action to counter terrorism; however, the attacks had little impact, economically or politically, on the three Indochinese states. At a third mini-summit in November 2004, Cambodia, Laos and Vietnam agreed to expand tripartite development projects, targeting their border provinces and focusing on agriculture, education, environmental conservation, health, industry, tourism and trade.[113]

Earlier, China, Laos, Myanmar and Thailand had concluded an Agreement on Commercial Navigation on the Lancang-Mekong River which took effect in June 2001 and was intended to develop the river as a major transportation means. In commenting on the Mekong agreement, Joern Kristensen, chief executive officer of the Mekong River Commission, highlighted the challenges involved in the potential opening of a major shipping route from Simao in Yunnan province to northeast Thailand.

> Nobody can deny that there is a need for social and economic development in the Greater Mekong Sub-region. And nobody would want to deprive the people living along the Mekong of their equal right to social development, food security and freedom from poverty.
>
> But it is necessary, when development is planned, that those involved keep in mind that the Mekong, with all its might, with its great old civilization and its richness in natural resources, is a truly inter-related, fragile and sensitive eco-system that calls for wise development and good management so that it will continue to cater for its ever growing population.[114]

Mekong River Commission scientists warned in March 2003 the lower Mekong basin was facing serious environmental degradation; however, when Mekong river levels later dropped to unusually low levels, MRC officials argued the culprit was inadequate rainfall and not upstream Chinese dams. Independent observers agreed low rainfall was partly to blame for low river levels, as was increased water use by growing populations; but Chinese dams on the upper stretches of the river, combined with the blasting of river rapids and other obstacles to improve navigation, were thought by many to be major contributors to downstream problems. Consequently, the impact of mainstream dams on Mekong water levels looked set to remain in the foreseeable future a major source of GMS dialog and discord.[115]

In February 2002, Cambodia, Laos, Thailand and Vietnam launched a regional planning initiative for the cross-border development of the lower Mekong river basin. Known as the Basin Development Plan, the process was designed by the Mekong River Commission to identify and seek investment for high priority, sustainable projects. Cambodian Prime Minister Hun Sen, in a March 2002 lecture at the National University of Singapore, called on ASEAN to play "big sister" to the smaller groupings in the region, encouraging faster development and ensuring synergy among their projects. Regarding the GMS, he urged ASEAN to help Cambodia, Laos and Vietnam to build an economic development triangle, arguing accelerated GMS development would reduce the development gap among ASEAN members. As economic growth picked up in Asia, ASEAN economic ministers in July 2002 adopted the so-called "10 minus X" principle, allowing member states able to open their markets in areas like aviation, telecommunications and financial services to move forward without waiting for the others. A recognition of the differing development stages of the ASEAN-10 grouping, the formula was a radical departure from past practice where long accepted procedure was to progress in unison.[116]

Meeting in Phnom Penh just prior to the annual ASEAN summit, GMS leaders in November 2002 endorsed a subregional power distribution agreement, laying the foundation for an ambitious program of hydropower development. Meant to facilitate electricity export from the Lao PDR to neighboring states, the integrated grid was hailed by proponents as a major contribution to making Laos "landlinked" as opposed to "land-locked." Critics feared the agreement would accelerate dam construction on the Mekong and its tributaries, precipitating ecological and social disaster. The foreign ministers of Cambodia, Laos, Thailand and Myanmar later met in Vientiane in August 2003 to develop a five-fold Economic Cooperation Strategy centered on investment and trade promotion, agricultural and industrial development, transportation links, tourism and human resource development. In a sweeping vision short of specific details, Southeast Asian leaders at the 2003 ASEAN summit in October pledged to establish a common market by 2020. To succeed, analysts agreed the lofty rhetoric to establish an economic community in far-off 2020 would necessitate swift and concrete action in areas like labor law, custom regulations and judicial reform. ASEAN leaders also agreed at the summit to endorse a set of shared sociopolitical values and principles, a first hint the grouping, like the European Union, might attempt to require members to adhere to certain minimum political standards. The declaration gave no clue as to what those shared values might be, and common political ground was scarce in an organization which included a military government in Myanmar, authoritarian communist regimes in Laos and Vietnam and a nascent democracy in Cambodia, not to mention incipient democracy in states like Brunei and Indonesia.[117]

Thereafter, the parade of agreements continued. In a one-day summit in the northern Burmese town of Pagan, leaders of Cambodia, Laos, Myanmar and Thailand in November 2003 signed another pact committing their nations to boosting trade and investment, improving cooperation in agriculture and industry, promoting tourism and developing human resources. In December 2003, Cambodia, Laos, Myanmar and Vietnam concluded an open skies agreement, allowing air carriers from each country to exploit markets in the others without trade barriers. In March 2004, the Mekong River Commission announced a new initiative, the Challenge Program on Water and Food, intended to improve the lives of the 55 million people living along the river and to protect the environment by finding new ways to grow more food using less water.[118]

With Laos scheduled to host the upcoming ASEAN Summit, Foreign Minister Somsavat in March 2004 reviewed progress toward creation of a Vientiane Action Plan to replace the Hanoi Plan of Action. In so doing, he pointed out an important lesson to be drawn from the Hanoi plan was that only one-third of its programs had been implemented. He also stressed the complexities involved in successfully promoting regional integration.

> The HPA [Hanoi Plan of Action] was drawn up during a much more peaceful political climate, but at a time when ASEAN was exposed to financial crisis, which brought about a plan with a strong emphasis on economy recovery. In preparing the VAP [Vientiane Action Plan], we are now faced with a complex political situation as a result of war, conflict and the use of force in many regions, and more gravely, the global threat of terrorism. On the economic front, the focus is now on the acceleration of increased sustained economic growth, intra-ASEAN integration and improved relations between ASEAN and other regional groupings.[119]

The ASEAN Ministerial Meeting in June 2004 closed with a joint communiqué reaffirming member commitment to the establishment of a European-style ASEAN Community by 2020, comprised of interrelated economic, security and sociocultural entities. Declaring progress in establishing an ASEAN Economic Community, the foreign ministers pared down a proposal for a complementary security grouping, exposing practical limits to the development of a regional organization similar in authority and responsibility to the European Union. Vietnam and other new members adamantly rejected proposed timetables for everything from democratic rule to the creation of national human rights commissions. A proposal to establish a regional peacekeeping force by 2012 was also shelved. In the end, concrete initiatives were reduced to little more than statements of principle with no timetables or deadlines established. With both the European Union and the United Nations urging ASEAN to push Myanmar to make democratic reforms, the grouping fell back on long-familiar arguments that its core policy of noninterference in the internal affairs of member states precluded it from chastising Myanmar and that constructive engagement was more effective than sanctions in bringing about reform. Cambodian Prime Minister Hun Sen later strengthened ASEAN's collective stance behind Myanmar, saying his government would not participate in an Asia-Europe forum unless the military-ruled state was also admitted.[120]

At the 2004 ASEAN summit in Vientiane, the original six ASEAN members agreed to accelerate free trade efforts in the region, scrapping tariffs between them by 2007, three years earlier than planned. In an adaptation of the so-called "10 minus X" principle, the remaining four member states, including Cambodia, Laos and Vietnam, were given until 2012 to follow. Observers agreed the moves were taken to improve ASEAN's economic position vis-à-vis China. Faced with increased Chinese economic competition, ASEAN also signed a landmark accord with China which aims to remove all tariffs by 2010, as part of a wider plan of action to cooperate in information technology, military affairs, politics, security, transportation and tourism. ASEAN also announced a Vientiane Action Program at the 2004 summit which fleshed out last year's agreement to create an ASEAN Community along the lines of a unified Europe.[121]

Longer term, there were reasons to be cautiously optimistic. General knowledge of and interest in the GMS will increase over time among ASEAN investors. In addition, the adjustments to regional frameworks for trade and investment required by ASEAN and AFTA will facilitate cross-border linkages and investment throughout the subregion. More-over, ASEAN should become over time more effective in developing mechanisms through ASEAN-MBDC, AEM-MITI and elsewhere that are more efficient in mobilizing and channeling resources to the GMS. Finally, the financial crisis at the end of the century highlighted the need for local economies to develop and expand capital markets in order to be less reliant on foreign capital for investment in areas like infrastructure devel-opment. While this will take time, there is every reason to believe that regional capital markets able to finance regional projects can and will develop.

# 7   Continuity and change

The 30-year war in Indochina largely defined the 30 years of relative peace which followed in Cambodia, Laos and Vietnam. But the twin themes of continuity and change which mark the contemporary relationship of these three states have their origins in the more distant past. With the creation of French Indochina in the second half of the nineteenth century, it became virtually impossible for nearly 100 years not to discuss Cambodia, Laos and Vietnam as a whole. Nonetheless, the preceding analysis has made clear the unique character of the revolutions, reforms and regional interests of each state. In so doing, it has highlighted the paradoxical nature of their relationship as they struggle to adapt and respond to the challenges and opportunities of a new millennium.

## Dreams of union

With the nineteenth-century occupation of Cambodia, Laos and Vietnam, the French government set out to recreate a space in the heart of Southeast Asia. The hyphenated name *Indo-Chine*, initially applied to the amalgamated territories of Annam, Cambodia, Cochinchina and Tonkin, suggested an empty space to be imagined, molded and developed. *Indo-Chine* was a region in transition, an in-between place, betwixt India and China, occupying the unknown zone of the hyphen, the gap. As the French consolidated their colonial rule, the hyphenated designation was gradually dropped as if to signal the creation of a new identity and society. The "in-between space," the unknown zone of the hyphen, became somewhere new, somewhere French; it became French Indochina. Formally adopted by decree in 1887, the politicized term *l'Indochine française* eliminated in a simple, linguistic sense both Chinese and Indian influence, replacing them with an entirely new French domain of cultural hegemony.[1]

From the outset, *l'Indochine française* was an artificial construct. Prior to French intervention in Vietnam, 1,000 years of Chinese rule were followed by 900 years of independence during which time the regions of Vietnam existed most often as separate and rival political societies. France occupied Cochinchina in 1862, designating it a colony, and established

protectorates over Annam and Tonkin in 1884. The French then established a protectorate over Cambodia in 1863. France also claimed Laos as
a tributary of Vietnam; and when French officials were unable to document their claim, they resorted to gunboat diplomacy to round out their
empire in 1893. In annexing the inland kingdoms of Laos, which almost
disappeared when neighboring states were consolidated earlier in the
nineteenth century, the French likely prevented Laos from being absorbed
by Thailand and Vietnam. The hill tribes of Indochina, a remote, isolated
people attached only loosely to Cambodia, Laos and Vietnam, were the
final component of the variegated colonial empire established by the
French. Despite obvious, fundamental social differences, the French set
out to unite the disparate, culturally distinct areas of what are now Cambodia, Laos and Vietnam under the umbrella term *l'Indochine française*.

French methods of governance varied from region to region; and while
French efforts to carry out a colonial civilizing mission (*mission civil-
isatrice*) resulted in a certain unity of policy in some areas, the comparison
remains largely one of contrasts. Not only were the cultures and societies
of Cambodia, Laos and Vietnam unique but French rule in each of the
components of its colonial regime was also fundamentally different. Fur-
thermore, the picture of French colonialism which emerges from the
limited indigenous literature available hardly squares with the image of
French Indochina as a model of modernity. In contrast to the suggestion
"that colonies were 'laboratories of modernity,' where disciplinary power
and the latest techniques of social engineering could be deployed,"
contemporary research more often points to the absence of modernist
impulses in key sectors of the imperial project.[2]

The full extent to which the colonial period and the subsequent 30-year
war transformed the traditional relationship of Vietnam and its neighbors
also must be recognized. Hanoi's twentieth-century ambitions to dominate
all of Indochina can be understood largely in terms of the French model.
One of the peculiarities of French colonial administration was its heavy
dependence on educated Vietnamese to staff the bureaucracies, not only
of Annam, Cochinchina and Tonkin, but also Cambodia and Laos. The
Vietnamese traveling throughout Indochina at the turn of the century,
often in the employ of their colonial masters, viewed the region in ways
that did not coincide with those of their French overseers or with ASEAN-
10 concepts promoted today. As increasing numbers of Vietnamese supported French colonial projects throughout Indochina, their contacts with
the peoples of Cambodia and Laos also increased, dramatically changing
their perceptions of the subregion.

In the aftermath of World War II, the Vietnamese leadership pursued a
revolutionary vision of the area as an Indochinese communist bloc, a view
increasingly at odds with the policies of their noncommunist neighbors,
especially Thailand. The result was a third regional conflict in the late
1970s which pitted Vietnamese troops against their former Chinese com-

rades-in-arms in the north and Thai-backed Cambodian communists in the south. By 1980, all that remained of Vietnam's post-WWII revolutionary vision was its so-called "special relationship" with the Lao PDR and tenuous ties to the remaining fragments of its pre-Geneva 1954 Cambodian allies.

A decade later, the 1991 Paris Accords marked the end of the Indochinese Communist Party's dream of Vietnam as the revolutionary edge of socialism in Southeast Asia. In agreeing to a comprehensive political settlement of the Cambodian conflict, the Vietnamese relinquished control of "the Indochinese epicentre of their revolutionary regional politics." In this sense, as an anonymous Vietnamese official told the French journalist, Jean-Claude Pomonti, the agreement marked "la fin de l'Indochine," the end of Indochina.[3]

Similarly, Vietnam's entry into ASEAN in 1995, followed by the entries of Laos in 1997 and Cambodia in 1999, marked the end of Hanoi's dream of building Southeast Asian socialism on Vietnamese terms. The road to ASEAN-10 marked a diplomatic triumph for a wider form of regionalism in that it constituted formal recognition in Cambodia, Laos and Vietnam that the Indochinese Communist Party's internationalist view of Indochina, as promoted by Ho Chi Minh in the 1930s, was finally dead. Vietnamese entry into ASEAN, followed by the accession of Laos and Cambodia, also confirmed the end of the Cold War, together with the conclusion of a long period in which ideology was the determining factor in regional relations.

## Economic reforms

Over the last two decades, economic reform in Cambodia, Laos and Vietnam has gone well beyond so-called socialist renovation or a mere fine-tuning of their previous command economies. What began around 1979 as minor repair to the existing economic system developed into a profound, enduring reform process which included the reduction, if not the elimination, of central planning, price deregulation and other features of an outward, market-based development model. Only a few years ago, the economies of Cambodia, Laos and Vietnam were significantly different from those of most other Asian states, but today, it is the similarities that are more striking.

Peasant families in all three states now enjoy access to land in some form of constitutionally guaranteed, long-term tenure with elements of ownership. In Cambodia, Laos and Vietnam, rural households are the main elements of agricultural production as they are in most Asian states. While cooperatives and collectivized farming have not totally disappeared from the scene, especially in Vietnam, they have receded into the background and are no longer the ruling institutions that once differentiated their farming practices from those of their Asian neighbors.

The people of Cambodia, Laos and Vietnam also enjoy an entirely new relationship to the market. They can generally choose what they grow to eat at home or sell in the marketplace with prices negotiated between the contracting parties. Where the state once controlled the production and distribution of resources, the market has now become the primary means to allocate resources for production and consumption. In the process, the role of the government, most especially in the agricultural sector, has become increasingly similar to that of other Asian states. Even in Laos and Vietnam, where the state remains a major actor in setting economic, political and social agendas, it is no longer as intrusive as it once was.

Likewise, the governments of Cambodia, Laos and Vietnam have redefined their role vis-à-vis the industrial sector. Shared characteristics of this new role include a progressive withdrawal from many state enterprises, increased autonomy for other state companies, deregulation of prices, greater reliance on markets, broader opportunities for the private sector and the active pursuit of foreign investment. State enterprise reform has gone hand in hand with banking reform because one without the other would not allow viable firms access to the credit they need and would not punish troubled firms engaged in distress financing. Conversely, in the absence of state enterprise reform, banking reform would be unlikely to produce a better allocation of capital because state enterprises, unrestrained by market forces, would continue to engage in short-term, expedient behavior. While Cambodia, Laos and Vietnam have demonstrated considerable determination to reorganize and rationalize the state sector, more work remains to be done in Laos and Vietnam. Laos has not conducted thoroughgoing structural changes and continues to subsidize state enterprises. Vietnam earmarked 2,143 state enterprises for restructuring in 2003–5 but was already well behind schedule after the first year. Once the backlog was cleared and the target reached, Vietnam would still be left with 1,866 state enterprises. Future reform measures must consider how best to continue equitization (privatization) in Vietnam as well as how best to manage those state enterprises not equitized.

Economic reforms have not occurred simultaneously in all three states, but the general direction of change has been the same. The end result has also been similar – modification beyond recognition of the former socialist system. Today, in Cambodia, Laos and Vietnam, socialism no longer constitutes an economic program or a blueprint for social and cultural transformation. Instead, it has been transformed in Laos and Vietnam into an element of political rhetoric which earnestly proclaims "the one-party state has no intention of allowing liberal-democratic reforms."[4] Cambodia is the exception in this regard. The 1993 general elections introduced an element of pluralism in the political system; thereafter, the economic policies of the Cambodian government eliminated virtually all remaining traces of socialism in the Marxist-Leninist sense.

The economic reform process in Cambodia, Laos and Vietnam has in many important respects been internally driven. Much of the change implemented was the product of peasant alienation or other discontent over the inefficiencies of the command economy and the authoritarian tone of the one-party state. Domestic pressure and bottom-up adaptations of the prevailing model played important roles in shaping reforms intended to break the low productivity stalemate. Despite the proliferation of foreign models and some pressure from allies, the timing and sequence of Vietnamese reforms, in particular, appear to have been drawn primarily from Vietnamese experience. Hanoi officials often spoke of learning from the South, and many of their ideas and policy models were sourced in southern Vietnam, a region which experienced a capitalist model more recently than any other communist-ruled state. Admittedly, many Vietnamese policies resembled those found in other command economies, but this was mostly because the problems they addressed and the institutional frameworks within which they worked were also much alike. Early on, selected reform measures undertaken by Cambodia and Laos mirrored the Vietnamese experience, but over time, both states increasingly developed local solutions to local problems.

At the same time, diverse regional and international developments, including economic reform in China, dramatic growth in neighboring Asian economies and the breakup of the Soviet Bloc, sanctioned and accelerated the reform process in all three cases. The "new world order" of the 1990s led to an entirely new international situation for Cambodia, Laos and Vietnam. As economic aid and political support from the Comecon states evaporated, Western trade, cooperation and finance became of decisive importance to the success of stabilization, reform and development efforts. In more recent times, the 1997–8 financial crisis, the SARS outbreak and the avian influenza (bird flu) epidemic impacted negatively on development plans, emphasizing the dynamic nature of the economic challenges facing these three states. On the positive side, the prevailing climate of uncertainty helped stimulate, out of necessity, economic efficiency whose need was recognized and introduced by the agenda-setting elite, most especially in Vietnam.

## Political reform

Economics and politics are intrinsically related dimensions of a single social reality, and the requirements of a protracted war decisively shaped until 1975 both the economic and political structures of Cambodia, Laos and Vietnam. The decision to wage war was "based on overriding political priorities" that produced "inevitable and enduring economic and social legacies." Victory was the only criterion for economic efficiency throughout the war; and in this, the communists were supremely successful. As a result, many communist leaders could not imagine that economic and political policies so effective in wartime would prove counterproductive in peace. And there was no way anyone inside or outside the Communist Party could openly discuss this risk.[5]

The governments of Cambodia, Laos and Vietnam have undergone dramatic and far-reaching economic reforms in recent years; however, the emphasis politically, with the notable exception of Cambodia, has remained on stability and control. Limited political reforms in Laos and Vietnam were undertaken within the framework of a one-party state, but the communist parties in both states remained unwilling to accommodate meaningful dialog or criticism. On the contrary, an important objective of the political reform process in both Laos and Vietnam has been to strengthen the credibility of the Party and the state as legitimate forces of change. In neither case have the restrained, sporadic reforms to date resulted in a noticeable shift toward greater popular participation in political life.

In Vietnam, there was a brief flowering of political reform after 1986, but this period was cut short in 1989 by China's massacre of pro-democracy demonstrators in Tiananmen Square and the collapse of communism in Eastern Europe. Thereafter, the Party insisted on retaining rule even as it adopted a goal of economic reform along market lines. There was widespread agreement the state had a key role to play in the reconstruction of Vietnam, but there was little recognition in Party circles that, to be successful, it would have to be a new and far different role from the one played in the past.

In April 2001, Nong Duc Manh replaced the much maligned Le Kha Phieu as general secretary of the Vietnam Communist Party and embarked on a program of legal reform and bureaucratic transparency. Having served for nine years as chairman of the National Assembly, Manh brought to his new post both seniority and considerable experience in consensus building. When national elections were held in May 2002, a revised candidate selection process placed a premium on high political, legal and ethical standards. For the first time, potential candidates were required to declare their assets in support of their bid for candidacy. General Secretary Manh worked hard to make Party members more accountable, attacking the pervasive corruption found at the highest levels of both Party and state. However, even as he pursued reforms intended to make the state more efficient and subject to law, it remained important to distinguish between political liberalization and the creation of what might be considered a law-governed state. In Vietnam under Manh, the objective remained one of preempting domestic opposition and keeping the Party in power, not bringing about its demise.

In Laos, the collapse of communism in Europe, culminating in the implosion of the Soviet Union, drove the Lao People's Revolutionary Party to reaffirm its ties with Asia's remaining communist states, notably China. To underscore the point, General Secretary Kaysone Phomvihane was the first foreign leader to visit Beijing after Tiananmen. Thereafter,

Lao PDR leaders repeatedly stressed the continuing supremacy of the Party, emphasizing that any and all political reform in Laos would occur under its auspices. When LPRP officials went to great lengths to make the 2002 National Assembly elections appear meaningful, for example, most observers viewed Lao conduct of the polls as indicative of a general shift on the part of Lao authorities toward being less embarrassed about the Party's role.

In a related event, the Lao government celebrated a national holiday in January 2003 to mark the birthday of fourteenth-century King Fa Ngum. This was the first time the communist regime had acknowledged the role of the past monarchy and marked a new phase in nation-building and the reconstruction of a Lao national identity. In seeking new sources of legitimacy from Buddhism to the monarchy, the communists signaled a determination to continue LPRP control of all aspects of life and society in Laos, allowing no other political parties to function.

The Lao People's Revolutionary Party and the Vietnam Communist Party may continue in the years ahead to use economic performance to retain governing legitimacy; however, experience would suggest they will find real limits to this development model. No communist-ruled society to date has been successful with a similar approach. At some point, increased respect for human rights and religious freedoms, in conjunction with democratic reforms, are virtually certain to become preconditions for Party survival in both states.

With the possible exception of elections held in 1955 after Cambodia received independence from France, the Cambodian people until the last decade had never experienced any form of truly democratic process or government. On the contrary, violence has long been the standard means for resolving political (and other) disputes in Cambodia. At the outset of the 1990s, Cambodia had experienced two decades of civil war in the wake of the overthrow of Prince Norodom Sihanouk in 1970, interrupted only by four years of "peace" under the Khmer Rouge, a period of terror and mass murder in which at least one million people died. Following the Vietnamese invasion and occupation of Cambodia in December 1978, competing factions in Cambodia continued their bloody conflict. Prospects for creating an enduring democratic government in this milieu were virtually nonexistent according to any known theory of democratic formation.

A fragile peace between warring factions, struck after 13 years of civil war, was only just holding when the United Nations sponsored elections in May 1993. Widely considered free and fair, more than four million people, an estimated 89 percent of registered voters, went to the polls. Exactly what Cambodians voted for in 1993 remains a subject of hot debate. What they received was a semblance of political pluralism in a shift from a one-party, Leninist state to a coalition government which brought a modicum of stability and a tentative political truce. In the process, Cambodia stepped back in time, becoming a constitutional monarchy with Norodom

Sihanouk returning to the throne he relinquished in 1955. Over the next few years, the actions of the Cambodian elite, in "Cambodia's most recent externally imposed political transition," were driven less by power sharing, an oxymoron when applied to Cambodian politics, than by power building. For much of this period, King Sihanouk was justly credited with holding together a fragile peace between Cambodia's competing factions.[6]

Violence again swept the Cambodian political system in July 1997. The Cambodian People's Party (CPP) led by co-premier Hun Sen executed a savage coup, shattering the organization and leadership of coalition partner and primary rival, the National United Front for an Independent, Neutral, Peaceful and Cooperative Cambodia (FUNCINPEC), led by Prince Norodom Ranariddh. Crushing the FUNCINPEC military organization and mangling its political structure, Hun Sen established himself in full control in Cambodia. Following a year in which the CPP consolidated its power, Hun Sen's party received a strong plurality in the July 1998 elections. A new coalition government was then formed with Hun Sen as prime minister and Prince Ranariddh as National Assembly president, a position with little political power.

Over the next four years, Hun Sen continued to consolidate his position as the single most powerful politician in Cambodia, marginalizing the role of King Sihanouk and supplanting the dwindling power of FUNCINPEC. The CPP swept both the February 2002 commune elections and the July 2003 general elections with the opposition Sam Rainsy Party outpolling FUNCINPEC for the first time. Increasing its plurality, the CPP failed to win the two-thirds majority necessary for Hun Sen to create his own government. And it took almost a year for CPP and FUNCINPEC to form a new coalition government. In the process, Hun Sen displayed a growing intolerance for any form of political opposition or dissent, an attitude which boded ill for the future of democracy in Cambodia. Enjoying a monopoly on political power and in control of all forms of security, Hun Sen appeared to be moving away from a maturing democratic process and toward a return to an effective one-party state in Cambodia.

Ironically, the People's Republic of China may in the end hold the key to democratic reform in Cambodia, Laos and Vietnam. Chinese support for the conservative leadership of the Vietnamese Communist Party has helped to stymie even modest reform efforts in Vietnam. Meaningful political reform in Vietnam is not necessarily contingent on a liberalization of the Chinese political system, but its prospects would likely improve if China initiated similar reforms. In turn, Vietnam would appear to be central to the adoption of related reforms in Laos. If Vietnam were to begin to implement truly democratic reforms, in the shape of a multi-party system with free and open elections, the Lao PDR would most likely follow suit given Hanoi's longtime political influence in Vientiane. Additional democracy in Vietnam would also deepen support in Cambodia for the rule of law and other conditions sustaining democratic civil society. In all three countries, any movement toward meaningful democratic reform would likely embolden donor states to make future assistance increasingly conditional on incremental reform steps.

## Regionalism

In Indochina, the anti-colonial struggle gave birth to a vision of close cooperation after independence. Cambodia, Laos and Vietnam remain linked today by friendship agreements concluded after 1975. Once viewed as fundamental, these agreements have become increasingly irrelevant as economic reforms have expanded, spawning wider regional and international initiatives. In the process, the prevailing concept of Indochina, born out of nineteenth-century French colonialism, became more and more anachronistic. The contemporary reform process in Cambodia, Laos and Vietnam thus signaled not the rebirth of an economic unit, but the end of an epoch. From the ashes of the old Indochina, a new phoenix arose grounded on free market principles in which old economies sought comparative advantage in new contexts.

Following France's defeat in the First Indochina War, the U.S. government aimed to be the prime mover in the development of the Mekong subregion, a goal later frustrated by its own defeat in the Second Indochina War. American initiatives in the 1950s and 1960s mirrored the French approach, focusing on south to north, east to west relationships and touting the economic benefits of large projects with subregional implications, most especially dam construction on the Mekong and its tributaries. A farsighted Ford Foundation Report published in 1961 emphasized the need for environmental and social studies to catch up to technical proposals for dam construction, a process which really only began in the 1990s.[7]

International lending agencies, like the Asian Development Bank (ADB) and the World Bank, championed throughout the 1990s elements of the earlier Franco-American approach. The notable exception was the inclusion of China's Yunnan province in the subregional grouping promoted by the Asian Development Bank. Bureaucrats from Manila to Washington, D.C. advocated subregional cooperation grounded largely on infrastructure development and integration in transportation, telecommunications, energy, trade and investment. It was only in December 2001 that ADB finally adopted a more balanced approach, addressing sensitive and complex issues, like human resource development and environmental degradation, and emphasizing the need to harmonize policies and procedures in addition to developing physical linkages. The new strategy took what ADB officials described as a "multisectoral and holistic" approach to regional cooperation, replacing the eight priority sectors of the 1990s with five strategic thrusts.[8]

This redirection of the earlier development model, aspects of which could be traced to the French colonial era, was welcomed in Cambodia, Laos and Vietnam. It reflected a more accurate understanding of their capabilities and requirements, as well as those of the other member states of the Greater Mekong Subregion. Unfortunately, with an estimated $15 billion in investment required over ten years, progress toward completion of the new plan has been necessarily slow. Investors remained hesitant to lend to countries with uncertain stability and poor credit records.

Similar to Indochina, ASEAN was a byproduct of the colonial occupation of most of Southeast Asia. As professor Mark Beeson has pointed out, "the very idea of a distinct Southeast Asian region, which ultimately provided a basis for the original ASEAN grouping and the subsequent ASEAN Plus Three initiative, was itself an artifact of British military planning during World War II." In this sense, "ASEAN did not so much create a Southeast Asian political space" as it indigenized "an existing one that had been given de facto expression by the activities of the colonial powers." Following World War II, the Cold War served to entrench external influences, dividing the region along ideological lines. The end of the Cold War opened new opportunities for a wider regionalism with new forms of cooperation and coordination grounded in formal political initiatives and agreements.[9] Cambodia, Laos and Vietnam took advantage of the changing circumstances to join ASEAN in the 1990s.

As a regional grouping, ASEAN-10 has promised much but delivered little in part because regional initiatives continue to be both driven and constrained by internal and external factors. The economic and political diversity of Southeast Asia make any form of cooperation more challenging and complex than it was in Europe. Intraregional trade and investment are modest, and the ASEAN economies are generally not complementary and often competitive. The possibilities for enhanced regionalism are also constrained, as they have been for more than a century, by the strategic concerns and tensions of outside players, particularly China, Japan and the United States. The war on terrorism, to take a contemporary example, has had a major impact on the region's development and sense of regional unity, once again demonstrating the difficulties involved in articulating and implementing a region-wide response to a strategic crisis. In this instance, the response of Southeast Asian states has been diverse and uneven with each country reacting to the war in ways that serve its own immediate political objectives.[10]

Geographically, Cambodia, Laos and Vietnam are situated in the fastest growing region in the world with Cambodia and Laos sandwiched between China, Thailand and Vietnam, three of the world's most dynamic economies. Developmentalists, politicians and academics often find the spatial content of development plans beguiling; but the reality is that business opportunities are relatively limited, especially in Cambodia and Laos. Mostly inhabited by poor farmers with limited spending power, low levels of education and few marketable skills, niches for profitable investment remain few and far between and geared largely to the exploitation of natural resources. Given their small populations, collectively 19 million people or only 4 percent of the ASEAN total, limited home markets and underdeveloped infrastructures further dampen overseas investment prospects. As a result, both Cambodia and Laos are at risk of becoming little more than a place to build a bridge, road or railway, a transshipment point between the more economically vibrant areas of China, Thailand and Vietnam. Consequently, their governments have reason to be both optimistic and wary of the benefits each can reap from inclusion in regional development programs. In the end, one of the most tangible benefits may be found in the diplomatic sphere where Cambodia and Laos will likely find centuries-old problems of dependence on China, Thailand or Vietnam to be more evenly balanced.

Broader regional issues include how best to deal with country-specific goals, for example Chinese construction of upstream Mekong dams, when they conflict with regional goals. No real forum exists to work out such conflicts. Moreover, there is limited support for challenging the ASEAN way of consultation and consensus building or the policy of noninterference in the internal affairs of member states. In addition, enormous uncertainty and legitimate concern exists as to the total impact of many proposed regional development projects, like the downstream economic, environmental and social impact of mainstream dams or the impact of road construction on HIV/AIDS transmission. Potential investors also continue to face serious obstacles, like the need for a strong legal framework and a transparent corporate culture to encourage and support investment.

A related issue is how best to ensure that development and growth plans in the Greater Mekong Subregion are compatible with related ASEAN schemes. A year-long study published in early 2004 by McKinsey and Company, a management consulting firm, argued ASEAN was losing its competitive edge because it remained "a collection of disparate markets." To make the region more competitive, the report recommended an accelerated integration scheme centered on the elimination of nontariff trade barriers, enhanced tariff reform, creation of a level playing field for capital and improved regional collaboration.[11] As ASEAN attempts to accelerate its integration process to regain its competitive position, poorer countries like Cambodia, Laos and Vietnam, unable to implement reforms as quickly as their neighbors, are in serious danger of falling further and further behind. It took ASEAN 25 years to establish the ASEAN Free Trade Area (AFTA) and another ten years for the ASEAN-6 to implement it. Even today, many businessmen rightly consider unconvincing AFTA's efforts to project Southeast Asia as a single, integrated market. Based on the ASEAN experience, the differences in social, economic, legal and political systems among the GMS countries in general, and Cambodia, Laos and Vietnam in particular, make achievement of a similar level of integration a challenging and lengthy process.

### Imperfect past, uncertain future

In discussing the economic and political reforms implemented in Cambodia, Laos and Vietnam over the last three decades, one is struck by parallel themes of continuity and change. All three states seek to build a new future while also accommodating the past. As their political economies modernize along different lines, they often demonstrate related characteristics, if not common traits. At the same time, they make different modifications and adjustments to exploit the unique strengths of their individual cultures and to mask their weaknesses in separate ways. In the process, all three states display a certain respect for hierarchy and an appreciation for order, moral responsibility and achievement.

In an economic condition not dissimilar to other Asian states, Cambodia, Laos and Vietnam must overcome related dilemmas, beginning with sound, growth-oriented macroeconomic policies. The Vietnamese case can be dealt with in short order as the economy has performed well in recent years with strong GDP growth achieved and macroeconomic stability maintained. Vietnam successfully managed both the Asian financial crisis in 1997–8 and the downturn in the world economy in 2001, displaying admirable adaptability in successive economic crises demanding very different responses.

The macroeconomic performance of the Lao PDR was reasonably good into the mid-1990s but deteriorated rapidly at the end of the decade. Internal factors initiated the decline which was then fueled by the Asian financial crisis. Soft budget constraints, revenue shortfalls and an increase in capital expenditure contributed to the deterioration. One lesson to be drawn from the Lao experience is that one-party rule can facilitate the creation and implementation of a rapid transition program, together with improved short-term macroeconomic performance. Longer term, the absence of transparency and democracy, together with the socioeconomic conditions found in a country like Laos, may have the reverse effect with the emergence of a bargaining economy contributing to macroeconomic instability.[12]

Blessed with substantial hydropower potential, the Lao PDR can anticipate relatively high growth rates if it can sustain a well-managed macroeconomic condition. Unlike other countries mired in slow growth, the challenge facing Laos is not so much generating growth as it is shaping growth to benefit all its citizens. A related dilemma is the perilous state of agricultural productivity and rural infrastructure as the two factors intensify the inequitable impact of rapid urban, industrial growth. If not addressed, the dual nature of the Lao economy, with standards of living improving in urban areas as they decline in rural ones, will exacerbate political pressures, compounding long-standing ethnic and social tensions.

In Cambodia, financial instability has been an acute problem for decades and the capacity to manage the economy by macroeconomic means has yet to be fully developed. A high level of dollarization, a situation in which the U.S. dollar is the dominant currency with the local riel playing a secondary role, is a unique feature of the economy. On the supply side, this condition is a product of sizable international assistance, private transfers and export earnings. On the demand side, it is encouraged by political uncertainty and limited confidence in the local currency. Dollarization helped limit the exchange rate impact of the external shock and inflationary pressures after 1997 but constitutes a serious complication for Cambodian officials hoping to create both sustainable growth and steadfast poverty reduction.

It must also be recognized that putting the macroeconomic houses of Cambodia, Laos and Vietnam in order, an ongoing challenge that is far from done, will not have a significant impact on that large portion of the rural population that is barely monetized. The subsistence population is not strongly affected by inflation rates nor is it affected immediately by improvements in the investment climate, banking sector or other institutional developments designed to attract foreign direct investment. On the contrary, the macroeconomic framework has its strongest and most rapid effect on the urban population, even when it sets the stage for programs with secondary effects on the general population. Consequently, the trickle down benefits to the bulk of the population, especially in Cambodia and Laos where a high percentage of people are dependent on agriculture, would be relatively small. This is not an argument against macroeconomic reform but rather a plea for understanding its short-term impact on the vast majority of citizens in agricultural economies.

In all three states, public sector spending must be brought in line with tax revenues, and inflation rates have to be carefully controlled. Some success in reducing the fiscal deficit has been achieved in Vietnam, but ongoing progress in containing inflation requires additional public sector retrenchment. Increased revenue generation in all three states is an essential leg of any broad-based program designed to correct the budget deficit. Accelerated human resource development is another requirement common to all three states. In Cambodia and Laos, the economy is kept afloat by a combination of bilateral and multilateral aid, a condition described by some observers as a form of cargo cult society in which citizens have come to see external aid as a permanent facet of the national economy. Increasing talk of donor fatigue in both Cambodia and Laos make any expectation of international aid ad infinitum, except assistance tied to specific projects or performance criteria, totally unrealistic.

Low-cost labor industries, especially garment making, are a major contributor to Cambodia's export revenues, as is rice which is beginning to be exported again although not at prewar levels. Tourism linked to the Angkor temple complex has also become an important foreign exchange earner, one that has come at the cost of environmental degradation, especially around Siem Reap. Timber removal in both Cambodia and Laos remains a corrupt, scandalous process, combining rapid deforestation and lost government revenues. Cambodia joined the World Trade Organization in September 2003, but the benefits of WTO membership are uncertain and likely to be long term. Optimists argue membership will generate badly needed foreign investment and broaden Cambodia's manufacturing base. Pessimists say it will prompt the government to lower tariffs, leading to increased agricultural imports which will impact the livelihood of already impoverished farmers. Most everyone agrees attracting investors to Cambodia will remain a hard sell given the weak legal infrastructure, uncertain political stability and rampant corruption.

The present tax system, which is incapable in all three countries of generating sufficient government revenues to cover essential expenditures, has been and will continue to be an important factor in ongoing macroeconomic difficulties. In Vietnam, the relationship between taxpayers and tax authorities has changed dramatically since the process of tax reform began. New tax regimes have been introduced, replacing systems more appropriate for the old economy, and administrative procedures have improved. The central objective has been to operate a tax system that generates adequate revenue within an internationally compatible and competitive system. The challenge for Vietnam is to continue to reform the tax system in a way which protects government revenues yet remains friendly to business. Cambodia and Laos face similar challenges in strengthening tax administration, revenue collection and expenditure management. In all three states, tax reforms are urgently needed which create a system capable of providing an adequate, stable source of revenue.

Trade policy also remains a common concern. Vietnam continues to pursue WTO membership, but its achievement of this objective is heavily dependent on more dramatic tariff reductions as well as increased flexibility in the areas of insurance, telecommunications and finance services. WTO member states are looking for trade conditions equivalent to or better than the market access Vietnam granted to the United States in 2000. In Laos, the sale of electricity to Thailand accounts for almost 30 percent of total exports and constitutes some 15 percent of government revenues. Completion of the Nam Theun 2 hydropower station, a problematic project scheduled for end 2009, could increase government revenues by another 5 percent. But hydropower is not the panacea for Laos. Thailand is the single customer, and maintenance and repair costs are high. Moreover, Laos faces core problems of productivity and production. It is unable to compete with its neighbors which means it imports more than it exports, threatening to institutionalize its dependence on foreign aid. In Cambodia, the garment industry, a pillar of the new economy, faces a serious threat of direct competition from China and Vietnam. Cambodia's market access will increase with WTO membership, but the garment industry cannot survive without improving its competitiveness.

Finally, all three states need to streamline both legal and policy environments to pave the way for increased foreign direct investment. Investment figures in Vietnam, despite a reputation for corruption, improved in recent years but are still below levels in the 1990s. Improved credit ratings and the composition of the foreign investment community, which is dominated by Asian investors, help account for Vietnam's recent success. Yet investors still complain about cumbersome administrative procedures and unequal service costs. In the wake of the Asian financial crisis, foreign direct investment approvals in Laos dropped sharply from $2.6 billion in 1996 to just $20 million in 2000. The loss of confidence caused the kip to plummet against the U.S. dollar, increasing the government's dependency on foreign aid to finance both public investment projects and a severe current account deficit. With some progress in macroeconomic stability and structural reforms, foreign direct investment levels in Laos improved in recent years, primarily in the hydropower sector. In Cambodia, investors continue to complain about high tax rates and corruption along with the inability of the government to treat investors in a consistent, transparent manner.

## A final word

The governments of Cambodia, Laos and Vietnam have succeeded in implementing economic reforms to the degree they have introduced major modifications to the structure of economic relations in their respective countries and the role of the state in their economies. The extent to which these governments have improved the livelihoods of their citizens is another issue. Their ability to build upon the economic reforms in place is also uncertain. Political reform is a separate but related issue which has proved to be even more challenging. In the political arena, too often it has been a question of *plus ça change, plus c'est la même chose*, or the more things change, the more they remain the same. All three states have clearly gone beyond the end of the beginning, but each must continue to build on the reforms in place if it is to progress down the road to sustained economic and political development. Once again, the devil is in the detail. A failure to accelerate current reforms would have the additional effect of jeopardizing already halting regional integration plans as the slouching "Tigers" of Asia look to restore their competitive edge in the global economy. Along the way, only one thing seems certain. The governments of Cambodia, Laos and Vietnam will surely need less continuity and more change.

# Notes

## 1 Same space, different dreams

1 Chiranan Prasertkul argues persuasively that southwestern China (Lower Yunnan) in the nineteenth century constituted a natural macroregion with parts of Burma, Laos, Thailand and Vietnam (*Yunnan Trade in the Nineteenth Century: Southwest China's Cross-boundaries Functional System*, Asian Studies Monograph 44, Chulalongkorn University, Bangkok, 1989).

2 Milton Osborne, *The Mekong: Turbulent Past, Uncertain Future*, New York, NY: Atlantic Monthly Press, 2000, pp. 64, 75–7. For a detailed look at early French exploration of the Mekong River see Milton Osborne, *River Road to China: The Mekong River Expedition, 1866–73*, London: George Allen & Unwin, 1975.

3 Osborne, *Mekong*, pp. 155–6. Along with stunning photographs, information on the culture, history and geography of the Mekong also can be found in John Hoskin and Allen W. Hopkins, *The Mekong: A River and Its People*, Bangkok: Post Publishing Company, 1991.

4 For an introduction to the Greater Mekong Subregion, see Asian Development Bank, *Subregional Economic Cooperation: Initial Possibilities for Cambodia, Lao PDR, Myanmar, Thailand, Viet Nam and the Yunnan Province of the People's Republic of China*, Manila: Asian Development Bank, 1993.

5 General economic data on Cambodia, Laos and Vietnam comes from a number of sources, including the Asian Development Bank, Central Intelligence Agency and World Bank.

6 Grant Evans, *The Politics of Ritual and Remembrance: Laos since 1975*, Honolulu, HI: University of Hawai'i Press, 1998, pp. 10, 49–50, 175–6.

7 Pierre Gourou, "For a French Indo-Chinese Federation," *Pacific Affairs*, vol. 20, no. 1, March 1947, pp. 18–19, quote 18.

8 Christopher E. Goscha, *Vietnam or Indochina? Contesting Concepts of Space in Vietnamese Nationalism, 1887–1954*, NIAS Report Series No. 28, Copenhagen: Nordic Institute of Asian Studies Publishing, 1999, p. 21; Gourou, "French Indo-Chinese Federation," p. 19.

9 Lauriston Sharp, "French Plan for Indochina," *Far Eastern Survey*, vol. 15, no. 13, 3 July 1946, pp. 193–4, quotes p. 194; Nicola J. Cooper, *France in Indochina: Colonial Encounters*, Oxford: Berg, 2001, pp. 29–42. The literature on colonial Indochina is rich but uneven. Among the more rewarding studies are the following: Pierre Brocheux and Daniel Hémery, *Indochine: La colonisation ambiguë (1858–1954)*, Paris: La Découverte, 1995; Alain Forest, *Le Cambodge et la Colonisation Française: Histoire d'une colonisation sans heurts (1897–1920)*, Paris: Éditions L'Harmattan, 1980; Philippe Hédy, *Histoire de L'Indochine: Le perle de l'empire, 1624–1954*, Paris: Albin Michel, 1998;

Hue-Tam Ho Tai, *Radicalism and the Origins of the Vietnamese Revolution*, Cambridge, MA: Harvard University Press, 1992; David G. Marr, *Vietnamese Anticolonialism 1885–1925*, Berkeley, CA: University of California Press, 1971; David G. Marr, *Vietnamese Tradition on Trial 1920–1945*, Berkeley, CA: University of California Press, 1981; Alfred W. McCoy, "French Colonialism in Laos, 1893–1945," in *Laos: War and Revolution*, ed. Nina S. Adams and Alfred W. McCoy, New York, NY: Harper Colophon Books, 1970, pp. 67–99; Patrice Morlat, *La répression coloniale au Vietnam (1908–1940)*, Paris: Éditions L'Harmattan, 1990; Martin J. Murray, *The Development of Capitalism in Colonial Indochina (1870–1940)*, Berkeley, CA: University of California Press, 1980; Ngo Van, *Viêt-nam, 1920–1945: Révolution et contre-révolution sous la domination coloniale*, Paris: Nautilus, 2000; Milton E. Osborne, *The French Presence in Cochinchina & Cambodia: Rule and Response (1859–1905)*, Ithaca, NY: Cornell University Press, 1969; Martin Stuart-Fox, "The French in Laos, 1887–1945," *Modern Asian Studies*, vol. 29, no. 1, February 1995, pp. 111–39; Truong Buu Lâm, *Colonialism Experienced: Vietnamese Writings on Colonialism, 1900–1931*, Ann Arbor, MI: University of Michigan Press, 2000.

10 Truong Buu Lâm, *Resistance, Rebellion, Revolution: Popular Movements in Vietnamese History*, Occasional Paper No. 75, Singapore: Institute of Southeast Asian Studies, 1984, pp. 27–36; Ngo Van, *Viêt-nam*, pp. 1–274; Hue-Tam Ho Tai, *Millenarianism and Peasant Politics in Vietnam*, Cambridge, MA: Harvard University Press, 1983, pp. 63–128; Geoffrey C. Gunn, *Rebellion in Laos: Peasant and Politics in a Colonial Backwater*, Boulder, CO: Westview Press, 1990, pp. 101–82; Ian Mabbett and David Chandler, *The Khmers*, Oxford: Blackwell, 1995, p. 234.

11 Murray, *Development*, pp. x, 90–1, 494–5, quote xi; Thomas E. Ennis, *French Policy and Developments in Indochina*, Chicago, IL: University of Chicago Press, 1936, pp. 111–48; Sharp, "French Plan," p. 194. For a poignant memoir of how life on a colonial rubber plantation brought one Vietnamese youth to the revolution, as well as an excellent example of the genre known as revolutionary prison memoirs, see Tran Tu Binh, *The Red Earth: A Vietnamese Memoir of Life on a Colonial Rubber Plantation*, Monographs in International Studies, Southeast Asia Series Number 66, Athens, OH: Ohio University Press, 1985.

12 Goscha, *Vietnam or Indochina*, pp. 24–6.

13 McCoy, "French Colonialism," pp. 82–3; Arthur J. Dommen, *Laos: Keystone of Indochina*, Boulder, CO: Westview Press, 1985, pp. 138–9. Recent scholarship suggests the oppressiveness of French colonial rule was not as all-encompassing as once thought. For example, Grant Evans concludes the *corvée* system touched the Lao population both unevenly and lightly (*A Short History of Laos: The Land in Between*, St Leonards, New South Wales: Allen & Unwin, 2002, pp. 51–2).

14 Osborne, *French Presence*, pp. 261–86, quote vii; David P. Chandler, "Cambodia in 1984: Historical Patterns Re-asserted?" *Southeast Asian Affairs 1985*, Singapore: Institute of Southeast Asian Studies, 1985, p. 179.

15 Arthur J. Dommen, *The Indochinese Experience of the French and the Americans: Nationalism and Communism in Cambodia, Laos, and Vietnam*, Bloomington, IN: Indiana University Press, 2001, pp. 22–5, quote p. 25.

16 Ho Chi Minh, "Appeal Made on the Occasion of the Founding of the Communist Party of Indochina (February 18, 1930)," in *Ho Chi Minh on Revolution: Selected Writings, 1920–66*, ed. Bernard B. Fall, New York, NY: Praeger Publishers, 1967, pp. 129–31; Thomas Engelbert and Christopher E. Goscha, *Falling Out of Touch: A Study on Vietnamese Communist Policy Towards an Emerging Cambodian Communist Movement, 1930–1975*, Clayton, Victoria: Monash University, 1995, pp. 5–9; Steven R. Heder, *Cambodian Communism*

*and the Vietnamese Model: Imitation and Independence, 1930–1975*, Bangkok: White Lotus Press, 2004, pp. 13–24; Huynh Kim Khánh, *Vietnamese Communism, 1925–1945*, Ithaca, NY: Cornell University Press, 1982, pp. 123–9. As David Chandler points out in the introduction to Engelbert and Goscha: "Marxism-Leninism made little headway among the royalist-Buddhist elite populations of Laos and Cambodia, many of whom, in any case, probably perceived the term 'Indo-China' as hegemonic rather than fraternal. To many Lao and Khmer, 'China' overshadowed 'Indo' " (*Out of Touch*, p. iii).

17 Engelbert and Goscha, *Out of Touch*, pp. 6–10, internal study quoted on p. 10. The debate between Vietnamese and Indochinese political lines cut across the full spectrum of Vietnamese nationalist discourse in the 1920s and 1930s (Engelbert and Goscha, *Out of Touch*, p. 8).

18 Engelbert and Goscha, *Out of Touch*, pp. 1–4, quote p. 3. This borrowing of the French model by Vietnamese nationalists in the 1920s and 1930s had important long-term consequences for Cambodian–Vietnamese and Lao–Vietnamese relations (Engelbert and Goscha, *Out of Touch*, p. 2, footnote 3).

19 Ben Kiernan, *How Pol Pot Came to Power: A History of Communism in Kampuchea, 1930–1975*, London: Verso, 1985, pp. 1–39; Geoffrey C. Gunn, *Political Struggles in Laos (1930–1954)*, Bangkok: Editions Duang Kamol, 1988, pp. 73–98; Christopher E. Goscha, *Thailand and the Southeast Asian Networks of the Vietnamese Revolution, 1885–1954*, Richmond, Surrey: Curzon Press, 1999, pp. 94–5, 148–51, 160–4; Murray, *Development*, p. 494; Engelbert and Goscha, *Out of Touch*, pp. 10–11.

20 Judith A. Stowe, *Siam Becomes Thailand: A Story of Intrigue*, Honolulu, HI: University of Hawai'i Press, 1991, pp. 37–9, 45–8; Goscha, *Thailand*, 76–83; David K. Wyatt, *Thailand: A Short History*, New Haven, CT: Yale University Press, 1982, p. 237; Engelbert and Goscha, *Out of Touch*, pp. 11–12.

21 Engelbert and Goscha, *Out of Touch*, pp. 12–18, quote 14; Huynh Kim Khánh, *Vietnamese Communism*, pp. 252, 263–9. On the early beginnings of Lao nationalism, see Soren Ivarsson, "Towards a New Laos: *Lao Nhay* and the Campaign for a National 'Reawakening' in Laos, 1941–45," in *Laos: Culture and Society*, ed. Grant Evans, Chiang Mai: Silkworm Books, 1999, pp. 61–78.

22 David G. Marr, *Vietnam 1945: The Quest for Power*, Berkeley, CA: University of California Press, 1995, pp. 471–539; Engelbert and Goscha, *Out of Touch*, pp. 18–21.

23 Goscha, *Vietnam or Indochina*, pp. 93–5, 102–3, quote p. 102.

24 Brocheux and Hémery, *Indochine*, pp. 345–7; Ellen J. Hammer, *The Struggle for Indochina*, Stanford, CA: Stanford University Press, 1954, pp. 31–2, 43–4; Sharp, "French Plan," pp. 194–5.

25 Gourou, "French Indo-Chinese Federation," p. 19.

26 As quoted in Sharp, "French Plan," p. 195.

27 David P. Chandler, *The Tragedy of Cambodian History: Politics, War and Revolution since 1945*, New Haven, CT: Yale University Press, 1991, pp. 26–8; V. M. Reddi, *A History of the Cambodian Independence Movement, 1863–1955*, Tirupati, India: Sri Venkateswara University, 1971, pp. 109–18.

28 Martin Stuart-Fox, *A History of Laos*, Cambridge: Cambridge University Press, 1997, pp. 66–7; Jean Deuve, *Le Laos 1945–1949: Contribution a l'histoire du mouvement Lao Issala*, Montpellier: Université Paul Valéry, n.d., p. 220; Gunn, *Political Struggles*, pp. 173–4.

29 Marr, *Vietnam 1945*, pp. 547–8; Sharp, "French Plan," pp. 196–7.

30 Goscha, *Vietnam or Indochina*, pp. 96–101, quotes p. 100.

31 Paul F. Langer and Joseph J. Zasloff, *North Vietnam and the Pathet Lao: Partners in the Struggle for Laos*, Cambridge, MA: Harvard University Press, 1970, pp. 23–105. The phrase "special relations" to characterize the association

between Laos and Vietnam was used as early as November 1973 (Arthur J. Dommen, "Social Science Research on Laos in the United States," in *New Laos, New Challenges*, ed. Jacqueline Butler-Diaz, Tempe, AZ: Arizona State University, 1998, p. 252).

32 MacAlister Brown and Joseph J. Zasloff, *Apprentice Revolutionaries: The Communist Movement in Laos, 1930–1985*, Stanford, CA: Hoover Institution Press, 1986, pp. 199–202.

33 Martin Stuart-Fox, *Buddhist Kingdom, Marxist State: The Making of Modern Laos*, Bangkok: White Lotus Press, 1996, pp. 197–201; Evans, *Politics of Ritual*, pp. 32–3. For a copy of the Lao–Vietnamese Treaty of Friendship and Cooperation, see Chang Pao-Min, *Kampuchea Between China and Vietnam*, Singapore: Singapore University Press, 1985, pp. 184–8.

34 Motoo Furuta, "The Indochina Communist Party's Division into Three Parties: Vietnamese Communist Policy Toward Cambodia and Laos, 1948–1951," in *Indochina in the 1940's and 1950's*, ed. Takashi Shiraishi and Motoo Furuta, Ithaca, NY: Cornell University Press, 1992, pp. 143–63; Gareth Porter, "Vietnamese Communist Policy Towards Kampuchea, 1930–1970," in *Revolution and Its Aftermath in Kampuchea: Eight Essays*, ed. David P. Chandler and Ben Kiernan, New Haven, CT: Yale University Southeast Asia Studies, 1983, pp. 57–98; Heder, *Cambodian Communism*, pp. 37–146.

35 R. B. Smith, "Cambodia in the Context of Sino-Vietnamese Relations," *Asian Affairs*, vol. 16, no. 3, October 1985, pp. 276–7; Heder, *Cambodian Communism*, pp. 5, 23–4, 132, 134–5; Kiernan, *How Pol Pot Came to Power*, pp. 198–235; Engelbert and Goscha, *Out of Touch*, pp. 67–84.

36 Peter M. Worthing, *Cambodia in Chinese Foreign Policy toward Vietnam*, Indochina Initiative Working Paper No. 4, Honolulu, HI: East-West Center, 1992, pp. 1–18; Smith, "Cambodia," pp. 277–8; Sheldon W. Simon, *War and Politics in Cambodia: A Communications Analysis*, Durham, NC: Duke University Press, 1974, pp. 74–88; Heder, *Cambodian Communism*, 156–7.

37 As quoted in Stephen J. Morris, *Why Vietnam Invaded Cambodia: Political Culture and the Causes of War*, Stanford, CA: Stanford University Press, 1999, p. 66.

38 Chang Pao-Min, *Kampuchea*, pp. 1–46; Morris, *Why Vietnam*, pp. 65–6; Smith, "Cambodia," pp. 273–87.

39 Nguyen Duy Trinh Speech, U.S. Department of Commerce, Office of Technical Services, *Joint Publications Research Service*, Washington, D.C., vol. 68, no. 992 (hereafter JPRS), as quoted in William J. Duiker, *Vietnam since the Fall of Saigon*, Athens, OH: Ohio University Center for International Studies, 1989, p. 129. Retired North Vietnamese Colonel Bui Tin was highly critical of Vietnamese attempts to foster a "special relationship" with its neighbors. He termed Vietnam the "big brother," Laos the "smallest of nephews" and Cambodia "just a poor relation." Bui Tin, *Following Ho Chi Minh: The Memoirs of a North Vietnamese Colonel*, Honolulu, HI: University of Hawai'i Press, 1995, pp. 127–8, quote p. 127.

40 For a copy of the Treaty of Peace, Friendship, and Co-operation between Kampuchea and Vietnam, see Chang Pao-Min, *Kampuchea*, pp. 194–8.

41 As quoted in Osborne, *Mekong*, p. 190.

42 U.S. Department of State, "Survey of Mekong River," *Bulletin*, vol. 34, no. 862, 2 January 1956, pp. 52–3.

43 C. Hart Schaaf and Russell H. Fifield, *The Lower Mekong: Challenge to Co-operation in Southeast Asia*, Princeton, NJ: D. Van Nostrand Company, 1963, pp. 84–6.

44 Ibid., pp. 82–4; Osborne, *Mekong*, pp. 190–1.

45 Schaff and Fifield, *Lower Mekong*, pp. 86–8.

46 Lloyd C. Gardner, *Pay Any Price: Lyndon Johnson and the Wars for Vietnam*, Chicago, IL: Ivan R. Dee, 1995, pp. 52–3.

47 Doris Kearns, *Lyndon Johnson and the American Dream*, New York, NY: Harper & Row, 1976, pp. 266–7; Lloyd C. Gardner, "From the Colorado to the Mekong," in *Vietnam: The Early Decisions*, ed. Lloyd C. Gardner and Ted Gittinger, Austin, TX: University of Texas Press, 1997, pp. 37–57.

48 Lyndon Baines Johnson, "United States Readiness for 'Unconditional Discussions' with the Governments Concerned in the Search for a Peaceful Settlement in Viet-Nam," Speech of 7 April 1965, Johns Hopkins University, Baltimore, MD, Document IX-110, *American Foreign Policy: Current Documents, 1965*, Washington, D.C.: U.S. Government, 1968, pp. 848–52, quotes pp. 850–1.

49 As quoted in Stanley Karnow, *Vietnam: A History*, New York, NY: Viking Press, 1983, p. 416; Gardner, "Colorado to Mekong," p. 53.

50 Speech before AFL-CIO, 22 March 1966, as quoted in Kearns, *Lyndon Johnson*, p. 267. On the interrelationship of these ideas to the Cold War imperatives of the U.S. government, see Mark Philip Bradley, *Imagining Vietnam & America: The Making of Postcolonial Vietnam, 1919–1950*, Chapel Hill, NC: University of North Carolina Press, 2000, p. 187.

51 Gardner, *Pay Any Price*, p. 298.

52 Pham Van Dong, "North Vietnamese Readiness to Negotiate on Viet-Nam Only after Recognition of Its Four-Point Basis for a Settlement," Speech of 8 April 1965, United Nations General Assembly, New York, Document IX-111, *American Foreign Policy: Current Documents, 1965*, Washington, D.C.: U.S. Government, 1968, pp. 852–3.

53 Vitit Muntarbhorn, "International Law and the Mekong River: Streamlining the Course through the Thai Middle Kingdom," in *Cooperation in the Mekong Development: Papers and Proceedings of the Seminar Held in Bangkok on 27–29 June 1991*, ed. Khien Theeravit, Sai Kham Mong, David Ruffolo and Benjamin Chiang, Bangkok: The Institute of Asian Studies, Chulalongkorn University, 1991, p. 19; Hoskin and Hopkins, *Mekong*, pp. 227–8.

54 For a copy of the *Statute*, see Schaff and Fifield, *Lower Mekong*, pp. 130–3.

55 Eugene R. Black, *Alternative in Southeast Asia*, London: Pall Mall Press, 1969, pp. 133–9; Schaff and Fifield, *Lower Mekong*, pp. 92–6; Osborne, *Mekong*, pp. 191–2.

56 Black, *Alternative*, pp. 134–5; Gardner, *Pay Any Price*, pp. 53, 191.

57 Bob Stensholt, "The Many Faces of Mekong Cooperation," in *Development Dilemmas in the Mekong Subregion*, ed. Bob Stensholt, Melbourne Workshop Proceedings, 1–2 October 1996, 2d ed., Clayton, Victoria: Monash University, 1996, pp. 199–205; Hoskin and Hopkins, *Mekong*, p. 229; Vitit Muntarbhorn, "International Law," pp. 19–21.

## 2 Rush to socialism

1 The radical approach adopted by the Khmer Rouge is beyond the scope of this study; therefore, the rise and demise of Democratic Kampuchea will be discussed only as it impacted on the socialist revolutions implemented after 1975 in Laos and Vietnam and after 1978 in Cambodia. On the economic and social reforms implemented by the Khmer Rouge, the following studies are recommended: Elizabeth Becker, *When the War Was Over: The Voices of Cambodia's Revolution and Its People*, New York, NY: Simon & Schuster, 1986; Craig Etcheson, *The Rise and Demise of Democratic Kampuchea*, Boulder, CO: Westview Press, 1984; Karl D. Jackson, ed., *Cambodia 1975–1978: Rendezvous with Death*, Princeton, NJ: Princeton University Press, 1989; Ben Kiernan, *The*

*Pol Pot Regime: Race, Power, and Genocide in Cambodia under the Khmer Rouge, 1975–79*, New Haven, CT: Yale University Press, 1996; Marie Alexandrine Martin, *Cambodia: A Shattered Society*, Berkeley, CA: University of California Press, 1994; Michael Vickery, *Cambodia 1975–1982*, Sydney: George Allen & Unwin, 1994.

2 "Program of the South Vietnam National Liberation Front," in Truong Nhu Tang, *A Viet Cong Memoir*, New York, NY: Vintage Books, 1986, pp. 322–8, quote p. 327. For an overview of the structure and functioning of wartime Marxist-Leninist groups in South Vietnam, see Ronald Bruce St John, "Marxist-Leninist Theory and Organization in South Vietnam," *Asian Survey*, vol. 20, no. 8, August 1980, pp. 812–28.

3 "National Salvation Manifesto of the Viet Nam Alliance of National, Democratic, and Peace Forces," *South Vietnam: From the NLF to the Provisional Revolutionary Government*, Vietnamese Studies, no. 23, 1968, pp. 358–9.

4 United States Mission in Vietnam, "The Action Program of the Provisional Revolutionary Government," *Viet-Nam Documents and Research Notes*, no. 60, June 1969, pp. 13–17, quote p. 16.

5 Truong Nhu Tang, *Viet Cong Memoir*, p. 283.

6 Robert K. Brigham, *Guerrilla Diplomacy: The NLF's Foreign Relations and the Viet Nam War*, Ithaca, NY: Cornell University Press, 1999, pp. 10–11, 128–31, quote p. x.

7 Ronald Bruce St John, "End of the Beginning: Economic Reform in Cambodia, Laos, and Vietnam," *Contemporary Southeast Asia*, vol. 19, no. 2, September 1997, p. 173; William J. Duiker, *Vietnam since the Fall of Saigon*, Athens, OH: Ohio University Center for International Studies, 1989, pp. 36–9; Gareth Porter, *Vietnam: The Politics of Bureaucratic Socialism*, Ithaca, NY: Cornell University Press, 1993, pp. 27–30.

8 Melanie Beresford, *Vietnam: Politics, Economics and Society*, New York, NY: Pinter Publishers, 1988, pp. 144–5; Adam Fforde and Suzanne H. Paine, *The Limits of National Liberation: Problems of Economic Management in the Democratic Republic of Vietnam*, London: Croom Helm, 1987, pp. 84–126. On the socioeconomic costs of early socialist policies in North Vietnam, see Andrew Vickerman, *The Fate of the Peasantry: Premature "Transition to Socialism" in the Democratic Republic of Vietnam*, New Haven, CT: Yale University Southeast Asia Studies, 1986; Adam Fforde, *The Agrarian Question in North Vietnam, 1974–1979: A Study of Cooperator Resistance to State Policy*, Armonk, NY: M.E. Sharpe, 1989; and Edwin E. Moise, *Land Reform in China and North Vietnam: Consolidating the Revolution at the Village Level*, Chapel Hill, NC: University of North Carolina Press, 1983.

9 Tran Thi Que, *Vietnam's Agriculture: The Challenges and Achievements*, Singapore: Institute of Southeast Asian Studies, 1998, pp. 25–6; Pham Xuan Nam and Be Viet Dang with Geoffrey B. Hainsworth, "The Ups and Downs of Vietnamese Agriculture and Rurality before Renovation," in *Socioeconomic Renovation in Viet Nam: The Origin, Evolution, and Impact of Doi Moi*, ed. Peter Boothroyd and Pham Xuan Nam, Singapore: Institute of Southeast Asian Studies, 2000, pp. 13–14; Melanie Beresford, *National Unification and Economic Development in Vietnam*, New York, NY: St. Martin's Press, 1989, pp. 90–129. On the land-to-the-tiller program, see Charles Stuart Callison, *Land-to-the-Tiller in the Mekong Delta: Economic, Social and Political Effects of Land Reform in Four Villages of South Vietnam*, Lanham, MD: University Press of America, 1983.

10 Stefan de Vylder and Adam Fforde, *Vietnam – An Economy in Transition*, Stockholm: Swedish International Development Authority, 1988, pp. 60–1, quote p. 61.

11 As quoted in Nguyen Van Canh, *Vietnam Under Communism, 1975–1982*, Stanford, CA: Hoover Institution Press, 1983, p. 25.

12 Tran Thi Que, *Vietnam's Agriculture*, p. 22.

13 Vo Nhan Tri, *Vietnam's Economic Policy since 1975*, Singapore: Institute of Southeast Asian Studies, 1990, pp. 1–57, especially pp. 44–6.

14 David G. Marr and Christine Pelzer White, "Introduction," in *Postwar Vietnam: Dilemmas in Socialist Development*, ed. David G. Marr and Christine Pelzer White, Ithaca, NY: Cornell Southeast Asia Program, 1988, pp. 3–4.

15 Ronald Bruce St John, "The Vietnamese Economy in Transition: Trends and Prospects," *Asian Affairs*, vol. 24, no. 3, October 1993, pp. 304–5.

16 Philip Taylor, *Fragments of the Present: Searching for Modernity in Vietnam's South*, Honolulu, HI: University of Hawai'i Press, 2001, pp. 23–55, quote p. 27.

17 Ngo Vinh Hai, "Postwar Vietnam: Political Economy," in *Coming to Terms: Indochina, the United States, and the War*, ed. Douglas Allen and Ngo Vinh Long, Boulder, CO: Westview Press, 1991, pp. 66–70; Vo Nhan Tri, *Vietnam's Economic Policy*, p. 71; Nguyen Tien Hung, *Economic Development of Socialist Vietnam, 1955–1980*, New York, NY: Praeger Publishers, 1977, pp. 167–70.

18 Vo Nhan Tri, "Party Policies and Economic Performance: The Second and Third Five-Year Plans Examined," in *Postwar Vietnam: Dilemmas in Socialist Development*, ed. David G. Marr and Christine P. White, Ithaca, NY: Cornell Southeast Asia Program, 1988, pp. 77–80; Dang T. Tran, *Socialist Economic Development and the Prospects for Economic Reform in Vietnam*, Indochina Initiative Working Paper No. 2, Honolulu, HI: East-West Center, 1991, pp. 12–16, 32; Ngo Vinh Long, "Vietnam," in *Coming to Terms: Indochina, the United States, and the War*, ed. Douglas Allen and Ngo Vinh Long, Boulder, CO: Westview Press, 1991, pp. 54–5.

19 Charles Harvie and Tran Van Hoa, *Vietnam's Reforms and Economic Growth*, New York, NY: St. Martin's Press, 1997, p. 36. For comparative statistics on state investment, see *Statistical Data of the Socialist Republic of Vietnam 1982*, Hanoi: General Statistical Office, 1983. As with most economies in transition, the accuracy, availability and consistency of statistical data for Vietnam, as well as for Cambodia and Laos, remains a problem. Therefore, the data cited in this study should be taken as an indication of magnitude and not at face value.

20 Andrew Vickerman, "A Note on the Role of Industry in Vietnam's Development Strategy," *Journal of Contemporary Asia*, vol. 2, 1985, p. 225; Vo Nhan Tri, *Vietnam's Economic Policy*, pp. 26–38; Beresford, *National Unification*, pp. 162–212.

21 Tran Thi Que, *Vietnam's Agriculture*, pp. 7–8.

22 Truong Chinh, "Toward Completion of National Reunification: The Substance, Objectives, and Urgent Problems To Be Solved, A Political Report to the Political Consultative Conference on National Reunification," *Vietnam Courier*, December 1975, p. 4; Tran Thi Que, *Vietnam's Agriculture*, pp. 24–5. In a very real sense, as Jayne Werner astutely observed, the agricultural collectives in Vietnam were not so much units of production as they were units of distribution ("Socialist Development: The Political Economy of Agrarian Reform in Vietnam," *Bulletin of Concerned Asian Scholars*, vol. 16, no. 2, April–June 1984, pp. 48–55).

23 Pham Xuan Nam and Be Viet Dang with Hainsworth, "Rural Development," 14.

24 Dang T. Tran, *Socialist Economic Development*, pp. 16–29.

25 United States Government, Foreign Broadcast Information Service, *Daily Report: Asia and Pacific (FBIS-APA)*, Dang Viet Chau, "Foreign Trade Minister Stresses Importance of Exports," FBIS-APA-78-250, 28 December 1978, pp. K11–K12, quote p. K12.

26 "Pham Van Dong Discusses Sino-Vietnamese, Cambodia Issues," FBIS-APA-79-004, 21 February 1979, pp. K10–K13, quote p. K12.

27 Ronald Bruce St John, *The Land Boundaries of Indochina: Cambodia, Laos and Vietnam*, International Boundaries Research Unit, University of Durham, Boundary and Territory Briefing, vol. 2, no. 6, 1998, pp. 22–9; Thu-huong Nguyen-vo, *Khmer–Viet Relations and the Third Indochina Conflict*, Jefferson, NC: McFarland & Company, 1992, pp. 64–80. For a detailed examination of the Cambodian–Vietnamese border issue, see Michel Blanchard, *Vietnam–Cambodge: Une frontière contestée*, Paris: L'Harmattan, 1999. Also valuable is Pierre-Lucien Lamant, "Le frontière entre le Cambodge et le Viêtnam du milieu du XIX^e siècle à nous jours," in *Les Frontières du Viêtnam: Histoire des frontières de la Péninsule Indochinoise*, ed. Pierre-Bernard Lafont, Paris: L'Harmattan, 1989, pp. 156–81.

28 Stephen J. Morris, *Why Vietnam Invaded Cambodia: Political Culture and the Causes of War*, Stanford, CA: Stanford University Press, 1999, p. 6. The literature on the Sino-Vietnamese rivalry and conflict is extensive. The following studies are recommended: Nayan Chanda, *Brother Enemy: The War after the War, A History of Indochina since the Fall of Saigon*, New York, NY: Macmillan Publishing Company, 1986; Chang Pao-Min, *Kampuchea Between China and Vietnam*, Singapore: Singapore University Press, 1985; King C. Chen, *Vietnam and China: 1938–1954*, Princeton, NJ: Princeton University Press, 1969; Philippe Franchini, *Le Sacrifice et l'espoir Cambodge, Laos et Viêt Nam: Le Sacrifice des peoples, 1975–1983*, Paris: Arthème Fayard, 1997; Anne Gilks, *The Breakdown of the Sino-Vietnamese Alliance, 1970–1979*, Institute of East Asian Studies, China Research Monograph 39, Berkeley, CA: University of California, 1992; Steven J. Hood, *Dragons Entangled: Indochina and the China-Vietnam War*, Armonk, NY: M.E. Sharpe, 1992; Qiang Zhai, *China & the Vietnam Wars, 1950–1975*, Chapel Hill, NC: University of North Carolina Press, 2000; Thu-huong Nguyen-vo, *Khmer–Viet Relations*. In addition, there are several essays on Sino-Vietnamese relations in Carlyle A. Thayer and Ramses Amer, ed., *Vietnamese Foreign Policy in Transition*, Singapore: Institute of Southeast Asian Studies, 1999.

29 "PRC Border Violations 24–30 December Draw Official Protest," FBIS-APA-79-001, 2 January 1979, pp. K1–K9; "Foreign Ministry, Government Reaction to PRC Invasion," FBIS-APA-79-036, 21 February 1979, pp. K1–K10; Harvie and Tran Van Hoa, *Vietnam's Reforms*, p. 40; Chanda, *Brother Enemy*, pp. 6–7; Gilks, *Breakdown*, pp. 224–33.

30 Virginia Thompson, *French Indo-China*, New York, NY: Octagon Books, 1968, pp. 127–8, 136–7, 141; Martin J. Murray, *The Development of Capitalism in Colonial Indochina (1870–1940)*, Berkeley, CA: University of California Press, 1980, pp. 220–2, 449–53; Charles Robequain, *The Economic Development of French Indo-China*, London: Oxford University Press, 1944, pp. 32–44.

31 Bernard B. Fall, "Viet-Nam's Chinese Problem," *Far Eastern Survey*, May 1958, pp. 65–72; Victor Purcell, *The Chinese in Southeast Asia*, 2d ed., London: Oxford University Press, 1944, pp. 215–16; Robert Scigliano, *South Vietnam: Nation Under Stress*, Boston, MA: Houghton Mifflin, 1963, pp. 4–5, 118–19.

32 Morris, *Why Vietnam*, pp. 175–9, 187–93, quote p. 187; Tran Khanh, *The Ethnic Chinese and Economic Development in Vietnam*, Singapore: Institute of Southeast Asian Studies, 1993, pp. 79–102; Vo Nhan Tri, *Vietnam's Economic Policy*, pp. 96–109; Taylor, *Fragments*, pp. 38–9.

33 Grant Evans, "Planning Problems in Peripheral Socialism: The Case of Laos," in *Laos: Beyond the Revolution*, ed. Joseph J. Zasloff and Leonard Unger, London: Macmillan Academic and Professional Ltd., 1991, p. 90; Nayan

Chanda, "Economic Changes in Laos, 1975–1980," in *Contemporary Laos: Studies in the Politics and Society of the Lao People's Democratic Republic*, ed. Martin Stuart-Fox, New York, NY: St. Martin's Press, 1982, p. 116.

34 Grant Evans, *Lao Peasants under Socialism*, New Haven, CT: Yale University Press, 1990, pp. 41–3, quote pp. 42–3.

35 On United States military involvement in Laos, see Timothy N. Castle, *At War in the Shadow of Vietnam: U.S. Military Aid to the Royal Lao Government, 1955–1975*, New York, NY: Columbia University Press, 1993; Jane Hamilton-Merritt, *Tragic Mountains: The Hmong, the Americans, and the Secret Wars for Laos, 1942–1992*, Bloomington, IN: Indiana University Press, 1993; Norman B. Hannah, *The Key to Failure: Laos & the Vietnam War*, Lanham, MD: Madison Books, 1987; Roger Warner, *The CIA's Secret War in Laos and Its Link to the War in Vietnam*, New York, NY: Simon & Schuster, 1995.

36 Jacques Decornoy, "Life in the Pathet Lao Liberated Zone," in *Laos: War and Revolution*, ed. Nina S. Adams and Alfred W. McCoy, New York, NY: Harper Colophon Books, 1970, pp. 411–23; Paul F. Langer and Joseph J. Zasloff, *North Vietnam and the Pathet Lao: Partners in the Struggle for Laos*, Cambridge, MA: Harvard University Press, 1970, pp. 106–28; Grant Evans, *A Short History of Laos: The Land in Between*, St Leonards, New South Wales: Allen & Unwin, 2002, pp. 128–33.

37 Mayoury Ngaosyvathn and Pheuiphanh Ngaosyvathn, *Kith and Kin Politics: The Relationship between Laos and Thailand*, Manila: Journal of Contemporary Asia Publishers, 1994, pp. 69–70.

38 Arthur J. Dommen, *Laos: Keystone of Indochina*, Boulder, CO: Westview Press, 1985, pp. 140–2; Evans, *Lao Peasants*, p. 44; Chanda, "Economic Changes," pp. 116–17; MacAlister Brown and Joseph J. Zasloff, *Apprentice Revolutionaries: The Communist Movement in Laos, 1930–1985*, Stanford, CA: Hoover Institution Press, 1986, pp. 196–7.

39 T. M. Burley, "Foreign Aid to the Lao People's Democratic Republic," in *Contemporary Laos: Studies in the Politics and Society of the Lao People's Democratic Republic*, ed. Martin Stuart-Fox, New York, NY: St. Martin's Press, 1982, pp. 129–36; Evans, "Planning Problems," p. 91.

40 Burley, "Foreign Aid," pp. 136–45; Evans, *Short History*, pp. 189–91. The available evidence does not support Fry's contention that "1975 to 1990 was basically an isolationist period for the Lao," with the exception of technical assistance and aid from the socialist bloc, "and there was little western contact with the Lao PDR." Gerald W. Fry, "The Future of the Lao PDR: Relations with Thailand and Alternative Paths to Internationalization," in *New Laos, New Challenges*, ed. Jacqueline Butler-Diaz, Tempe, AZ: Arizona State University, 1998, p. 157.

41 MacAlister Brown and Joseph J. Zasloff, "Dependency in Laos," *Current History*, vol. 75, no. 442, December 1978, pp. 202–7, 228; MacAlister Brown and Joseph J. Zasloff, "Laos in 1975: People's Democratic Revolution-Lao Style," *Asian Survey*, vol. 16, no. 2, February 1976, pp. 197–9. For a more detailed examination of post-1975 resistance to the revolutionary government in Laos, see Bernard Hamel, *Résistances au Vietnam, Cambodge et Laos (1975–1980)*, Paris: Éditions L'Harmattan, 1994.

42 Yves Bourdet, *The Economics of Transition in Laos: From Socialism to ASEAN Integration*, Northampton, MA: Edward Elgar, 2000, pp. 35–6; MacAlister Brown and Joseph J. Zasloff, "Laos 1976: Faltering First Steps toward Socialism," *Asian Survey*, vol. 17, no. 2, February 1977, pp. 107–9; St John, "End of the Beginning," pp. 174–5.

43 Christian Taillard, "Les transformations récentes des politiques agricoles en Chine et dans les pays socialistes de la peninsula indochinoise (1978–1982),"

*Études rurales*, vol. 89–91, January–September 1983, pp. 127–8; Brown and Zasloff, *Apprentice Revolutionaries*, pp. 197–8.

44 Evans, *Lao Peasants*, pp. 44–5; Martin Stuart-Fox, *Buddhist Kingdom, Marxist State: The Making of Modern Laos*, Bangkok: White Lotus Press, 1996, p. 111; Bourdet, *Economics*, p. 36.

45 *Sieng Pasasonh*, 31 December 1976, as quoted in Stuart-Fox, *Buddhist Kingdom*, p. 111; MacAlister Brown and Joseph J. Zasloff, "Laos 1977: The Realities of Independence," *Asian Survey*, vol. 18, no. 2, February 1978, pp. 168–9.

46 Martin Stuart-Fox, "Laos in 1981: Economic Prospects and Problems," *Southeast Asian Affairs 1982*, Singapore: Institute of Southeast Asian Studies, 1982, pp. 229–33; Evans, "Planning Problems," pp. 96–7.

47 W. Randall Ireson, "Evolving Village-State Relations in the Lao PDR: Time, Space, and Ethnicity," in *New Laos, New Challenges*, ed. Jacqueline Butler-Diaz, Tempe, AZ: Arizona State University, 1998, pp. 46–7, quote p. 46; Evans, *Politics of Ritual*, pp. 11–12; Fry, "Future of the Lao PDR," pp. 156–7.

48 Evans, *Short History*, pp. 177–87; Brown and Zasloff, "Laos in 1975," pp. 195–6; Ireson, "Evolving Village-State Relations," pp. 46–52; Evans, *Politics of Ritual*, p. 12.

49 Pierre-Bernard Lafont, "Buddhism in Contemporary Laos," in *Contemporary Laos: Studies in the Politics and Society of the Lao People's Democratic Republic*, ed. Martin Stuart-Fox, New York, NY: St. Martin's Press, 1982, pp. 148–62; Evans, *Lao Peasants*, pp. 185–8; Martin Stuart-Fox and Rod Bucknell, "Politicization of the Buddhist Sangha in Laos," *Journal of Southeast Asian Studies*, vol. 13, no. 1, March 1982, pp. 60–80; Evans, *Politics of Ritual*, pp. 61–3; Martin Stuart-Fox, "Marxism and Theravada Buddhism: The Legitimation of Political Authority in Laos," *Pacific Affairs*, vol. 56, no. 3, Fall 1983, pp. 428–54.

50 Evans, *Politics of Ritual*, pp. 12–14, quote p. 14.

51 Gilks, *Breakdown*, pp. 159–68; Evans, *Lao Peasants*, pp. 46–9; Brown and Zasloff, "Laos 1977," pp. 172–3.

52 Bourdet, *Economics*, p. 37; Brown and Zasloff, "Laos 1976," p. 109; Evans, *Lao Peasants*, pp. 220–7.

53 Murray Hiebert, "Laos: Flexible Policies Spark Tenuous Recovery," *Indochina Issues*, vol. 37, May 1983, p. 2; Chanda, "Economic Changes," pp. 122–3; Martin Stuart-Fox, "The Initial Failure of Agricultural Cooperativization in Laos," *Asia Quarterly*, vol. 4, 1980, pp. 279–84.

54 Stuart-Fox, "Initial Failure," p. 285.

55 St John, "End of the Beginning," p. 175; Evans, "Planning Problems," pp. 96–9.

56 Brown and Zasloff, *Apprentice Revolutionaries*, pp. 212–13; Stuart-Fox, *Buddhist Kingdom*, pp. 135–6; Chanda, "Economic Changes," p. 124; Stuart-Fox, "Initial Failure," p. 296.

57 Kaysone Phomvihane, "Speech to Supreme People's Council, Parts I & II," FBIS-APA-80-013, 18 January 1980, pp. I1–I33, quote p. I19.

58 Ibid., p. I23; Stuart-Fox, "Laos in 1981," pp. 230–1.

59 Kaysone Phomvihane, "Speech to Supreme People's Council, Parts III & IV," FBIS-APA-80-028, Supplement No. 36, 8 February 1980, pp. 1–41, quote p. 5.

60 Murray Hiebert, "'Socialist Transformation' in Laos," *Current History*, vol. 79, no. 461, December 1980, pp. 175–6; Stuart-Fox, "Laos in 1981," pp. 231–2.

61 Evans, *Lao Peasants*, pp. 55–6, quote p. 55; Stanley S. Bedlington, "Laos in 1980: The Portents Are Ominous," *Asian Survey*, vol. 21, no. 1, January 1981, pp. 110–11.

62 *Vietnam News Agency*, 8 February 1976, British Broadcasting Corporation, Summary of World Broadcasts, Far East, 5131/A3, p. 1, as quoted in Gilks, *Breakdown*, pp. 159–60.

63 Joint Statement, *Vietnam News Agency*, 11 February 1976, British Broadcasting Corporation, Summary of World Broadcasts, Far East, 5133/A3, pp. 4–5, as quoted in Gilks, *Breakdown*, p. 159.
64 For a copy of the Lao-Vietnamese Treaty of Friendship and Cooperation, see Chang Pao-Min, *Kampuchea*, pp. 184–8.
65 St John, *Land Boundaries*, pp. 30–2. On the Lao–Vietnamese border, see Bernard Gay, *La nouvelle frontière lao-vietnamienne: Les accords de 1977–1990*, Paris: L'Harmattan, 1995.
66 *New York Times*, 23 July 1978.
67 "President Souphanouvong Addresses Opening of Heroes Congress," FBIS-APA-79-069, 9 April 1979, pp. I2–I5, quote p. I4.
68 Hiebert, "Socialist Transformation," p. 178. Hiebert suggests there was opposition within the Lao leadership to the strong tilt toward Vietnam but not enough to disrupt the unity of men who had worked together for over three decades.
69 Brown and Zasloff, "Dependency," p. 207.
70 Hiebert, "Socialist Transformation," p. 177; MacAlister Brown and Joseph J. Zasloff, "Laos 1979: Caught in Vietnam's Wake," *Asian Survey*, vol. 20, no. 2, February 1980, pp. 103–7; Bedlington, "Laos in 1980," pp. 106–7.
71 Brown and Zasloff, "Dependency," pp. 202–7, 228, quote p. 206.
72 Arthur J. Dommen, "Laos: Vietnam's Satellite," *Current History*, vol. 77, no. 452, December 1979, pp. 201–2, 225, quotes pp. 201–2.
73 De Vylder and Fforde, *Vietnam*, pp. 61–2, quote p. 62.
74 Porter, *Vietnam*, pp. 29–30.
75 Stuart-Fox, *Buddhist Kingdom*, pp. 138–41, 163.

## 3 Tentative reforms

1 "Condensed Political Report of the Central Committee to the Fifth VCP Congress," FBIS-APA-82-060, 29 March 1982, pp. K6–K18, quote p. K9.
2 "Council of Ministers Promulgates New Economic Policies," FBIS-APA-79-155, 9 August 1979, pp. K5–K8, quotes pp. K5–K6.
3 Max Spoor, "Reforming State Finance in Post-1975 Vietnam," *Journal of Development Studies*, vol. 24, no. 4, 1988, pp. 107–10.
4 Stefan de Vylder and Adam Fforde, *Vietnam – An Economy in Transition*, Stockholm: Swedish International Development Authority, 1988, p. 62. In a centralized political system like Vietnam, "spontaneous bottom-up" reforms are difficult if not impossible without some level of top-down support. Unfortunately, the exact location and extent of early Party support for the output contract system remains unclear.
5 Melanie Beresford, *Vietnam: Politics, Economics and Society*, New York, NY: Pinter Publishers, 1988, pp. 160–1, quote p. 161; Tran Thi Que, *Vietnam's Agriculture: The Challenges and Achievements*, Singapore: Institute of Southeast Asian Studies, 1998, pp. 28–45; Pham Xuan Nam and Be Viet Dang with Geoffrey B. Hainsworth, "Rural Development in Viet Nam: The Search for Sustainable Livelihoods," in *Socioeconomic Renovation in Viet Nam: The Origin, Evolution, and Impact of Doi Moi*, ed. Peter Boothroyd and Pham Xuan Nam, Singapore: Institute of Southeast Asian Studies, 2000, p. 15.
6 Jozef M. Van Brabant, "Reforming a Socialist Developing Country: The Case of Vietnam," *Economics of Planning*, vol. 23, 1990, pp. 211–13; Dang T. Tran, *Socialist Economic Development and the Prospects for Economic Reform in Vietnam*, Indochina Initiative Working Paper Series, Working Paper No. 2, Honolulu, HI: East–West Center, 1991, pp. 26–8; Melanie Beresford, "Household and Collective in Vietnamese Agriculture," *Journal of Contemporary Asia*, vol. 15, no. 1, 1985, pp. 5–36.

7 David Wurfel, *"Doi Moi* in Comparative Perspective," in *Reinventing Viet-namese Socialism: Doi Moi in Comparative Perspective*, ed. William S. Turley and Mark Selden, Boulder, CO: Westview Press, 1993, pp. 23–4.

8 Beresford, *Vietnam*, pp. 161–2; Nguyen Xuan Oanh and Philip Donald Grub, *Vietnam: The New Investment Frontier in Southeast Asia*, Singapore: Times Academic Press, 1992, pp. 42–3; Jayne Werner, "Socialist Development: The Political Economy of Agrarian Reform in Vietnam," *Bulletin of Concerned Asian Scholars*, vol. 16, no. 2, April–June 1984, pp. 49–52.

9 As quoted in Tran Thi Que, *Vietnam's Agriculture*, p. 36.

10 Vo-Tong Xuan, "Rice Production, Agricultural Research, and the Environment," in *Vietnam's Rural Transformation*, ed. Benedict J. Tria Kerkvliet and Doug J. Porter, Boulder, CO: Westview Press, 1995, pp. 185–200, quote pp. 188–9.

11 "Condensed Political Report of the Central Committee to the Fifth VCP Congress," FBIS-APA-82-060, 29 March 1982, pp. K6–K18, quote p. K12.

12 World Bank, *Viet Nam: Transition to the Market: An Economic Report*, Report No. 11902-VN, 15 September 1993, p. 26.

13 Wurfel, *"Doi Moi,"* p. 24; Nguyen Van Huy and Tran Van Nghia, "Government Policies and State-Owned Enterprise Reform," in *State-Owned Enterprise Reform in Vietnam: Lessons from Asia*, ed. Ng Chee Yuen, Nick J. Freeman and Frank H. Huynh, Singapore: Institute of Southeast Asian Studies, 1996, pp. 38–9.

14 Charles Harvie and Tran Van Hoa, *Vietnam's Reforms and Economic Growth*, New York, NY: St. Martin's Press, 1997, 45–7; Wurfel, *"Doi Moi,"* pp. 24–5; Beresford, *Vietnam*: pp. 163–4.

15 Beresford, *Vietnam*: pp. 164–5.

16 "Truong Chinh's Opening Speech," FBIS-APA-82-060, 29 March 1982, pp. K1–K6, quote p. K2.

17 Wurfel, *"Doi Moi,"* p. 25; Kimura Tetsusaburo, *The Vietnamese Economy, 1975–86*, Tokyo: Institute of Developing Economies, 1989, p. 48.

18 Harvie and Tran Van Hoa, *Vietnam's Reforms*, pp. 47–8; Beresford, *Vietnam*: p. 165.

19 De Vylder and Fforde, *Vietnam*, p. 66; Vo Nhan Tri, "Party Policies and Economic Performance: The Second and Third Five-Year Plans Examined," in *Postwar Vietnam: Dilemmas in Socialist Development*, ed. David G. Marr and Christine P. White, Ithaca, NY: Cornell Southeast Asia Program, 1988, pp. 84–9; Dang T. Tran, *Socialist Economic Development*, pp. 29–30.

20 Wurfel, *"Doi Moi,"* pp. 26–7; Pham Xuan Nam and Be Viet Dang with Hainsworth, "Rural Development," p. 16.

21 Vo Nhan Tri, *Vietnam's Economic Policy since 1975*, Singapore: Institute of Southeast Asian Studies, 1990, p. 242.

22 Carlyle A. Thayer, "Recent Political Developments: Constitutional Change and the 1992 Elections," in *Vietnam and the Rule of Law*, ed. Carlyle A. Thayer and David G. Marr, Canberra: Australian National University, 1993, p. 74.

23 Vu Tuan Anh, *Development in Vietnam: Policy Reforms and Economic Growth*, Singapore: Institute of Southeast Asian Studies, 1994, p. 9.

24 Pacific Basin Research Institute, *Toward a Market Economy in Viet Nam: Economic Reforms and Development Strategies*, Rockville, MD: Pacific Basin Research Institute, 1993, pp. 7–11, quote p. 10.

25 Dang T. Tran, *Vietnam: Socialist Economic Development, 1955–1992*, San Francisco, CA: Institute for Contemporary Studies Press, 1994, p. 39.

26 Carlyle A. Thayer, "Introduction," in *Vietnam and the Rule of Law*, ed. Carlyle A. Thayer and David G. Marr, Canberra: Australian National University, 1993, p. 1.

27 Vo Nhan Tri, *Vietnam's Economic Policy*, pp. 125–80; Tran, *Vietnam*, pp. 32–66.
28 Martin Stuart-Fox, "Laos in 1981: Economic Prospects and Problems," *Southeast Asian Affairs 1982*, Singapore: Institute of Southeast Asian Studies, 1982, p. 229; MacAlister Brown and Joseph J. Zasloff, *Apprentice Revolutionaries: The Communist Movement in Laos, 1930–1985*, Stanford, CA: Hoover Institution Press, 1986, p. 202.
29 "Part I of Kaysone Speech at SPC Plenary Session," FBIS-APA-81-016, 26 January 1981, pp. I2–I18, quotes pp. I14–I17.
30 "Part II of Kaysone Speech at SPC Plenary Session," FBIS-APA-81-021, 2 February 1981, pp. I8–I19, quotes pp. I10–I11.
31 Ibid., pp. I11–I12.
32 Martin Stuart-Fox, "Laos: The First Lao Five Year Plan," *Asian Thought and Society*, vol. 6, no. 17–18, 1981, pp. 272–3; Stuart-Fox, "Laos in 1981," pp. 234–5.
33 Brown and Zasloff, *Apprentice Revolutionaries*, pp. 202, 208; Stuart-Fox, "Laos: First Lao Five Year Plan," p. 273.
34 As quoted in Stuart-Fox, "Laos: First Lao Five Year Plan," pp. 272–6, quotes pp. 272–3.
35 As quoted in Stuart-Fox, "Laos in 1981," pp. 236–7, quotes p. 237.
36 "Last Installment of Kaysone's SPC Speech," FBIS-APA-81-030, 13 February 1981, pp. I6–I22, quote pp. I19–I20.
37 Brown and Zasloff, *Apprentice Revolutionaries*, p. 202; Stuart-Fox, "Laos in 1981," pp. 238–42; MacAlister Brown and Joseph J. Zasloff, "Laos: Gearing Up for National Development, An Overview," *Southeast Asian Affairs 1985*, Singapore: Institute of Southeast Asian Studies, 1985, pp. 192–4.
38 Ronald Bruce St John, "End of the Beginning: Economic Reform in Cambodia, Laos and Vietnam," *Contemporary Southeast Asia*, vol. 19, no. 2, September 1997, p. 175; Yves Bourdet, *The Economics of Transition in Laos: From Socialism to ASEAN Integration*, Northampton, MA: Edward Elgar Publishing, 2000, pp. 38–9; Grant Evans, "Planning Problems in Peripheral Socialism: The Case of Laos," in *Laos: Beyond the Revolution*, ed. Joseph J. Zasloff and Leonard Unger, London: Macmillan Academic and Professional Ltd., 1991, p. 101; MacAlister Brown, "Laos: Bottoming Out," *Current History*, vol. 82, no. 483, April 1983, pp. 154–7, 180–2; Brown and Zasloff, "Laos: Gearing Up," pp. 202–3; Murray Hiebert, "Laos: Flexible Policies Spark Tenuous Recovery," *Indochina Issues*, vol. 37, May 1983, pp. 3–4.
39 Yves Bourdet, "Rural Reforms and Agricultural Productivity in Laos," *Journal of Developing Area*, vol. 29, no. 2, January 1995, pp. 179–80; Richard Vokes and Armand Fabella, "Lao PDR," in *From Centrally Planned to Market Economies: The Asian Approach*, vol. 3: *Lao PDR, Myanmar and Viet Nam*, ed. Pradumna B. Rana and Naved Hamid, Hong Kong: Oxford University Press for the Asian Development Bank, 1996, pp. 96–9; Carlyle A. Thayer, "Laos in 1983: Pragmatism in the Transition to Socialism," *Asian Survey*, vol. 24, no. 1, January 1984, pp. 51–2.
40 William Worner, "Economic Reform and Structural Change in Laos," *Southeast Asian Affairs 1989*, Singapore: Institute of Southeast Asian Studies, 1989, p. 199; Stuart-Fox, "Laos: First Lao Five Year Plan," pp. 272–3; Evans, "Planning Problems," p. 103.
41 "Report on the Economic and Social Situation, Development Strategy and Assistance Needs (1986–90)," I, Principal Report prepared for the Second Round Table Conference of the least-developed Asian and Pacific countries, LPDR, April 1986, p. 25, as quoted in Ng Shui Meng, "Laos in 1986: Into the Second Decade of National Reconstruction," *Southeast Asian Affairs 1987*, Singapore: Institute of Southeast Asian Studies, 1987, pp. 182–3.

42  Ng Shui Meng, "Laos in 1986," pp. 181–3.
43  Martin Stuart-Fox, *Laos: Politics, Economics and Society*, Boulder, CO: Lynne Rienner, 1986, pp. 97–105; Bourdet, "Rural Reforms," pp. 168–70; Hiebert, "Laos: Flexible Policies," pp. 6–7; Brown and Zasloff, "Laos: Gearing Up," 204–5; Bourdet, *Economics*, pp. 41–2. On cross-border trade in northwestern Laos, see Andrew Walker, *The Legend of the Golden Boat: Regulation, Trade and Traders in the Borderlands of Laos, Thailand, China and Burma*, Honolulu, HI: University of Hawai'i Press, 1999.
44  Charles A. Joiner, "Laos in 1986: Administrative and International Partially Adaptive Communism," *Asian Survey*, vol. 27, no. 1, January 1987, pp. 105–6; Ng Shui Meng, "Laos in 1986," p. 180; Martin Stuart-Fox, "Laos in 1985: Time to Take Stock," *Southeast Asian Affairs 1986*, Singapore: Institute of Southeast Asian Studies, 1986, pp. 167–8.
45  Stuart-Fox, "Laos in 1981," p. 240.
46  Thayer, "Laos in 1983," pp. 53–5; Brown and Zasloff, *Apprentice Revolutionaries*, p. 212.
47  Arthur J. Dommen, "Laos in 1985: The Year of the Census," *Asian Survey*, vol. 26, no. 1, January 1986, pp. 114–17; Brown and Zasloff, *Apprentice Revolutionaries*, pp. 202–3, 208–12; T. M. Burley, "Foreign Aid to the Lao People's Democratic Republic," in *Contemporary Laos: Studies in the Politics and Society of the Lao People's Democratic Republic*, ed. Martin Stuart-Fox, New York, NY: St. Martin's Press, 1982, pp. 140–1; Brown and Zasloff, "Laos: Gearing Up," pp. 206–7.
48  Brown and Zasloff, "Laos: Gearing Up," p. 204; Brown and Zasloff, *Apprentice Revolutionaries*, p. 216.
49  Carlyle A. Thayer, "Laos in 1982: The Third Congress of the Lao People's Revolutionary Party," *Asian Survey*, vol. 23, no. 1, January 1983, pp. 84–93; Grant Evans, *The Politics of Ritual and Remembrance: Laos since 1975*, Honolulu, HI: University of Hawai'i Press, 1998, p. 28.
50  Brown and Zasloff, "Laos: Gearing Up," pp. 189–91.
51  Dommen, "Laos in 1985," pp. 112–14; Arthur J. Dommen, "Laos in 1984: The Year of the Thai Border," *Asian Survey*, vol. 25, no. 1, January 1985, pp. 120–1; Thayer, "Laos in 1983," pp. 49–51.
52  Evans, *Politics of Ritual*, pp. 63–4, quotes p. 63; Martin Stuart-Fox, "Marxism and Theravada Buddhism: The Legitimation of Political Authority in Laos," *Pacific Affairs*, vol. 56, no. 3, Fall 1983, pp. 450–4.
53  Chanthou Boua, "Observations of the Heng Samrin Government, 1980–1982," in *Revolution and Its Aftermath in Kampuchea: Eight Essays*, ed. David P. Chandler and Ben Kiernan, New Haven, CT: Yale University Southeast Asia Studies, 1983, pp. 280–2; Evan Gottesman, *Cambodia After the Khmer Rouge: Inside the Politics of Nation Building*, New Haven, CT: Yale University Press, 2003, pp. 42–4; Kishore Mahbubani, "The Kampuchean Problem: A Southeast Asian Perception," *Foreign Affairs*, vol. 62, no. 2, Winter 1983/84, pp. 407–25; Margaret Slocomb, *The People's Republic of Kampuchea, 1979–1989: The Revolution after Pol Pot*, Chiang Mai: Silkworm Books, 2003, pp. 34, 41, 45.
54  For a copy of the Kampuchea–Vietnam Treaty of Peace, Friendship, and Cooperation, see Chang Pao-Min, *Kampuchea Between China and Vietnam*, Singapore: Singapore University Press, 1985, pp. 194–8, quotes pp. 194, 196; Patrick Raszelenberg and Peter Schier, *The Cambodia Conflict: Search for a Settlement, 1979–1991, An Analytical Chronology*, Hamburg: Institute of Asian Affairs, 1995, pp. 21–4.
55  Charles H. Twining, "The Economy," in *Cambodia, 1975–1978: Rendezvous with Death*, ed. Karl D. Jackson, Princeton, NJ: Princeton University Press, 1989, pp. 109–50; Slocomb, *People's Republic of Kampuchea*, pp. 48, 51;

Michael Vickery, "Cambodia," in *Coming to Terms: Indochina, the United States and the War*, ed. Douglas Allen and Ngô Vinh Long, Boulder, CO: Westview Press, 1991, p. 109.

56 Kimmo Kiljunen, "Power Politics and the Tragedy of Kampuchea During the Seventies," *Bulletin of Concerned Asian Scholars*, vol. 17, no. 2, April–June 1985, pp. 51–3; Slocomb, *People's Republic of Kampuchea*, pp. 91–123; Boua, "Observations," pp. 259–90; Vickery, "Cambodia," pp. 110–12.

57 Vickery, "Cambodia," p. 109.

58 Slocomb, *People's Republic of Kampuchea*, pp. 179–82; Justus M. van der Kroef, "Cambodia: From 'Democratic Kampuchea' to 'People's Republic,'" *Asian Survey*, vol. 19, no. 8, August 1979, pp. 737–8; Gottesman, *Cambodia*, pp. 71–2; Boua, "Observations," pp. 283–5; Marie Alexandrine Martin, *Cambodia: A Shattered Society*, Berkeley, CA: University of California Press, 1994, pp. 237–8.

59 Börje Ljunggren, "Market Economies under Communist Regimes: Reform in Vietnam, Laos and Cambodia," in *The Challenge of Reform in Indochina*, ed. Börje Ljunggren, Cambridge, MA: Harvard University Press, 1993, pp. 64–5; Michael Vickery, "Notes on the Political Economy of the People's Republic of Kampuchea (PRK)," *Journal of Contemporary Asia*, vol. 20, no. 4, 1990, pp. 451–2; Boua, "Observations," pp. 268–83; Sheridan T. Prasso, *The Riel Value of Money: How the World's Only Attempt to Abolish Money Has Hindered Cambodia's Economic Development*, Asia Pacific Issues No. 49, Honolulu, HI: East–West Center, 2001.

60 Boua, "Observations," pp. 266, 271, 273; Vickery, "Cambodia," pp. 109–12.

61 As quoted in Viviane Frings, *Allied and Equal: The Kampuchean People's Revolutionary Party's Historiography and Its Relations with Vietnam (1979–1991)*, Working Paper No. 90, Clayton, Victoria: Monash University, 1994, p. 3.

62 Frings, *Allied and Equal*, pp. 1–4, 32–3, quote p. 1; Anthony Barnett, "Cambodian Possibilities," *International Journal of Politics*, vol. 16, no. 3, Fall 1986, pp. 81–2; Ea Méng-Try, "Kampuchea: A Country Adrift," *Population and Development Review*, vol. 7, no. 2, June 1981, pp. 221–2; Gottesman, *Cambodia*, pp. 159–64.

63 Boua, "Observations," p. 285.

64 David J. Steinberg, *Cambodia*, New Haven, CT: Human Relations Area Files Press, 1959, pp. 195–211; Alain Forest, *Le Cambodge et la Colonisation Française: Histoire d'une colonisation sans heurts (1897–2000)*, Paris, Éditions L'Harmattan, 1980: pp. 269–331; Robert J. Muscat, *Cambodia: Post-Settlement Reconstruction and Development*, New York, NY: Columbia University, 1989, pp. 10–12; Boua, "Observations," p. 262.

65 Viviane Frings, *The Failure of Agricultural Collectivization in the People's Republic of Kampuchea (1979–1989)*, Working Paper No. 80, Clayton, Victoria: Monash University, 1993, pp. 1–4, 15–22; St John, "End of the Beginning," p. 176; World Bank, *Cambodia: Agenda for Rehabilitation and Reconstruction*, Washington, D.C.: World Bank, 1992; Vickery, "Notes," pp. 446–9; Gottesman, *Cambodia*, pp. 90–5.

66 Boua, "Observations," pp. 265–71, quote pp. 265–6.

67 Patcharawalai Wongboonsin, *et al.*, *Current Indochinese Economies*, Bangkok: Chulalongkorn University, 1992, pp. 40–1, 48; Slocomb, *People's Republic of Kampuchea*, pp. 263–4; St John, "End of the Beginning," p. 176; Frings, *Failure*, pp. 20–2, 35–40.

68 Michael Vickery, *Kampuchea: Politics, Economics and Society*, Boulder, CO: Lynne Rienner, 1986, p. 171; Mahbubani, "Kampuchean Problem," pp. 407–9.

69 Ronald Bruce St John, "Cambodian Foreign Policy: New Directions," *Asian Affairs*, vol. 16, no. 1, January–March 1994, pp. 57–60; Muthiah Alagappa,

"The Major Powers and Southeast Asia," *International Journal*, vol. 44, no. 3, Summer 1989, pp. 562–9; David W. P. Elliott, "Deadlock Diplomacy: Thai and Vietnamese Interests in Kampuchea," *International Journal of Politics*, vol. 16, no. 3, Fall 1986, pp. 39–76; R. B. Smith, "Cambodia in the Context of Sino-Vietnamese Relations," *Asian Affairs*, vol. 16, no. 3, October 1985, pp. 273–87; Michael Eiland, "Cambodia in 1985: From Stalemate to Ambiguity," *Asian Survey*, vol. 26, no. 1, January 1986, pp. 118–25.

70  William Bach, "A Chance in Cambodia," *Foreign Policy*, vol. 62, Spring 1986, pp. 75–6; St John, "Cambodian Foreign Policy," pp. 67–8; Vickery, *Kampuchea*, pp. 171–3; MacAlister Brown and Joseph J. Zasloff, *Cambodia Confounds the Peacemakers, 1979–1998*, Ithaca, NY: Cornell University Press, 1998, pp. 10–24; Chang Pao-Min, *Kampuchea*, pp. 113–56. Vickery rightly considered the U.S. claim to be following ASEAN on Cambodia to be a "smokescreen," arguing the United States was often pushing, not following ASEAN. Michael Vickery, *Cambodia: A Political Survey*, Department of Political and Social Change, Discussion Paper Series No. 14, Canberra: Australian National University, 1994, p. 4.

71  Sorpong Peou, *Intervention & Change in Cambodia: Towards Democracy?* Singapore: Institute of Southeast Asian Studies, 2000, pp. 132–45; Muthiah Alagappa, "Regionalism and the Quest for Security," *Journal of International Affairs*, vol. 46, no. 2, Winter 1993, pp. 448–58; Hood, *Dragons Entangled*, pp. 58–80.

72  Tim Huxley, "Cambodia in 1986: The PRK's Eighth Year," *Southeast Asian Affairs 1987*, Singapore: Institute of Southeast Asian Studies, 1987, pp. 163–4.

73  Vickery, *Kampuchea*, pp. 146–8; Huxley, "Cambodia in 1986," pp. 164–5; Muscat, *Cambodia*, pp. 51–4; Boua, "Observations," pp. 271–4.

74  Vickery, *Kampuchea*, pp. 148–51; Huxley, "Cambodia in 1986," pp. 165–6.

75  Huxley, "Cambodia in 1986," pp. 166–7.

76  Mabbett and Chandler, *Khmers*, pp. 253–4, quote p. 254; St John, "End of the Beginning," pp. 185–6.

77  David P. Chandler, "Cambodia in 1984: Historical Patterns Re-asserted?," *Southeast Asian Affairs 1985*, Singapore: Institute of Southeast Asian Studies, 1985, p. 182.

78  Frings, *Allied and Equal*, pp. 3–4.

79  As quoted in the *Far Eastern Economic Review*, 6 April 1979; Brown and Zasloff, "Laos: Gearing Up," p. 195.

80  Thayer, "Laos in 1983," p. 56; Mya Than, "Economic Co-operation in the Greater Mekong Subregion," *Asian-Pacific Economic Literature*, vol. 11, no. 2, November 1997, pp. 41–3.

81  Brown and Zasloff, "Laos: Gearing Up," pp. 195–6; Dommen, "Laos in 1984," pp. 119–20.

## 4 Reform accelerates

1  "Vo Van Kiet's Economic Report at CPV Congress," FBIS-APA-86-246, 23 December 1986, pp. K8–K24; Ronald Bruce St John, "The Vietnamese Economy in Transition: Trends and Prospects," *Asian Affairs*, vol. 24, no. 3, October 1993, pp. 306–7; Zdenek Drabek, "A Case Study of a Gradual Approach to Economic Reform: The Viet Nam Experience of 1985–88," Asia Regional Series, Internal Discussion Paper 74, Washington, D.C.: World Bank, 1990, p. 1.

2  Dang T. Tran, *Vietnam: Socialist Economic Development, 1955–1992*, San Francisco, CA: Institute for Contemporary Studies Press, 1994, pp. 66–7.

3  "Agricultural Accomplishments in 1988 Listed," JPRS-SEA-89-022, 31 May

1989, p. 56; Florence Yvon-Tran, "The Chronicle of a Failure: Collectivization in Northern Vietnam, 1958–1988," in *Viêt-Nam Exposé: French Scholarship on Twentieth-Century Vietnamese Society*, ed. Gisele L. Bousquet and Pierre Brocheux, Ann Arbor, MI: University of Michigan Press, 2002, pp. 331–55; Drabek, "Case Study," pp. 1–2, 4–5, 7–9.

4 "Council of Ministers Issues Decision on Economic Work," JPRS-SEA-89-024, 29 June 1989, pp. 66–7; "State Planning Commission Chairman Pham Van Khai on Vietnam's Economy," JPRS-SEA-89-026, 28 July 1989, pp. 42–3; Drabek, "Case Study," pp. 36–7.

5 Socialist Republic of Vietnam, *Fundamental Laws and Regulations of Vietnam*, Hanoi: THẾ GIỚI Publishers, 1993, pp. 243–75; World Bank, *Viet Nam: Transition to the Market: An Economic Report*, Report No. 11902-VN, 15 September 1993, pp. 32–3.

6 World Bank, *Viet Nam: Transition*, p. 27.

7 Benedict R. Tria Kerkvliet, "Village-State Relations in Vietnam: The Effect of Everyday Politics on Decollectivization," *Journal of Asian Studies*, vol. 54, no. 2, May 1995, pp. 396–418.

8 Lewis M. Stern, *Renovating the Vietnamese Communist Party: Nguyen Van Linh and the Programme for Organizational Reform, 1987–91*, New York, NY: St. Martin's Press, 1993, pp. 1–26; Lewis M. Stern, "The Vietnamese Communist Party in 1986: Party Reform Initiatives, the Scramble towards Economic Revitalization, and the Road to the Sixth National Congress," *Southeast Asian Affairs 1987*, Singapore: Institute of Southeast Asian Studies, 1987, pp. 345–63.

9 Stern, *Renovating*, pp. 27–53.

10 Ibid., pp. 55–89; Ronald J. Cima, "Vietnam in 1988: The Brink of Renewal," *Asian Survey*, vol. 29, no. 1, January 1989, pp. 65–7.

11 David G. Marr, "Where is Vietnam Coming From?" in *Doi Moi: Vietnam's Renovation Policy and Performance*, ed. Dean K. Forbes, Terence H. Hull, David G. Marr and Brian Brogan, Canberra: Australian National University, 1991, p. 18; David Elliott, "Vietnam's 1991 Party Elections," *Asian Affairs*, vol. 19, no. 3, Fall 1992, pp. 159–68.

12 D. M. Leipziger, "Awakening the Market: Viet Nam's Economic Transition," World Bank Discussion Paper 157, Washington, D.C.: World Bank, 1992, pp. 3–9; United Nations Development Programme, *Report on the Economy of Vietnam*, December 1990, pp. 18–19.

13 Carlyle A. Thayer, "Introduction," in *Vietnam and the Rule of Law*, ed. Carlyle A. Thayer and David G. Marr, Canberra: Australian National University, 1993, p. 16; Ken Atkinson, "Vietnam: A Faster Reformer than China," *Business Asia*, 26 April 1993, p. 12; Ngo Ba Thanh, "The 1992 Constitution and the Rule of Law," in *Vietnam and the Rule of Law*, ed. Carlyle A. Thayer and David G. Marr, Canberra: Australian National University, 1993, pp. 89, 94.

14 Ronald Bruce St John, "Policy of the United States on Vietnam," *Congressional Record: Proceedings and Debates of the 102d Congress. First Session*, vol. 137, no. 73, 15 May 1991, pp. S5959–60; Private Interview, Pham Chi Lan, Deputy Secretary General, Chamber of Commerce and Industry, Socialist Republic of Vietnam, Hanoi, 24 October 1990; David Wurfel, "*Doi Moi in Comparative Perspective*," in *Reinventing Vietnamese Socialism: Doi Moi in Comparative Perspective*, ed. William S. Tusley and Mark Selden, Boulder, CO: Westview Press, 1993, p. 33.

15 Socialist Republic of Vietnam, "Law on Foreign Investment in Vietnam," *Selection of Fundamental Laws and Regulations of Vietnam* 2d ed., Hanoi: THẾ GIỚI Publishers, 1993, pp. 59–74; Private Interview, Nguyen Long Trao, Deputy General Director, Saigon Export Processing Zone, Socialist Republic of Vietnam, Ho Chi Minh City, 28 March 1991.

16 David Dollar, "Vietnam: Successes and Failures of Macroeconomic Stabiliza-tion," in *The Challenge of Reform in Indochina*, ed. Börje Ljunggren, Cam-bridge, MA: Harvard University Press, 1993, pp. 207–31; Adrian Wood, "Deceleration of Inflation with Acceleration of Price Reform: Vietnam's Remarkable Recent Experience," *Cambridge Journal of Economics*, vol. 13, 1989, pp. 563–71; Adam Fforde, *Vietnam: Economic Commentary and Analysis (a bi-annual appraisal of the Vietnamese economy)*, London: ADUKI Ltd., 1992, pp. 11–15, 25–30, 34–5.

17 St John, "Vietnamese Economy," pp. 308–9; Private Interview, Le Ngoc Hoan, Vice Minister, Ministry of Transport and Communications, Socialist Republic of Vietnam, Hanoi, 26 October 1990; Karl H. Englund, "External Assistance in the Context of Vietnam's Development Effort," in *Postwar Vietnam: Dilemmas in Socialist Development*, ed. David G. Marr and Christine P. White, Ithaca, NY: Cornell Southeast Asia Program, 1988, pp. 225–31.

18 *Draft Political Report to the Seventh Communist Party of Vietnam Congress*, 5 April 1991, mimeograph; Elliott, "Vietnam's 1991 Party Elections," pp. 159–68; Dennis Duncanson, "The Legacy of Ho Chi Minh," *Asian Affairs*, vol. 23, no. 1, February 1992, p. 52.

19 Brantly Womack, "Reform in Vietnam: Backwards Towards the Future," *Government and Opposition*, vol. 27, no. 2, Spring 1992, pp. 177–8; "VN Meeting On Economic Policy, Constitution Ends," *Bangkok Post*, 7 December 1991; "On the Draft Amendments to the 1980 Constitution," *Vietnam Courier*, August 1991, p. 2.

20 Socialist Republic of Vietnam, *The Constitution of 1992*, Hanoi: THÊ GIÓI Publishers, 1993, p. 18; Levien Do, "Vietnam's Revised Constitution: Impact on Foreign Investment," in *Vietnam and the Rule of Law*, ed. Carlyle A. Thayer and David G. Marr, Canberra: Australian National University, 1993, pp. 116–25; "Foreign-Invested Hanoi Projects Approved," FBIS-EAS-93-116, 18 June 1993, pp. 57–8.

21 Vo Van Kiet, "Speech by Chairman of the Council of Ministers to Thai Busi-ness Circle," Bangkok, 28 October 1991, mimeograph; World Bank, *Viet Nam: Transition*, pp. 25–6.

22 Marie-Sybille de Vienne, *L'économie du Viet-Nam (1955–1995): Bilan et prospective*, Paris: CHEAM, 1994, pp. 149–51; Nguyen Tien Hung, *Vietnam: Reforming the State Enterprises: Toward an Agenda for Privatisation*, Bangkok: Post Books, 1995, pp. 14–26; Ngo Ba Thanh, "1992 Constitution," p. 93.

23 World Bank, *Viet Nam: Transition*, p. 37; Thayer, "Introduction," p. 5; Private Interview, Le Tung Hieu, Deputy General Director, Ministry of Heavy Indus-try, Socialist Republic of Vietnam, Ho Chi Minh City, 28 March 1991.

24 Socialist Republic of Vietnam, "Land Law," *Selection of Fundamental Laws and Regulations of Vietnam*, 2d ed., Hanoi: THÊ GIÓI Publishers, 1993, pp. 283–314; World Bank, *Viet Nam: Transition*, p. 32.

25 Thayer, "Introduction," p. 12; Nguyen Qui Binh, "Real Estate Laws in Vietnam," in *Vietnam and the Rule of Law*, ed. Carlyle A. Thayer and David G. Marr, Canberra: Australian National University, 1993, pp. 148–59; World Bank, *Viet Nam: Transition*, p. 33.

26 Private Interview, Bai Danh Lun, Minister, Ministry of Transport and Commu-nications, Socialist Republic of Vietnam, Hanoi, 26 October 1990; Jozef M. Van Brabant, "Reforming a Socialist Developing Country: The Case of Vietnam," *Economic of Planning*, vol. 33, 1990, pp. 209–29; Socialist Republic of Vietnam, "Ordinance on the State Bank of Vietnam," *Fundamental Laws and Regula-tions of Vietnam*, Hanoi: THÊ GIÓI Publishers, 1993, pp. 460–76.

27 Pacific Basin Research Institute, *Toward a Market Economy in Vietnam: Eco-nomic Reforms and Development Strategies*, Rockville: MD: Pacific Basin

Research Institute, 1993, pp. 27–8; Nguyen Xuan Oanh and Philip Donald Grub, *Vietnam: The New Investment Frontier in Southeast Asia*, Singapore: Times Academic Press, 1992, pp. 12–19.

28  "Hanoi 'Non-State Economic Sector' Prospering," FBIS-EAS-93-085, 5 May 1993, pp. 69–70; Frederick Z. Brown, "Winning in Vietnam," *SAIS Review*, vol. 13, no. 1, Winter-Spring 1993, pp. 66–9; Dorothy R. Avery, "Vietnam in 1992: Win Some; Lose Some," *Asian Survey*, vol. 33, no. 1, January 1993, pp. 71–2.

29  "Guidelines and Tasks of the Second Five-Year Plan (1986–90) for Economic and Social Development of the Lao People's Democratic Republic," Fourth Party Congress, Vientiane, 1986, mimeograph, pp. 10–15; Ng Shui Meng, "Laos in 1986: Into the Second Decade of National Reconstruction," *Southeast Asian Affairs 1987*, Singapore: Institute of Southeast Asian Studies, 1987, p. 183; MacAlister Brown, "Easing the Burden of Socialist Struggle in Laos," *Current History*, vol. 86, no. 519, April 1987, pp. 152–5, 177.

30  "Guidelines and Tasks of the Second Five-Year Plan," pp. 15–16; Ng Shui Meng, "Laos in 1986," pp. 183–4.

31  "Guidelines and Tasks of the Second Five-Year Plan," pp. 17–18; Private Interview, Phetsamone Viraphanth, Director, Department of International Relations, Ministry of Communication, Transport, Post and Construction, Lao People's Democratic Republic, Vientiane, 17 October 1990.

32  "Guidelines and Tasks of the Second Five-Year Plan," p. 19; Private Interview, Bounleuang Insisienmay, Deputy Director, Department of Foreign Trade and Tourism, Lao People's Democratic Republic, Vientiane, 16 October 1990.

33  "Political Report of the Central Committee by the Lao People's Revolutionary Party Presented at Its Fourth Party Congress by Comrade Kaysone Phomvihane, General Secretary," Fourth Party Congress, Vientiane, 1986, mimeograph, p. 68, as quoted in Ng Shui Meng, "Laos in 1986," p. 185.

34  Ibid.

35  Charles A. Joiner, "Laos in 1987: New Economic Management Confronts the Bureaucracy," *Asian Survey*, vol. 28, no. 1, January 1988, pp. 96–8; Ng Shui Meng, "Laos in 1986," p. 186.

36  Bernard Funck, "Laos: Decentralization and Economic Control," in *The Challenge of Reform in Indochina*, ed. Börge Ljunggren, Cambridge, MA: Harvard University Press, 1993, pp. 129–32; United Nations Development Program, "The Economy of Laos: An Overview," in *Laos: Beyond the Revolution*, ed. Joseph J. Zasloff and Leonard Unger, London: Macmillan, 1991, pp. 75–9.

37  Private Interview, Liang Insisiengmay, Director, Tax Department, Lao People's Democratic Republic, Vientiane, 11 December 1990; Martin Stuart-Fox, "Laos in 1988: In Pursuit of New Directions," *Asian Survey*, vol. 29, no. 1, January 1989, pp. 82–3; Grant Evans, "Planning Problems in Peripheral Socialism: The Case of Laos," in *Laos: Beyond the Revolution*, ed. Joseph J. Zasloff and Leonard Unger, New York, NY: St. Martin's Press, 1991, p. 104; Yves Bourdet, *The Economics of Transition in Laos: From Socialism to ASEAN Integration*, Northampton, MA: Edward Elgar Publishing, 2000, p. 43.

38  UNDP, "Economy of Laos," pp. 68–9; William Worner, "Economic Reform and Structural Change in Laos," *Southeast Asian Affairs 1989*, Singapore: Institute of Southeast Asian Studies, 1989, p. 200.

39  W. Randall Ireson, "Laos: Building a Nation under Socialism," *Indochina Issues*, vol. 79, February 1988, pp. 1–7; Worner, "Economic Reform," pp. 198–9.

40  Patcharawalai Wongboonsin, *et al.*, *Current Indochinese Economies*, Bangkok: Chulalongkorn University, 1992, p. 75.

41  Worner, "Economic Reform," p. 199; Evans, "Planning Problems," pp. 106–8.

42 Yves Bourdet, "Reforming Laos' Economic System," *Economic Systems*, vol. 16, no. 1, April 1992, p. 69.

43 Private Interview, Bountiem Phissamay, First Vice Minister, Ministry of External Economic Relations, Lao People's Democratic Republic, Vientiane, 10 December 1990; Bourdet, *Economics*, pp. 14–15.

44 Private Interview, Bounnhang Sengchandavong, Deputy Director, Office of the Foreign Investment Management Committee, Ministry of External Economic Relations, Lao People's Democratic Republic, 11 December 1990; Ian Livingston, "Industrial Development in Laos: New Policies and New Possibilities," in *Laos' Dilemmas and Options: The Challenge of Economic Transition in the 1990s*, ed. Mya Than and Joseph L. H. Tan, Singapore: Institute of Southeast Asian Studies, 1997, pp. 128–53.

45 Geoffrey C. Gunn, "Laos in 1989: Quiet Revolution in the Marketplace," *Asian Survey*, vol. 30, no. 1, January 1990, pp. 81–3; Stuart-Fox, "Laos in 1988," p. 84; Worner, "Economic Reform," pp. 187–208.

46 Private Interview, Sitaheng Rasphone, Vice Minister, Ministry of Agriculture and Forestry, Lao People's Democratic Republic, Vientiane, 3 March 1992; Ireson, "Laos," pp. 3–4; Stuart-Fox, "Laos in 1988," pp. 81–3; Worner, "Economic Reform," pp. 198–9.

47 UNDP, "Economy of Laos," p. 78.

48 Siriphan Kitiprawat, "Business Opportunities in Laos Today," *Bangkok Bank Monthly Review*, vol. 33, no. 11, November 1992, pp. 18–19.

49 "Boost for Foreign Investment," *Vientiane Times*, vol. 1, no. 3, 15–21 April 1994, pp. 6–7; Private Interview, Himmakone Manodham, Vice Minister, Ministry of Communication, Transport, Post and Construction, Lao People's Democratic Republic, Vientiane, 12 December 1990; Yves Bourdet, "Reforming," p. 70.

50 Siriphan, "Business Opportunities in Laos," pp. 14–22; Yves Bourdet, "Reforming," pp. 70–2; Michael Bogdan, "Legal Aspects of the Reintroduction of a Market Economy in Laos," *Review of Socialist Law*, vol. 17, no. 2, 1991, pp. 101–3.

51 Private Interview, Bountheuang Mounlasy, Deputy Director, Ministry of External Economic Relations, Lao People's Democratic Republic, Vientiane, 12 December 1990; UNDP, "Economy of Laos," pp. 77–9; Worner, "Economic Reform," pp. 197–8.

52 Ronald Bruce St John, *The Land Boundaries of Indochina: Cambodia, Laos and Vietnam*, International Boundaries Research Unit, University of Durham, Boundary and Territory Briefing, vol. 2, no. 6, 1998, pp. 38–9; MacAlister Brown and Joseph J. Zasloff, "Laos 1990: Socialism Postponed but Leadership Intact," *Southeast Asian Affairs 1991*, Singapore: Institute of Southeast Asian Studies, 1991, pp. 153–4; Ng Shui Meng, "Laos: Taking the Pragmatic Road," *Southeast Asian Affairs 1990*, Singapore: Institute of Southeast Asian Studies, 1990, pp. 159–60; Joiner, "Laos in 1987," pp. 103–4.

53 Worner, "Economic Reform," pp. 206–7, quote p. 207; Murray Hiebert, "Steps to a Summit: Vietnam, Thailand Prepare for Landmark Agreements," *Far Eastern Economic Review*, 3 October 1991, p. 15; Joiner, "Laos in 1987," pp. 101–3.

54 Pichai Chuensuksawadi, Nattaya Chetchotiros and Supapohn Kanwerayotin, "PM's Indochina Policy," *Bangkok Post*, 16 August 1990; Stuart-Fox, "Laos in 1988," p. 85; Ng Shui Meng, "Laos in 1986," pp. 190–1.

55 Worner, "Economic Reform," pp. 207–8; Evans, "Planning Problems," p. 118.

56 Brown and Zasloff, "Laos 1990," pp. 156–7; Stuart-Fox, "Laos in 1988," pp. 85–6; Ng Shui Meng, "Laos in 1986," p. 191.

57 Ronald Bruce St John, "Japan's Moment in Indochina: Washington Initiative

... Tokyo Success," *Asian Survey*, vol. 35, no. 7, July 1995, pp. 674–5; Ng Shui Meng, "Laos: Pragmatic Road," pp. 160–1; Worner, "Economic Reform," pp. 205–6; Anuraj Manibhandu, "After Cambodia, More Region-Building," *Bangkok Post*, 29 December 1991.

58 Martin Stuart-Fox, "Laos at the Crossroads," *Indochina Issues*, vol. 92, March 1991, p. 5; Stan Sesser, "Forgotten Country," *The New Yorker*, August 20, 1990, pp. 39–68, especially p. 48; Stuart-Fox, "Laos in 1988," p. 87; Bourdet, *Economics*, pp. 2–3.

59 "People Urged to Participate," FBIS-EAS-88-095, 17 May 1988, pp. 36–7, quotes p. 36; Ng Shui Meng, "Laos: Pragmatic Road," pp. 147–8.

60 "Leaders Cast Votes," FBIS-EAS-88-123, 27 June 1988, p. 40; Worner, "Economic Reform," pp. 203–4.

61 Brown and Zasloff, "Laos 1990," pp. 144–5, as quoted on p. 144.

62 Martin Stuart-Fox, "The Constitution of the Lao People's Democratic Republic," *Review of Socialist Law*, vol. 17, no. 4, 1991, pp. 299–317; Manynooch N. Faming, "An Interpretation of the Constitution of the Lao People's Democratic Republic," in *New Laos, New Challenges*, ed. Jacqueline Butler-Diaz, Tempe, AZ: Arizona State University Press, 1998, pp. 22–39; Ng Shui Meng, "Laos: Pragmatic Road," pp. 148–51.

63 Stuart-Fox, "Constitution," p. 317; Brown and Zasloff, "Laos 1990," pp. 145–6.

64 Economist Intelligence Unit, *Indochina*, vol. 4, 1988, p. 18; Stuart-Fox, "Laos in 1988," p. 88; Worner, "Economic Reform," p. 204.

65 Grant Evans, *The Politics of Ritual and Remembrance: Laos since 1975*, Honolulu, HI: University of Hawai'i Press, 1998, pp. 64–5, quotes p. 65.

66 Article 9 of Lao PDR constitution.

67 Patrick Raszelenberg and Peter Schier, *The Cambodia Conflict: Search for a Settlement, 1979–1991, An Analytical Chronology*, Hamburg: Institute of Asian Affairs, 1995, p. 88; Michael Vickery, "Notes on the Political Economy of the People's Republic of Kampuchea (PRK)," *Journal of Contemporary Asia*, vol. 20, no. 4, 1990, pp. 442–56.

68 Michael Vickery, *Kampuchea: Politics, Economics and Society*, Boulder, CO: Lynne Rienner, 1986, pp. 151–2, quote p. 151.

69 Evan Gottesman, *Cambodia After the Khmer Rouge: Inside the Politics of Nation Building*, New Haven, CT: Yale University Southeast Asia Studies, 1983, pp. 212–15; Margaret Slocomb, *The People's Republic of Kampuchea, 1979–1989: The Revolution after Pol Pot*, Chiang Mai: Silkworm Books, 2003, pp. 195–8; Jacques Bekaert, *Cambodian Diary: Tales of a Divided Nation, 1983–1986*, Bangkok: White Lotus Press, 1997, pp. 183–6, 191–3, 213–17, 241–6.

70 Raoul M. Jennar, "The People's Republic of Kampuchea," *The Cambodian Constitutions (1953–1993)*, Bangkok: White Lotus Press, 1995, pp. 89–110, quote p. 101.

71 Tim Huxley, "Cambodia in 1986: The PRK's Eighth Year," *Southeast Asian Affairs 1987*, Singapore: Institute of Southeast Asian Studies, 1987, pp. 170–2; Bekaert, *Cambodian Diary: Tales*, pp. 256–8; Grant Evans and Kelvin Rowley, *Red Brotherhood at War: Vietnam, Cambodia and Laos since 1975*, New York, NY: Verso, 1990, pp. 231–44, 272–84.

72 Steven Erlanger, "The Endless War: The Return of the Khmer Rouge," *New York Times Magazine*, 5 March 1989, pp. 25–7, 50–2, quote pp. 25–7.

73 Khatharya Um, "Cambodia in 1988: The Curved Road to Settlement," *Asian Survey*, vol. 29, no. 1, January 1989, p. 80; Sophal Ear, "Cambodia's Economic Development in Historical Perspective," August 1995, mimeograph pp. 87–8, 90–1.

74 Gottesman, *Cambodia*, pp. 272–6; Viviane Frings, "Cambodia After Decollec-

tivization (1989–1992)," *Journal of Contemporary Asia*, vol. 24, no. 1, January 1994, pp. 49–66; Slocomb, *People's Republic of Kampuchea*, pp. 216–17.

75 Jacques Népote and Marie-Sybille de Vienne, *Cambodge, Laboratoire d'une crise*, Paris: Centre des Hautes Études sur l'Afrique et l'Asie Modernes, 1993, pp. 86–7; Jennar, *Cambodian Constitutions*, p. 115.

76 Viviane Frings, *The Failure of Agricultural Collectivization in the People's Republic of Kampuchea (1979–1989)*, Working Paper No. 80, Clayton, Victoria: Monash University, 1993, p. 41.

77 H. D. S. Greenway, "Report from Cambodia: The Tiger and the Crocodile," *The New Yorker*, 17 July 1989, pp. 72–83, quote p. 76.

78 Ear, "Cambodia's Economic Development," p. 85; World Bank, *Cambodia: Agenda for Rehabilitation and Reconstruction*, 1 June 1992, pp. 18–19; Frings, *Failure*, pp. 40–3.

79 Siriphan Kitiprawat, "Cambodia Today: Economy and Business Opportunities," *Bangkok Bank Monthly Review*, vol. 34, no. 1, January 1993, p. 19; Mya Than, "Rehabilitation and Economic Reconstruction in Cambodia," *Contemporary Southeast Asia*, vol. 14, no. 3, December 1992, p. 271.

80 World Bank, *Cambodia: Agenda*, pp. 20, 26–9; Börje Ljunggren, "Market Economies under Communist Regimes: Reform in Vietnam, Laos and Cambodia," in *The Challenge of Reform in Indonesia*, ed. Börje Ljunggren, Cambridge, MA: Harvard University Press, 1993, p. 88; Népote and de Vienne, *Cambodge*, pp. 106–13.

81 Ronald Bruce St John, "Cambodian Foreign Policy: New Directions," *Asian Affairs*, vol. 16, no. 1, January–March 1994, pp. 55–74; Marie Alexandrine Martin, *Cambodia: A Shattered Society*, Berkeley, CA: University of California Press, 1994, pp. 263–5; Michael Vickery, "Notes," pp. 453–4; Mya Than, "Rehabilitation," pp. 269–86.

82 Sina Than, "Cambodia 1990: Towards a Peaceful Solution?" *Southeast Asian Affairs 1991*, Singapore: Institute of Southeast Asian Studies, 1991, pp. 98–102; Siriphan, "Cambodia Today," pp. 14–21.

83 Michael Haas, "The Paris Conference on Cambodia, 1989," *Bulletin of Concerned Asian Scholars*, vol. 23, no. 2, April–June 1991, p. 42; Raszelenberg and Schier, *Cambodia Conflict*, pp. 170–82, 212–18; Jacques Bekaert, *Cambodian Diary: A Long Road to Peace, 1987–1993,* Bangkok: White Lotus Press, 1998, pp. 129–31.

84 Khatharya Um, "Cambodia in 1989: Still Talking but No Settlement," *Asian Survey*, vol. 30, no. 1, January 1990, pp. 96–104, quote pp. 97–8.

85 Gottesman, *Cambodia*, pp. 308–9; Um, "Cambodia in 1989," pp. 96–8; MacAlister Brown and Joseph J. Zasloff, *Cambodia Confounds the Peacemakers, 1979–1998*, Ithaca, NY: Cornell University Press, 1998, pp. 53–9.

86 Private Interview, Richard H. Solomon, Assistant Secretary of State for East Asian and Pacific Affairs, U.S. Department of State, Bangkok, 29 July 1991; Sorpong Peou, *Conflict Neutralization in the Cambodia War: From Battlefield to Ballot-box*, New York, NY: Oxford University Press, 1997, pp. 37–47, 112–74; Haas, "Paris Conference," pp. 52–3.

87 Arthur J. Dommen, "UN Bias and Cambodian Peace," *Global Affairs*, vol. 7, no. 4, Fall 1992, pp. 120–35; Jennar, "State of Cambodia (1989–1993)," *Cambodian Constitutions*, pp. 111–33; Gottesman, *Cambodia*, pp. 303–4.

88 UN Document A/46/608-S/23177, 30 October 1991. For the texts of the four Paris peace accords, see Raszelenberg and Schier, *Cambodia Conflict*, pp. 570–605.

89 Janet E. Heininger, *Peacekeeping in Transition: The United Nations in Cambodia*, New York, NY: Twentieth Century Fund Press, 1994, pp. 56–62; Raszelenberg and Schier, *Cambodia Conflict*, pp. 567–70, 603–5.

90 Frank Frost, "Cambodia: From UNTAC to Royal Government," *Southeast Asian Affairs 1994*, Singapore: Institute of Southeast Asian Studies, 1994, pp. 79–82; Caroline Hughes, *UNTAC in Cambodia: The Impact on Human Rights*, Occasional Paper No. 92, Singapore: Institute of Southeast Asian Studies, 1996, pp. 31–71; Peou, *Conflict Neutralization*, pp. 192–3, 221–9.

91 William Shawcross, *Cambodia's New Deal*, Contemporary Issues Paper No. 1, Washington, D.C.: Carnegie Endowment for International Peace, 1994, pp. 20–3, quote p. 23; *Report of the Secretary-General on the Conduct and Results of the Elections in Cambodia*, United Nations Security Council S/25913, 10 June 1993.

92 Nate Thayer, "New Govt: Who's Really in Control?" *Phnom Penh Post*, 19 November–2 December 1993; "Sihanouk Addresses New Government at Ceremony," FBIS-EAS-93-128, 7 July 1993, pp. 37–46; Brown and Zasloff, *Cambodia*, pp. 165–210.

93 Khatharya Um, "Cambodia in 1993: Year Zero Plus One," *Asian Survey*, vol. 34, no. 1, January 1994, pp. 72–81; "National Assembly Approves Economic Reforms," FBIS-EAS-93-129, 8 July 1993, pp. 35–6; Zachary Abuza, "The Khmer Rouge Quest for Economic Independence," *Asian Survey*, vol. 33, no. 10, October 1993, pp. 1010–21; Ker Munthit, "Interim Coalition Faces Cash Crunch," *Phnom Penh Post*, 2–15 July 1993.

94 St John, "Japan's Moment," pp. 678–9; "Tokyo FM Is Upbeat," *Phnom Penh Post*, 21 October–3 November, 1994; Jonathan Friedland, "Someone to Trust: Cambodia's Free-Market Plan Wins Over Donors," *Far Eastern Economic Review*, 24 March 1994, p. 47.

95 Leszek Buszynski, "Thailand's Foreign Policy: Management of a Regional Vision," *Asian Survey*, vol. 34, no. 8, August 1994, pp. 721–37; Surin Maisrikrod, "The 'Peace Dividend' in Southeast Asia: The Political Economy of New Thai-Vietnamese Relations," *Contemporary Southeast Asia*, vol. 16, no. 1, June 1994, pp. 46–66; St John, *Land Boundaries*, p. 29.

96 Thayer, "Introduction," p. 1; Ngo Ba Thanh, "1992 Constitution," pp. 81–115. See David Koh's review of *Vietnam and the Rule of Law* in *Contemporary Southeast Asia*, vol. 16, no. 1, June 1994, pp. 108–12.

## 5  End of the beginning

1 Ronald Bruce St John, "Japan's Moment in Indochina: Washington Initiative ... Tokyo Success," *Asian Survey*, vol. 35, no. 7, July 1995, pp. 678–9; Masaya Shiraishi, *Japanese Relations with Vietnam: 1951–1987*, Ithaca, NY: Cornell Southeast Asia Program, 1990, pp. 84–7.

2 Brantly Womack, "Vietnam in 1995: Successes in Peace," *Asian Survey*, vol. 36, no. 1, January 1996, pp. 73–82; Allan E. Goodman, "Vietnam's Post-Cold War Diplomacy and the U.S. Response," *Asian Survey*, vol. 33, no. 8, August 1993, pp. 832–47.

3 Adam Fforde and Stefan de Vylder, *From Plan to Market: The Economic Transition in Vietnam*, Boulder, CO: Westview Press, 1996, pp. 281–302; International Monetary Fund, *World Economic Outlook (May 1999)*, Washington, D.C.: International Monetary Fund, 1999, p. 147; Institute of Southeast Asian Studies, *Regional Outlook: Southeast Asia, 2000–2001*, Singapore: Institute of Southeast Asian Studies, 2000, p. 95.

4 International Monetary Fund, *World Economic Outlook (May 1999)*, p. 155; Vo Dai Luoc, "The Fight against Inflation: Achievements and Problems," in *Reinventing Vietnamese Socialism: Doi Moi in Comparative Perspective*, ed. William S. Turley and Mark Selden, Boulder, CO: Westview Press, 1993, pp. 107–17.

5 Asian Development Bank, *Asian Development Outlook, 1995 and 1996*, Manila: Asian Development Bank, 1995, pp. 125–6; Siriphan Kitiprawat, "Business Opportunities in Vietnam Today," *Bangkok Bank Monthly Review*, vol. 34, no. 3, March 1993, pp. 12–19.

6 Private Interview, Le Dang Doanh, Central Institute for Economic Management, Socialist Republic of Vietnam, Hanoi, 12 June 1996; Vo Dai Luoc, "Monetary Stabilization: The Vietnamese Experience," in *Vietnam in a Changing World*, ed. Irene Norlund, Carolyn L. Gates and Vu Cao Dam, Richmond, Surrey: Curzon Press, 1995, pp. 71–84.

7 Ha Thang, "Trade Deficit Plunge Brings New Year Cheer," *Vietnam Investment Review*, 29 December 1997–4 January 1998; Institute of Southeast Asian Studies, *Regional Outlook: Southeast Asia, 2000–2001*, p. 95.

8 Womack, "Vietnam in 1995," pp. 77–8, quote p. 76.

9 Thaveeporn Vasavakul, "Vietnam: The Third Wave of State Building," *Southeast Asian Affairs 1997*, Singapore: Institute of Southeast Asian Studies, 1997, pp. 337–45.

10 Zachary Abuza, "Leadership Transition in Vietnam since the Eighth Party Congress: The Unfinished Congress," *Asian Survey*, vol. 38, no. 12, December 1998, pp. 1105–12.

11 Thaveeporn Vasavakul, "Vietnam's One-Party Rule and Socialist Democracy?" *Southeast Asian Affairs 1998*, Singapore: Institute of Southeast Asian Studies, 1998, pp. 311–13; Abuza, "Leadership Transition," pp. 1113–15.

12 Private Interview, Tran Ngoc Hien, Vice President, Ho Chi Minh National Academy for Political Science, Socialist Republic of Vietnam, Hanoi, 12 June 1996; Jeremy Grant, "Hanoi Leadership Finalised," *Financial Times*, 8 January 1998; Abuza, "Leadership Transition," pp. 1115–17.

13 Mark Sidel, "Vietnam in 1998: Reform Confronts the Regional Crisis," *Asian Survey*, vol. 39, no. 1, January–February 1999, pp. 89–95; Melina Nathan, "Vietnam: Is Globalization a Friend or a Foe?" *Southeast Asian Affairs 1999*, Singapore: Institute of Southeast Asian Studies, 1999, pp. 34–41.

14 "Vietnam: Worse Than Imagined," *Far Eastern Economic Review*, 15 January 1998, p. 57; David H. D. Truong, "Striving towards *Doi Moi* II," *Southeast Asian Affairs 1998*, Singapore: Institute of Southeast Asian Studies, 1998, pp. 328–39.

15 Jeremy Grant, "Hanoi Sticks to 9% Target," *Financial Times*, 31 March 1998; Nguyen Tri Dung, "Growth Rates Maintained but More Hard Work Ahead," *Vietnam Investment Review*, 29 December 1997–4 January 1998.

16 Carlyle A. Thayer, "Vietnam: The Politics of Immobilism Revisited," *Southeast Asian Affairs 2000*, Singapore: Institute of Southeast Asian Studies, 2000, pp. 311–16; Nathan, "Vietnam," pp. 341–4; Jeremy Grant, "Vietnam's Leaders Are Losing Their Way," *Financial Times*, 13 February 1998.

17 Nguyen Tri Dung, "Bleak Economic Outlook on the Cards Says Top Minister," *Vietnam Investment Review*, 13–19 July 1998; Anya Schffrin, "Vietnam's Prime Minister Says Economic Reform Will Be Gradual," *Asian Wall Street Journal*, 25 March 1998.

18 World Bank, *Vietnam: Rising to the Challenge, An Economic Report*, Report No. 18632-VN, 25 November 1998; Ha Thang, "Crunch Time Looms, Warns World Bank," *Vietnam Investment Review*, 6–12 July 1998.

19 Institute of Southeast Asian Studies, *Regional Outlook: Southeast Asia, 2001–2002*, p. 86; Minh Nhung, "Optimistic Growth Targets Far from Reality," *Vietnam Investment Review*, 29 December 1997–4 January 1998.

20 Socialist Republic of Vietnam, "1993 Land Law," *Selection of Fundamental Laws and Regulations of Vietnam*, 2d ed., Hanoi: THẾ GIỚI Publishers, 1993, pp. 283–314; Douglas Pike, "Vietnam in 1993: Uncertainty Closes In," *Asian*

*Survey*, vol. 34, no. 1, January 1994, p. 67; United Nations Development Program, *Catching Up: Capacity Development for Poverty Elimination in Viet Nam*, Hanoi: UNDP/UNICEF, 1996, pp. 37–49.

21 Nguyen Ngoc Tuan, Ngo Tri Long and Ho Phuong, "Restructuring of State-Owned Enterprises towards Industrialization and Modernization in Vietnam," in *State-Owned Enterprise Reform in Vietnam: Lessons from Asia*, ed. Ng Chee Yuen, Nick J. Freeman and Frank H. Huynh, Singapore: Institute of Southeast Asian Studies, 1996, pp. 19–37.

22 Phan Van Tiem and Nguyen Van Thanh, "Problems and Prospects of State Enterprise Reform, 1996–2000," in *State-Owned Enterprise Reform in Vietnam: Lessons from Asia*, ed. Ng Chee Yuen, Nick J. Freeman and Frank H. Huynh, Singapore: Institute of Southeast Asian Studies, 1996, pp. 3–18, quote p. 16.

23 Nathan, "Vietnam," pp. 341–4; Nguyen Manh Hung, "PM Approves Forced Equitisation of SOEs," *Vietnam Investment Review*, 6–12 July 1998; "Hanoi to Speed Privatizations," *International Herald Tribune*, 23 February 1998.

24 Institute of Southeast Asian Studies, *Regional Outlook: Southeast Asia, 1999–2000*, pp. 58–9; International Monetary Fund, *World Economic Outlook (May 2000)*, Washington, D.C.: International Monetary Fund, 2000, p. 219.

25 Ngoc Dung, "Jobless Rate Surges to All Time Record," *Vietnam Investment Review*, 13–19 July 1998; Institute of Southeast Asian Studies, *Regional Outlook: Southeast Asia, 1999–2000*, pp. 62–3.

26 Nick J. Freeman, "Vietnam: Better Managing Reform," *Southeast Asian Affairs 1996*, Singapore: Institute of Southeast Asian Studies, 1996, pp. 398–9, quote p. 398; Carolyn L. Gates and David H. D. Truong, "Vietnam in ASEAN: Economic Reform, Openness and Transformation," *ASEAN Economic Bulletin*, vol. 13, no. 2, November 1996, pp. 159–68.

27 Private Interview, Le Van Bang, Vietnamese Ambassador to the United States, Indianapolis, IN, 23 April 1996; Institute of Southeast Asian Studies, *Regional Outlook: Southeast Asia, 2001–2002*, p. 86; Luu Tien Hai, "Ministry Looks to Boost Exports with Tax Breaks," *Vietnam Investment Review*, 6–12 July 1998.

28 Ha Thang, "Adjusted Dong Forces Up Inflation," *Vietnam Investment Review*, 31 August–6 September 1998; Institute of Southeast Asian Studies, *Regional Outlook: Southeast Asia, 1999–2000*, p. 61.

29 Nathan, "Vietnam," p. 342; Nguyen Tuan Dung, "Foreign Direct Investment in Vietnam," in *Vietnam Assessment: Creating a Sound Investment Climate*, ed. Suiwah Leung, Singapore: Institute of Southeast Asian Studies, 1996, pp. 69–89.

30 "Foreigners Ditching Vietnam Amid Pervasive Economic Gloom," *Japan Times*, 27 December 1998; Dang Tu Suong, "Doors Slam as Rep Offices Shut," *Vietnam Investment Review*, 13–19 July 1998.

31 Zachary Abuza, *Renovating Politics in Contemporary Vietnam*, Boulder, CO: Lynne Rienner Publishers, 2002, pp. 217–19; Nathan, "Vietnam," p. 341.

32 Jonathan Birchall, "Rifts Show in Vietnamese Leadership," *Financial Times*, 12 August 1998; Abuza, *Renovating Politics*, pp. 217–18.

33 Sidel, "Vietnam in 1998," pp. 96–8; Freeman, "Vietnam," p. 398; "MFN Status On-line as US Votes Against Veto," *Vietnam Investment Review*, 29 June–5 July 1998.

34 Jonathan Birchall, "Vietnam Visit by UN Human Rights Envoy Ends in Disarray," *Financial Times*, 30 October 1998; Jonathan Birchall, "Test for Vietnam on Religious Freedom," *Financial Times*, 17–18 October 1998.

35 Li Ma, "China and Vietnam: Coping with the Threat of Peaceful Evolution," in *Vietnamese Foreign Policy in Transition*, ed. Carlyle A. Thayer and Ramses

Amer, Singapore: Institute of Southeast Asian Studies, 1999, pp. 44–67, quote p. 58.

36 "Vietnam: Border Tensions Rise," *Far Eastern Economic Review*, 5 February 1998, p. 13; Ramses Amer, "Sino-Vietnamese Relations: Past, Present and Future," in *Vietnamese Foreign Policy in Transition*, ed. Carlyle A. Thayer and Ramses Amer, Singapore: Institute of Southeast Asian Studies, 1999, pp. 68–129.

37 "Highway Link Plan Gears Up," *Vietnam Investment Review*, 24–30 August 1998; Nathan, "Vietnam," p. 348; Ramses Amer, "Vietnam and Its Neighbours: The Border Dispute Dimension," *Contemporary Southeast Asia*, vol. 17, no. 3, December 1995, pp. 309–11.

38 Jonathan Birchall, "Hanoi Pleads for Cambodia," *Financial Times*, 15 December 1998; Martin Wikfalk, "Opposition Takes Issue with VN Border Talks," *Phnom Penh Post*, 17–23 July 1998; "Cambodian PM Mounts Upbeat Visit," *Vietnam Investment Review*, 8–14 June 1998; Nathan, "Vietnam," p. 348.

39 Ronald Bruce St John, *The Land Boundaries of Indochina: Cambodia, Laos and Vietnam*, International Boundaries Research Unit, University of Durham, Boundary and Territory Briefing, vol. 2, no. 6, 1998, p. 32; Thaveeporn Vasavakul, "Vietnam," p. 356.

40 "Hanoi Summit Opens New Window of Opportunity," *Vietnam Investment Review*, 21–27 December 1998; David Wurfel, "Between China and ASEAN: The Dialectics of Recent Vietnamese Foreign Policy," in *Vietnamese Foreign Policy in Transition*, ed. Carlyle A. Thayer and Ramses Amer, Singapore: Institute of Southeast Asian Studies, 1999, pp. 148–69.

41 Private Interview, Himmakone Manodham, Vice Minister, Ministry of Communication, Transport, Post, and Construction, Lao People's Democratic Republic, Vientiane, 15 June 1992; Richard Vokes and Armand Fabella, "Lao PDR," in *From Centrally Planned to Market Economies: The Asian Approach*, vol. 3, *Lao PDR, Myanmar and Viet Nam*, edited by Pradumna B. Rana and Naved Hamid, New York: Oxford University Press, pp. 20–1.

42 Martin Stuart-Fox, "Laos 1991: On the Defensive," *Southeast Asian Affairs 1992*, Singapore: Institute of Southeast Asian Studies, 1992, pp. 168–70, 174–7; Vokes and Fabella, "Lao PDR," pp. 20–1.

43 Arthur J. Dommen, "Laos: Consolidating the Economy," *Southeast Asian Affairs 1994*, Singapore: Institute of Southeast Asian Studies, 1994, p. 168; Martin Stuart-Fox, "Laos: Towards Subregional Integration," *Southeast Asian Affairs 1995*, Singapore: Institute of Southeast Asian Studies, 1995, p. 186.

44 Private Interview, Sitaheng Rasphone, Vice Minister, Ministry of Agriculture and Forestry, Lao People's Democratic Republic, Vientiane, 3 March 1992; Dommen, "Laos: Consolidating," p. 169.

45 Lao People's Democratic Republic, *Law on the Promotion and Management of Foreign Investment in the Lao PDR*, Vientiane, 14 March 1994, mimeograph; Suchint Chaimungkalanont, "New Foreign Investment Law in Laos," *The Standard Chartered Indochina Monitor*, July 1994, pp. 20–1.

46 World Bank, *Lao People's Democratic Republic Country Economic Memorandum*, Report No. 12554-LA, 24 March, 1994, pp. 102–5.

47 Khamsouk Sundara, "New Laos – Economic Challenges," in *New Laos, New Challenges*, ed. Jacqueline Butler-Diaz, Tempe, AZ: Arizona State University Press, 1998, pp. 77–82; Vokes and Fabella, "Lao PDR," p. 4; Andrea Thalemann, "Laos: Between Battlefield and Marketplace," *Journal of Contemporary Asia*, vol. 27, no. 1, 1997, pp. 85–105.

48 Mark Nguyen, "Laos: Back to a Land of Three Kingdoms," *Southeast Asian Affairs 1996*, Singapore: Institute of Southeast Asian Studies, 1996, pp. 211–12; Yves Bourdet, "Laos: The Sixth Party Congress, and After?"

*Southeast Asian Affairs 1997*, Singapore: Institute of Southeast Asian Studies, 1997, pp. 146–50.

49 Yves Bourdet, "Rural Reforms and Agricultural Productivity in Laos," *Journal of Developing Areas*, vol. 29, no. 2, January 1995, pp. 161–82; World Bank, *Lao PDR Agricultural Sector Memorandum*, Report No. 13675-LA, 23 March 1995, pp. 1–53; Yves Bourdet, *The Economics of Transition in Laos: From Socialism to ASEAN Integration*, Northampton, MA: Edward Elgar Publishing, pp. 80–1.

50 Yves Bourdet, "The Dynamics of Regional Disparities in Laos: The Poor and the Rich," *Asian Survey*, vol. 38, no. 7, July 1998, pp. 629–52; Randi Jerndal and Jonathan Rigg, "From Buffer State to Crossroads State: Spaces of Human Activity and Integration in the Lao PDR," in *Laos: Culture and Society*, ed. Grant Evans, Chiang Mai: Silkworm Books, 1999, pp. 43–7.

51 J. Malcolm Dowling and Charissa N. Castillo, "Recent Economic Developments in Southeast Asia," *Southeast Asian Affairs 1996*, Singapore: Institute of Southeast Asian Studies, 1996, pp. 26–8; Bourdet, "Laos: Sixth Party Congress," pp. 150–1.

52 Yves Bourdet, "Laos in 1995: Reform Policy, Out of Breath?" *Asian Survey*, vol. 36, no. 1, January 1996, pp. 89–91; Jeremy Grant, "Laos authorities find economic success difficult to manage," *Financial Times*, 31 August 1995; Nguyen, "Laos," p. 210; Bourdet, "Laos: Sixth Party Congress," pp. 151–5.

53 Martin Stuart-Fox, "Laos in 1997: Into ASEAN," *Asian Survey*, vol. 38, no. 1, January 1998, pp. 76–7; Bourdet, *Economics*, pp. 5–6; Peter Waldman, "Dam Proposed for Laos Is of Immense Meaning to an Array of Interests," *Wall Street Journal*, 12 August 1977.

54 World Bank, *Memorandum of the President of the International Development Association to the Executive Directors on a Country Assistance Strategy of the World Bank Group for the Lao People's Democratic Republic*, Report No. 19098-LA, 30 March 1999, pp. 1–2; Nick J. Freeman, "Laos: No Safe Haven from the Regional Tumult," *Southeast Asian Affairs 1998*, Singapore: Institute of Southeast Asian Studies, 1998, pp. 142–52.

55 Bourdet, *Economics*, pp. 80–1, quote 80; Ngozi Okonjo-Iweala, Victoria Kwakwa, Andrea Beckwith and Zafar Ahmed, "Impact of Asia's Financial Crisis on Cambodia and the Lao PDR," *Finance & Development*, vol. 36, no. 3, September 1999, p. 3.

56 As quoted in Bertil Lintner, "Home-Grown Crisis: Laos fails to face up to its economic woes," *Far Eastern Economic Review*, 30 July 1998, pp. 52–3; Bourdet, *Economics*, pp. 4, 80.

57 Andreas Schneider, "Laos: A Million Elephants, A Million Tourists?" *Southeast Asian Affairs 1999*, Singapore: Institute of Southeast Asian Studies, 1999, pp. 147–56; Carlyle A. Thayer, "Laos in 1998: Continuity under New Leadership," *Asian Survey*, vol. 39, no. 1, January–February 1999, pp. 39–41.

58 Stephen T. Johnson, "Laos in 1992: Succession and Consolidation," *Asian Survey*, vol. 33, no. 1, January 1993, p. 76; Bruce Lambert, "Kaysone Phomvihan, Communist Who Ruled Laos, Is Dead at 71," *New York Times*, 22 November 1992.

59 Grant Evans, *The Politics of Ritual and Remembrance: Laos since 1975*, Honolulu, HI: University of Hawai'i Press, 1998, pp. 25–31, quotes p. 24.

60 Johnson, "Laos in 1992," pp. 76–7, quote p. 77; Bourdet, *Economics*, pp. 2–3; Vokes and Fabella, "Lao PDR," p. 117.

61 Vokes and Fabella, "Lao PDR," pp. 117–18.

62 Arthur J. Dommen, "Laos in 1993: The Revolution on Hold," *Asian Survey*, vol. 34, no. 1, January 1994, pp. 82–3; Dommen, "Laos: Consolidating," p. 172.

63 Stuart-Fox, "Laos: Toward Subregional Integration," pp. 188, 190; Henry Kamm, "Communism in Laos: Poverty and a Thriving Elite," *New York Times*, 30 July 1995.

64 Bourdet, "Laos in 1995," quote p. 92; Nguyen, "Laos," p. 198.

65 Bourdet, *Economics*, pp. 2–3, quote p. 3; Bourdet, "Laos: Sixth Party Congress," pp. 143–4; Ted Bardacke, "Military tightens its grip on Laos," *Financial Times*, 21 March 1996.

66 "Change of Face: Reform gets an authoritarian overlay," *Far Eastern Economic Review*, 18 April 1996, p. 22; Bourdet, "Laos: Sixth Party Congress," pp. 144–5.

67 Stuart-Fox, "Laos in 1997," pp. 75–6; Randi Jerndal and Jonathan Rigg, "Making Space in Laos: Constructing a National Identity in a 'Forgotten' Country," *Political Geography*, vol. 17, no. 7, 1998, pp. 823–6; Evans, *Politics of Ritual*, pp. 65–8.

68 Schneider, "Laos," pp. 145–7; Thayer, "Laos in 1998," pp. 38–9; Bertil Lintner, "Two Steps Back: Election slate portends a slowdown in reform," *Far Eastern Economic Review*, 18 December 1997, p. 32; Freeman, "Laos: No Safe Haven," pp. 141–2.

69 Thayer, "Laos in 1998," p. 41; Stuart-Fox, "Laos in 1997," p. 78; Stuart-Fox, "Laos: Toward Subregional Integration," p. 191.

70 Schneider, "Laos," p. 158; Thayer, "Laos in 1998," p. 41; Stuart-Fox, "Laos: Toward Subregional Integration," pp. 191–2; Sai Namkok, "Relations with Thailand Viewed," FBIS-EAS-93-109, 9 June 1993, pp. 37–8.

71 Stuart-Fox, "Laos in 1997," p. 79; "Cambodia's Ranariddh, Hun Sen Arrives for Visit," FBIS-EAS-93-143, 28 July 1993, p. 72; Dommen, "Laos: Consolidating," p. 174.

72 Thayer, "Laos in 1998," p. 41; Stuart-Fox, "Laos in 1997," p. 79; Bourdet, "Laos: Sixth Party Congress," p. 156; Stuart-Fox, "Laos: Toward Subregional Integration," p. 192.

73 Freeman, "Laos: No Safe Haven," p. 154; Bertil Lintner, "Ties that Bind," *Far Eastern Economic Review*, 9 February 1995, pp. 18–19; "Li Signs Pact over Border with Laos," *China Daily*, 4 December 1993; Johnson, "Laos in 1992," p. 81.

74 Freeman, "Laos: No Safe Haven," p. 154; "Laos blasts US over Radio Free Asia," *Vietnam Investment Review*, 25–31 August 1997; Nguyen, "Laos," p. 209; Stuart-Fox, "Laos: Toward Subregional Integration," p. 193; Johnson, "Laos in 1992," pp. 81–2.

75 Bourdet, "Laos: Sixth Party Congress," pp. 156–7; "Japanese Minister Promises Increased Aid," FBIS-EAS-93-079, 27 April 1993, p. 58.

76 Royal Government of Cambodia, *National Programme to Rehabilitate and Develop Cambodia*, Phnom Penh, February 1994, p. 1.

77 Royal Government of Cambodia, *Constitution of the Kingdom of Cambodia*, Phnom Penh, October 1993.

78 The vision and the scope of the *National Programme* were impressive, but there was little new in the approach. All of its central ideas had been discussed in the years prior to the 1993 elections. For example, see World Bank, *Cambodia: Agenda for Rehabilitation and Reconstruction*, Washington, D.C.: World Bank, 1992 and United Nations Development Program, *Cambodia's Rehabilitation Needs: Discussions with Donor Countries*, New York, NY, 11 November 1991, mimeograph.

79 Sam Rainsy, "Medium and Long-Term Development Needs of Cambodia: Progress in the Economic Reform Policy," Second Meeting of the International Committee on the Reconstruction of Cambodia (ICORC), Tokyo, 10 March 1994, mimeograph.

80 Kingdom of Cambodia, Ministry of Economics and Finance, *Announcement No. 018*, Phnom Penh, 31 December 1993, mimeograph.

81 Kingdom of Cambodia, Office of the Minister of State, *Announcement concerning the Profits Tax, House and Land Rent Tax, and Turnover Tax, No. 012*, Phnom Penh, 9 March 1994, mimeograph.

82 Kingdom of Cambodia, Ministry of Economics and Finance, *Proposed New Taxes*, Phnom Penh, 1 May 1994, mimeograph; Asian Development Bank, *Asian Development, Outlook 1995 and 1996*, p. 97.

83 State of Cambodia, Council of State, *Banking Laws*, Phnom Penh, 1992, mimeograph; Cambodia, *National Programme*, pp. 11–13.

84 Rainsy, "Medium and Long-Term Development," p. 4; Michael Ward, "Inflation Management and Stabilization: The Cambodian Experience," in *Macroeconomic Management in Southeast Asia's Transitional Economies*, ed. Manuel F. Montes, Romeo A. Reyes and Somsak Tambunlertchai, Kuala Lumpur: Asian and Pacific Development Centre, 1995, pp. 71–104.

85 Radsady Om, "One Year After the Election: The Position of Cambodia in the Southeast Asian Region," Institute of Asian Studies, Chulalongkorn University, Bangkok, Thailand, 17 June 1994; "The New Investment Law," *Phnom Penh Post*, 12–25 August 1994. The Ministry of Economics and Finance drew on a wide variety of Third World and First World investment codes to draft the Cambodian approach. Private Interview, Senior Official, Ministry of Economics and Finance, Royal Government of Cambodia, Phnom Penh, 15 June 1994.

86 David Doran, "The Council for Development of Cambodia," *Phnom Penh Post*, 25 August–7 September 1995.

87 Michael Hayes, "Econ Reforms Creep Ahead," *Phnom Penh Post*, 16–29 May 1997; Susan Postlewaite, "ADB Board Worried about Tattered Economy," *Phnom Penh Post*, 22 September–5 October 1995.

88 Cambodia, *National Programme*, pp. 40–2.

89 Kingdom of Cambodia, Ministry of Economics and Finance, *Revenue from Exports of Timber*, Phnom Penh, 27 April 1994, mimeograph.

90 Anugraha Palan, "Defence Secretly Holds Out on Logs," *Phnom Penh Post*, 21 October–3 November 1994.

91 Kirk Talbott, "Logging in Cambodia: Politics and Plunder," in *Cambodia and the International Community: The Quest for Peace, Development, and Democracy*, ed. Frederick Z. Brown and David G. Timberman, New York, NY: Asia Society, 1998, pp. 149–68; Ted Bardacke, "Cambodia Failing To Curb Illegal Logging," *Financial Times*, 16 September 1997.

92 Matthew Grainger, Christine Chaumeau and Ker Munthit, "A Ruby Tuesday in Pailin," *Phnom Penh Post*, 31 October–14 November 1996.

93 Mang Channo, "Shrimp Farmers Ripping Away Mangroves," *Phnom Penh Post*, 24 March–6 April 1995.

94 Cambodia, *National Programme*, pp. 16–22.

95 Caroline Hughes, *The Political Economy of Cambodia's Transition, 1991–2001*, London: RoutledgeCurzon, 2003, pp. 60–7; David W. Roberts, *Political Transition in Cambodia, 1991–99: Power, Elitism and Democracy*, Richmond, Surrey: Curzon, 2001, pp. 115–18; Abdulgaffar Peang-Meth, "Understanding Cambodia's Political Developments," *Contemporary Southeast Asia*, vol. 19, no. 3, December 1997, pp. 293–5.

96 Jason Barber and Ker Munthit, "King Brokers Sirivudh's Departure," *Phnom Penh Post*, 15–28 December 1995; Pierre P. Lizée, "Cambodia in 1995: From Hope to Despair," *Asian Survey*, vol. 36, no. 1, January 1996, pp. 84–6; Frederick Z. Brown and Laura McGrew, "Cambodia: The Royal Government on

Trial," *Southeast Asian Affairs 1995*, Singapore: Institute of Southeast Asian Studies, 1995, pp. 132–3.

97 Joakim Öjendal, "Democracy Lost? The Fate of the U.N.-implanted Democracy in Cambodia," *Contemporary Southeast Asia*, vol. 18, no. 2, September 1996, pp. 204–7; Brown and McGrew, "Cambodia," pp. 135–6; Roberts, *Political Transition*, pp. 121–49.

98 Lao Mong Hay, "Building Democracy in Cambodia: Problems and Prospects," in *Cambodia and the International Community: The Quest for Peace, Development and Democracy*, ed. Frederick Z. Brown and David G. Timberman, New York, NY: Asia Society, 1998, pp. 172–5; Sheridan T. Prasso, "Cambodia: A Heritage of Violence," *World Policy Journal*, vol. 11, no. 3, Fall 1994, pp. 71–7.

99 Nate Thayer, "Compassion Fatigue," *Far Eastern Economic Review*, 16 February 1995, p. 19; Lizée, "Cambodia in 1995," p. 86.

100 "Intrigue and Conflict Bring Politics to a Boil," *Phnom Penh Post*, 29 November–12 December 1996; Sorpong Peou, "Cambodia: A New Glimpse of Hope?" *Southeast Asian Affairs 1997*, Singapore: Institute of Southeast Asian Studies, 1997, pp. 83–90; MacAlister Brown and Joseph J. Zasloff, *Cambodia Confounds the Peacemakers, 1979–1998*, Ithaca, NY: Cornell University Press, 1998, pp. 239–62.

101 Khatharya Um, "One Step Forward, Two Steps Back: Cambodia and the Elusive Quest for Peace," *Southeast Asian Affairs 1998*, Singapore: Institute of Southeast Asian Studies, 1998, pp. 71–85, quote p. 71.

102 Sorpong Peou, "Hun Sen's Pre-emptive Coup: Causes and Consequences," *Southeast Asian Affairs 1998*, Singapore: Institute of Southeast Asian Studies, 1998, pp. 86–102; Hughes, *Political Economy*, pp. 117–23; Roberts, *Political Transition*, pp. 126–49; Chea Sotheacheath and Christine Chaumeau, "Hardliners Split as PMs Quarrel," *Phnom Penh Post*, 13–26 June 1997.

103 Um, "One Step Forward," p. 71.

104 Ted Bardacke, Heather Bourbeau and Gwen Robinson, "Hun Sen Calls for Elections in Cambodia," *Financial Times*, 14 July 1997; Jason Barber, "Democracy from the Barrel of a Gun," *Phnom Penh Post*, 12–24 July 1997; Sarpong Peou, *Intervention & Change in Cambodia: Towards Democracy?*, Singapore: Institute of Southeast Asian Studies, 2000, pp. 336–71.

105 Asian Development Bank, *Asian Development Outlook, 1995 and 1996*, pp. 97–8; Brown and McGrew, "Cambodia," pp. 139–43.

106 Martha M. Hamilton, "Tough Sell: The 'New' Cambodia," *International Herald Tribune*, 18–19 February 1995; Peou, "Cambodia," pp. 90–5; Harish Mehta, "Cambodia: A Year of Consolidation," *Southeast Asian Affairs 1996*, Singapore: Institute of Southeast Asian Studies, 1996, pp. 120–3.

107 Elizabeth Moorthy, "Foreign Aid – A Guide for the Bemused," *Phnom Penh Post*, 15–28 August 1997; *Memorandum of Economic and Financial Policies for 1997*, reprinted in *Phnom Penh Post*, 16–29 May 1997.

108 Ngozi Okonjo-Iweala et al., "Impact of Asia's Financial Crisis," pp. 3–5; William Barnes, "Cambodia Finance Support Suspended," *Financial Times*, 24 September 1997.

109 Matthew Grainger, "Thais Forced To Play Key Role in Breaking the KR," *Phnom Penh Post*, 23 August–5 September 1996; Peou, "Cambodia," pp. 95–6; Ker Munthit, "Thai-Khmer Border Pact Signed by Army," *Phnom Penh Post*, 6–19 October 1995.

110 Sody Lay Rusden Quinn, "The Cambodian Fear of Vietnam," *Phnom Penh Post*, 21 November–4 December 1997; "Cambodia Shrinking," *Boundary and Security Bulletin*, vol. 4, no. 2, Summer 1996, p. 41; Zachary Abuza, "The

Khmer Rouge and the Crisis of Vietnamese Settlers in Cambodia," *Contemporary Southeast Asia*, vol. 16, no. 4, March 1995, pp. 433–45.

111 Michael Hayes, "Watching Beijing Playing Its Cards," *Phnom Penh Post*, 23 August–5 September 1996.

112 Peou, "Cambodia," pp. 97–8, quote p. 98; Christine Chaumeau, "Chinese Deals with Hun Sen Draw Fire," *Phnom Penh Post*, 19 December 1997–1 January 1998; "Cambodia, South Korea Ties," *Financial Times*, 31 October 1997.

113 Brown and Zasloff, *Cambodia*, pp. 267–8.

114 As quoted in Ker Munthit, "MFN to be lobbied in Senate: Lord," *Phnom Penh Post*, 26 January–8 February 1996; Elizabeth Moorthy, "Ambassador under Fire from DC while US Officials Target Hun Sen," *Phnom Penh Post*, 29 August–11 September 1997; Brown and Zasloff, *Cambodia*, pp. 265–6; Peou, "Cambodia: A New Glimpse of Hope?" pp. 99–100.

115 Seth Mydans, "Cambodia Poses Quandary for World Diplomats," *New York Times*, 12 July 1997; Peou, "Cambodia: A New Glimpse of Hope?" p. 99; Eduardo Lachica, "Cambodia's Aid Request May Raise Reform Issues," *Asian Wall Street Journal Weekly*, 8 July 1996.

116 Kay Möller, "Cambodia and Burma: The ASEAN Way Ends Here," *Asian Survey*, vol. 38, no. 12, December 1998, pp. 1087–104, quotes p. 1098; Jason Barber and Huw Watkin, "Hun Sen Left Seatless at UN," *Phnom Penh Post*, 26 September–9 October 1997.

117 "Mekong project comes under fire," *Financial Times*, 12 May 1997; Ann Danaiya Usher, "The Race for Power in Laos: The Nordic Connections," in *Environmental Change in South-East Asia: People, Politics and Sustainable Development*, ed. Michael J. G. Parnwell and Raymond L. Bryant, London: Routledge, 1996, pp. 123–44; Tyson R. Roberts, "Mekong Mainstream Hydropower Dams: Run-of-the-River or Ruin-of-the-River?" *Natural History Bulletin of the Siam Society*, vol. 43, 1995, pp. 9–19.

118 *Agreement on the Cooperation for the Sustainable Development of the Mekong River Basin*, 5 April 1995, mimeograph; Mya Than and George Abonyi, "The Greater Mekong Subregion: Co-operation in Infrastructure and Finance," in *ASEAN Enlargement: Impacts and Implications*, ed. Mya Than and Carolyn L. Gates, Singapore: Institute of Southeast Asian Studies, 2001, p. 132.

119 Milton Osborne, *The Mekong: Turbulent Past, Uncertain Future*, New York, NY: Atlantic Monthly Press, 2000, p. 16; E. C. Chapman and He Daming, "Downstream Implications of China's Dams on the Lancang Jiang (Upper Mekong) and Their Potential Significance for Greater Regional Cooperation, Basin-Wide," in *Development Dilemmas in the Mekong Subregion*, ed. Bob Stensholt, Clayton, Victoria: Monash University, 1996, pp. 16–25.

120 Asian Development Bank, *Subregional Economic Cooperation: Initial Possibilities for Cambodia, Lao PDR, Myanmar, Thailand, Viet Nam and Yunnan Province of the People's Republic of China*, Manila: Asian Development Bank, 1993, quote pp. i–ii.

121 Mya Than, "Economic Co-operation in the Greater Mekong Subregion," *Asian-Pacific Economic Literature*, vol. 11, no. 2, November 1997, pp. 43–5.

122 Asian Development Bank, *Subregional Economic Cooperation: Initial Possibilities*, pp. xiv–xvi, 55–85, quote p. 11.

123 Ibid., pp. 47–50.

124 Ibid., pp. 52–3, quote p. 52.

125 Asian Development Bank, *Economic Cooperation in the Greater Mekong Subregion: Proceedings of the Second Conference on Subregional Economic Cooperation Among Cambodia, Lao People's Democratic Republic, Myanmar, Thailand, Viet Nam and Yunnan Province of the People's Republic*

*of China, 30–31 August 1993*, Manila: Asian Development Bank, 1993, pp. 21–4, quote p. 22.

126 Asian Development Bank, *Economic Cooperation: Proceedings of Second Conference*, pp. 25–35.

. 127 Asian Development Bank, *Economic Cooperation: Proceedings of Second Conference*, pp. 37–41, quote p. 39; Bou Saroeun, "Huge Viet Dam Devastates Se San Valley," *Phnom Penh Post*, 9–22 June 2000.

128 Asian Development Bank, *Economic Cooperation in the Greater Mekong Subregion, Toward Implementation: Proceedings of the Third Conference on Subregional Economic Cooperation Among Cambodia, People's Republic of China, Lao People's Democratic Republic, Myanmar, Thailand and Vietnam, 20–23 April 1994*, Manila: Asian Development Bank, 1994, pp. 85–379; Ted Bardacke, "Past muddies Mekong regional deal," *Financial Times*, 26 October 1995. The proceedings of ministerial, forum and working group meetings are available on the Asian Development Bank website (http://www.adb.org).

129 Mya Than, "Economic Co-operation," pp. 47–8, 55; Mya Than and Abonyi, "Greater Mekong Subregion," pp. 132–3.

130 Mya Than, *The Golden Quadrangle of the Mainland Southeast Asia*, Institute of Southeast Asian Studies Working Papers in Economics and Finance no. 3, Singapore: Institute of Southeast Asian Studies, 1996, quote p. 1.

131 "ADB targets private project finance," *Financial Times*, 12 May 1997; "Mekong countries all set for direct telecom linkup," *Straits Times*, 6 August 1996; "Asean formulates Mekong growth plan," *Vietnam Investment Review*, 20–26 May 1996.

132 Peter Hinton, "Is It Possible to 'Manage' a River? Reflections from the Mekong," in *Development Dilemmas in the Mekong Subregion*, ed. Bob Stensholt, Clayton, Victoria: Monash University, 1996, pp. 49–56, quote p. 49; "Initiative Overload," *Economist*, 7 September 1996; Teiichi Miyauchi, "Basin Nations Struggle for Leading Role," *Nikkei Weekly*, 21 October 1996.

133 Ricardo M. Tan, Filologo Pante, Jr. and George Abonyi, "Economic Co-operation in the Greater Mekong Subregion," in *Regional Co-operation and Integration in Asia*, ed. Kiichiro Fukasaku, Paris: Organization for Economic Cooperation and Development, 1995, pp. 232–5.

134 Mya Than, "Economic Co-operation," pp. 40–1, quote p. 41.

135 Tan, Pante and Abonyi, "Economic Co-operation," p. 239, quote p. 229.

136 Mya Than and Abonyi, "Greater Mekong Subregion," pp. 128, 154–5.

137 "Water and Conflict in Asia?" Seminar Report, Asia-Pacific Center for Security Studies, Honolulu, Hawai'i, 17 September 1999, pp. 14–16, quotes pp. 14, 16.

138 Anya Schiffrin, "Vietnam's Prime Minister Says Economic Reform Will Be Gradual," *Asian Wall Street Journal*, 25 March 1998.

## 6 Challenges and prospects

1 Carlyle A. Thayer, "Vietnam: The Politics of Immobilism Revisited," *Southeast Asian Affairs 2000*, Singapore: Institute of Southeast Asian Studies, 2000, pp. 311–12; World Bank, *Vietnam: Country Assistance Evaluation*, Report No. 23288, 21 November 2001, pp. 1–4, 16–19; Institute of Southeast Asian Studies, *Regional Outlook: Southeast Asia, 2000–2001*, Singapore: Institute of Southeast Asian Studies, 2000, pp. 80–1.

2 World Bank, *Memorandum of the President of the International Development Association and the International Finance Corporation to the Executive Directors on a Country Assistance Strategy Progress Report for the Socialist Republic of Vietnam*, Report No. 22887-VN, 28 September 2001; Duong

Phong, "Growing need for *doi moi*, phase two," *Vietnam Investment Review*, 10–16 January 2000.

3 Thayer, "Vietnam: Politics of Immobilism," pp. 312–13; "Concern over pace of reform in Vietnam," *Financial Times*, 25 February 2000.

4 Brantly Womack, "Vietnam in 1996: Reform Immobilism," *Asian Survey*, vol. 37, no. 1, January 1997, pp. 79–87, quotes pp. 86–7; Thayer, "Vietnam: Politics of Immobilism," p. 311.

5 Thayer, "Vietnam: Politics of Immobilism," quotes p. 314; Institute of Southeast Asian Studies, *Regional Outlook: Southeast Asia, 2000–2001*, pp. 81–2; Quan Xuan Dinh, "The Political Economy of Vietnam's Transformation Process," *Contemporary Southeast Asia*, vol. 22, no. 2, August 2000, pp. 360–88.

6 Asian Development Bank, *Regional and Country Highlights: Viet Nam in 2000* (http://www.adb.org); Wayne Arnold, "Vietnam's Trade Imbalance and Economy Keep Growing," *New York Times*, 27 December 2000; Duong Nguyen, "Economic engine 'heavily reliant' on export fuelling," *Vietnam Investment Review*, 20–26 November 2000.

7 Russell Hiang-Khng Heng, "Vietnam: Light at the End of the Tunnel?" *Southeast Asian Affairs 2001*, Singapore: Institute of Southeast Asian Studies, 2001, pp. 359–60; David E. Sanger, "Huge Crowd in Hanoi for Clinton, Who Speaks of 'Shared Suffering,'" *New York Times*, 18 November 2000.

8 Institute of Southeast Asian Studies, *Regional Outlook: Southeast Asia, 2001–2002*, p. 85.

9 "Agreement between the United States of America and the Socialist Republic of Vietnam on Trade Relations," 13 July 2000 (http://www.ustr.gov); Carlyle A. Thayer, "Vietnam in 2000: Toward the Ninth Party Congress," *Asian Survey*, vol. 41, no. 1, January–February 2001, pp. 185–6; Emiko Fukase and Will Martin, *The Effect of the United States' Granting Most Favored Nation Status to Vietnam*, World Bank Policy Research Working Paper 2219, November 1999.

10 Amy Kazmin, "Hanoi prepares for first stock market," *Financial Times*, 22 June 2000; Heng, "Vietnam: Light," p. 360.

11 Ang Cheng Guan, "Vietnam: Another Milestone and the Country Plods On," *Southeast Asian Affairs 2002*, Singapore: Institute of Southeast Asian Studies, 2002, pp. 346–7; "Economic and political renovation to be prioritized," *Nhân Dân*, 4 March 2002; World Bank, Asian Development Bank and United Nations Development Program, *Vietnam 2010: Entering the 21st Century*, 2001 (http://www.worldbank.org).

12 Keith Bradsher, "Vietnam Seeks Global Aid to Fight Bird Flu," *New York Times*, 3 February 2005; "Vietnam's economy: The good pupil," *Economist*, 6 May 2004; Bao Giang, "Economic growth: PM raises the bar," *Vietnam Investment Review*, 12–18 January 2004; Asian Development Bank, *Asia Development Outlook 2004* (http://www.adb.org); Adam Fforde, "Vietnam in 2003: The Road to Ungovernability?" *Asian Survey*, vol. 44, no. 1, January–February 2004, pp. 122–4.

13 Dinh Van An, "SOE reform still a critical task," *Vietnam Investment Review*, 22–28 March 2004; Jeff Moore, "Vietnam must seize the day on FDI," *Asia Times*, 10 March 2004; Nguyen Manh Hung, "Vietnam: Facing the Challenge of Integration," *Southeast Asian Affairs 2004*, Singapore: Institute of Southeast Asian Studies, 2004, pp. 298–302.

14 Quan Xuan Dinh, "Political Economy," pp. 365–72, quotes p. 370; Thayer, "Vietnam: Politics of Immobilism," pp. 314–16; "Elder statesman joins call for internal focus," *Vietnam Investment Review*, 22–28 February 1999.

15 Carlyle A. Thayer, "Vietnam in 2001: The Ninth Party Congress and After,"

*Asian Survey*, vol. 42, no. 1, January–February 2002, pp. 81–2; "Vietnam Veterans Seek Fresh Blood," *Far Eastern Economic Review*, 11 January 2001, p. 8; Thayer, "Vietnam in 2000," pp. 182–5; Duong Phong, "Pre-Congress Plenum outlines targets," *Vietnam Investment Review*, 10–16 July 2000.

16 Amnesty International, "No sanctuary: The plight of the Montagnard minority," ASA 41/011/2002, 18 December 2002 (http://web.amnesty.org); Thayer, "Vietnam in 2001," p. 82; David Koh, "The Politics of a Divided Party and Parkinson's State in Vietnam," *Contemporary Southeast Asia*, vol. 23, no. 3, December 2001, pp. 543–8; Margot Cohen, "Thunder from the Highlands," *Far Eastern Economic Review*, 1 March 2001, pp. 24–5.

17 "New spring in step of Party leadership," *Vietnam Investment Review*, 23–29 April 2001; Thayer, "Vietnam in 2001," pp. 82–4; Koh, "Politics," pp. 541–2. Abuza argued Phieu's downfall was also influenced by systemic changes in the Vietnamese political system (Zachary Abuza, "The Lessons of Le Kha Phieu: Changing Rules in Vietnamese Politics," *Contemporary Southeast Asia*, vol. 24, no. 1, April 2002, pp. 121–45).

18 Thayer, "Vietnam in 2001," pp. 85–86, quote p. 86; Ang Cheng Guan, "Vietnam," pp. 345–7; Ha Thang, "Defining orientations of a socialist market economy," *Vietnam Investment Review*, 23–29 April 2001.

19 Amnesty International, "Socialist Republic of Vietnam: Renewed concern for the Montagnard minority," ASA 41/005/2004, 28 April 2004 (http://web.amnesty.org); Human Rights Watch, "Vietnam: Violence against Montagnards during Easter Week Protests," 14 April 2004 (http://hrw.org); Thayer, "Vietnam in 2001," pp. 85–6.

20 Carlyle A. Thayer, "Vietnam: The Stewardship of Nong Duc Manh," *Southeast Asian Affairs 2003*, Singapore: Institute of Southeast Asian Studies, 2003, pp. 315–16; "Newly elected leaders vow to hasten economic push," *Vietnam Investment Review*, 29 July–4 August 2002; Regina M. Abrami, "Vietnam in 2002: On the Road to Recovery," *Asian Survey*, vol. 43, no. 1, January–February 2003, p. 99.

21 Asian Development Bank, *Country Strategy and Program Update, 2004–2006: Socialist Republic of Viet Nam*, July 2003 (http://www.adb.org); Thayer, "Vietnam: Stewardship," pp. 316–18.

22 Margot Cohen, "Crime-Fighting For the Masses," *Far Eastern Economic Review*, 19 June 2003, pp. 22–3; "Trial of a Crime Boss Shines a Spotlight on Corruption in Vietnam," *New York Times*, 24 February 2003; Abrami, "Vietnam in 2002," pp. 97–8.

23 Thayer, "Vietnam: Stewardship," pp. 321–4; Seth Mydans, "Vietnam: Jail Term for Internet Dissent," *New York Times*, 9 November 2002; "Fear over Hanoi's Internet Curbs," *Far Eastern Economic Review*, 31 October 2002, p. 10.

24 "Trying to Kill a Revolution," *Far Eastern Economic Review*, 24 June 2004, p. 8; Fforde, "Vietnam in 2003," p. 128; Human Rights Watch, "Vietnam: Independent Investigation of Easter Week Atrocities Needed Now," 27 May 2004 (http://hrw.org).

25 As quoted in "Party General Secretary delivers closing speech at the plenary session," *Nhân Dân*, 11 November 2002; Ngoc Tram, "Party vows to continue war on corruption," *Vietnam Investment Review*, 15–21 March 2004.

26 Thayer, "Vietnam: Stewardship," pp. 313–15, 324–5; Institute of Southeast Asian Studies, *Regional Outlook: Southeast Asia, 2004–2005*, pp. 42–3.

27 As quoted in "Party General Secretary delivers closing speech at the plenary session," *Nhân Dân*, 11 November 2002.

28 Fforde, "Vietnam in 2003," pp. 125–8; Nguyen Manh Hung, "Vietnam," pp. 302–7.

29 As quoted in Xuan Son, "'Let's develop together,' says Chinese leader," *Vietnam Investment Review*, 4–10 March 2002; Tul Pinkaew and Ranjana Wangvipula, "China upset by 'friendly' amendment," *Bangkok Post*, 26 November 2004; Ramses Amer, "Assessing Sino-Vietnamese Relations through the Management of Contentious Issues," *Contemporary Southeast Asia*, vol. 26, no. 2, August 2004, pp. 328–37; "Vietnam: Tour to Disputed Islands," *New York Times*, 20 April 2004; "Vietnam, China Communist Parties reaffirm good neighbourliness," *Nhân Dân*, 30 August 2003; Ronald Bruce St John, "Land Boundaries of Indochina," *Boundary and Security Bulletin*, vol. 9, no. 1, Spring 2001, pp. 100–1.

30 Le Minh, "Thailand offers a helping hand in the integration game," *Vietnam Investment Review*, 29 March–4 April 2004; Supalak Ganjanakhundee, "Seeking more substantial cooperation with Vietnam," *Nation*, 20 February 2004.

31 Lach Chantha, "Anxious refugees watch U.S.–Vietnam tug of war," *Voice of Cambodia*, 30 March 2002; "President leaves Phnom Penh for Siem Reap," *Nhân Dân*, 28 November 2001; Ang Cheng Guan, "Vietnam," pp. 351–2.

32 "Vietnamese Govt Figures Call for Trade Zone on Border with Laos," *Yahoo! News Asia*, 29 October 2003; "Viet Nam, Laos Leaders Stress Need To Boost Bilateral Ties," *Vietnam News Agency*, 17 February 2000.

33 Sergei Blagov, "Russian missiles to guard skies over Vietnam," *Asia Times*, 4 September 2003; "Russia wishes to enhance co-operation," *Nhân Dân*, 9 October 2002; Thayer, "Vietnam in 2001," 87.

34 Tu Giang, "Deal to draw fresh Japanese investment," *Vietnam Investment Review*, 8–14 December 2003; "Viet Nam, Japan exchange views on foreign affairs and defence," *Viet Nam Agency*, 26 February 2003.

35 "Vietnam: U.S. Airline Starts Flights," *New York Times*, 11 November 2004; "Admiral's Landmark Visit to Danang," *Far Eastern Economic Review*, 19 February 2004, p. 8; "U.S. and Vietnam Reach an Accord on Establishing Direct Air Service," *New York Times*, 10 October 2003; Thayer, "Vietnam in 2000," pp. 187–8.

36 Emily Parker, "The Textile Offensive," *Wall Street Journal*, 3 January 2005; David M. Lenard, "US makes a meal of shrimp dispute," *Asia Times*, 9 December 2004; "Half Measures: Vietnam's human-rights record goes under U.S. lens," *Far Eastern Economic Review*, 29 July 2004, p. 8; Edward Alden, "US to put tariffs on China shrimps," *Financial Times*, 7 July 2004; "Vietnam Faces Garment Quotas," *Far Eastern Economic Review*, 25 March 2004, p. 10; Alan Boyd, "Vietnam tightens control on religion," *Asia Times*, 4 October 2003.

37 Supalak Ganjanakhundee, "Poorest Four in Tourism Push," *Nation*, 29 November 2004; "This Week – Vietnam," *Far Eastern Economic Review*, 25 September 2003, pp. 14–15; Ang Cheng Guan, "Vietnam," pp. 351–2; Thayer, "Vietnam in 2001," p. 87.

38 Yves Bourdet, "Laos in 2000: The Economics of Political Immobilism," *Asian Survey*, vol. 41, no. 1, January–February 2001, pp. 166–7; Carlyle A. Thayer, "Laos in 1999: Economic Woes Drive Foreign Policy," *Asian Survey*, vol. 40, no. 1, January–February 2000, pp. 43–4.

39 Bertil Lintner and Shawn W. Crispin, "Brothers in Arms," *Far Eastern Economic Review*, 11 May 2000, p. 8; Institute of Southeast Asian Studies, *Regional Outlook: Southeast Asia, 2000–2001*, pp. 24, 73–4; Thayer, "Laos in 1999," pp. 44–7.

40 Bourdet, "Laos in 2000," pp. 167–8; Asian Development Bank, *Lao People's Democratic Republic: Economic Performance in 2000* (http://www.adb.org); By Pansivongsay, "Market economy critique," *Vientiane Times*, 1 July 2000.

41 Asian Development Bank, *Asian Development Outlook 2004* (http://www.adb.org); Nick J. Freeman, "Laos: Exiguous Evidence of Economic Reform and Development," *Southeast Asian Affairs 2004*, Singapore: Institute of Southeast Asian Studies, 2004, pp. 125–8; Carlyle A. Thayer, "Laos in 2003: Counterrevolution Fails to Ignite," *Asian Survey*, vol. 44, no. 1, January–February 2004, pp. 112–13; Yves Bourdet, "Laos in 2001: Political Introversion and Economic Respite," *Asian Survey*, vol. 42, no. 1, January–February 2002, pp. 110–12.

42 Alan Boyd, "Laos dam still in limbo," *Asia Times*, 14 October 2004; Peter Stephens, "World Bank is not close to deciding on dam project as was reported," *Nation*, 13 February 2004; World Bank, "The Proposed Nam Theun 2 Hydropower Project," January 2004 (http://www.worldbank.org); Bertil Lintner, "Dam the Poverty," *Far Eastern Economic Review*, 11 December 2003, p. 52.

43 Jenina Joy Chavez Malaluan and Shalmali Guttal, "Structural Adjustment in the Name of the Poor: The PRSP Experience in the Lao PDR, Cambodia and Vietnam," *Focus on the Global South*, January 2002, pp. 4–7, quote p. 6 (http://www.focusweb.org).

44 Institute of Southeast Asian Studies, *Regional Outlook: Southeast Asia, 2004–2005*, pp. 71–2; Carlyle A. Thayer, "Laos in 2002: Regime Maintenance through Political Stability," *Asian Survey*, vol. 43, no. 1, January–February 2003, pp. 121–2; "PM explains measures to reform banking system," *Vientiane Times*, 4 July 2002.

45 Bourdet, "Laos in 2000," p. 168; Institute of Southeast Asian Studies, *Regional Outlook: Southeast Asia, 2004–2005*, p. 70; Catherine Aubertin, "Institutionalizing Duality: Lowlands and uplands in the Lao PDR," *International Institute for Asian Studies (IIAS) Letter 24*, February 2001, pp. 11–12. On regional disparities in Laos, see Yves Bourdet, The *Economics of Transition in Laos: From Socialism to ASEAN Integration*, Northampton, MA: Edward Elgar, 2000, pp. 133–58.

46 Bertil Lintner, "Aid-Dependent," *Far Eastern Economic Review*, 3 July 2003, p. 49; Thayer, "Laos in 2002," p. 122; Songrit Pongern, "Laos needs consistent foreign aid to fight poverty," *Yahoo! News Singapore*, 23 April 2000; Bourdet, "Laos in 2000," pp. 169–70.

47 Quoted in Grant Evans, "Laos moving along at snail's pace," *Bangkok Post*, 21 June 2003.

48 Kulachada Chaipipat, "Tiny splash sets wave in motion," *Nation*, 24 March 2000; Thayer, "Laos in 1999," pp. 44–5; "Protests Stir in Laos," *Far Eastern Economic Review*, 18 November 1999, p. 8.

49 Bertil Lintner, "Laos: Signs of Unrest," *Southeast Asian Affairs 2001*, Singapore: Institute of Southeast Asian Studies, 2001, pp. 178–82; Rajiv Chandrasekaran, "Mysterious Bomb Blasts Shake Remote Laos," *Washington Post*, 27 December 2000; "Hanoi Steps In Against Rebels in Laos," *International Herald Tribune*, 3 June 2000.

50 William Barnes, "Laos newly willing to lay itself bare," *Financial Times*, 13 December 2000; Barbara Crossette, "Exiled Laotian Prince Seeks a New Role," *New York Times*, 13 August 2000; Achara Ashayagachat and Bhanravee Tansubhapol, "Laos blames overseas Hmong," *Bangkok Post*, 1 July 2000.

51 As quoted in Saritdet Marukatat, "Logging on in Laos: Criticism gains a forum," *Bangkok Post*, 1 December 2000; John Armstrong, "Elusive Laos minister granted asylum in NZ," *New Zealand Herald*, 7 November 2000.

52 Evgeny Belenky, "Forget heavy-handed, a good time had by all," *Bangkok Post*, 8 December 2000; Matthew Pennington, "Communists in Laos Still In

Power," *Washington Post*, 1 December 2000; Grant Evans, "Demoralisation but No Revolt in Laos," *Nation*, 16 August 2000.

53  Shawn W. Crispin and Bertil Lintner, "Behind the Bombings," *Far Eastern Economic Review*, 27 July 2000, p. 9; Lintner, "Laos: Signs of Unrest," pp. 180–1; Bourdet, "Laos in 2000," pp. 164–6; "Internecine Conflict? Not Likely," *Lan-Xang*, 22 July 2000.

54  Nick J. Freeman, "Laos: Sedately Seguing into the Twenty-first Century," *Southeast Asian Affairs 2002*, Singapore: Institute of Southeast Asian Studies, 2002, pp. 145–8; Sunai Phasuk, "Lao Party Congress faces stiff challenges," *Nation*, 19 March 2001.

55  Bourdet, "Laos in 2001," pp. 108–9, quote p. 108; Freeman, "Laos: Sedately Seguing," p. 147; "Lao deputy premier in Thailand reviews democracy development efforts," *Nation*, 3 December 2001; Don Pathan, "Change in Laos glacial, but old guard stays put," *Nation*, 17 March 2001.

56  Fred Thurlow, "For Laos, it's steady as she goes," *Asia Times*, 16 March 2001; "Resolution of Seventh Party Congress," *Vientiane Times*, 15 March 2001; Bourdet, "Laos in 2001," pp. 109–10.

57  Kulachada Chaipipat, "The choice of new Lao premier is a sign of pragmatism," *Nation*, 2 April 2001; Saritdet Marukatat and Bhanravee Tansubhapol, "Finance minister becomes PM," *Bangkok Post*, 28 March 2001; Songrit Pongern, "Laos shuffles cabinet in party faction compromise," *Reuters*, 27 March 2001.

58  Bertil Lintner, "Laos: Mired in Economic Stagnation?" *Southeast Asian Affairs 2003*, Singapore: Institute of Southeast Asian Studies, 2003, pp. 136–9; "Laos endorses Feb 24 election results," *Japan Today*, 15 March 2002.

59  Supalak Ganjanakhundee, "Surprise cabinet reshuffle in Laos," *Nation*, 19 January 2003; Freeman, "Laos: Exiguous Evidence," pp. 125–6; Thayer, "Laos in 2002," pp. 120–1.

60  Catherine Raymond, "Homage to a King in Laos," *Mandala*, vol. 22, Summer 2003, pp. 4–5, quotes p. 4; Somsack Pongkhao, "Fa Ngoum not a revival of monarchy," *Vientiane Times*, 14 January 2003; Thayer, "Laos in 2003," pp. 110–11. On Fa Ngum, see Peter and Sanda Simms, *The Kingdom of Laos: Six Hundred Years of History*, Richmond, Surrey: Curzon Press, 1999, pp. 23–41.

61  Institute of Southeast Asian Studies, *Regional Outlook: Southeast Asia, 2004–2005*, p. 18; Thayer, "Laos in 2003," p. 111; "Communist Laos to Hold First Town Elections in Decentralization Move," *Manila Times*, 22 April 2003; "Lao National Assembly Approves Revised Constitution," *Vietnam News Agency*, 8 May 2003.

62  Thierry Falise, "Rare Glimpses of Forgotten Rebels," *New York Times*, 14 September 2003; Grant Evans, "Laos is getting a bad rap from the world's media," *Bangkok Post*, 8 July 2003; Thayer, "Laos in 2003," pp. 111–12.

63  Meuangkham Noradeth, "Easy border access brings higher AIDS risks," *Vientiane Times*, 15 March 2004; Ellen Nakashima, "Finally, a Life Out of the Mountains," *Washington Post*, 7 March 2004; Amnesty International, "Starvation As A Weapon Of War Against Civilians," ASA26/013/2003, 2 October 2003 (http://web.amnesty.org).

64  Institute of Southeast Asian Studies, *Regional Outlook: Southeast Asia, 2000–2001*, pp. 75–7.

65  "Chinese vice-premier ends visit to Laos," *Shanghai Daily*, 20 March 2004; "Chinese, Lao leaders confer in Beijing," *Xinhua News Agency*, 13 July 2003; "China hails new Lao leaders," *Vientiane Times*, 28 March 2001.

66  As quoted in "Viet Nam gives priority to relationship with Laos, says president," *Vietnam News Agency*, 14 June 2001; "Vietnam 'joins rebel fight,'" *South China Morning Post*, 3 June 2000.

67  Bourdet, "Laos in 2001," pp. 112–13, quote p. 113; "Vietnam announces cash aid for Laos," *Washington Times*, 12 April 2002.
68  As quoted in "Lao Chairman addresses Viet Nam's National Assembly session," *Vietnam News Agency*, 10 June 2003; Le Minh, "Local investors plan to power Laos," *Vietnam Investment Review*, 8–14 March 2004.
69  "Vietnam, Laos Agree to Cross-Border Wildlife Protection," *Associated Press*, 19 November 2004.
70  Institute of Southeast Asian Studies, *Regional Outlook: Southeast Asia, 2003–2004*, pp. 20–1, quote p. 21; Saritdet Marukatat, "Getting along with the neighbors," *Bangkok Post*, 16 December 2002; "Thai Princess tours caves of Lao leaders," *Vientiane Times*, 26 November 2002.
71  Thongchai Chaiyasa, "Trade boost awaited after bridge opens," *Bangkok Post*, 29 October 2004; "Thailand stands by decision to deport 16 Laotians," *Yahoo! News Asia*, 7 July 2004; Bhanravee Tansubhapol, "Deals done to boost trust," *Bangkok Post*, 21 March 2004.
72  "Laos and Cambodia to further boost bilateral cooperation," *Vietnam News Agency*, 15 February 2004; "Milestones for Laos and Cambodia," *Vietnam News Agency*, 11 April 2003.
73  Lao Veterans of America, "Joint Communiqué on Laos," 7–8 February 2005 (http://www.laoveterans.com); Mike Taugher, "Laotians oppose lifting trade cap," *Mercury News*, 26 January 2003; Judy Sarasohn, "Lobbying Against Trade With Laos," *Washington Post*, 20 June 2002; Lao Human Rights Council, "Religious Persecution in Vietnam and Laos," 24 February 2002 (http://www.laohumanrights.org).
74  "Congress approves trade relations with Laos," *Financial Times*, 20–21 November 2004; Seth Mydans, "Indochina War Refugees Find Homes at Last, in U.S.," *New York Times*, 8 August 2004; "Legislation Promises Laos A New Deal," *Far Eastern Economic Review*, 1 April 2004, p. 8; Alan Boyd, "The dark side of trade with Laos," *Asia Times*, 4 November 2003.
75  "ADB approves 17.7 million US dollar loan to Laos for road improvement," *Yahoo! News Asia*, 29 June 2004; "Vice-Premier highly values Japan's aid," *Vientiane Times*, 24 January 2003; Asian Development Bank, *Lao People's Democratic Republic: Country Strategy and Program Update (2004–2006)*, July 2003, (http://www.adb.org).
76  "Russian Foreign Minister arrives in Laos," *Novosti*, 29 November 2004; "Russia writes off most of Laotian debts," *Pravada*, 24 June 2003; "India extends $10m. loan to Laos," *Hindu*, 16 June 2003; "Laos shares Russia's opposition to NATO enlargement," *Financial Times*, 28 August 2001; "Laos, North Korea issue joint communiqué at end of Kim Yong-nam's visit," *Financial Times*, 18 July 2001.
77  Institute of Southeast Asian Studies, *Regional Outlook: Southeast Asia, 2000–2001*, pp. 71–2; James Eckardt, "Economy given two months to melt-down," *Phnom Penh Post*, 16–29 October 1998.
78  Joseph J. Zasloff, "Emerging Stability in Cambodia," *Asian Affairs: An American Review*, vol. 28, no. 4, Winter 2002, pp. 196–7; Bill Bainbridge, "Economy grows despite corruption," *Phnom Penh Post*, 31 August–13 September 2001; Institute of Southeast Asian Studies, *Regional Outlook: Southeast Asia, 2001–2002*, pp. 74–6; World Bank, *Cambodia: Country Assistance Evaluation*, Report No. 21354, 16 November 2000 (http://www.worldbank.org).
79  World Bank, "Cambodia Consultative Group meeting results: Aid partnership supports Cambodian development efforts," 26 May 2000 (http://www.worldbank.org); Toshiyasu Kato, Jeffrey A. Kaplan, Chan Sophal and Real Sopheap, *Cambodia: Enhancing Governance for Sustainable Development*, Asian Development Bank, October 2000 (http://www.adb.org).

80 Martin Godfrey, Toshiyasu Kato, Chan Sophal, Long Vou Piseth, Pon Dorina, Tep Saravy, Tia Savora and So Sovannarit, *Technical Assistance and Capacity Development in an Aid-dependent Economy: The Experience of Cambodia*, Working Paper 15, Phnom Penh: Cambodia Development Resource Institute, 2000, p. 123; Bertil Lintner, "Kicking the Habit," *Far Eastern Economic Review*, 2 August 2001, p. 52; Irene V. Langran, "Cambodia in 2000: New Hopes Are Challenged," *Asian Survey*, vol. 41, no. 1, January–February 2001, pp. 159–60.

81 Asian Development Bank, *Asian Development Outlook 2004: Cambodia*, pp. 69–71 (http://www.adb.org); Institute of Southeast Asian Studies, *Regional Outlook: Southeast Asia, 2003–2004*, pp. 53–5; Patrick Falby, "Questions over repaying Cambodia's debt," *Phnom Penh Post*, 29 August–11 September 2003; Robert B. Albritton, "Cambodia in 2003: On the Road to Democratic Consolidation," *Asian Survey*, vol. 44, no. 1, January–February 2004, pp. 107–8; Kheang Un and Judy Ledgerwood, "Cambodia in 2002: Decentralization and Its Effects on Party Politics," *Asian Survey*, vol. 43, no. 1, January–February 2003, pp. 118–19.

82 Liam Cochrane, "WTO approved; now for the laws," *Phnom Penh Post*, 10–23 September 2004; Tin Maung Maung Than, "Cambodia: Strongman, Terrible Man, Invisible Man, and Politics of Power Sharing," *Southeast Asian Affairs 2004*, Singapore: Institute of Southeast Asian Studies, 2004, pp. 80–2; Asian Development Bank, *Cambodia: Country Strategy and Program Update, 2004–2006*, July 2003, pp. 1–2 (http://www.adb.org); Albritton, "Cambodia in 2003," pp. 107–8.

83 Elena Lesley, "Safeguarding the Cambodian Dream," *Phnom Penh Post*, 17–30 December 2004; Institute of Southeast Asian Studies, *Regional Outlook: Southeast Asia, 2004–2005*, pp. 64–6; Asian Development Bank, *Country Assistance Program Evaluation for Cambodia*, January 2004, pp. iii–iv (http://www.adb.org); Alan Boyd, "The heavy price of WTO membership," *Asia Times*, 29 September 2003.

84 "The brutal truth of Aids in Cambodia," *BBC News*, 12 July 2004; Staffan Lindberg, "Why FDI has plummeted," *Phnom Penh Post*, 2–15 July 2004; Liam Cochrane, "ADB's Malik fires parting shot over good governance," *Phnom Penh Post*, 23 April–6 May 2004; Richard Wood, "Corruption 'sucking vitality' from country," *Phnom Penh Post*, 9–22 April 2004.

85 Pierre P. Lizée, "Testing the Limits of Change: Cambodia's Politics After the July Elections," *Southeast Asian Affairs 1999*, Singapore: Institute of Southeast Asian Studies, 1999, pp. 80–6, quotes pp. 79–80.

86 Caroline Hughes, "Surveillance and Resistance in the Cambodian Elections: The Prisoners' Dilemma?" *Southeast Asian Affairs 1999*, Singapore: Institute of Southeast Asian Studies, 1999, pp. 92–108; Michael Hayes, "Another chapter opens as Hun Sen gives Prince Ranariddh the deal," *Phnom Penh Post*, 27 November–11 December 1998; Lizée, "Testing the Limits," pp. 84–6.

87 Milton Osborne, "Cambodia: Hun Sen Consolidates Power," *Southeast Asian Affairs 2000*, Singapore: Institute of Southeast Asian Studies, 2000, pp. 101–11, quote p. 103; John Marston, "Cambodia: Transnational Pressures and Local Agendas," *Southeast Asian Affairs 2002*, Singapore: Institute of Southeast Asian Studies, 2002, pp. 95–6; Caroline Hughes, "Cambodia: Democracy or Dictatorship?" *Southeast Asian Affairs 2001*, Singapore: Institute of Southeast Asian Studies, 2001, pp. 113–14.

88 Langran, "Cambodia in 2000," pp. 157, 159; Hughes, "Cambodia," pp. 119–20, 201; Sue Downie and Damien Kingsbury, "Political Development and the Re-emergence of Civil Society in Cambodia," *Contemporary Southeast Asia*, vol. 23, no. 1, April 2001, pp. 43–64.

89  Kheang Un and Judy Ledgerwood, "Cambodia in 2001: Toward Democratic Consolidation?" *Asian Survey*, vol. 42, no. 1, January–February 2002, pp. 100–1; Vong Sokheng and Bill Bainbridge, "King signs KR law, but obstacles loom," *Phnom Penh Post*, 17–30 August 2001; Marston, "Cambodia," pp. 99–100. For background on the Khmer Rouge trials, see Stephen R. Heder, "Hun Sen and Genocide Trials in Cambodia: International Impacts, Impunity, and Justice," in *Cambodia Emerges from the Past: Eight Essays*, ed. Judy Ledgerwood, Dekalb, IL: Northern University Press, 2002, pp. 176–223.

90  Stephen R. Heder, "Dealing with Crimes against Humanity: Progress or Illusion?" *Southeast Asian Affairs 2001*, Singapore: Institute of Southeast Asian Studies, 2001, pp. 129–41; Seth Mydans, "Khmer Rouge Trials Won't Be Fair, Critics Say," *New York Times*, 10 February 2002.

91  Sam Rith, "UN seeks money for KR Trial," *Phnom Penh Post*, 14–27 January 2005; Alan Sipress, "Khmer Rouge Trials Stalled by Political Deadlock," *Washington Post*, 5 May 2004.

92  International Crisis Group, *Cambodia: The Elusive Peace Dividend*, Asia Report No. 8, 11 August 2000, pp. 20–3, quote p. 23; James Watson and Sam Rith, "Ex-soldiers replace striking workers," *Phnom Penh Post*, 23 April–6 May 2004; Amy Kazmin, "World Bank cuts Cambodia loan in demobilisation scandal," *Financial Times*, 9 July 2003; Hughes, "Cambodia," pp. 121–2.

93  Amy Kazmin, "Rough road ahead as Cambodia prepares for local elections," *Financial Times*, 2 August 2001; Marston, "Cambodia," pp. 96–9; Un and Ledgerwood, "Cambodia in 2001," pp. 101–2; Hughes, "Cambodia," pp. 115–16.

94  Milton Osborne, "Cambodia: Hun Sen Firmly in Control," *Southeast Asian Affairs 2003*, Singapore: Institute of Southeast Asian Studies, 2003, pp. 84–6; Rajesh Kumar, "Election winner: 'the grassroots,'" *Phnom Penh Post*, 15–28 February 2002.

95  Un and Ledgerwood, "Cambodia in 2002," pp. 114–16, quote p. 115; Leo Dobbs, "Better Than No Polls At All," *Far Eastern Economic Review*, 7 February 2002, pp. 24–5.

96  Institute of Southeast Asian Studies, *Regional Outlook: Southeast Asia, 2003–2004*, p. 13; Osborne, "Hun Sen Firmly in Control," pp. 86–7; Raoul M. Jennar, *The Cambodian Constitutions (1953–1993)*, Bangkok: White Lotus Press, 1995, pp. 10, 137–42; Un and Ledgerwood, "Cambodia in 2002," p. 116.

97  Cheang Sokha, "Buddhist monks focus of war against smoking," *Phnom Penh Post*, 7–20 May 2004; Eric Unmacht, "Monks Behaving Badly," *Far Eastern Economic Review*, 5 December 2002, pp. 64–6.

98  Liam Cochrane, "Religious freedom reigns in Cambodia," *Phnom Penh Post*, 24 September–7 October 2004; Nadezda Bektimirova, "The Sangha in Politics: Challenges and Consequences," *Phnom Penh Post*, 21 November–4 December 2003; Amy Kazmin, "Buddhist monks find collective voice but urged to keep a vow of silence," *Financial Times*, 25 July 2003.

99  Liam Cochrane and Sam Rith, "Govt dismisses UN terrorism warning," *Phnom Penh Post*, 5–18 November 2004; Luke Hunt, "Cham Offensive," *Far Eastern Economic Review*, 29 July 2004, pp. 50–2; "Security fears over Cambodian Muslims," *Bangkok Post*, 2 May 2004; Bjorn Blengsli, "Trends in the Islamic Community," *Phnom Penh Post*, 6–19 June 2003.

100  Albritton, "Cambodia in 2003," pp. 103–5; Human Rights Watch, *Don't Bite the Hand that Feeds You: Coercion, Threats, and Vote-Buying in Cambodia's National Elections*, Briefing Paper, July 2003 (http://www.hrw.org).

101  Jennar, *Cambodian Constitutions*, pp. 21, 25; Institute of Southeast Asian Studies, *Regional Outlook: Southeast Asia, 2004–2005*, p. 10.

102  "Corruption report paints grim picture," *Phnom Penh Post*, 3–16 December

2004; Luke Hunt and Michael Hayes, "New government formed after Chea Sim leaves the country," *Phnom Penh Post*, 16–29 July 2004; Vong Sokheng and Richard Wood, "Jumbo cabinet ends stalemate," *Phnom Penh Post*, 2–15 July 2004; Amy Kazmin, "Coalition deal in Cambodia ends 11-month post-election standoff," *Financial Times*, 29 June 2004.

103  Liam Cochrane, "Sihamoni crowned new King," *Phnom Penh Post*, 5–18 November 2004; Julio A. Jeldres, "Constitutional crisis looms in Cambodia," *Asia Times*, 12 August 2004; Nelson Rand and Vincent MacIsaac, "In Cambodia, Hun Sen is in the driver's seat," *Asia Times*, 19 July 2004; "King Sihanouk withdraws threat to abdicate," *Straits Times*, 12 July 2004.

104  Michael Coren and Cheang Sokha, "Cambodia seeks seat on UN Security Council," *Phnom Penh Post*, 29 December 2003–1 January 2004; Kavi Chongkittavorn, "Regional Perspective: Asean summit boosts Cambodia's image," *Nation*, 21 October 2002; Zasloff, "Emerging Stability," pp. 198–9.

105  Luke Hunt, "Montagnards curdle in a Vietnamese coffee pot," *Phnom Penh Post*, 16–29 July 2004; Michael Coren, "Yali Falls: Cambodia appeals to Vietnam," *Phnom Penh Post*, 21 November–4 December 2003; Michael Coren and Chea Chou, "Vietnamese lose vote as race card played," *Phnom Penh Post*, 1–14 August 2003; Greg Torode, "Hanoi strongman returns to old warring ground," *South China Morning Post*, 9 June 1999.

106  Vong Sokheng, "Hun Sen leads CPP officials to China," *Phnom Penh Post*, 23 April–6 May 2004; Osborne, "Hun Sen Firmly in Control," pp. 89–90; "China writes off Cambodian debt," *Financial Times*, 4 November 2002; Zasloff, "Emerging Stability," p. 198; Tom Fawthrop, "Middle kingdom puts squeeze on little kingdom," *Phnom Penh Post*, 25 May–7 June 2001.

107  Kheang Un, "The Anti-Thai Riots: Sparking Khmer Nationalism," *Mandala*, vol. 22, Summer 2003, pp. 1–2; Amy Kazmin, "Cambodia apology helps ease Thai relations," *Financial Times*, 5 February 2003; "Mobs go berserk in anti-Thai frenzy," *Phnom Penh Post*, 31 January–13 February 2003; Marston, "Cambodia," p. 104.

108  "McCain Statement on Cambodian Prime Minister Hun Sen's Threats against Democratic Opposition," Press Release, 23 July 2004 (http://mccain.senate.gov); Liam Cochrane, "Global report card on trafficking," *Phnom Penh Post*, 26 March–8 April 2004; Jon Bugge, "US funds courses for Chams," *Phnom Penh Post*, 5–18 December 2003.

109  Mya Than and George Abonyi, "The Greater Mekong Subregion: Co-operation in Infrastructure and Finance," in *ASEAN Enlargement: Impacts and Implications*, ed. Mya Than and Carolyn L. Gates, Singapore: Institute of Southeast Asian Studies, 2001, pp. 143–50, quote p. 146; Nick J. Freeman, "Greater Mekong Sub-region and the 'Asian Crisis': Caught between Scylla and Charybdis," *Southeast Asian Affairs 1999*, Singapore: Institute of Southeast Asian Studies, 1999, pp. 32–51.

110  "Hanoi stresses ASEAN non-interference over Myanmar," *Reuters*, 17 October 2000; Robin Ramcharan, "ASEAN and Non-interference: A Principle Maintained," *Contemporary Southeast Asia*, vol. 22, no. 1, April 2000, pp. 60–88.

111  "German Fin Min Says 'No Chance' to Asian Version of EU," *Yahoo! Finance Asia*, 16 January 2001; Dan Murphy, "Southeast Asian nations dance to different tunes," *Christian Science Monitor*, 25 November 2000.

112  "Cambodia Hosts Sub-Regional Meeting on Airline Cooperation," *Xinhua News Agency*, 22 March 2001; "New flight links Asian capitals," *Los Angeles Times*, 14 January 2001; Institute of Southeast Asian Studies, *Regional Outlook: Southeast Asia, 2000–2001*, pp. 75–7; Nguyen Son, "2002 finish date on Laos link highway," *Vietnam Investment Review*, 20–26 November 2000.

113 Supalak Ganjanakhundee, "Poorest Four in Tourism Push," *Nation*, 29 November 2004; "Indochinese PMs meet down south," *Vietnam Investment Review*, 28 January–8 February 2002; "Cambodia, Vietnam, Laos pledge cooperation at summit," *Kyodo News Service*, 26 January 2002; "Regional economies running out of puff," *Vietnam Investment Review*, 15–21 October 2001.

114 Joern Kristensen, "Making best use of the Mekong poses a huge challenge," *Bangkok Post*, 21 May 2001; "Thailand, Laos, Vietnam, Japan to examine Mekong bridge site," *Kyodo News Service*, 14 November 2001.

115 Rajat M. Nag, "On the Mekong, a new era quietly takes shape," *International Herald Tribune*, 17 January 2005; Piyaporn Wongruang and Tul Pinkaew, "Mekong commission downplays impact of Chinese dams," *Bangkok Post*, 20 November 2004; Richard Wood, "Mekong dams a disaster," *Phnom Penh Post*, 22 October–4 November 2004; Luke Hunt, "Mekong River report damns Chinese dams," *Phnom Penh Post*, 30 July–12 August 2004; "Drought, not Chinese dams, blamed for lower flows in the Mekong," *Yahoo! News Asia*, 27 March 2004.

116 As quoted in Shefali Rekhi, "Hun Sen urges Asean to help region's smaller groups," *Straits Times*, 12 March 2002; Chin Kin Wah, "Southeast Asia in 2002: From Bali to Iraq – Co-operating for Security," *Southeast Asian Affairs 2003*, Singapore: Institute of Southeast Asian Studies, 2003, pp. 3–23; "ASEAN economic ministers reach consensus on two main issues," *Nhân Dân*, 9 July 2002.

117 Richard Stubbs, "ASEAN in 2003: Adversity and Response," *Southeast Asian Affairs 2004*, Singapore: Institute of Southeast Asian Studies, 2004, pp. 9–10; Amy Kazmin and Shawn Donnan, "Nations set deadline of 2020 for single market," *Financial Times*, 8 October 2003; "Four nations in economic dialogue," *Nation*, 2 August 2003; "Meeting held to boost infrastructure development for Laos, Vietnam, Cambodia triangle," *Nhân Dân*, 27 December 2002.

118 Grant Peck, "Program launched to support agriculture, environment along Mekong Basin," *Associated Press*, 11 March 2004; "Cambodia, Laos, Myanmar and Thailand sign Bagan Declaration, agreements," *New Light of Myanmar*, 13 November 2003; "Thailand fosters economic partnership with neighbors," *Yahoo! News Asia*, 12 November 2003.

119 As quoted in Phonekeo Vorakhoun, "Vientiane Action Plan pivotal to upcoming ASEAN Summit," *Vientiane Times*, 12 March 2004.

120 "ASEAN Insecurity," *Far Eastern Economic Review*, 15 July 2004; "Cambodian PM backs Myanmar in Asia-Europe spat," *Yahoo! News Asia*, 7 July 2004; "ASEAN Ministerial Meeting closes," *Vietnam Agency*, 1 July 2004. For a defense of the "ASEAN way," see Hiro Katsumata, "Reconstruction of Diplomatic Norms in Southeast Asia: The Case for Strict Adherence to the 'ASEAN Way,'" *Contemporary Southeast Asia*, vol. 25, no. 1, April 2003, pp. 104–21.

121 Jane Perlez, "Chinese Premier Signs Trade Pact at Southeast Asian Summit," *New York Times*, 30 November 2004; Evelyn Iritani, "New Trade Pact Could Cut Clout of U.S. in Asia," *Los Angeles Times*, 30 November 2004; Sun Shangwu, "China, Asean to advance free trade," *China Daily*, 29 November 2004; Michael Vatikiotis, "A Diplomatic Offensive," *Far Eastern Economic Review*, 5 August 2004, pp. 28–30.

## 7 Continuity and change

1 Nicola J. Cooper, *France in Indochina: Colonial Encounters*, Oxford: Berg, 2001, pp. 1–2, 43, quote p. 1.

2 Peter Zinoman, *The Colonial Bastille: A History of Imprisonment in Vietnam, 1862–1940*, Berkeley, CA: University of California Press, 2001, pp. 5–8, quote p. 6; Truong Buu Lâm, *Colonialism Experienced: Vietnamese Writings on Colonialism, 1900–1931*, Ann Arbor, MI: University of Michigan Press, 2000; Patrice Morlat, *La répression coloniale au Vietnam (1908–1940)*, Paris: Éditions L'Harmattan, 1990.

3 Christopher E. Goscha, *Thailand and the Southeast Asian Networks of the Vietnamese Revolution, 1885–1954*, Richmond, Surrey: Curzon Press, 1999, pp. 371–2, quote p. 372; Jean-Claude Pomonti, "La fin de l'Indochine," *Le Monde*, 9 July 1992, as cited by Goscha, *Thailand*, p. 372.

4 Grant Evans, *The Politics of Ritual and Remembrance: Laos since 1975*, Honolulu, HI: University of Hawai'i Press, 1998, p. 2.

5 Gabriel Kolko, *Vietnam: Anatomy of a Peace*, London: Routledge, 1997, pp. 20–1, quote p. 20.

6 David W. Roberts, *Political Transition in Cambodia, 1991–99: Power, Elitism and Democracy*, Richmond, Surrey: Curzon Press, 2001, pp. 1–5, quote p. 3.

7 C. Hart Schaaf and Russell H. Fifield, *The Lower Mekong: Challenge to Cooperation in Southeast Asia*, Princeton, NJ: D. Van Nostrand Company, 1963, p. 123.

8 Asian Development Bank, *Building on Success: A Strategic Framework for the Next Ten Years of the Greater Mekong Subregion Economic Cooperation Program*, November 2002, pp. 19–29 (http://www.adb.org).

9 Mark Beeson, "ASEAN Plus Three and the Rise of Reactionary Regionalism," *Contemporary Southeast Asia*, vol. 25, no. 2, August 2003, pp. 251–68, quotes p. 254.

10 Ibid., pp. 264–5; Zachary Abuza, *Militant Islam in Southeast Asia: Crucible of Terror*, Boulder, CO: Lynne Rienner, 2003, p. 224.

11 Adam Schwarz and Roland Villinger, "Integrating Southeast Asia's Economies," *McKinsey Quarterly*, vol. 1, 2004, pp. 1–9, quote p. 3 (www.mckinseyquarterly.com).

12 Yves Bourdet, *The Economics of Transition in Laos: From Socialism to ASEAN Integration*, Northampton, MA: Edward Elgar Publishing, 2000, pp. 79–81.

# Select bibliography

## Reports, plans and papers

Amnesty International, "No Sanctuary: The Plight of the Montagnard Minority," ASA41/011/2002, 18 December 2002, accessed online at http://web.amnesty.org.
—— "Starvation As A Weapon Of War Against Civilians," ASA26/013/2003, 2 October 2003, accessed online at http://web.amnesty.org.
—— "Socialist Republic of Vietnam: Renewed concern for the Montagnard minority," ASA41/005/2004, 28 April 2004, accessed online at http://web.amnesty.org.
Asia-Pacific Center for Security Studies, "Water and Conflict in Asia?" Seminar Report, Asia-Pacific Center for Security Studies, Honolulu, Hawai'i, 17 September 1999, mimeograph.
Asian Development Bank, *Asian Development Outlook*, Manila: Asian Development Bank, various countries and years.
—— *Cambodia, Country Economic Review*, various years.
—— *Key Indicators of Developing Asian and Pacific Countries*, various years.
—— *Lao People's Democratic Republic, Country Assistance Plan*, various years.
—— *Regional and Country Highlights*, various countries and years.
—— *Socialist Republic of Vietnam, Country Economic Review*, various years.
—— *Economic Cooperation in the Greater Mekong Subregion: Proceedings of the Second Conference on Subregional Economic Cooperation Among Cambodia, Lao People's Democratic Republic, Myanmar, Thailand, Viet Nam and Yunnan Province of the People's Republic of China, 30–31 August 1993*, Manila: Asian Development Bank, 1993.
—— *Subregional Economic Cooperation: Initial Possibilities for Cambodia, Lao PDR, Myanmar, Thailand, Viet Nam and the Yunnan Province of the People's Republic of China*, Manila: Asian Development Bank, 1993.
—— *Economic Cooperation in the Greater Mekong Subregion: Toward Implementation: Proceedings of the Third Conference on Subregional Economic Cooperation Among Cambodia, People's Republic of China, Lao People's Democratic Republic, Myanmar, Thailand and Vietnam, 20–23 April 1994*, Manila: Asian Development Bank, 1994.
—— *Subregional Economic Cooperation among Cambodia, People's Republic of China, Lao People's Democratic Republic, Myanmar, Thailand and Vietnam*, Manila: Asian Development Bank, 1994.
—— *Economic Cooperation in Greater Mekong Subregion: Facing the Challenges*, Manila: Asian Development Bank, 1996.

—— *Sustaining Momentum: Economic Cooperation in the Greater Mekong Subregion*, Manila: Asian Development Bank, 1996.

—— *Proceedings of the Seventh Conference on Subregional Economic Cooperation*, Manila: Asian Development Bank, 1997.

—— *Lao People's Democratic Republic: Economic Performance in 2000*, accessed online at http://www.adb.org.

—— *Regional and Country Highlights: Vietnam in 2000*, accessed online at http://www.adb.org.

—— *Cambodia, Country Assistance Evaluation*, Report No. 21354, 16 November 2000.

—— *Building on Success: A Strategic Framework for the Next Ten Years of the Greater Mekong Subregion Economic Cooperation Program*, Manila: Asian Development, 2002, accessed online at http://www.adb.org.

—— *Cambodia: Country Strategy and Program Update, 2004–2006*, July 2003, accessed online at http://www.adb.org.

—— *Country Strategy and Program Update, 2004–2006: Socialist Republic of Viet Nam*, July 2003, accessed online at http://www.adb.org.

—— *Lao People's Democratic Republic: Country Strategy and Program Update (2004–2006)*, July 2003, accessed online at http://www.adb.org.

—— *Country Assistance Program Evaluation for Cambodia*, January 2004, accessed online at http://www.adb.org.

Calavan, Michael, Sergio Diaz Briquets and Jerald O'Brien, *Cambodian Corruption Assessment*, USAID and Casals & Associates, IQC Contract No. DFD-I-00-03-00139-00, Task Order No. 801, May–June 2004.

Cambodia, Council of State, *Banking Laws*, Phnom Penh, 1992, mimeograph.

—— Royal Government of Cambodia, *Constitution of the Kingdom of Cambodia*, Phnom Penh, October 1993.

—— Ministry of Economics and Finance, *Announcement No. 018*, Phnom Penh, 31 December 1993, mimeograph.

—— Royal Government of Cambodia, *National Programme to Rehabilitate and Develop Cambodia*, Phnom Penh, February 1994, mimeograph.

—— Office of the Minister of State, *Announcement concerning the Profits Tax, House and Land Rent Tax and Turnover Tax, No. 012*, Phnom Penh, 9 March 1994, mimeograph.

—— Ministry of Economics and Finance, *Revenue from Exports of Timber*, Phnom Penh, 27 April 1994, mimeograph.

—— Ministry of Economics and Finance, *Proposed New Taxes*, Phnom Penh, 1 May 1994, mimeograph.

De Zamaróczy, Mario and Sopanha Sa, *Economic Policy in a Highly Dollarized Economy: The Case of Cambodia*, International Monetary Fund Occasional Paper No. 219, 23 September 2003.

Dodsworth, John R., Erich Spitäller, Michael Braulke, Keon Hyok Lee, Kenneth Miranda, Christian Mulder, Hisanobu Shishido and Krishna Srinivasan, *Vietnam: Transition to a Market Economy*, International Monetary Fund Occasional Paper No. 135, March 1996.

Drabek, Zdenek, *A Case Study of a Gradual Approach to Economic Reform: The Viet Nam Experience of 1985–88*, Asia Regional Series, Internal Discussion Paper, Report No. 74. Washington, D.C.: World Bank, 1990.

Fukase, Emiko and Will Martin, *The Effect of the United States' Granting Most*

*Favored Nation Status to Vietnam*, World Bank Policy Research Working Paper 2219, November 1999.

Godfrey, Martin, Toshiyasu Kato, Chan Sophal, Long Vou Piseth, Pon Dorina, Tep Saravy, Tia Savora and So Sovannarit, *Technical Assistance and Capacity Development in an Aid-dependent Economy: The Experience of Cambodia*, Working Paper 15, Phnom Penh: Cambodia Development Resource Institute, 2000.

Human Rights Watch, *Don't Bite the Hand that Feeds You: Coercion, Threats, and Vote-Buying in Cambodia's National Elections*, Briefing Paper, July 2003, accessed online at http://hrw.org.

—— "Vietnam: Violence against Montagnards during Easter Week Protests," Press Release, 14 April 2004, accessed online at http://hrw.org.

—— "Vietnam: Independent Investigation of Easter Week Atrocities Needed Now," Briefing Paper, 27 May 2004, accessed online at http://hrw.org.

Institute of Southeast Asian Studies, *Regional Outlook: Southeast Asia*, Singapore: Institute of Southeast Asian Studies, various years.

International Crisis Group, *Cambodia: The Elusive Peace Dividend*, Asia Report No. 8, 11 August 2000.

International Monetary Fund, *World Economic Outlook*, Washington, D.C.: International Monetary Fund, various years.

Kato, Toshiyasu, Jeffrey A. Kaplan, Chan Sophal and Real Sopheap, *Cambodia: Enhancing Governance for Sustainable Development*, Asian Development Bank, October 2000, accessed online at http://www.adb.org.

Lao Human Rights Council, "Religious Persecution in Vietnam and Laos," 24 February 2002, accessed online at http://www.laohumanrights.org.

Lao People's Democratic Republic, *Law on the Promotion and Management of Foreign Investment*, Vientiane, 14 March 1994, mimeograph.

Lao Veterans of America, "Joint Communiqué on Laos," 7–8 February 2005, accessed online at http://www.laoveterans.com.

Leipziger, D. M., *Awakening the Market: Viet Nam's Economic Transition*, World Bank Discussion Paper 157, Washington, D.C.: World Bank, 1992.

Lichtenstein, Natalie G., *A Survey of Viet Nam's Legal Framework in Transition*, World Bank Policy Research Working Paper 1291, April 1994.

Lipworth, Gabrielle and Erich Spitäller, *Viet Nam – Reform and Stabilization, 1986–92*, International Monetary Fund Working Paper WP/93/46, May 1993.

Malaluan, Jenina Joy Chavez and Shalmali Guttal, "Structural Adjustment in the Name of the Poor: The PRSP Experience in the Lao PDR, Cambodia and Vietnam," *Focus on the Global South*, January 2002, pp. 1–18, accessed online at http://www.focusweb.org.

Okonjo-Iweala, Ngozi, Victoria Kwakwa, Andrea Beckwith and Zafor Ahmed, "Impact of Asia's Financial Crisis on Cambodia and the Lao PDR," *Finance & Development*, vol. 36, no. 3, September 1999, pp. 1–8, accessed online at http://www.imf.org/external/pubs/ft/fandd/1999/09/okonjo.htm.

Polaski, Sandra, *Cambodia Blazes a New Path to Economic Growth and Job Creation*, Carnegie Endowment for International Peace Paper 51, October 2004.

Rainsy, Sam, "Medium and Long-Term Development Needs of Cambodia: Progress in the Economic Reform Policy," Second Meeting of the International Committee on the Reconstruction of Cambodia (ICORC), Tokyo, 10 March 1994, mimeograph.

St John, Ronald Bruce, "Policy of the United States on Vietnam," *Congressional Record: Proceedings and Debates of the 102d Congress, First Session*, vol. 137, no. 73, 15 May 1991, pp. S5959–60.

Socialist Republic of Vietnam, *Statistical Data of the Socialist Republic of Vietnam*, Hanoi: General Statistical Office, various years.

—— *The Constitution of 1992*, Hanoi: THẾ GIỚI Publishers, 1993.

—— *Fundamental Laws and Regulations of Vietnam*, Hanoi: THẾ GIỚI Publishers, 1993.

—— *Selection of Fundamental Laws and Regulations of Vietnam*, 2d ed., Hanoi: THẾ GIỚI Publishers, 1995.

—— *Draft Political Report of the Central Committee (VIIth Tenure) to the VIIIth National Congress*, Hanoi, 1996, mimeograph.

United Nations Development Program, *Report on the Economy of Vietnam*, December 1990.

—— *Cambodia's Rehabilitation Needs: Discussions with Donor Countries*, New York, 11 November 1991.

—— "The Economy of Laos: An Overview," in *Laos: Beyond the Revolution*, edited by Joseph J. Zasloff and Leonard Unger, London: Macmillan Academic and Professional, 1991, pp. 67–83.

—— *Catching Up: Capacity Development for Poverty Elimination in Viet Nam*. Hanoi: UNDP/UNICEF, 1996.

United States of America, *American Foreign Policy: Current Documents*, Washington, D.C.: U.S. Government, various years.

—— *Foreign Broadcast Information Service, Daily Report: Asia and Pacific (FBIS-APA)*, various years.

—— *Joint Publications Research Service: East Asia and Southeast Asia (JPRS-SEA)*, various years.

—— Department of State, "Survey of the Mekong River," *Bulletin*, vol. 34, no. 862, 2 January 1956, pp. 52–3.

—— *Foreign Economic Trends and Their Implications for the United States (Laos)*, FET 91-58, September 1991.

—— *Agreement between the United States of America and the Socialist Republic of Vietnam on Trade Relations*, 13 July 2000, accessed online at http://www.ustr.gov.

United States Mission in Vietnam, "The Action Program of the Provisional Revolutionary Government," *Viet-Nam Documents and Research Notes*, no. 60, June 1969.

Viet Nam Alliance of National, Democratic and Peace Forces, "National Salvation Manifesto of the Viet Nam Alliance of National, Democratic, and Peace Forces," *South Vietnam: From the NLF to the Provisional Revolutionary Government*, Vietnamese Studies, no. 8, August 1980, pp. 358–9.

World Bank, *Report on the Economy of Vietnam*, Washington, D.C.: World Bank, 1990.

—— *Cambodia: Agenda for Rehabilitation and Reconstruction*, June 1992.

—— *Vietnam: Transition to the Market: An Economic Report*, Report No. 11902-VN, 15 September 1993.

—— *Lao People's Democratic Republic Country Economic Memorandum*, Report No. 12554-LA, 24 March 1994.

—— *Viet Nam: Public Sector Management and Private Sector Incentives: An Economic Report*, Report No. 13143-VN, 26 September 1994.

—— *Cambodia Rehabilitation Program: Implementation and Outlook, A World Bank Report for the 1995 ICORC Conference*, Report No. 13965-KH, 27 February 1995.

—— *Lao PDR Agricultural Sector Memorandum*, Report No. 13675-LA, 23 March 1995.

—— *Lao PDR Social Development Assessment and Strategy*, Report No. 13992-LA, 15 August 1995.

—— *Vietnam: Deepening Reform for Growth: An Economic Report*, Report No. 17031-VN, 31 October 1997.

—— *Vietnam: Rising to the Challenge, An Economic Report*, Report No. 18632-VN, 25 November 1998.

—— *Memorandum of the President of the International Development Association to the Executive Directors on a Country Assistance Strategy of the World Bank Group for the Lao People's Democratic Republic*, Report No. 19098-LA, 30 March 1999.

—— "Cambodia Consultative Group meeting results: Aid partnership supports Cambodian development efforts," 26 May 2000, accessed online at http://www.worldbank.org.

—— *Cambodia: Country Assistance Evaluation*, Report No. 21354, 16 November 2000, accessed online at http://www.worldbank.org.

—— *Memorandum of the President of the International Development Association and the International Finance Corporation to the Executive Directors on a Country Assistance Strategy Progress Report for the Socialist Republic of Vietnam*, Report No. 22887-VN, 28 September 2001.

—— *Vietnam: Country Assistance Evaluation*, Report No. 23288, 21 November 2001.

—— "The Proposed Nam Theun Project," January 2004, accessed online at http://www.worldbank.org.

—— *Cambodia: Seizing the Global Opportunity*, Prepared for the Royal Cambodian Government by the World Bank Group, 12 August 2004.

—— *Cambodia at the Crossroads: Strengthening Accountability to Reduce Poverty*, 15 November 2004.

World Bank, Asian Development Bank, UNDP, *Vietnam 2010: Entering the 21st Century*, Vietnam Development Report, 2001, accessed online at http://www.worldbank.org.

## Books and articles

Abrami, Regina M., "Vietnam in 2002: On the Road to Recovery," *Asian Survey*, vol. 43, no. 1, January–February 2003, pp. 91–100.

Abuza, Zachary, "The Khmer Rouge Quest for Economic Independence," *Asian Survey*, vol. 33, no. 10, October 1993, pp. 1010–21.

—— "The Khmer Rouge and the Crisis of Vietnamese Settlers in Cambodia," *Contemporary Southeast Asia*, vol. 16, no. 4, March 1995, pp. 433–45.

—— "Leadership Transition in Vietnam Since the Eighth Party Congress: The Unfinished Congress," *Asian Survey*, vol. 38, no. 12, December 1998, pp. 1105–21.

—— "The Lessons of Le Kha Phieu: Changing Rules in Vietnamese Politics," *Contemporary Southeast Asia*, vol. 24, no. 1, April 2002, pp. 121–45.

—— *Renovating Politics in Contemporary Vietnam*, Boulder, CO: Lynne Rienner Publishers, 2002.

—— *Militant Islam in Southeast Asia: Crucible of Terror*, Boulder, CO: Lynne Rienner Publishers, 2003.

Alagappa, Muthiah, "The Major Powers and Southeast Asia," *International Journal*, vol. 44, no. 3, Summer 1989, pp. 562–9.

—— "Regionalism and the Quest for Security: ASEAN and the Cambodian Conflict," *Journal of International Affairs*, vol. 46, no. 2, Winter 1993, pp. 439–67.

Albritton, Robert B., "Cambodia in 2003: On the Road to Democratic Consolidation," *Asian Survey*, vol. 44, no. 1, January–February 2004, pp. 102–9.

Allen, Douglas and Ngo Vinh Long, ed., *Coming to Terms: Indochina, the United States, and the War*, Boulder, CO: Westview Press, 1991.

Amer, Ramses, "Vietnam and Its Neighbors: The Border Dispute Dimension," *Contemporary Southeast Asia*, vol. 17, no. 3, December 1995, pp. 298–318.

—— "Sino-Vietnamese Relations: Past, Present and Future," in *Vietnamese Foreign Policy in Transition*, edited by Carlyle A. Thayer and Ramses Amer, Singapore: Institute of Southeast Asian Studies, 1999, pp. 68–129.

—— "Assessing Sino-Vietnamese Relations through the Management of Contentious Issues," *Contemporary Southeast Asia*, vol. 26, no. 2, 2004, pp. 320–45.

Ang Cheng Guan, "Vietnam: Another Milestone and the Country Plods On," *Southeast Asian Affairs 2002*, Singapore: Institute of Southeast Asian Studies, 2002, pp. 345–56.

Aubertin, Catherine, "Institutionalizing Duality: Lowlands and Uplands in the Lao PDR," *International Institute for Asian Studies (IIAS) Letter 24*, February 2001.

Avery, Dorothy R., "Vietnam in 1992: Win Some; Lose Some," *Asian Survey*, vol. 33, no. 1, January 1993, pp. 67–74.

Bach, William, "A Chance in Cambodia," *Foreign Policy*, vol. 62, Spring 1986, pp. 75–95.

Bao Ninh, *The Sorrow of War*, London: Secker & Warburg, 1993.

Barnett, Anthony, "Cambodian Possibilities," *International Journal of Politics*, vol. 16, no. 3, Fall 1986, pp. 77–109.

Becker, Elizabeth, *When the War Was Over: The Voices of Cambodia's Revolution and Its People*, New York, NY: Simon & Schuster, 1986.

Bedlington, Stanley S., "Laos in 1980: The Portents Are Ominous," *Asian Survey*, vol. 21, no. 1, January 1981, pp. 102–11.

Beeson, Mark, "ASEAN Plus Three and the Rise of Reactionary Regionalism," *Contemporary Southeast Asia*, vol. 25, no. 2, August 2003, pp. 251–68.

Bekaert, Jacques, *Cambodian Diary: Tales of a Divided Nation, 1983–1986*, Bangkok: White Lotus Press, 1997.

—— *Cambodian Diary: A Long Road to Peace, 1987–1993*, Bangkok: White Lotus Press, 1998.

Beresford, Melanie, "Household and Collective in Vietnamese Agriculture," *Journal of Contemporary Asia*, vol. 15, no. 1, 1985, pp. 5–36.

—— *Vietnam: Politics, Economics, and Society*, London: Pinter Publishers, 1988.

—— *National Unification and Economic Development in Vietnam*, New York, NY: St. Martin's Press, 1989.

Black, Eugene R., *Alternative in Southeast Asia*, London: Pall Mall Press, 1969.

Blanchard, Michel, *Vietnam-Cambodge: Une frontière contestée*, Paris: L'Harmattan, 1999.

Bogdan, Michael, "Legal Aspects of the Re-Introduction of a Market Economy in Laos," *Review of Socialist Law*, vol. 17, no. 2, 1991, pp. 101–23.

Boua, Chanthou, "Observations of the Heng Samrin Government, 1980–1982," in *Revolution and Its Aftermath in Kampuchea: Eight Essays*, edited by David P. Chandler and Ben Kiernan, New Haven, CT: Yale University Southeast Studies, 1983, pp. 259–90.

Bourdet, Yves, "Reforming Laos' Economic System," *Economic Systems*, vol. 16, no. 1, April 1992, pp. 63–88.

—— "Rural Reforms and Agricultural Productivity in Laos," *Journal of Developing Areas*, vol. 29, no. 2, January 1995, pp. 161–82.

—— "Laos in 1995: Reform Policy, Out of Breath?" *Asian Survey*, vol. 36, no. 1, January 1996, pp. 89–94.

—— "Laos: The Sixth Party Congress, and After?" in *Southeast Asian Affairs 1997*, Singapore: Institute of Southeast Asian Studies, 1997, pp. 143–60.

—— "The Dynamics of Regional Disparities in Laos: The Poor and the Rich," *Asian Survey*, vol. 38, no. 7, July 1998, pp. 629–52.

—— *The Economics of Transition in Laos: From Socialism to ASEAN Integration*, Northampton, MA: Edward Elgar Publishing, 2000.

—— "Laos in 2000: The Economics of Political Immobilism," *Asian Survey*, vol. 41, no. 1, January–February 2001, pp. 164–70.

—— "Laos in 2001: Political Introversion and Economic Respite," *Asian Survey*, vol. 42, no. 1, January–February 2002, pp. 107–14.

Bradley, Mark Philip, *Imagining Vietnam and America: The Making of Postcolonial Vietnam, 1919–1950*, Chapel Hill, NC: University of North Carolina Press, 2000.

Brigham, Robert K., *Guerrilla Diplomacy: The NLF's Foreign Relations and the Viet Nam War*, Ithaca, NY: Cornell University Press, 1999.

Brocheux, Pierre and Daniel Hémery, *Indochine: La colonisation ambiguë (1858–1954)*, Paris: La Découverte, 1995.

Brown, Frederick Z., "Winning in Vietnam," *SAIS Review*, vol. 13, no. 1, Winter-Spring 1993, pp. 61–76.

Brown, Frederick Z. and Laura McGrew, "Cambodia: The Royal Government on Trial," *Southeast Asian Affairs 1995*, Singapore: Institute of Southeast Asian Studies, 1995, pp. 127–46.

Brown, MacAlister, "Laos: Bottoming Out," *Current History*, vol. 82, no. 483, April 1983, pp. 154–7, 180–2.

—— "Easing the Burden of Socialist Struggle in Laos," *Current History*, vol. 86, no. 519, April 1987, pp. 152–5, 177.

Brown, MacAlister and Joseph J. Zasloff, "Laos in 1975: People's Democratic Revolution – Lao Style," *Asian Survey*, vol. 16, no. 2, February 1976, pp. 193–9.

—— "Laos 1976: Faltering First Steps toward Socialism," *Asian Survey*, vol. 17, no. 2, February 1977, pp. 107–15.

—— "Laos 1977: The Realities of Independence," *Asian Survey*, vol. 18, no. 2, February 1978, pp. 164–74.

—— "Dependency in Laos," *Current History*, vol. 75, no. 442, December 1978, pp. 202–7, 228.

—— "Laos 1979: Caught in Vietnam's Wake," *Asian Survey*, vol. 20, no. 2, February 1980, pp. 103–11.

—— "Laos: Gearing up for National Development, An Overview," *Southeast*

*Asian Affairs 1985*, Singapore: Institute of Southeast Asian Studies, 1985, pp. 189–208.

—— *Apprentice Revolutionaries: The Communist Movement in Laos, 1930–1985*, Stanford, CA: Hoover Institution Press, 1986.

—— "Laos 1990: Socialism Postponed but Leadership Intact," *Southeast Asian Affairs 1991*, Singapore: Institute of Southeast Asian Studies, 1991, pp. 141–58.

—— *Cambodia Confounds the Peacemakers, 1979–1998*, Ithaca, NY: Cornell University Press, 1998.

Bui Tin, *Following Ho Chi Minh: The Memoirs of a North Vietnamese Colonel*, Honolulu, HI: University of Hawai'i Press, 1995.

Burley, T. M., "Foreign Aid to the Lao People's Democratic Republic," in *Contemporary Laos: Studies in the Politics and Society of the Lao People's Democratic Republic*, edited by Martin Stuart-Fox, New York, NY: St. Martin's Press, 1982, pp. 129–47.

Buszynski, Leszek, "Thailand's Foreign Policy: Management of a Regional Vision," *Asian Survey*, vol. 34, no. 8, August 1994, pp. 721–37.

Callison, Charles Stuart, *Land-to-the-Tiller in the Mekong Delta: Economic, Social and Political Effects of Land Reform in Four Villages of South Vietnam*, Lanham, MD: University Press of America, 1983.

"Cambodia Shrinking," *Boundary and Security Bulletin*, vol. 4, no. 2, Summer 1996, p. 41.

Castle, Timothy N., *At War in the Shadow of Vietnam: U.S. Military Aid to the Royal Lao Government, 1955–1975*, New York, NY: Columbia University Press, 1993.

Chanda, Nayan, "Economic Changes in Laos, 1975–1980," in *Contemporary Laos: Studies in the Politics and Society of the Lao People's Democratic Republic*, edited by Martin Stuart-Fox, New York, NY: St. Martin's Press, 1982, pp. 116–28.

—— *Brother Enemy: The War after the War, A History of Indochina since the Fall of Saigon*, New York, NY: Macmillan Publishing Company, 1986.

Chandler, David, *The Friends Who Tried To Empty the Sea: Eleven Cambodian Folk Stories*, Centre of Southeast Asian Studies, Working Paper No. 8, Clayton, Victoria: Monash University, 1976.

—— "Cambodia in 1984: Historical Patterns Re-asserted?" *Southeast Asian Affairs 1985*, Singapore: Institute of Southeast Asian Studies, 1985, pp. 177–86.

—— *The Tragedy of Cambodian History: Politics, War and Revolution since 1945*, New Haven, CT: Yale University Press, 1991.

Chang Pao-Min, *Kampuchea Between China and Vietnam*, Singapore: Singapore University Press, 1985.

Chapman, E. C. and He Daming, "Downstream Implications of China's Dams on the Lancang Jiang (Upper Mekong) and Their Potential Significance for Greater Regional Cooperation, Basin-Wide," in *Development Dilemmas in the Mekong Subregion*, edited by Bob Stensholt, Clayton, Victoria: Monash University, 1996, pp. 16–25.

Chen, King C., *Vietnam and China: 1938–1954*, Princeton, NJ: Princeton University Press, 1969.

Chien-peng (C.P.) Chung, "Southeast Asia-China Relations: Dialectics of 'Hedging' and 'Counter-Hedging,'" *Southeast Asian Affairs 2004*, Singapore: Institute of Southeast Asian Studies, 2004, pp. 35–60.

Chin Kin Wah, "Southeast Asia in 2002: From Bali to Iraq – Co-operating for Security," *Southeast Asian Affairs 2003*, Singapore: Institute of Southeast Asian Studies, 2003, pp. 3–23.

Chiranan Prasertkul, *Yunnan Trade in the Nineteenth Century: Southwest China's Cross-boundaries Functional System*, Asian Studies Monograph 44, Chulalongkorn University, Bangkok, 1989.

Cima, Ronald J., "Vietnam in 1988: The Brink of Renewal," *Asian Survey*, vol. 29, no. 1, January 1989, pp. 64–72.

Cooper, Nicola J., *France in Indochina: Colonial Encounters*, Oxford: Berg, 2001.

Cross, Mary and Frances FitzGerald, *Vietnam: Spirits of the Earth*, New York, NY: Bulfinch Press, 2001.

Dahm, Henrich, *French and Japanese Economic Relations with Vietnam since 1975*, Richmond, Surrey: Curzon Press, 1999.

Dakin, Brett, *Another Quiet American: Stories of Life in Laos*, Bangkok: Asia Books, 2003.

Dang T. Tran, *Socialist Economic Development and the Prospects for Economic Reform in Vietnam*, Indochina Initiative Working Paper No. 2, Honolulu, HI: East-West Center, 1991.

—— *Vietnam: Socialist Economic Development, 1955–1992*, San Francisco, CA: Institute for Contemporary Studies Press, 1994.

Decornoy, Jacques, "Life in the Pathet Lao Liberated Zone," in *Laos: War and Revolution*, edited by Nina S. Adams and Alfred W. McCoy, New York, NY: Harper Colophon Books, 1970, pp. 411–23.

Deuve, Jean, *Le Laos 1945–1949: Contribution a l'histoire du mouvement Lao Issala*, Montpellier: Université Paul Valéry, n.d.

De Vienne, Marie-Sybille, *L'économie du Viêt-Nam (1955–1995): Bilan et prospective*, Paris: CHEAM, 1994.

De Vylder, Stefan and Adam Fforde, *Viet Nam: An Economy in Transition*, Stockholm: Swedish International Development Authority, 1988.

Dollar, David, "Vietnam: Successes and Failures of Macroeconomic Stabilization," in *The Challenge of Reform in Indochina*, edited by Börge Ljunggren, Cambridge, MA: Harvard University Press, 1993, pp. 207–31.

Dommen, Arthur J., "Laos: Vietnam's Satellite," *Current History*, vol. 77, no. 452, December 1979, pp. 201–2, 225.

—— "Laos in 1984: The Year of the Thai Border," *Asian Survey*, vol. 25, no. 1, January 1985, pp. 114–21.

—— *Laos: Keystone of Indochina*, Boulder, CO: Westview Press, 1985.

—— "Laos in 1985: The Year of the Census," *Asian Survey*, vol. 26, no. 1, January 1986, pp. 112–17.

—— "UN Bias and Cambodian Peace," *Global Affairs*, vol. 7, no. 4, Fall 1992, pp. 120–35.

—— "Laos: Consolidating the Economy," *Southeast Asian Affairs 1994*, Singapore: Institute of Southeast Asian Studies, 1994, pp. 167–86.

—— "Laos in 1993: The Revolution on Hold," *Asian Survey*, vol. 34, no. 1, January 1994, pp. 82–6.

—— "Social Science Research on Laos in the United States," in *New Laos, New Challenges*, edited by Jacqueline Butler-Diaz, Tempe, AZ: Arizona State University, 1998, pp. 249–77.

—— *The Indochinese Experience of the French and the Americans: Nationalism and Communism in Cambodia, Laos, and Vietnam*, Bloomington, IN: Indiana University Press, 2001.

Dowling, J. Malcolm and Charissa N. Castillo, "Recent Economic Developments in Southeast Asia," *Southeast Asian Affairs 1996*, Singapore: Institute of Southeast Asian Studies, 1996, pp. 21–39.

Downie, Sue and Damien Kingsbury, "Political Development and the Re-emergence of Civil Society in Cambodia," *Contemporary Southeast Asia*, vol. 23, no. 1, April 2001, pp. 43–64.

Duiker, William J., *Vietnam since the Fall of Saigon*, Athens, OH: Ohio University Center for International Studies, 1989.

—— *Ho Chi Minh: A Life*, New York, NY: Hyperion, 2000.

Duncanson, Dennis, "The Legacy of Ho Chi Minh," *Asian Affairs* (Journal of the Royal Society for Asian Affairs), vol. 23, no. 1, February 1992, pp. 49–62.

Duong Thu Huong, *Paradise of the Blind*, New York: Penguin Books, 1994.

Ea Méng-Try, "Kampuchea: A Country Adrift," *Population and Development Review*, vol. 7, no. 2, June 1981, pp. 209–25.

Ear, Sophal, "Cambodia's Economic Development in Historical Perspective: A Contribution to the Study of Cambodia's Economy," August 1995, mimeograph.

Eiland, Michael, "Cambodia in 1985: From Stalemate to Ambiguity," *Asian Survey*, vol. 26, no. 1, January 1986, pp. 118–25.

Elliott, David W. P., "Deadlock Diplomacy: Thai and Vietnamese Interests in Kampuchea," *International Journal of Politics*, vol. 16, no. 3, Fall 1986, pp. 39–76.

—— "Vietnam's 1991 Party Elections," *Asian Affairs: An American Review*, vol. 19, no. 3, Fall 1992, pp. 159–68.

Engelbert, Thomas and Christopher E. Goscha, *Falling Out of Touch: A Study on Vietnamese Communist Policy Towards an Emerging Cambodian Communist Movement, 1930–1975*, Clayton, Victoria: Monash University, 1995.

Englund, Karl H., "External Assistance in the Context of Vietnam's Development Effort," in *Postwar Vietnam: Dilemmas in Socialist Development*, edited by David G. Marr and Christine P. White, Ithaca, NY: Cornell Southeast Asia Program, 1988, pp. 225–31.

Ennis, Thomas E., *French Policy and Developments in Indochina*, Chicago, IL: University of Chicago Press, 1936.

Etcheson, Craig, *The Rise and Demise of Democratic Kampuchea*, Boulder, CO: Westview Press, 1984.

Evans, Grant, *Lao Peasants under Socialism*, New Haven, CT: Yale University Press, 1990.

—— "Planning Problems in Peripheral Socialism: The Case of Laos," in *Laos: Beyond the Revolution*, edited by Joseph J. Zasloff and Leonard Unger, New York, NY: St. Martin's Press, 1991, pp. 84–130.

—— *Lao Peasants under Socialism and Post-Socialism*, Chiang Mai: Silkworm Books, 1995.

—— *The Politics of Ritual and Remembrance: Laos since 1975*, Honolulu, HI: University of Hawai'i Press, 1998.

—— ed., *Laos: Culture and Society*, Chiang Mai: Silkworm Books, 1999.

—— *A Short History of Laos: The Land in Between*, St Leonards, New South Wales: Allen & Unwin, 2002.

Evans, Grant and Kelvin Rowley, *Red Brotherhood at War: Vietnam, Cambodia and Laos since 1975*, New York, NY: Verso, 1990.

Fall, Bernard B., "Viet-Nam's Chinese Problem," *Far Eastern Survey*, May 1958, pp. 65–72.

Faming, Manynooch N., "An Interpretation of the Constitution of the Lao People's Democratic Republic," in *New Laos, New Challenges*, edited by Jacqueline Butler-Diaz, Tempe, AZ: Arizona State University, 1998, pp. 9–39.

Fforde, Adam, *The Agrarian Question in North Vietnam, 1974–1979: A Study of Cooperator Resistance to State Policy*, Armonk, NY: M.E. Sharpe, 1989.

—— *Vietnam: Economic Commentary and Analysis (a bi-annual appraisal of the Vietnamese Economy)*, London: ADUKI, 1992.

—— "Vietnam in 2003: The Road to Ungovernability?" *Asian Survey*, vol. 44, no. 1, January–February 2004, pp. 121–9.

Fforde, Adam and Suzanne H. Paine, *The Limits of National Liberation: Problems of Economic Management in the Democratic Republic of Vietnam*, London: Croom Helm, 1987.

Fforde, Adam and Stefan de Vylder, *From Plan to Market: The Economic Transition in Vietnam*, Boulder, CO: Westview Press, 1996.

Forest, Alain, *Le Cambodge et la Colonisation Française: Histoire d'une colonisation sans heurts (1897–1920)*, Paris: L'Harmattan, 1980.

Franchini, Phillippe, *Le Sacrifice et l'espoir Cambodge, Laos et Viêt Nam: Le Sacrifice des peuples, 1975–1983*, Paris: Arthème Fayard, 1997.

Freeman, Michael, *Cambodia*, London: Reaktion, 2004.

Freeman, Nick J., "Vietnam: Better Managing Reform," *Southeast Asian Affairs 1996*, Singapore: Institute of Southeast Asian Studies, 1996, pp. 385–402.

—— "Laos: No Safe Haven from the Regional Tumult," *Southeast Asian Affairs 1998*, Singapore: Institute of Southeast Asian Studies, 1998, pp. 141–57.

—— "Greater Mekong Sub-region and the 'Asian Crisis': Caught between Scylla and Charybdis," *Southeast Asian Affairs 1999*, Singapore: Institute of Southeast Asian Studies, 1999, pp. 32–51.

—— "Laos: Sedately Seguing into the Twenty-first Century," *Southeast Asian Affairs 2002*, Singapore: Institute of Southeast Asian Studies, 2002, pp. 145–56.

—— "Laos: Exiguous Evidence of Economic Reform and Development," *Southeast Asian Affairs 2004*, Singapore: Institute of Southeast Asian Studies, 2004, pp. 125–35.

Frings, Viviane, *The Failure of Agricultural Collectivization in the People's Republic of Kampuchea (1979–1989)*, Working Paper No. 80, Clayton, Victoria: Monash University, 1993.

—— *Allied and Equal: The Kampuchean People's Revolutionary Party's Historiography and its Relations with Vietnam (1979–1991)*, Working Paper No. 90, Clayton, Victoria: Monash University, 1994.

—— "Cambodia After Decollectivization (1989–1992)," *Journal of Contemporary Asia*, vol. 24, no. 1, 1994, pp. 49–66.

Frost, Frank, "Cambodia: From UNTAC to Royal Government," *Southeast Asian Affairs 1994*, Singapore: Institute of Southeast Asian Studies, 1994, pp. 79–101.

Fry, Gerald W., "The Future of the Lao PDR: Relations with Thailand and Alternative Paths to Internationalization," in *New Laos, New Challenges*, edited by Jacqueline Butler-Diaz, Tempe, AZ: Arizona State University, 1998, pp. 147–79.

Funck, Bernard, "Laos: Decentralization and Economic Control," in *The Challenge of Reform in Indochina*, edited by Börge Ljunggren, Cambridge, MA: Harvard University Press, 1993, pp. 123–48.

Furuta, Motoo, "The Indochina Communist Party's Division into Three Parties: Vietnamese Communist Policy toward Cambodia and Laos, 1948–1951," in *Indochina in the 1940's and 1950's*, edited by Takashi Shiraishi and Motoo Furuta, Ithaca, NY: Cornell University Press, 1992, pp. 143–63.

Gardner, Lloyd C., *Pay Any Price: Lyndon Johnson and the Wars for Vietnam*, Chicago, IL: Ivan R. Dee, 1995.

—— "From the Colorado to the Mekong," in *Vietnam: The Early Decisions*, edited by Lloyd C. Gardner and Ted Gittinger, Austin, TX: University of Texas Press, 1997, pp. 37–57.

Gates, Carolyn L. and David H. D. Truong, "Vietnam in ASEAN: Economic Reform, Openness and Transformation," *ASEAN Economic Bulletin*, vol. 13, no. 2, November 1996, pp. 159–68.

Gay, Bernard, *La nouvelle frontière lao-vietnamienne: Les accords de 1977–1990*, Paris: L'Harmattan, 1995.

Gilks, Anne, *The Breakdown of the Sino-Vietnamese Alliance, 1970–1979*, Institute of East Asian Studies, China Research Monograph 39, Berkeley, CA: University of California, 1992.

Godfrey, Martin, Toshiyasu Kato, Chan Sophal, Long Vou Piseth, Pon Dorina, Tep Saravy, Tia Savor and So Sovannarity, *Technical Assistance and Capacity Development in an Aid-dependent Economy: The Experience of Cambodia*, Working Paper 15, Phnom Penh: Cambodia Development Resource Institute, 2000.

Goodman, Allan E., "Vietnam's Post-Cold War Diplomacy and the U.S. Response," *Asian Survey*, vol. 33, no. 8, August 1993, pp. 832–47.

Goscha, Christopher E., *Thailand and the Southeast Asian Networks of the Vietnamese Revolution, 1885–1954*, Richmond, Surrey: Curzon Press, 1999.

—— *Vietnam or Indochina? Contesting Concepts of Space in Vietnamese Nationalism, 1887–1954*, Nordic Institute of Asian Studies Report Series No. 28, Copenhagen: Nordic Institute of Asian Studies Publishing, 1999.

Gottesman, Evan, *Cambodia After the Khmer Rouge: Inside the Politics of Nation Building*, New Haven, CT: Yale University Press, 2003.

Gourou, Pierre, "For a French Indo-Chinese Federation," *Pacific Affairs*, vol. 20, no. 1, March 1947, pp. 18–29.

Greene, Graham, *The Quiet American*, New York, NY: Random House, 1955.

Greenway, H. D. S., "Report from Cambodia: The Tiger and the Crocodile," *The New Yorker*, 17 July 1989, pp. 72–83.

Gunn, Geoffrey C., *Political Struggles in Laos (1930–1954)*, Bangkok: Duang Kamol, 1988.

—— "Laos in 1989: Quiet Revolution in the Marketplace," *Asian Survey*, vol. 30, no. 1, January 1990, pp. 81–7.

—— *Rebellion in Laos: Peasant and Politics in a Colonial Backwater*, Boulder, CO: Westview Press, 1990.

Haas, Michael, "The Paris Conference on Cambodia, 1989," *Bulletin of Concerned Asian Scholars*, vol. 23, no. 2, April–June 1991, pp. 42–53.

Hamel, Bernard, *Résistances au Vietnam, Cambodge et Laos (1975–1980)*, Paris: L'Harmattan, 1994.

Hamilton-Merritt, Jane, *Tragic Mountains: The Hmong, the Americans, and the Secret Wars for Laos, 1942–1992*, Bloomington, IN: Indiana University Press, 1993.

Hammer, Ellen J., *The Struggle for Indochina*, Stanford, CA: Stanford University Press, 1954.

Hannah, Norman B., *The Key to Failure: Laos & the Vietnam War*, Lanham, MD: Madison Books, 1987.

Harvie, Charles and Tran Van Hoa, *Vietnam's Reforms and Economic Growth*, New York, NY: St. Martin's Press, 1997.

Heder, Stephen R., "Dealing with Crimes Against Humanity: Progress or Illusion?" *Southeast Asian Affairs 2001*, Singapore: Institute of Southeast Asian Studies, 2001, pp. 129–41.

—— "Hun Sen and Genocide Trials in Cambodia: International Impacts, Impunity, and Justice," in *Cambodia Emerges from the Past: Eight Essays*, edited by Judy Ledgerwood, DeKalb, IL: Northern Illinois University, 2002, pp. 176–223.

—— *Cambodian Communism and the Vietnamese Model: Imitation and Independence, 1930– 1975*, Bangkok: White Lotus Press, 2004.

Hédy, Philippe, *Histoire de L'Indochine: Le perle de l'empire, 1624–1954*, Paris: Albin Michel, 1998.

Heininger, Janet E., *Peacekeeping in Transition: The United Nations in Cambodia*, New York, NY: Twentieth Century Fund Press, 1994.

Heng, Russell Hiang-Khng, "Vietnam: Light at the End of the Economic Tunnel?" *Southeast Asian Affairs 2001*, Singapore: Institute of Southeast Asian Studies, 2001, pp. 357–68.

Hiebert, Murray, " 'Socialist Transformation' in Laos," *Current History*, vol. 79, no. 461, December 1980, pp. 175–9, 194–5.

—— "Laos: Flexible Policies Spark Tenuous Recovery," *Indochina Issues*, vol. 37, May 1983, pp. 1–7.

Hinton, Peter, "Is It Possible to 'Manage' a River? Reflections from the Mekong," in *Development Dilemmas in the Mekong Subregion*, edited by Bob Stensholt, Clayton, Victoria: Monash University, 1996, pp. 49–56.

Ho Chi Minh, "Appeal Made on the Occasion of the Founding of the Communist Party of Indochina (February 18, 1930)," in *Ho Chi Minh on Revolution: Selected Writings, 1920–66*, edited by Bernard B. Fall, New York, NY: Praeger Publishers, 1967, pp. 129–31.

Hood, Steven J., *Dragons Entangled: Indochina and the China-Vietnam War*, Armonk, NY: M.E. Sharpe, 1992.

Hoskin, John and Allen W. Hopkins, *The Mekong: A River and Its People*, Bangkok: Post Publishing Company, 1991.

Hue-Tam Ho Tai, *Millenarianism and Peasant Politics in Vietnam*, Cambridge, MA: Harvard University Press, 1983.

—— *Radicalism and the Origins of the Vietnamese Revolution*, Cambridge, MA.: Harvard University Press, 1992.

Hughes, Caroline, *UNTAC in Cambodia: The Impact on Human Rights*, Occasional Paper No. 92, Singapore: Institute of Southeast Asian Studies, 1996.

—— "Surveillance and Resistance in the Cambodian Elections: The Prisoners' Dilemma?" *Southeast Asian Affairs 1999*, Singapore: Institute of Southeast Asian Studies, 1999, pp. 92–108.

—— "Cambodia: Democracy or Dictatorship?" *Southeast Asian Affairs 2001*, Singapore: Institute of Southeast Asian Studies, 2001, pp. 113–28.

—— *The Political Economy of Cambodia's Transition, 1991–2001*, London: RoutledgeCurzon, 2003.

Huxley, Tim, "Cambodia in 1986: The PRK's Eighth Year," *Southeast Asian Affairs 1987*, Singapore: Institute of Southeast Asian Studies, 1987, pp. 161–73.

Huynh Kim Khanh, *Vietnamese Communism, 1925–1945*, Ithaca, NY: Cornell University Press, 1982.

Ireson, W. Randall, "Laos: Building a Nation under Socialism," *Indochina Issues*, vol. 79, February 1988, pp. 1–7.

—— "Evolving Village-State Relations in the Lao PDR: Time, Space, and Ethnicity," in *New Laos, New Challenges*, edited by Jacqueline Butler-Diaz, Tempe, AZ: Arizona State University, 1998, pp. 41–71.

Ivarsson, Soren, "Towards a New Laos: *Lao Nhay* and the Campaign for a National 'Reawakening' in Laos, 1941–45," in *Laos: Culture and Society*, edited by Grant Evans, Chiang Mai: Silkworm Books, 1999, pp. 61–78.

Jackson, Karl D., ed., *Cambodia, 1975–1978: Rendezvous with Death*, Princeton, NJ: Princeton University Press, 1989.

Jamieson, Neil L., *Understanding Vietnam*, Berkeley, CA: University of California Press, 1993.

Jennar, Raoul M., *The Cambodian Constitutions (1953–1993)*, Bangkok: White Lotus Press, 1995.

Jerndal, Randi and Jonathan Rigg, "Making Space in Laos: Constructing a National Identity in a 'Forgotten' Country," *Political Geography*, vol. 17, no. 7, 1998, pp. 809–31.

—— "From Buffer State to Crossroads State: Spaces of Human Activity and Integration in the Lao PDR," in *Laos: Culture and Society*, edited by Grant Evans, Chiang Mai: Silkworm Books, 1999, pp. 35–60.

Johnson, Stephen T., "Laos in 1992: Succession and Consolidation," *Asian Survey*, vol. 33, no. 1, January 1993, pp. 75–82.

Joiner, Charles A., "Laos in 1986: Administrative and International Partially Adaptive Communism," *Asian Survey*, vol. 27, no. 1, January 1987, pp. 104–14.

—— "Laos in 1987: New Economic Management Confronts the Bureaucracy," *Asian Survey*, vol. 28, no. 1, January 1988, pp. 95–104.

Karnow, Stanley, *Vietnam: A History*, New York, NY: Penguin Books, 1984.

Katsumata, Hiro, "Reconstruction of Diplomatic Norms in Southeast Asia: The Case for Strict Adherence to the ASEAN Way," *Contemporary Southeast Asia*, vol. 25, no. 1, April 2003, pp. 104–21.

Kaysone Phomvihane, *Revolution in Laos: Practice and Prospects*, Moscow: Progress Publishers, 1981.

Kearns, Doris, *Lyndon Johnson and the American Dream*, New York, NY: Harper & Row, 1976.

Kerkvliet, Benedict J. Tria, "Rural Society and State Relations," in *Vietnam's Rural Transformation*, edited by Benedict J. Tria Kerkvliet and Doug J. Porter, Boulder, CO: Westview Press, 1995, pp. 65–96.

—— "Village-State Relations in Vietnam: The Effect of Everyday Politics on Decollectivization," *Journal of Asian Studies*, vol. 54, no. 2, May 1995, pp. 396–418.

Kerkvliet, Benedict J. Tria and David G. Marr, ed., *Beyond Hanoi: Local Government in Vietnam*, Singapore: Institute of Southeast Asian Studies, 2004.

Kerkvliet, Benedict J. Tria and Doug J. Porter, ed., *Vietnam's Rural Transformation*, Boulder, CO: Westview Press, 1995.

Khamsouk Sundara, "New Laos – Economic Challenges," in *New Laos, New Challenges*, edited by Jacqueline Butler-Diaz, Tempe, AZ: Arizona State University, 1998, pp. 73–83.

Kiernan, Ben, *How Pol Pot Came to Power: A History of Communism in Kampuchea, 1930–1975*, London: Verso, 1985.

—— *The Pol Pot Regime: Race, Power, and Genocide in Cambodia under the Khmer Rouge, 1975–79*, New Haven, CT: Yale University Press, 1996.

Kiljunen, Kimmo, "Power Politics and the Tragedy of Kampuchea During the Seventies," *Bulletin of Concerned Asian Scholars*, vol. 17, no. 2, April–June 1985, pp. 49–64.

Kimura Tetsusabureo, *The Vietnamese Economy, 1975–86*, Tokyo: Institute of Developing Nations, 1989.

Koh, David, "The Politics of a Divided Party and Parkinson's State in Vietnam," *Contemporary Southeast Asia*, vol. 23, no. 3, December 2001, pp. 533–51.

Kolko, Gabriel, *Vietnam: Anatomy of a Peace*, London: Routledge, 1997.

Lafont, Pierre-Bernard, "Buddhism in Contemporary Laos," in *Contemporary Laos: Studies in the Politics and Society of the Lao People's Democratic Republic*, edited by Martin Stuart-Fox, New York, NY: St. Martin's Press, 1982, pp. 148–62.

Lamant, Pierre-Lucien, "Le frontière entre le Cambodge and le Viêtnam du milieu du XIXᵉ siècle à nous jours," in *Les Frontières du Viêtnam: Histoire des frontières de la Péninsule Indochinoise*, edited by Pierre-Bernard Lafont, Paris: L'Harmattan, 1989, pp. 156–81.

Langer, Paul F. and Joseph J. Zasloff, *North Vietnam and the Pathet Lao: Partners in the Struggle for Laos*, Cambridge, MA: Harvard University Press, 1970.

Langran, Irene V., "Cambodia in 2000: New Hopes Are Challenged," *Asian Survey*, vol. 41, no. 1, January–February 2001, pp. 156–63.

Lao Mong Hay, "Building Democracy in Cambodia: Problems and Prospects," in *Cambodia and the International Community: The Quest for Peace, Development and Democracy*, edited by Frederick Z. Brown and David G. Timberman, New York, NY: Asia Society, 1998, pp. 169–86.

Ledgerwood, Judy, ed., *Cambodia Emerges from the Past: Eight Essays*, Southeast Asia Publications, DeKalb, IL: Northern Illinois University, 2002.

Levien Do, "Vietnam's Revised Constitution: Impact on Foreign Investment," in *Vietnam and the Rule of Law*, edited by Carlyle A. Thayer and David G. Marr, Canberra: Australian National University, 1993, pp. 116–25.

Li Ma, "China and Vietnam: Coping with the Threat of Peaceful Evolution," in *Vietnamese Foreign Policy in Transition*, edited by Carlyle A. Thayer and Ramses Amer, Singapore: Institute of Southeast Asian Studies, 1999, pp. 44–67.

Lintner, Bertil, "Laos: Signs of Unrest," *Southeast Asian Affairs 2001*, Singapore: Institute of Southeast Asian Studies, 2001, pp. 177–86.

—— "Laos: Mired in Economic Stagnation?" *Southeast Asian Affairs 2003*, Singapore: Institute of Southeast Asian Studies, 2003, pp. 135–45.

Livingston, Ian, "Industrial Development in Laos: New Policies and New Possibilities," in *Laos' Dilemmas and Options: The Challenge of Economic Transition in the 1990s*, edited by Mya Than and Joseph L. H. Tan, Singapore: Institute of Southeast Asian Studies, 1997, pp. 128–53.

Lizée, Pierre P., "Cambodia in 1995: From Hope to Despair," *Asian Survey*, vol. 36, no. 1, January 1996, pp. 83–8.

—— "Testing the Limits of Change: Cambodia's Politics after the July Elections," *Southeast Asian Affairs 1999*, Singapore: Institute of Southeast Asian Studies, 1999, pp. 79–91.

Ljunggren, Börje, ed., *The Challenge of Reform in Indochina*, Cambridge, MA: Harvard University Press, 1993.

—— "Market Economies under Communist Regimes: Reform in Vietnam, Laos, and Cambodia," in *The Challenge of Reform in Indochina*, edited by Börje Ljunggren, Cambridge, MA: Harvard University Press, 1993, pp. 39–121.

Ma Van Khang, *Against the Flood*, Willimantic, CT: Curbstone, 2000.

Mabbett, Ian and David Chandler, *The Khmers*, Oxford: Blackwell, 1995.

Mahbubani, Kishore, "The Kampuchean Problem: A Southeast Asian Perception," *Foreign Affairs*, vol. 62, no. 2, Winter 1983/84, pp. 407–25.

Marr, David G., *Vietnamese Anticolonialism 1885–1925*, Berkeley, CA: University of California Press, 1971.

—— *Vietnamese Tradition on Trial 1920–1945*, Berkeley, CA: University of California Press, 1981.

—— "Where is Vietnam Coming From?" in *Doi Moi: Vietnam's Renovation Policy and Performance*, edited by Dean K. Forbes, Terence H. Hull, David G. Marr and Brian Brogan, Canberra: Australian National University, 1991, pp. 12–20.

—— *Vietnam 1945: The Quest for Power*, Berkeley, CA: University of California Press, 1995.

Marr, David G. and Christine P. White, "Introduction," in *Postwar Vietnam: Dilemmas in Socialist Development*, edited by David G. Marr and Christine P. White, Ithaca, NY: Cornell Southeast Asia Program, 1988, pp. 1–11.

—— ed., *Postwar Vietnam: Dilemmas in Socialist Development*, Ithaca, NY: Cornell Southeast Asia Program, 1988.

Marston, John, "Cambodia: Transnational Pressures and Local Agendas," *Southeast Asian Affairs 2002*, Singapore: Institute of Southeast Asian Studies, 2002, pp. 95–108.

Martin, Marie Alexandrine, *Cambodia: A Shattered Society*, Berkeley, CA: University of California Press, 1994.

McCoy, Alfred W., "French Colonialism in Laos, 1893–1945," in *Laos: War and Revolution*, edited by Nina S. Adams and Alfred W. McCoy, New York, NY: Harper & Row, 1970, pp. 67–99.

Mehta, Harish, "Cambodia: A Year of Consolidation," *Southeast Asian Affairs 1996*, Singapore: Institute of Southeast Asian Studies, 1996, pp. 113–29.

Moise, Edwin E., *Land Reform in China and North Vietnam: Consolidating the Revolution at the Village Level*, Chapel Hill, NC: University of North Carolina Press, 1983.

Möller, Kay, "Cambodia and Burma: The ASEAN Way Ends Here," *Asian Survey*, vol. 38, no. 12, December 1998, pp. 1087–104.

Morlat, Patrice, *La répression coloniale au Vietnam (1908–1940)*, Paris: L'Harmattan, 1990.

Morris, Stephen J., *Why Vietnam Invaded Cambodia: Political Culture and the Causes of War*, Stanford, CA: Stanford University Press, 1999.

Murray, Martin J., *The Development of Capitalism in Colonial Indochina (1870–1940)*, Berkeley, CA: University of California Press, 1980.

Muscat, Robert J., *Cambodia: Post-Settlement Reconstruction and Development*, New York, NY: Columbia University, 1989.

Mya Than, "Rehabilitation and Economic Reconstruction in Cambodia," *Contemporary Southeast Asia*, vol. 14, no. 3, December 1992, pp. 269–86.

—— *The Golden Quadrangle of the Mainland Southeast Asia*, ISEAS Working Papers in Economics and Finance no. 3, Singapore: Institute of Southeast Asian Studies, 1996.

—— "Economic Co-operation in the Greater Mekong Subregion," *Asian-Pacific Economic Literature*, vol. 11, no. 2, November 1997, pp. 40–57.

Mya Than and George Abonyi, "The Greater Mekong Subregion: Co-operation in Infrastructure and Finance," in *ASEAN Enlargement: Impacts and Implications*, edited by Mya Than and Carolyn L. Gates, Singapore: Institute of Southeast Asian Studies, 2001, pp. 128–63.

Mya Than and Joseph L. H. Tan, ed., *Vietnam's Dilemmas and Options: The Challenge of Economic Transition in the 1990s*, Singapore: Institute of Southeast Asian Studies, 1993.

—— *Laos' Dilemmas and Options: The Challenge of Economic Transition in the 1990s*, Singapore: Institute of Southeast Asian Studies, 1997.

Nathan, Melina, "Vietnam: Is Globalization a Friend or Foe?" *Southeast Asian Affairs 1999*, Singapore: Institute of Southeast Asian Studies, 1999, pp. 339–57.

Népote, Jacques and Marie-Sybille de Vienne, *Cambodge, Laboratoire d'une crise*, Paris: Centre des Hautes Études sur l'Afrique et l'Asie Modernes, 1993.

Ng Chee Yuen, Nick J. Freeman and Frank H. Huynh, eds, *State-Owned Enterprise Reform in Vietnam: Lessons from Asia*, Singapore: Institute of Southeast Asian Studies, 1996.

Ng Shui Meng, "Laos in 1986: Into the Second Decade of National Reconstruction," *Southeast Asian Affairs 1987*, Singapore: Institute of Southeast Asian Studies, 1987, pp. 177–93.

—— "Laos: Taking the Pragmatic Road," *Southeast Asian Affairs 1990*, Singapore: Institute of Southeast Asian Studies, 1990, pp. 147–62.

Ngaosyvathn, Mayoury and Pheuiphanh Ngaosyvathn, *Kith and Kin Politics: The Relationship between Laos and Thailand*, Manila: Journal of Contemporary Asia Publishers, 1994.

Ngo Ba Thanh, "The 1992 Constitution and the Rule of Law," in *Vietnam and the Rule of Law*, edited by Carlyle A. Thayer and David G. Marr, Canberra: Australian National University, 1993, pp. 81–115.

Ngo Van, *Viêt-nam, 1920–1945: Révolution et contre-révolution sous la domination coloniale*, Paris: Nautilus, 2000.

Ngo Vinh Hai, "Postwar Vietnam: Political Economy," in *Coming to Terms: Indochina, the United States, and the War*, edited by Douglas Allen and Ngo Vinh Long, Boulder, CO: Westview Press, 1991, pp. 65–88.

Ngo Vinh Long, "Vietnam," in *Coming to Terms: Indochina, the United States, and the War*, edited by Douglas Allen and Ngo Vinh Long, Boulder, CO: Westview Press, 1991, pp. 9–64.

Nguyen, Mark, "Laos: Back to a Land of Three Kingdoms," *Southeast Asian Affairs 1996*, Singapore: Institute of Southeast Asian Studies, 1996, pp. 197–214.

Nguyen Manh Hung, "Vietnam: Facing the Challenge of Integration," *Southeast*

*Asian Affairs 2004*, Singapore: Institute of Southeast Asian Studies, 2004, pp. 297–311.

Nguyen Ngoc Tuan, Ngo Tri Long and Ho Phuong, "Restructuring of State-Owned Enterprises towards Industrialization and Modernization in Vietnam," in *State-Owned Enterprise Reform in Vietnam: Lessons from Asia*, edited by Ng Chee Yuen, Nick J. Freeman and Frank H. Huynh, Singapore: Institute of Southeast Asian Studies, 1996, pp. 19–37.

Nguyen Qui Binh, "Real Estate Laws in Vietnam," in *Vietnam and the Rule of Law*, edited by Carlyle A. Thayer and David G. Marr, Canberra: Australian National University, 1993, pp. 148–59.

Nguyen Tien Hung, *Economic Development of Socialist Vietnam, 1955–1980*, New York, NY: Praeger Publishers, 1977.

—— *Vietnam, Reforming the State Enterprises: Toward an Agenda for Privatisation*, Bangkok: Post Books, 1995.

Nguyen Tuan Dung, "Foreign Direct Investment in Vietnam," in *Vietnam Assessment: Creating a Sound Investment Climate*, edited by Suiwah Leung, Singapore: Institute of Southeast Asian Studies, 1996, pp. 69–89.

Nguyen Van Canh, *Vietnam Under Communism, 1975–1982*, Stanford, CA: Hoover Institution Press, 1983.

Nguyen Van Huy and Tran Van Nghia, "Government Policies and State-Owned Enterprise Reform," in *State-Owned Enterprise Reform in Vietnam: Lessons from Asia*, edited by Ng Chee Yuen, Nick J. Freeman and Frank H. Huynh, Singapore: Institute of Southeast Asian Studies, 1996, pp. 38–62.

Nguyen Xuan Oanh and Philip Donald Grub, *Vietnam: The New Investment Frontier in Southeast Asia*, Singapore: Times Academic Press, 1992.

Norindr, Panivong, *Phantasmatic Indochina: French Colonial Ideology in Architecture, Film, and Literature*, Durham, NC: Duke University Press, 1996.

Norlund, Irene, Carolyn L. Gates and Vu Cao Dam, eds, *Vietnam in a Changing World*, Richmond, Surrey: Curzon Press, 1995.

Öjendal, Joakim, "Democracy Lost? The Fate of the U.N.-implanted Democracy in Cambodia," *Contemporary Southeast Asia*, vol. 18, no. 2, September 1996, pp. 193–218.

Osborne, Milton, *The French Presence in Cochinchina and Cambodia: Rule and Response (1859–1905)*, Ithaca, NY: Cornell University Press, 1969.

—— *River Road to China: The Mekong River Expedition, 1866–73*, London: George Allen & Unwin, 1975.

—— "Cambodia: Hun Sen Consolidates Power," *Southeast Asian Affairs 2000*, Singapore: Institute of Southeast Asian Studies, 2000, pp. 101–11.

—— *The Mekong: Turbulent Past, Uncertain Future*, New York, NY: Atlantic Monthly Press, 2000.

—— "Cambodia: Hun Sen Firmly in Control," *Southeast Asian Affairs 2003*, Singapore: Institute of Southeast Asian Studies, 2003, pp. 83–94.

Pacific Basin Research Institute, *Toward a Market Economy in Viet Nam: Economic Reforms and Development Strategies*, Rockville, MD: Pacific Basin Research Institute, 1993.

Patcharawalai Wongboonsin, *et al.*, *Current Indochinese Economies*, Bangkok: Chulalongkorn University, 1992.

Peang-Meth, Abdulgaffar, "Understanding Cambodia's Political Developments," *Contemporary Southeast Asia*, vol. 19, no. 3, December 1997, pp. 286–308.

Peou, Sorpong, "Cambodia: A New Glimpse of Hope?" *Southeast Asian Affairs 1997*, Singapore: Institute of Southeast Asian Studies, 1997, pp. 83–103.

—— *Conflict Neutralization in the Cambodia War: From Battlefield to Ballot-box*, New York, NY: Oxford University Press, 1997.

—— "Hun Sen's Pre-emptive Coup: Causes and Consequences," *Southeast Asian Affairs 1998*, Singapore: Institute of Southeast Asian Studies, 1998, pp. 86–102.

—— *Intervention & Change in Cambodia: Towards Democracy?* Singapore: Institute of Southeast Asian Studies, 2000.

Pham Xuan Nam and Be Viet Dang with Geoffrey B. Hainsworth, "Rural Development in Viet Nam: The Search for Sustainable Livelihoods," in *Socioeconomic Renovation in Viet Nam: The Origin, Evolution, and Impact of Doi Moi*, edited by Peter Boothroyd and Pham Xuan Nam, Singapore: Institute of Southeast Asian Studies, 2000, pp. 10–16.

Phan Van Tiem and Nguyen Van Thanh, "Problems and Prospects of State Enterprise Reform, 1996–2000," in *State-Owned Enterprise Reform in Vietnam: Lessons from Asia*, edited by Ng Chee Yuen, Nick J. Freeman and Frank H. Huynh, Singapore: Institute of Southeast Asian Studies, 1996, pp. 3–18.

Pike, Douglas, "Vietnam in 1993: Uncertainty Closes In," *Asian Survey*, vol. 34, no. 1, January 1994, pp. 64–71.

Porter, Gareth, "Vietnam's Ethnic Chinese and the Sino-Vietnamese Conflict," *Bulletin of Concerned Asian Scholars*, vol. 12, no. 4, October–December 1980, pp. 55–9.

—— "Vietnamese Communist Policy Towards Kampuchea, 1930–1970," in *Revolution and Its Aftermath in Kampuchea: Eight Essays*, edited by David P. Chandler and Ben Kiernan, New Haven, CT: Yale University Southeast Asia Studies, 1983, pp. 57–98.

—— *Vietnam: The Politics of Bureaucratic Socialism*, Ithaca, NY: Cornell University Press, 1993.

Prasso, Sheridan. T., "Cambodia: A Heritage of Violence," *World Policy Journal*, vol. 11, no. 3, Fall 1994, pp. 71–7.

—— *The Riel Value of Money: How the World's Only Attempt to Abolish Money Has Hindered Cambodia's Economic Development*, Asia Pacific Issues No. 49, Honolulu, HI: East-West Center, 2001.

Purcell, Victor, *The Chinese in Southeast Asia*, 2d ed., London: Oxford University Press, 1965.

Qiang Zhai, *China & the Vietnam Wars, 1950–1975*, Chapel Hill, NC: University of North Carolina Press, 2000.

Quan Xuan Dinh, "The Political Economy of Vietnam's Transformation Process," *Contemporary Southeast Asia*, vol. 22, no. 2, August 2000, pp. 360–88.

Ramcharan, Robin, "ASEAN and Non-interference: A Principle Maintained," *Contemporary Southeast Asia*, vol. 22, no. 1, April 2000, pp. 60–88.

Raszelenberg, Patrick and Peter Schier, *The Cambodia Conflict: Search for a Settlement, 1979–1991, An Analytical Chronology*, Hamburg: Institute of Asian Affairs, 1995.

Raymond, Catherine, "Homage to a King in Laos," *Mandala*, vol. 22, Summer 2003, pp. 4–5.

Reddi, V. M, *A History of the Cambodian Independence Movement, 1863–1955*, Tirupati, India: Sri Venkateswara University, 1971.

Robequain, Charles, *The Economic Development of French Indo-China*, London: Oxford University Press, 1944.

Roberts, David W., *Political Transition in Cambodia 1991–99: Power, Elitism and Democracy*, Richmond, Surrey: Curzon Press, 2001.

Roberts, Tyson R., "Mekong Mainstream Hydropower Dams: Run-of-the-River or Ruin-of-the-River?" *Natural History Bulletin of the Siam Society*, vol. 43, 1995, pp. 9–19.

St John, Ronald Bruce, "Marxist-Leninist Theory and Organization in South Vietnam," *Asian Survey*, vol. 20, no. 8, August 1980, pp. 812–28.

—— "The Vietnamese Economy in Transition: Trends and Prospects," *Asian Affairs* [Journal of the Royal Society for Asian Affairs], vol. 24, no. 3, October 1993, pp. 304–14.

—— "Preah Vihear and the Cambodia-Thailand Borderland," *IBRU Boundary and Security Bulletin*, vol. 1, no. 4, January 1994, pp. 64–8.

—— "Cambodian Foreign Policy: New Directions," *Asian Affairs* [Dhaka], vol. 16, no. 1, January–March 1994, pp. 55–74.

—— "Recent Economic Reforms in Indochina," Paper delivered at the Asia-Pacific Business Forum, Hudson Institute, September 1994.

—— "New Economic Order in Indochina," *Asian Affairs: An American Review*, vol. 21, no. 4, Winter 1995, pp. 227–40.

—— "Japan's Moment in Indochina: Washington Initiative ... Tokyo Success," *Asian Survey*, vol. 35, no. 7, July 1995, pp. 668–81.

—— "The Political Economy of the Royal Government of Cambodia," *Contemporary Southeast Asia*, vol. 17, no. 3, December 1995, pp. 265–81.

—— "Review," *Bulletin of Concerned Asian Scholars*, vol. 28, no. 3–4, July–December 1996, pp. 116–23.

—— "End of the Beginning: Economic Reform in Cambodia, Laos and Vietnam," *Contemporary Southeast Asia*, vol. 19, no. 2, September 1997, pp. 172–89.

—— "Japan's New Role in Indochina," *Asia-Pacific Magazine*, vol. 11, 1998, pp. 38–41.

—— *The Land Boundaries of Indochina: Cambodia, Laos and Vietnam*, International Boundaries Research Unit, University of Durham, Boundary and Territory Briefing, vol. 2, no. 6, 1998.

—— "Misreading the Tea Leaves in Hanoi," *Northwestern Journal of International Affairs*, vol. 1, Winter 1999, pp. 41–7.

—— "Land Boundaries of Indochina," *Boundary and Security Bulletin*, vol. 9, no. 1, Spring 2001, pp. 97–107.

Schaaf, C. Hart and Russell H. Fifield, *The Lower Mekong: Challenge to Co-operation in Southeast Asia*, Princeton, NJ: D. Van Nostrand Company, 1963.

Schneider, Andreas, "Laos: A Million Elephants, A Million Tourists?" *Southeast Asian Affairs 1999*, Singapore: Institute of Southeast Asian Studies, 1999, pp. 145–61.

Schwarz, Adam and Roland Villinger, "Integrating Southeast Asia's Economies," *McKinsey Quarterly*, vol. 1, 2004, pp. 1–9, accessed online at http://www.mckinseyquarterly.com.

Scigliano, Robert, *South Vietnam: Nation Under Stress*, Boston, MA: Houghton Mifflin, 1963.

Sesser, Stan, "Forgotten Country," *The New Yorker*, 20 August 1990, pp. 39–68.

Sharp, Lauriston, "French Plan for Indochina," *Far Eastern Survey*, vol. 15, no. 13, 3 July 1946, pp. 193–7.

Shawcross, William, *Cambodia's New Deal*, Contemporary Issues Paper No. 1, Washington, D.C.: Carnegie Endowment for International Peace, 1994.

Shiraishi, Masaya, *Japanese Relations with Vietnam, 1951–1987*, Ithaca, NY: Cornell Southeast Asia Program, 1990.

Short, Philip, *Pol Pot: Anatomy of a Nightmare*, New York: Holt Henry and Company, 2004.

Sidel, Mark, "Vietnam in 1998: Reform Confronts the Regional Crisis," *Asian Survey*, vol. 39, no. 1, January–February 1999, pp. 89–98.

Simms, Peter and Sanda, *The Kingdom of Laos: Six Hundred Years of History*, Richmond, Surrey: Curzon Press, 1999.

Simon, Sheldon W., *War and Politics in Cambodia: A Communications Analysis*, Durham, NC: Duke University Press, 1974.

Siriphan Kitiprawat, "Business Opportunities in Laos Today," *Bangkok Bank Monthly Review*, vol. 33, no. 11, November 1992, pp. 15–22.

—— "Cambodia Today: Economy and Business Opportunities," *Bangkok Bank Monthly Review*, vol. 34, no. 1, January 1993, pp. 14–21.

—— "Business Opportunities in Vietnam Today," *Bangkok Bank Monthly Review*, vol. 34, no. 3, March 1993, pp. 12–19.

Slocomb, Margaret, *The People's Republic of Kampuchea, 1979–1989: The Revolution after Pol Pot*, Chiang Mai: Silkworm Books, 2003.

Smith, R. B., "Cambodia in the Context of Sino-Vietnamese Relations," *Asian Affairs* [Journal of the Royal Society for Asian Affairs], vol. 16, no. 3, October 1985, pp. 273–87.

Spoor, Max, "Reforming State Finance in Post-1975 Vietnam," *Journal of Development Studies*, vol. 24, no. 4, 1988, pp. 107–10.

Steinberg, David J., *Cambodia*, New Haven, CT: Human Relations Area Files Press, 1959.

Stensholt, Bob, "The Many Faces of Mekong Cooperation," in *Development Dilemmas in the Mekong Subregion*, edited by Bob Stensholt, Melbourne Workshop Proceedings, 1–2 October 1996, 2d ed., Clayton, Victoria: Monash University, 1996, pp. 199–205.

Stern, Lewis M., "The Vietnamese Communist Party in 1986: Party Reform Initiatives, the Scramble towards Economic Revitalization, and the Road to the Sixth National Congress," *Southeast Asian Affairs 1987*, Singapore: Institute of Southeast Asian Studies, 1987, pp. 345–63.

—— *Renovating the Vietnamese Communist Party: Nguyen Van Linh and the Programme for Organizational Reform, 1987–91*, New York, NY: St. Martin's Press, 1993.

Stowe, Judith A., *Siam Becomes Thailand: A Story of Intrigue*, Honolulu, HI: University of Hawai'i Press, 1991.

Stuart-Fox, Martin, "The Initial Failure of Agricultural Cooperativization in Laos," *Asia Quarterly*, vol. 4, 1980, pp. 273–99.

—— "Laos: The First Lao Five Year Plan," *Asian Thought and Society*, vol. 6, no. 17–18, 1981, pp. 272–6.

—— "Laos in 1981: Economic Prospects and Problems," *Southeast Asian Affairs 1982*, Singapore: Institute of Southeast Asian Studies, 1982, pp. 229–42.

—— ed., *Contemporary Laos: Studies in the Politics and Society of the Lao People's Democratic Republic*, New York, NY: St. Martin's Press, 1982.

—— "Marxism and Theravada Buddhism: The Legitimation of Political Authority in Laos," *Pacific Affairs*, vol. 56, no. 3, Fall 1983, pp. 428–54.

—— "Laos in 1985: Time to Take Stock," *Southeast Asian Affairs 1986*, Singapore: Institute of Southeast Asian Studies, 1986, pp. 165–81.

—— *Laos: Politics, Economics and Society*, Boulder, CO: Lynne Rienner Publishers, 1986.

—— "Laos in 1988: In Pursuit of New Directions," *Asian Survey*, vol. 29, no. 1, January 1989, pp. 81–8.

—— "Laos at the Crossroads," *Indochina Issues*, vol. 92, March 1991, pp. 1–8.

—— "The Constitution of the Lao People's Democratic Republic," *Review of Socialist Law*, vol. 17, no. 4, 1991, pp. 299–317.

—— "Laos 1991: On the Defensive," *Southeast Asian Affairs 1992*, Singapore: Institute of Southeast Asian Studies, 1992, pp. 163–80.

—— "The French in Laos, 1887–1945," *Modern Asian Studies*, vol. 29, no. 1, February 1995, pp. 111–39.

—— "Laos: Towards Subregional Integration," *Southeast Asian Affairs 1995*, Singapore: Institute of Southeast Asian Studies, 1995, pp. 177–95.

—— *Buddhist Kingdom, Marxist State: The Making of Modern Laos*, Bangkok: White Lotus Press, 1996.

—— *A History of Laos*, New York, NY: Cambridge University Press, 1997.

—— "Laos in 1997: Into ASEAN," *Asian Survey*, vol. 38, no. 1, January 1998, pp. 75–9.

—— *Historical Dictionary of Laos*, 2d ed., Lanham, MD: Scarecrow Press, 2001.

—— "Southeast Asia and China: The Role of History and Culture in Shaping Future Relations," *Contemporary Southeast Asia*, vol. 26, no. 1, 2004, pp. 116–39.

Stuart-Fox, Martin and Rod Bucknell, "Politicization of the Buddhist Sangha in Laos," *Journal of Southeast Asian Studies*, vol. 13, no. 1, March 1982, pp. 60–80.

Stubbs, Richard, "ASEAN in 2003: Adversity and Response," *Southeast Asian Affairs 2004*, Singapore: Institute of Southeast Asian Studies, 2004, pp. 3–17.

Suchint Chaimungkalanont, "New Foreign Investment Law in Laos," *Standard Chartered Indochina Monitor*, July 1994, pp. 20–4.

Surin Maisrikrod, "The 'Peace Dividend' in Southeast Asia: The Political Economy of New Thai-Vietnamese Relations," *Contemporary Southeast Asia*, vol. 16, no. 1, June 1994, pp. 46–66.

Taillard, Christian, "Les transformations récentes des politiques agricoles en Chine et dans les pays socialistes de la peninsula indochinoise (1978–1982)," *Études rurales*, vol. 89–91, January–September 1983, pp. 111–43.

—— *Le Laos: stratégies d'un État-tampon*, Montpellier: Groupement d'Intérêt Public RECLUS, 1989.

Talbott, Kirk, "Logging in Cambodia: Politics and Plunder," in *Cambodia and the International Community: The Quest for Peace, Development, and Democracy*, edited by Frederick Z. Brown and David G. Timberman, New York, NY: Asia Society, 1998, pp. 149–68.

Tan, Ricardo M., Filologo Pante, Jr. and George Abonyi, "Economic Co-operation in the Greater Mekong Subregion," in *Regional Co-operation and*

*Integration in Asia*, edited by Kiichiro Fukasaku, Paris: Organization for Economic Co-operation and Development, 1995, pp. 223–48.

Taylor, Philip, *Fragments of the Present: Searching for Modernity in Vietnam's South*, Honolulu, HI: University of Hawai'i Press, 2001.

—— ed., *Social Inequality in Vietnam and the Challenges to Reform*, Singapore: Institute of Southeast Asian Studies, 2004.

Terzani, Tiziano, *A Fortune-Teller Told Me*, New York, NY: Three Rivers Press, 1997.

Thalemann, Andrea, "Laos: Between Battlefield and Marketplace," *Journal of Contemporary Asia*, vol. 27, no. 1, 1997, pp. 85–105.

Thaveeporn Vasavakul, "Vietnam: The Third Wave of State Building," *Southeast Asian Affairs 1997*, Singapore: Institute of Southeast Asian Studies, 1997, pp. 337–63.

—— "Vietnam's One-Party Rule and Socialist Democracy?" *Southeast Asian Affairs 1998*, Singapore: Institute of Southeast Asian Studies, 1998, pp. 309–27.

Thayer, Carlyle A., "Laos in 1982: The Third Congress of the Lao People's Revolutionary Party," *Asian Survey*, vol. 23, no. 1, January 1983, pp. 84–93.

—— "Laos in 1983: Pragmatism in the Transition to Socialism," *Asian Survey*, vol. 24, no. 1, January 1984, pp. 49–59.

—— "Introduction," in *Vietnam and the Rule of Law*, edited by Carlyle A. Thayer and David G. Marr, Canberra: Australian National University, 1993, pp. 1–20.

—— "Recent Political Developments: Constitutional Change and the 1992 Elections," in *Vietnam and the Rule of Law*, edited by Carlyle A. Thayer and David G. Marr, Canberra: Australian National University, 1993, pp. 50–80.

—— "Laos in 1998: Continuity under New Leadership," *Asian Survey*, vol. 39, no. 1, January–February 1999, pp. 38–42.

—— "Laos in 1999: Economic Woes Drive Foreign Policy," *Asian Survey*, vol. 40, no. 1, January–February 2000, pp. 43–8.

—— "Vietnam: The Politics of Immobilism Revisited," *Southeast Asian Affairs 2000*, Singapore: Institute of Southeast Asian Studies, 2000, pp. 311–26.

—— "Vietnam in 2000: Toward the Ninth Party Congress," *Asian Survey*, vol. 41, no. 1, January–February 2001, pp. 181–8.

—— "Vietnam in 2001: The Ninth Party Congress and After," *Asian Survey*, vol. 42, no. 1, January–February 2002, pp. 81–9.

—— "Laos in 2002: Regime Maintenance through Political Stability," *Asian Survey*, vol. 43, no. 1, January–February 2003, pp. 120–6.

—— "Vietnam: The Stewardship of Nong Duc Manh," *Southeast Asian Affairs 2003*, Singapore: Institute of Southeast Asian Studies, 2003, pp. 313–26.

—— "Laos in 2003: Counterrevolution Fails to Ignite," *Asian Survey*, vol. 44, no. 1, January–February 2004, pp. 110–14.

Thayer, Carlyle A. and Ramses Amer, ed., *Vietnamese Foreign Policy in Transition*, Singapore: Institute of Southeast Asian Studies, 1999.

Thayer, Carlyle A. and David G. Marr, ed., *Vietnam and the Rule of Law*, Research School of Pacific Studies, Department of Political and Social Change, Political and Social Change Monograph 19, Canberra: Australian National University, 1993.

Thompson, Virginia, *French Indo-China*, New York, NY: Octagon Books, 1968.

Thu-huong Nguyen-vo, *Khmer-Viet Relations and the Third Indochina Conflict*, Jefferson, NC: McFarland & Company, 1992.

Tin Maung Maung Than, "Cambodia: Strongman, Terrible Man, Invisible Man, and Politics of Power Sharing," *Southeast Asian Affairs 2004*, Singapore: Institute of Southeast Asian Studies, 2004, pp. 73–86.

Tran Khanh, *The Ethnic Chinese and Economic Development in Vietnam*, Singapore: Institute of Southeast Asian Studies, 1993.

Tran Thi Que, *Vietnam's Agriculture: The Challenges and Achievements*, Singapore: Institute of Southeast Asian Studies, 1998.

Tran Tu Binh, *The Red Earth: A Vietnamese Memoir of Life on a Colonial Rubber Plantation*, Monographs in International Studies, Southeast Asia Series Number 66, Athens, OH: Ohio University Press, 1985.

Truong, David H. D., "Striving Towards *Doi Moi* II," *Southeast Asian Affairs 1998*, Singapore: Institute of Southeast Asian Studies, 1998, pp. 328–39.

Truong Buu Lâm, *Resistance, Rebellion, Revolution: Popular Movements in Vietnamese History*, Occasional Paper No. 75, Singapore: Institute of Southeast Asian Studies, 1984.

—— *Colonialism Experienced: Vietnamese Writings on Colonialism, 1900–1931*, Ann Arbor, MI: University of Michigan Press, 2000.

Truong Nhu Tang, *A Viet Cong Memoir*, New York, NY: Vintage Books, 1986.

Turley, William S. and Mark Selden, ed., *Reinventing Vietnamese Socialism: Doi Moi in Comparative Perspective*, Boulder, CO: Westview Press, 1993.

Twining, Charles H., "The Economy," in *Cambodia, 1975–1978: Rendezvous with Death*, edited by Karl D. Jackson, Princeton, NJ: Princeton University Press, 1989, pp. 109–50.

Um, Khatharya, "Cambodia in 1988: The Curved Road to Settlement," *Asian Survey*, vol. 29, no. 1, January 1989, pp. 73–80.

—— "Cambodia in 1989: Still Talking but No Settlement," *Asian Survey*, vol. 30, no. 1, January 1990, pp. 96–104.

—— "Cambodia in 1993: Year Zero Plus One," *Asian Survey*, vol. 34, no. 1, January 1994, pp. 72–81.

—— "One Step Forward, Two Steps Back: Cambodia and the Elusive Quest for Peace," *Southeast Asian Affairs 1998*, Singapore: Institute of Southeast Asian Studies, 1998, pp. 71–85.

Un, Kheang, "The Anti-Thai Riots: Sparking Khmer Nationalism," *Mandala*, vol. 22, Summer 2003, pp. 1–2.

Un, Kheang and Judy Ledgerwood, "Cambodia in 2001: Toward Democratic Consolidation?" *Asian Survey*, vol. 42, no. 1, January–February 2002, pp. 100–6.

—— "Cambodia in 2002: Decentralization and Its Effects on Party Politics," *Asian Survey*, vol. 43, no. 1, January–February 2003, pp. 113–19.

Usher, Ann Danaiya, "The Race for Power in Laos: The Nordic Connections," in *Environmental Change in South-East Asia: People, Politics and Sustainable Development*, edited by Michael J. G. Parnwell and Raymond L. Bryant, London: Routledge, 1996, pp. 123–44.

Van Brabant, Jozef M., "Reforming a Socialist Developing Country: The Case of Vietnam," *Economics of Planning*, vol. 23, 1990, pp. 209–29.

Van der Kroef, Justus M., "Cambodia: From 'Democratic Kampuchea' to 'People's Republic,'" *Asian Survey*, vol. 19, no. 8, August 1979, pp. 731–50.

Vickerman, Andrew, "A Note on the Role of Industry in Vietnam's Development Strategy," *Journal of Contemporary Asia*, vol. 2, 1985, pp. 224–34.

—— *The Fate of the Peasantry: Premature "Transition to Socialism" in the Demo-*

*cratic Republic of Vietnam*, New Haven, CT: Yale University Southeast Asia Studies, 1986.

Vickery, Michael, *Kampuchea: Politics, Economics and Society*, Boulder, CO: Lynne Rienner Publishers, 1986.

—— "Notes on the Political Economy of the People's Republic of Kampuchea (PRK)," *Journal of Contemporary Asia*, vol. 20, no. 4, 1990, pp. 435–65.

—— "Cambodia," in *Coming to Terms: Indochina, the United States, and the War*, edited by Douglas Allen and Ngo Vinh Long, Boulder, CO: Westview Press, 1991, pp. 89–128.

—— *Cambodia: A Political Survey*, Research School of Pacific Studies, Department of Political and Social Change, Discussion Paper Series No. 14, Canberra: Australian National University, 1994.

—— *Cambodia 1975–1982*, Sydney: George Allen & Unwin, 1994.

Vitit Muntarbhorn, "International Law and the Mekong River: Streamlining the Course through the Thai Middle Kingdom," in *Cooperation in the Mekong Development: Papers and Proceedings of the Seminar Held in Bangkok on 27–29 June 1991*, edited by Khien Theeravit, Sai Kham Mong, David Ruffolo and Benjamin Chiang, Bangkok: The Institute of Asian Studies, Chulalongkorn University, 1991, pp. 11–24.

Vo Dai Luoc, "The Fight against Inflation: Achievements and Problems," in *Reinventing Vietnamese Socialism: Doi Moi in Comparative Perspective*, edited by William S. Turley and Mark Selden, Boulder, CO: Westview Press, 1993, pp. 107–17.

—— "Monetary Stabilization: The Vietnamese Experience," in *Vietnam in a Changing World*, edited by Irene Norlund, Carolyn L. Gates and Vu Cao Dam, Richmond, Surrey: Curzon Press, 1995, pp. 71–84.

Vo Nhan Tri, "Party Policies and Economic Performance: The Second and Third Five-Year Plans Examined," in *Postwar Vietnam: Dilemmas in Socialist Development*, edited by David G. Marr and Christine P. White, Ithaca, NY: Cornell Southeast Asia Program, 1988, pp. 77–89.

—— *Vietnam's Economic Policy since 1975*, Singapore: Institute of Southeast Asian Studies, 1990.

Vokes, Richard and Armand Fabella, "Lao PDR," in *From Centrally Planned to Market Economies: The Asian Approach*, vol. 3, *Lao PDR, Myanmar and Viet Nam*, edited by Pradumna B. Rana and Naved Hamid, New York, NY: Oxford University Press, 1996, pp. 1–148.

Vo-Tong Xuan, "Rice Production, Agricultural Research, and the Environment," in *Vietnam's Rural Transformation*, edited by Benedict J. Tria Kerkvliet and Doug J. Porter, Boulder, CO: Westview Press, 1995, pp. 185–200.

Vu Tuan Anh, *Development in Vietnam: Policy Reforms and Economic Growth*, Singapore: Institute of Southeast Asian Studies, 1994.

Walker, Andrew, *The Legend of the Golden Boat: Regulation, Trade and Traders in the Borderlands of Laos, Thailand, China and Burma*, Honolulu, HI: University of Hawai'i Press, 1999.

Ward, Michael, "Inflation Management and Stabilization: The Cambodian Experience," in *Macroeconomic Management in Southeast Asia's Transitional Economies*, edited by Manuel F. Montes, Romeo A. Reyes and Somsak Tambunlertchai, Kuala Lumpur: Asian and Pacific Development Centre, 1995, pp. 71–104.

Warner, Roger, *The CIA's Secret War in Laos and Its Link to the War in Vietnam*, New York, NY: Simon & Schuster, 1995.

Werner, Jayne, "Socialist Development: The Political Economy of Agrarian Reform in Vietnam." *Bulletin of Concerned Asian Scholars*, vol. 16, no. 2, April–June 1984, pp. 48–55.

Womack, Brantly, "Reform in Vietnam: Backwards Towards the Future," *Government and Opposition*, vol. 27, no. 2, Spring 1992, pp. 177–89.

—— "Vietnam in 1995: Successes in Peace," *Asian Survey*, vol. 34, no. 1, January 1996, pp. 73–82.

—— "Vietnam in 1996: Reform Immobilism," *Asian Survey*, vol. 37, no. 1, January 1997, pp. 79–87.

Wood, Adrian, "Deceleration of Inflation with Acceleration of Price Reform: Vietnam's Remarkable Recent Experience," *Cambridge Journal of Economics*, vol. 13, 1989, pp. 563–71.

Worner, William, "Economic Reform and Structural Change in Laos," *Southeast Asian Affairs 1989*, Singapore: Institute of Southeast Asian Studies, 1989, pp. 187–208.

Worthing, Peter M., *Cambodia in Chinese Foreign Policy toward Vietnam*, Indochina Initiative Working Paper No. 4, Honolulu, HI: East-West Center, 1992.

Wurfel, David, *"Doi Moi* in Comparative Perspective," in *Reinventing Vietnamese Socialism: Doi Moi in Comparative Perspective*, edited by William S. Turley and Mark Selden, Boulder, CO: Westview Press, 1993, pp. 19–52.

—— "Between China and ASEAN: The Dialectics of Recent Vietnamese Foreign Policy," in *Vietnamese Foreign Policy in Transition*, edited by Carlyle A. Thayer and Ramses Amer, Singapore: Institute of Southeast Asian Studies, 1999, pp. 148–69.

Wyatt, David K., *Thailand: A Short History*, New Haven, CT: Yale University Press, 1982.

Yvon-Tran, Florence, "The Chronicle of a Failure: Collectivization in Northern Vietnam, 1958–1988, in *Viêt-Nam Exposé: French Scholarship on Twentieth-Century Vietnamese Society*, edited by Gisele L. Bousquet and Pierre Brocheux, Ann Arbor, MI: University of Michigan Press, 2002, pp. 331–55.

Zasloff, Joseph J., "Emerging Stability in Cambodia,".*Asian Affairs: An American Review*, vol. 28, no. 4, Winter 2002, pp. 187–200.

Zasloff, Joseph J. and Leonard Unger, ed., *Laos: Beyond the Revolution*, New York, NY: St. Martin's Press, 1991.

Zinoman, Peter, *The Colonial Bastille: A History of Imprisonment in Vietnam, 1862–1940*, Berkeley, CA: University of California Press, 2001.

## Interviews

Ashley, David, Senior Official, Ministry of Economics and Finance, Royal Government of Cambodia, Phnom Penh, 15 June 1994.

Bai Danh Lun, Minister, Ministry of Transport and Communications, Socialist Republic of Vietnam, Hanoi, 26 October 1990.

Bounleuang Insisienmay, Deputy Director, Department of Foreign Trade, Ministry of Trade and Tourism, Lao People's Democratic Republic, Vientiane, 16 October 1990.

Bounnhang Sengchandavong, Deputy Director, Office of the Foreign Investment Management Committee, Ministry of External Economic Relations, Lao People's Democratic Republic, Vientiane, 11 December 1990.

Bountheuang Mounlasy, Deputy Director, Ministry of Foreign Economic Relations, Lao People's Democratic Republic, Vientiane, 12 December 1990.

Bountiem Phissamay, First Vice Minister, Ministry of External Economic Relations, Lao People's Democratic Republic, Vientiane, 10 December 1990.

Himmakone Manodham, Vice Minister, Ministry of Communication, Transport, Post, and Construction, Lao People's Democratic Republic, Vientiane, 12 December 1990 and 15 June 1992.

Hoang Trong Quang, Deputy Director, Ministry of Water Resources, Socialist Republic of Vietnam, Hanoi, 25 October 1990.

Khamphan Simmalavong, Deputy Minister, Foreign Trade and Tourism, Ministry of Commerce, Lao People's Democratic Republic, Vientiane, 3 March 1992.

Le Dang Doanh, President, Central Institute for Economic Management, Socialist Republic of Vietnam, Hanoi, 12 June 1996.

Le Ngoc Hoan, Vice Minister, Ministry of Transport and Communications, Socialist Republic of Vietnam, Hanoi, 26 October 1990.

Le Tung Hieu, Deputy General Director, Ministry of Heavy Industry, Socialist Republic of Vietnam, Ho Chi Minh City, 28 March 1991.

Le Van Bang, Ambassador, Embassy of Vietnam (Washington, D.C.), Socialist Republic of Vietnam, Washington, D.C., 25 April 1991 and Indianapolis, Indiana, 23 April 1996.

Liang Insisiengmay, Director, Tax Department, Lao People's Democratic Republic, Vientiane, 11 December 1990.

Nguyen Cao Tam, Deputy General Manager, Ministry of Water Resources, Socialist Republic of Vietnam, Ho Chi Minh City, 27 March 1991.

Nguyen Long Trao, Deputy General Director, Saigon Export Processing Zone, Socialist Republic of Vietnam, Ho Chi Minh City, 28 March 1991.

Nguyen Van Luong, Vice Director, Transport Engineering Design Institute, Socialist Republic of Vietnam, Hanoi, 22 October 1990.

Nokham Ratanavong, Director, Department of Foreign Trade, Ministry of Commerce and Tourism, Lao People's Democratic Republic, Vientiane, 2 March 1992.

Pham Chi Lan, Deputy Secretary General, Chamber of Commerce and Industry, Socialist Republic of Vietnam, Hanoi, 24 October 1990.

Pham Van Dinh, Director, Ministry of Transport and Communications, Socialist Republic of Vietnam, Hanoi, 22 October 1990.

Phetsamone Viraphanth, Director, Department of International Relations, Ministry of Communication, Transport, Post and Construction, Lao People's Democratic Republic, Vientiane, 17 October 1990.

Radsady Om, Chairman, Foreign Affairs and Information Committee, National Assembly of Cambodia, Bangkok, 17 June 1994.

Sitaheng Rasphone, Vice Minister, Ministry of Agriculture and Forestry, Lao People's Democratic Republic, Vientiane, 3 March 1992.

Solomon, Richard H., Assistant Secretary of State for East Asian and Pacific Affairs, State Department, United States of America, Bangkok, 29 July 1991.

Tran Ngoc Hien, Vice President, Ho Chi Minh National Academy for Political Science, Hanoi, 12 June 1996.

## Newspapers, periodicals and news agencies

*Asia Times* (www.atimes.com)
*Asian Wall Street Journal* (www.awsj.com.hk)
*Associated Press* (www.ap.org)
*BBC News* (www.bbc.co.uk)
*Bangkok Post* (www.bangkokpost.com)
*Boston Globe* (www.boston.com)
*China Daily* (www.chinadaily.com)
*Christian Science Monitor* (www.csmonitor.com)
*The Economist* (www.economist.com)
*Far Eastern Economic Review* (www.feer.com)
*Financial Times* (www.ft.com)
*The Hindu* (www.hinduonnet.com)
*The Philadelphia Inquirer* (www.philly.com)
*International Herald Tribune* (www.iht.com)
*Japan Today* (www.japantoday.com)
*Kyodo News Service* (www.kyodonews.com)
*Manila Times* (www.manilatimes.net)
*The Mercury News* (www.bayarea.com)
*Laos Daily* (www.laosdaily.com)
*Laos Post* (http://laospost.com)
*Le Monde* (www.lemonde.fr)
*The Nation* (www.nationmultimedia.com)
*The New York Times* (www.nytimes.com)
*New Zealand Herald* (www.nzherald.co.nz)
*Nhân Dân* (www.nhandan.org.vn)
*People's Daily* (www.peoplesdaily.com)
*Phnom Penh Post* (www.phnompenhpost.com)
*Pioneer Press* (www.twincities.com)
*Pravada* (http://newsfromrussia.com)
*The Providence Journal* (www.projo.com)
*Radio Free Asia Khmer* (www.rfa.org)
*Reuters* (http://reuters.com)
*Shanghai Daily* (http://english.eastday.com)
*South China Morning Post* (www.scmp.com)
*Star Tribune* (www.startribune.com)
*Straits Times* (http://straitstimes.asia1.com)
*The Times* (www.timesonline.co.uk)
*The Times of India* (www.timesofindia.com)
*Vientiane Times* (www.vientianetimes.com)
*Vietnam Investment Review* (www.vir.com)
*Vietnam News Agency* (www.vnagency.com.vn)
*The Wall Street Journal* (http://online.wsj.com)
*Washington Post* (www.washingtonpost.com)
*Washington Times* (www.washtimes.com)
*Xinhua News Agency* (www.xinhuanet.com)
*Yahoo! Finance Asia* (http://asia.biz.yahoo.com)
*Yahoo! News Asia* (http://asia.news.yahoo.com)
*Yahoo! News Singapore* (http://sg.news.yahoo.com)

## E-lists and Websites

Amnesty International (http://web.amnesty.org)
Asian Development Bank (www.adb.org)
Cambodia Daily (www.cambodiadaily.com)
Cambodia Development Resource Institute (www.cdri.org.kh)
Cambodia News (www.the cambodianews.net)
Comité des frontière du Cambodge (www.cfcambodge.org)
Focus on the Global South (www.focusweb.org)
Human Rights Watch (http://hrw.org)
Institute of Southeast Asian Studies (www.iseas.edu.sg)
International Crisis Group (www.icg.org)
International Monetary Fund (www.imf.org)
Khmer Intelligence (www.khmerintelligence.org)
World Bank (www.worldbank.org)

# Author's note

Ronald Bruce St John is an independent scholar specializing in the political economy of developing states. He served in Vietnam as a military intelligence officer during the Second Indochina War. He later worked as an advisor, consultant and researcher in Southeast Asia for over three decades and remains a frequent visitor to Cambodia, Laos and Vietnam. He holds a B.A. in political science from Knox College and an M.A. and Ph.D. in international relations from the Graduate School of International Studies, University of Denver. He has been an affiliate professor at the Institute of International Studies, Bradley University, since 1982 and served as a consultant for a variety of U.S. government agencies, Fortune 500 companies, *National Geographic Magazine* and *The New York Times*. Dr. St John has published more than 300 books and articles, including *Libya and the United States: Two Centuries of Strife* (Penn Press, 2002), *La Política Exterior del Perú* (AFSDP, 1999), *Historical Dictionary of Libya* (Scarecrow, 1998), *The Foreign Policy of Peru* (Lynne Rienner, 1992), and *Qaddafi's World Design: Libyan Foreign Policy, 1969–1987* (Saqi, 1987). His articles have appeared in a number of scholarly journals, including *Asian Affairs*, *Asian Affairs: An American Review*, *Asian Survey*, *Boundary and Security Bulletin*, *Bulletin of Concerned Asian Scholars*, *Contemporary Southeast Asia*, *Journal of Libyan Studies*, *Journal of the Siam Society*, *Middle East Journal*, *Middle East Policy*, *Orbis*, *Política Internacional* and *The World Today*. He has also authored a variety of essays in the current editions of the *Africa Contemporary Record*, *Encyclopedia of Religious Practices*, *Governments of the World* and *Encyclopedia of the Modern Middle East and North Africa*.

# Index